Federico Fellini

. . . .

Federico Fellini

Essays in Criticism

Edited by

PETER BONDANELLA
Indiana University

New York
OXFORD UNIVERSITY PRESS
1978

Copyright © 1978 by Oxford University Press, Inc.

Library of Congress Cataloging in Publication Data
Main entry under title:
Federico Fellini.

   Bibliography: p.
   Filmography: p.
   1. Fellini, Federico—Addresses, essays, lec-
tures. I. Bondanella, Peter, 1943-
PN1998.A3F336   791.43'0233'0924   76-57481
ISBN 0-19-502273-4
ISBN 0-19-502274-2 pbk.

Printed in the United States of America.

For M. M. and D. B.

Contents

· ·

1. Fellini on Fellini: Interviews and Statements about Film Art

· ·

2. Perspectives on Individual Films

. . . .

3. Themes and Techniques

. . . .

4. Fellini Bibliography and Filmography   303

Preface

Although Federico Fellini is surely the most popular Italian director in the English-speaking world, much of the important critical material on his works was located until very recently either in film journals (some of which had a relatively small circulation) or in books written in Italian or French, which were often inaccessible to the reading public. Because of the undeniable importance of Fellini to the history of the cinema, this collection of essays is intended to make available a representative selection of the critical literature that has appeared in Italian, French, and English during the past two decades.

Several criteria have guided the editorial decisions. First and foremost, the articles included here were judged to be fundamental statements about the nature and scope of Fellini's films that would elicit a critical response from the reader and lead to a deeper understanding of the evolution of Fellini's characteristic themes and artistic style. In this regard, there is an emphasis upon three of Fellini's works in this collection—*La Strada, 8½,* and *Fellini Satyricon.* The emphasis reflects not only the objective fact that many of the best critical studies devoted to Fellini analyze these three films but also my more subjective and personal belief that critical debate on Fellini's place in film history should concentrate upon these three works.

Second, an effort has been made to present an international selection of materials that would include all of the important national criticisms pertinent to Fellini, as well as a variety of methodologies and approaches. Thus, the collection includes essays reflecting Marxist, religious, historical, philosophical, psychological, literary, and semiological points of view. They focus upon a number of specific problems within various films or groups of films, including the relationship of Fellini's work to literature or the figurative arts, the place of music in his cinema, and his most characteristic imagery, camera movements, and techniques. In a real sense, the scope of this volume reflects the historical development of Fellini criticism from 1950 to the present, just as the subject matter ranges from *Variety Lights* to *Casanova.* In most cases, I have reprinted articles with few changes, except for correcting factual or typographical mistakes. The minor stylistic inconsistencies which remain in terminology (neo-realism, neorealism), names (Oswaldo, Osvaldo; Encolpius, Encolpio) and in film titles (*Le notti di Cabiria, Le Notti di Cabiria, The Nights of Cabiria*) should not be confusing.

A final comment is in order concerning the five critical statements by Fellini himself. Other interviews with Fellini, published in English, often tend to portray him as a madcap Latin genius or an incurable Romantic who somehow (and quite by accident) manages to bring order out of his chaotic life to produce work after work of merit. One expects "serious" critical opinion from the late Pier Paolo Pasolini or Bernardo Bertolucci, but even the most serious of film critics often seems to view Fellini in the role Fellini himself provides for his spectators in such works as *Fellini: A Director's Notebook, The Clowns,* and *Roma.* But this role is simply that, a role—it is the *character* Federico Fellini portrayed by the *actor* Federico Fellini as manipulated by the *director* Federico Fellini. The role should not be confused with the man behind the camera. Fellini's critical remarks on neorealism, his distinction between art films by authors and films made for television, as well as the artistic and philosophical motivations of such works as *Fellini Satyricon, Amarcord,* and *Casanova,* some printed here for the first time in English, are critical statements worthy of comparison to any of those contained in this anthology. The image of Fellini that emerges from his own remarks here and from those of the many critics, writers, and scholars represented in this volume is the true one—that of a great artist who is engaged in resolving the artistic problems of his medium while he is involved in the fundamental social and political concerns of his era. There is, however, more than the self-conscious intellectual or the socially aware artist evident in the films of Federico Fellini. In addition, there is a humanism and warmth in his works common to all the great comic geniuses of our culture. Perhaps this quality derives from the sense of complicity and compassion Fellini feels for everything and everyone he depicts, criticizes, or satirizes. But it is his almost magic capacity to capture rare moments of poetic truth in unforgettable images, in addition to this special cinematic humanism, which marks Fellini as one of the cinema's most remarkable creative spirits.

Peter Bondanella

Bloomington, Ind.
January 1977

Acknowledgments

This work owes much to the patient advice and encouragement of John Wright, Jean Shapiro, and Pat Golin of Oxford University Press, as well as to Hugo Kunoff and Jill Caldwell of the Indiana University Library. Donald Krim, Peter Meyer, and George Schumacher (among others) helped to provide me with prints of Fellini's works for my film courses at rates that made the very existence of such courses and this book possible. Conversations with Carolyn and Harry Geduld of Indiana University and Ben Lawton of Purdue University provided stimulating insights into the nature of film art in general and Fellini in particular. A special note of thanks is due to Lucio Bartolai, my teaching assistant in the Italian film course I began at Indiana University in 1974, and to the many students who have since enrolled in the course and who have helped me to test some of the ideas and translations contained in this book. My wife, Julia, provided French translations for several key essays and helped to ensure that my own translations from the Italian were readable. Finally, a note of gratitude is due to Federico Fellini himself, who agreed to the translation of important critical materials hitherto unavailable in English and who has provided us all with matchless artistic entertainment, surely the only justification for the existence of the present work.

P. B.

1

Fellini on Fellini

*Interviews and Statements
on Film Art*

1. My Experiences as a Director   *Federico Fellini*

I think I may honestly say that what I mostly owe to Roberto Rossellini's teaching is his example of humility, or better, a way of facing reality in a totally simplified way; an effort of not interfering with one's own ideas, culture, feelings.[1] When I happened to meet Rossellini, I was not attracted at all by the film world as I was a journalist at the time and was interested in quite different things. I had definitely no idea that I might direct my life to films.

I had already written stories, film subjects, scripts, but my co-operation remained always so far a very external one, as I never really entered this field with my own feelings and love.

When I happened to go on a set to see an actress or a friend, or when I was asked there by a film director, while one of my scripts was being staged, I always felt actually uneasy and was not able to realise clearly what all those people were about.

In short, I considered the life of a cast and their way of working quite uncongenial to my nature, quite far from my mind, so that I was not attracted in the least. Of course, I never thought I might become a film director myself.

When I came in touch with Rossellini, I saw at first a completely new world, the loving eyes through which Rossellini observed everything to make things alive through his framings. It was actually through his attitude that I thought that, after all, films may be created without deceits, without presumptions, without thinking of sending around quite definite messages. In a way, that it was possible to look at somebody or something, to consider a situation or some characters in an extremely simple way, and to try and relate what had been actually seen.

I do repeat that the most important thing I got from Rossellini was a lesson of humility.

Of course, getting in touch with him, and having then become truly friends (ours has been the most passionate, the most adventurous kind of friendship), I also learnt quite a number of other things; and, as I
. . . .

From *International Film Annual*, No. 3, ed. William Whitebait (London: John Calder, 1959), pp. 29-35. Reprinted by permission of Calder and Boyars Ltd. Publishers.

had with him my first experience as an assistant film director, I had the chance of realising that I myself might screen my stories, that filming would not be so difficult. I definitely realised that the camera, the film apparatus on the whole are not so very mysterious, so terribly technical. It was just a matter of relating quite simply what one was looking at.

I staged *Paisà* together with Amidei, and then I followed this film as an assistant. My contribution to Rossellini's work has been altogether marginal, as he had quite clear ideas, knew very well all he wanted, and we were just like two very good friends talking and discussing their opinions. Sometimes I may have given him a hint to turn in a certain direction or directed his attention to some particular situation, but nothing more. For instance, when Rossellini was directing the first episode of *Paisà* at Majori (a small village on the Amalfitan coast) I discovered a little convent of Franciscan friars and, since as a young boy I had often been sent to a boarding-school kept by friars, I entered it full of curiosity and actually discovered a charming place, very much resembling a picture. There were five or six friars, very poor, extremely simple. I don't exactly recollect, now, whether the idea of that episode was already written in the story or if it was suggested by this little convent. I remember anyway that, one evening, I took Rossellini to dine with me in the convent, so that I started to suggest to him the possibility of filming an episode. At first, the idea was to achieve a meeting between two quite different ways of conceiving religion, through a meeting between American chaplains and Italian friars; between an active belief, as that of military priests should be, and this kind of faith, so meditative, a life of prayers only, as it was lived in some little mediaeval convents that are to be found here and there in Italy. The idea was there, but not yet the episode.

I wrote the episode in that convent.

You ask me whether I think I am a neo-realistic film director. Well yes, but it is necessary, to begin with, to agree about the actual meaning of neo-realism. In my opinion, the only real neo-realist is Rossellini, the only one, I think, who actually reached a powerful manner of expression (a few days ago I saw *Paisà* once more and I think it really is grand), the only one that expressed himself in an efficient and inimitable way. It would not be too long to take in consideration that, from his way of looking at reality, a new current arose which was influenced and moved in several directions.

If, by neo-realism, we mean an attitude of sincerity to the ideas we intend to develop or the characters whose story we want to tell, I do believe I am a neo-realistic film director.

As for the films acted by Giulietta, the forming of the character is entirely based upon her possibilities as an actress. On the whole, when I imagine a story, I already have a clear idea about who will be the principal actors to impersonate my characters. For instance, *I Vitelloni* was written to fit Sordi, Trieste, Interlenghi, and my brother, Riccardo. When I was making the script, there was only one character for whom I had no actor in mind, and it was the part afterwards played by Franco Fabrizi. I made several essays and then decided to give it to Franco. So that, whenever I write a story, I already have in my mind which actor I am going to ask to perform a character.

But it happens sometimes that, when the script is ready, the actor I have had in my mind is no longer available, as it happened for *Il Bidone*. When I wrote it, I thought the character might be acted by Humphrey Bogart, but at the last moment, for reasons too long to relate, this actor happened to be engaged. So I had to address myself to Broderick Crawford, though I had so far seen only his photos, having not seen *Tutti gli uomini del Re* (*All the King's Men*). They had to show me this film, when Crawford arrived in Italy. I had, therefore, to modify the character, so that it might fit Crawford, his possibilities and his heavy features, so very different from Bogart's who was, as you certainly recollect, an actor very much like a lean wolf, with a hollow face. I think he might probably have expressed more forcibly the desolation of an ill-spent life.

In short, Bogart's tense, scowling melancholy would probably have been more effectual than Crawford's melancholy. When Crawford was starring, I had to change something, and I am always quite willing to do that, as I think that what is unforeseen, unexpected, turns sometimes to be a positive factor in making a work successful. When it is impossible for me to have the actor I would like, or when I can't find just the face I fancied, I turn quite easily to a new solution.

What I mean, in short, is this: that I never make (this is, maybe, the only "system" I recognise in my working way) the mistake—as I think it is a mistake—to fit the actor to the character, but I always do just the reverse, namely, I try to fit the character to the actor. I never require of the actor to do a particular interpretative effort, I mean that I don't stubbornly require a phrase to be uttered in a predetermined way. When Giulietta acted as Gelsomina, it was the only instance when I obliged an actress having an exuberant, aggressive, rather explosive nature to act as a creature overwhelmed with shyness, having only a small light of reason, and making gestures always full of affection and grotesquerie. It was quite a job. I may well say that Giulietta has made a far greater interpretative effort here than in *Cabiria*, as Gelsomina is really an interpretation, while performing Cabiria, she was much nearer to the character with her own impetuosity, her fanciful imagination, her prolixity in talking.

When I direct the actors, I generally show them the whole action and try to give the phrase the value I think it should have. Sometimes though, so as not to influence, not to compel another person to imitate me, I prefer to see what he would do spontaneously. On this matter, there is another thing I wish to tell you. Most of my inspirations about the way the actors should act come just when the work is stopped for a break, during the very moments when the actor is sitting down or having a snack or courting a little actress or sitting by himself or going to 'phone or falling asleep.

It is therefore rather difficult to fix exactly the moment of inspiration, but I could recall how the finale of *Notti di Cabiria* was born. It was not conceived just as a finale, but more exactly it came as the inspiring idea of the whole film. I have been reproached by some leftist journalists for having, in face of reality, an evasive, shunning attitude, for not suggesting any aim or definite solution with my stories. Apart from the somewhat hysterical anger that naturally arises in reading things we do not expect, I performed an act of humility and told myself: it is quite true that Zavattini and Vittorio De Sica suggest subscribing to a certain political party (I don't mean to be witty): they indoctrinate their characters, they show a way, and this means that they have a definite idea, which I have not. Therefore, of course, their films and their characters give, in the end, greater satisfaction than mine. So I told myself: maybe they are right, I am not able to tell my characters: "Look, buy that particular paper, or now go and get married, now go to church." . . . I am not able to tell them a single thing.

On the whole, it is a rather inhuman attitude an author shows to his characters. So that, recalling my good will (as if I wanted, for once, to tell one of my characters: "Look here, act in this particular way"), I thought: what have I to tell him?—and after having thought for a long while, I perceived there was not a single thing I could suggest to him, for I am not able to instruct myself. So that, the only thing I might offer my characters, who are always so very much oppressed with sorrows and misfortunes, is my sympathy. I might, in a word, say: "Listen, I could not explain what is wrong, but I sympathise with you and sing a serenade for you." I thought, concerning the *Notti di Cabiria*: "I wish to make a film about the adventures of an unlucky woman, who, in spite of everything, confusedly hopes, in a somewhat childish way, for a better life, in one direction." And when the film is over, I want to say to her: "Listen, I took you through such a terrible amount of trouble, but you are so charming to me that I want to have you sing a little song." This is how, following this rather childish idea, I imagined a scene. She was a woman, an unlucky character, who, at the end of an adventure more dreadful than the others, having lost in such a final way her confidence in reality and in the humanity surrounding her, was totally wasted. And I thought to myself: would it not be possible that—at a certain moment—this character might be persuaded that somebody comes and tells her, in a sympathetic and kind way: "You are right"?—this is how the character of Cabiria was born and her adventures became the adventures of a prostitute, living like a rat in terrible surroundings, being crushed by reality all the time, but going innocently and having this mysterious faith through life.

About the end of this film, I got the idea of letting her meet some elves, very young of course, symbolising a future mankind, who kindly, teasing her a little, but candidly, play for her a song in token of gratitude. This idea has been, on the whole, the origin of the film.

Concerning my work with Giulietta, I can say that she is not only the interpreter of my films, but she was the inspirer as well. By this I don't mean that her co-operation has been like Pinelli's, Flaiano's, Rondi's, but she has been an inspirer of a deeper significance, really an inspiring Muse.

La Strada and *Le notti di Cabiria* have actually been inspired by my life with Giulietta, by what I think of her, by my ideas about her, by her humanity, by what nearly is her meaning in my life.

My preference for Maestro Rota arises from the fact that I think him to be rather congenial to my stories and my characters; and that we work together in a very cheerful way (I don't mean the results, just the way our work is developed). I don't suggest to him musical themes, as I am no music connoisseur. Anyway, as my ideas about the film I am preparing are clear in every detail, my work with Rota proceeds just like the co-operation for the dialogues.

I remain near his piano, while he is there, and I tell him exactly what I wish. Of course, I can't tell him the motives, I can only suggest to him and make precise my wishes. I can say that, among film musicians, he is maybe the humblest, for he really writes a music extremely functional in my opinion. He is not conceited, nor proud like many musicians, who just want to have their own music admired. He is quite aware that the music is, in a film, an accessory, a secondary feature that in certain moments may be a protagonist, but which in general is just meant to back the action.

Brunello Rondi is a most valuable co-operator because, though he does not co-operate in the script (as usual, I avail myself of two dialogue-writers, Pinelli and Flaiano, and I am remarkably satisfied with them), his work comes somewhat later, when shooting begins. This is the moment when Brunello steps in to supply hints and suggestions. It is a co-operation on an active plan, not just theoretical; as the shots of the scenes are being made, Brunello, following the film, gives me quite a number of suggestions. . . . His co-operation is remarkably valuable to me, and I am sincerely grateful to him.

I can't be always quite objective to my films, for a very simple reason: I don't consider myself to be a professional film director, as my films are just the expression of a craftsman. I think I am actually a story-teller or singer. I make my films because I like to tell lies, to imagine fairy-tales, to tell about what I have seen and people I have met. I mostly like to tell about myself. So that, in a way, I make my films relating episodes in my life, so frankly that I am even a gossip, and I may even, sometimes, cause uneasiness with my confessions, profuse and most likely unasked for. This attitude, which inspires my work, prevents me consequently from judging it objectively, for it would be like asking me: "Do you prefer your marriage or your military service? Do you prefer the years spent in the high school or your first love adventures"? I could not say, because I prefer everything; since, being different episodes of my life, I think all of them valuable. I have a sort of paralysing feeling for everything concerning me, and therefore for my films. You might think this to be rather extravagant, but I do declare it is quite sincere. Anyway, from a sentimental point of view, I may well acknowledge that the film I love best is *La Strada*. First of all, because I believe it to be my most representative film, the most autobiographical one, and also for private and sentimental reasons, because its realisation cost me more trouble than the others. It has been the most trying one also because of the hardships I met to find a producer. Among the characters, the one I prefer is of course Gelsomina. This leads me to answer to the question: how did you get the idea of the episode of the sick child, unexpectedly discovered by Gelsomina?—

it is a remembrance of my childhood, just as it happened, when I lived at Gambettola (I spent most of my childhood in the country), a small place near Rimini, at my grandmother's. Once I went with some wild peasant boys to a farm beyond the hill. This farm had once been a convent. Going around this large, romantic building, full of magical spots, of corridors, vaults, in a garret, among the apples that had been put there to ripen and the sacks of maize, there was something like a dog's bed—it could not even be called a bed—a kind of pallet, where an idiot child was lying. The peasants, who always have a defensive instinct against those who do not work, and thence against the creatures born unfit, had removed as far as possible this child, in the hope, maybe, that it might starve. I was deeply impressed by this sight, it caused me a grievous shock and I reproduced it in my film *La Strada*. How important is this episode in the story? Most likely I put it there to let Gelsomina realise the right feeling of her loneliness. There is a party going on in the farm. Gelsomina is a creature who likes to be with people and wishes to join their songs, their cheerfulness. She is led by a crowd of shouting little children and they take her to see the sick child. I think that the apparition of such a lonely, delirious creature—something very mysterious—joined to the scene, showing Gelsomina curiously looking at the child, stresses strikingly Gelsomina's loneliness.

You ask me why—in my opinion—*Lo Sceicco Bianco* and *Il Bidone* proved not to be altogether successful with the public. As *Lo Sceicco Bianco* (apart from the practical reasons, that is to say that the distributors went out of business before distributing the film and that the cast was maybe not striking enough to attract the attention of the public), is a film against the "cartoons" (I don't mean the "cartoons" as a journalistic expression, but as an attitude, as a fashion), it has most likely perturbed a part of the public, those who go to the movies wishing to find a conformist, conventional reality, of a sentimental kind. *Lo Sceicco Bianco* most likely had bad luck, for it failed to meet the prejudices of the public.

As for *Il Bidone*, well, I still don't understand quite clearly why it failed to achieve commercial success. When I think it over, I believe the reason of its failure may be this: quite likely the public, attracted by the title, as happened for the other film *I Vitelloni*, thought it to be a sort of humorous tale, and to be confronted with merry, attractive rascals, jokers more than hardened criminals, as actually I tried to represent them. Thence, I think the first discomfort, the first disappointment arose.

Secondly, the public may have not liked this film, since it does not follow the usual conventional ways in a story concerning the life of a bad man, who is expected—I wonder why—to be redeemed at the end.

Till now, I am glad to say, my freedom to do what I wanted has never been restrained. Maybe some patience was required, but I never had to renounce anything (not even a shot) and always managed to do what I wanted. The producer of course always tries to justify his presence, with suggestions at any rate, but we have merely to know just what we want. To be true as far as possible to our own selves and to remember this: that, between film director and producer, the first is always right. If one is perfectly aware of this (of course, not in a fanatical way), if one is objectively aware of having some good qualities and the wish of expressing a world, it is essential for him to make sure that he has the first and last word, that he comes out with everything he has in mind, and that he listens to nobody's advice, when once the film is started, because at this moment even the most affectionate advice may prove to be untimely and altogether wrong.

Which of my characters do I believe might be further developed? I am very fond of the characters of my films, so that when a film is ended, I still muse, and imagine other stories concerning the life of its characters. . . . And maybe I don't do anything about it. But most likely the character that might have had further developments (but it has had none so far) is Moraldo. I thought of a film for this character, called *Moraldo in Town*, and it should be a continuation of *I Vitelloni*. It should tell Moraldo's adventures in Rome, the adventures of a young man trying to find his own self, a young man without a faith, without prejudice, completely free, like an animal venturing for the first time in a wood to seek out the meaning of life. But then I did not make this film and I don't think I ever will, because I have not yet found this meaning of life myself and therefore I don't know what the conclusion of Moraldo's history might be. On the day I think I have reached my own conclusion, or a conclusion at any rate, that I might convey to others, then perhaps I shall film *Moraldo in Town*.

NOTE

1. Some years later, Fellini clarified his definition of humility and his relationship to the neo-realism of Rossellini in an interview given to Belgian television in 1962: "It is therefore perfectly right to have an attitude of humility toward life, that is, to really be able to look at life. But then,

once you're in front of the camera, you ought to abandon this humility completely; on the contrary, you ought to be arrogant, tyrannical, you ought to become a sort of god, in total command not only of the actors, but also of the objects and the lights. This is why, in my view, the confusion created by neo-realism was a very serious matter, because if you have an attitude of humility not only toward life but toward the camera as well, carrying the idea to its logical conclusion, you wouldn't need a director at all." For the complete text, see Suzanne Budgen, *Fellini* (London: British Film Institute, 1966), pp. 85-95.—EDITOR

. . . .

2. Fellini on Television: *A Director's Notebook* and *The Clowns*

Federico Fellini

My experience in television has made me understand that when one works in that medium, it is necessary to remember such a series of conditions that, all in all—perhaps also because of my character and my means of self-expression—I don't know whether "the game is really worth the candle"—to put it as one should (not) say. In reality, now that I have completed A *Director's Notebook* and *The Clowns*, I realize that in the past, I had not reflected sufficiently on this question: what is television? In short, I had never ever even seen this television! That is, I had always seen it as a piece of furniture—that's it, something which furnished a corner of the house. Sometimes I stopped in front of it to look at certain particularly interesting news broadcasts; certain somewhat cruel close-ups of singers where their gold teeth showed; or those ferocious TV quiz games like spectacles at the Circus Maximus—the questions posed in order to savor the embarrassment of the competitor or his sudden lapse of memory. I used to look at these things with curiosity. But, in reality, I never asked myself what must be the viewpoint of anyone who tries to reach such an apathetic pit of spectators as that of television viewers. It is necessary to keep a number of factors in mind. Too many factors! First of all, from the view-

. . . .

From *Fellini TV: Block-Notes di un regista/I Clowns di Federico Fellini*, ed. Renzo Renzi (Bologna: Cappelli Editore, 1972), pp. 209–13. Copyright © 1976 by Diogenes Verlag AG Zurich. All rights reserved. Translated by Peter Bondanella.

point of communications, with whom does one communicate and how does one communicate? At first, I thought it might be very stimulating for an author to attempt to achieve a more intimate relationship with his public—in fact, to arrive at the home of that spectator, to speak right to him (you imagine him, perhaps, in bed); therefore, the relationship is even more private and secret, and this condition might ensure for the communication its own extraordinary suggestiveness. In reality, it is not at all true that things are like that. That is fiction. It is not true that one arrives at such a direct, friendly relationship. First of all, the fact of entering into these homes removes its religious character from the communication, if I may put it that way. I mean to say that when a certain number of people gather in one spot where, after raising a curtain or lighting a stage, someone appears who tells a story, then, in fact, the communication of a message occurs.

At the theater or the cinema, this ritual has the potential of being realized more or less casually; in other words, the "meeting place" becomes a church, a suitable place for receiving the communication or the message. This condition does not exist in television. It cannot exist and, therefore, the sacred aspect of the spectacle is lacking.

In the meantime, the public does not leave home and go to your house. It is you who goes to their house: this places you in a condition of inferiority. And where is it that you are going? Are you perhaps entering into this intimacy which is so fondly anticipated because you think you will be able to say that your story has arrived in a more direct manner? Not at all! In fact, in the first place, you must win over the domineering attitude of the spectator. Whoever owns the television is the master of the television. This is something that does not occur either in the theater or at the cinema, where the spectator does not feel himself to be the master. On the contrary, the spectator must leave home, stand in line, buy the ticket, enter the dark, sit down, be completely dressed and not in one's undershorts or housecoat with slippers; the spectator cannot bring the children, or if he brings them, they are obliged (at least in theory) to behave themselves correctly. There is, in summation, a climate of respect that ought to predispose one to a certain kind of listening.

Not so with television. There you are—you have to come in with good manners—immediately obliged to interest or amuse people who are in their homes and who are, therefore, at the table, eating, or talking on the telephone. You as an author cannot ignore this fact, and therefore, you must immediately be very amusing or very interesting, as certain jongleurs or acrobats were forced to be who had to attract

the attention of people in the town squares who were going about their
own business . . . and who, in the final analysis, would stop to look
from far off with diffidence and, moreover, with an attitude of con-
descending tolerance. Therefore, let me repeat: you must keep in mind
that you are addressing a public which must *immediately* be interested
or amused. For this public, this master—as he has purchased you—if
you do not amuse him immediately, he shuts you off or changes the
channel; he turns you off and eats his spaghetti. Bear in mind besides
this that you must speak and tell your secret stories to people who, just
because they are in their own homes, have the complete right to make
all the comments they wish at the top of their voices and, moreover,
to insult you, or worse, to ignore you. Then, I ask, is it possible to try
to be oneself, to be faithful to one's own world, to one's own stylistics
in a similar situation, knowing, that is, that you must make a racket
to attract attention, that you are forced to say the most amusing thing
immediately, that you must not lose time, etc.? I do not think that it
is possible. There, now: anyone who sets himself to talking about television must bear this atmosphere in mind, this morphology of its communications. That is, let us repeat: the necessary ritual is lacking, as is
the breach of trust in reverse on the part of the public. The television
viewer, in short, is the master of the television set; in fact, if he wishes,
he can even throw it out the window.

Then there are the technical aspects. For instance, there is the small
format and, consequently, the impossibility of long shots or scenes in
which the actors become too small. From this arises another syntax, another way of telling a story, a much more simplified one like a series of
pictures. These pictures, in their turn, must not even possess an excessive interconnection, for if one of these spectators in his bathrobe is
distracted or talks with his neighbor or his wife, or quarrels with his
son . . . etc., you must bear in mind that each picture must be introduced with a long-winded, tired, repetitive, stretched-out rhythm in
order that all the possible distractions may be permitted. That is, television does not have the nervous cinematographic rhythm in which one
image slides after another, every image is required by another, and one
is produced by the other. No. In television, this cannot be done. Moreover, it is necessary to remember, especially for the objects that are
filmed, the fact that television eats up two frames per second, and
therefore, it is necessary to harmonize all the actions with a slower
cadence in order to reproduce them with a rhythm that gives them the
appearance of normal motion.

In short, for a man of the cinema—that is, for anyone who feels he must and can express himself only with images—there exist precise expressive problems. For me, in fact, the cinema is this—images. Light is my basic element. I have said it so many times: for me, light comes even before the theme, even before the actors selected for the various roles. Light is really everything: it is substance, sentiment, style, description. It is everything. The image is expressed with light. Well, in television this functioning of light, which is for me fundamental, is not at the heart of the operation itself, for in television the possibility of illuminating faces and objects in a graphic or psychological manner or however the devil you, as an author, feel it is right to express yourself does not exist. No, nothing of this—away with medium lights, shadows, and back lighting, since these effects would never be seen. In television one must see everything with clarity. The expressive operation of which I was speaking, basic to the cinema, is not required, is not possible in television, nor is it even appreciated. Therefore, in television the image has an illustrative character. It is an illustration, not an expression. Rossellini was correct, then, when he understood immediately that the most direct method of communicating—and the best means of employing television—was to produce illustrated instructions—that is, a kind of lecture with slides which are emphasized from time to time by a simple editing. Roberto is correct when he says that television has a didactic function, which allows it to pass easily from didacticism to the didactic moment, thus achieving a cultural operation at the level of information.

But for anyone, like myself, who believes in expression and not in information (and not even in the information that arises from expression), television seems to have limits which are too confining. Therefore, I consider the experience that I had with *The Clowns* a failure,[1] and I think that if I shall do other things, I shall try a completely different path.

Perhaps I have looked at television from a perspective which is too aristocratic, too private and personal, as always. In substance, I had told myself: the cinema practically always entails a very laborious organization, whereas I often have the desire to express myself immediately, with spontaneity; perhaps working for television and taking apart the cumbersome technical, organizational, and logistical apparatus of the film director may serve to guarantee expressive capacities, to allow one to try new stylistic experiences. This is a kind of avant-garde private experimentation, as in a laboratory. From a psychological viewpoint besides, the fact of knowing that I am working for television gives me a sense of frivolity which actually seems healthy.

In a certain sense this was true. In fact, I must make an effort to remember that I am making a little film for television when, instead, I am making a real film, because this film would profit from this nonchalant, less committed condition of mine. Commitment is, in fact, profoundly damaging because it kills spontaneity. It renders one so self-conscious and rationally convinced that everything which is accomplished has a precise goal that it demolishes spontaneity—that is, the main quality of the creative temperament.

In conclusion, I have thought about television in the way that I have remarked upon above. The experience that I had with it has taught me, instead, that it is something completely different from the cinema. And I do not know exactly what television authors are: that is, authors who have used this particular medium and have succeeded in creating a work containing a specific interpretation of reality and have, therefore, performed an artistic operation—in television, I do not know who might be television authors. Perhaps, unconscious of it himself, the only television author is Mike Bogiorno,[2] insofar as he proposes over and over again with his little shape so distorted and delirious an image of our country or, perhaps, of the human condition. That is, the bit of ferocity, ignorance, competition, and superficial erudition that comes through, an unconscious interpretation of our very provincial country, is enough to cause us to declare that he is a television author insofar as he has succeeded in executing an interpretative work. His TV quiz game is, all in all, a rather artistic example in the sense that he makes himself the interpreter of a certain kind of madness and offers it over and over again in a disquieting spectacle. If not him, then whom can we cite, an example of which one might say—there's one, he is recognizable? Bah! Perhaps it is necessary to state that television does not have this task of being a more or less compliant medium for the exhibitionism, the vanity, and the narcissism of an author. It does not require aesthetic objects to be judged by aesthetic criteria. Television lies here: in the television newscasts, in the news, in the immediately presented document which at times may exist in a visionary condition superior to that mediated vision of an author. Or else it lies in these experiences: studying in a face the embarrassment of a close-up held fixed and cruelly at length; investigating how a person swallows saliva, fear, hope, delusion, mortification. There you are, radiography: the close-up with this machine that analyzes, that produces psychological X rays . . . *Canzonissima*,[3] for example. It would be sufficient to change the lights a bit to make of this program a great Expressionist spectacle.[4]

NOTES

1. Not that I deny *The Clowns*—let's be clear. On the contrary, I especially consider the little film a success.
2. A well-known master of ceremonies in Italy at the time this essay was written.—EDITOR
3. A program based upon a competition between Italian pop singers and their songs.—EDITOR
4. When Fellini made *A Director's Notebook* and *The Clowns* (both in color), Italian television did not yet have the capacity to transmit images in color.—EDITOR.

. . . .

3. Preface to *Satyricon*   *Federico Fellini*

Many years ago at school I read the *Satyricon* by Petronius for the first time, with all the energy and greedy curiosity a schoolboy can muster. That reading has remained with me as a vivid memory, and its interest has evolved to become a constant and mysterious challenge.

After the lapse of many years I reread the *Satyricon* recently, with perhaps a less greedy curiosity but with the same enjoyment as before. This time more than just a temptation to make a film out of it, there was a need, an enthusiastic certainty.

The encounter with that world and that society turned out to be a joyful affair, a stimulation of fantasy, an encounter rich in themes of remarkable relevance to modern society.

In fact it seems we can find disconcerting analogies between Roman society before the final arrival of Christianity—a cynical society, impassive, corrupt and frenzied—and society today, more blurred in its external characteristics only because it is internally more confused. Then as now we find ourselves confronting a society at the height of its splendor but revealing already the signs of a progressive dissolution; a society in which politics is only the sordid, routine administration of
. . . .

From *Fellini's Satyricon* by Federico Fellini, ed. Dario Zanelli, trans. Eugene Walter (New York: Ballantine Books, 1970), pp. 43-46. Copyright © 1970 by Ballantine Books, a division of Random House, Inc. Reprinted by permission of the publisher.

Satyricon: Trimalchio (Mario Romagnoli) and his wife Fortunata (Magali Noël) at the sumptuous banquet made famous by Petronius' book. (Museum of Modern Art/Film Stills Archive)

a common affluence and an end in itself; where big business intrudes at all levels in the brutality of its instruments and the vulgarity of its ends; a society in which all beliefs—religious, philosophical, ideological and social—have crumbled, and been displaced by a sick, wild and impotent eclecticism; where science is reduced to a frivolous and meaningless bundle of notions or to a gloomy and fanatical elitism. If the work of Petronius is the realistic, bloody and amusing description of the customs, characters and general feel of those times, the film we want to freely adapt from it could be a fresco in fantasy key, a powerful and evocative allegory—a satire of the world we live in today. Man never changes, and today we can recognise all the principal characters of the drama: Encolpius and Ascyltus, two hippie students, like any of those hanging around today in Piazza di Spagna, or in Paris, Amsterdam or London, moving on from adventure to adventure, even the most gruesome, without the least remorse, with all the natural innocence and splendid vitality of two young animals. Their revolt, though having nothing in common with traditional revolts—neither the faith, nor the desperation, nor the drive to change or destroy—is nevertheless a revolt and is expressed in terms of utter ignorance of and estrangement from the society surrounding them. They live from day to day, taking problems as they come, their life interests alarmingly confined to the elementaries: they eat, make love, stick together, bed down anywhere. They make a living by the most haphazard expedients, often downright illegal ones. They are drop-outs from every system, and recognize no obligations, duties or restrictions. Their ignorance, except for the few scraps of scientific knowledge they have picked up, can be disconcerting. They are totally insensible to conventional ties like the family (usually built less on affection than on blackmail): they don't even practice the cult of friendship, which they consider a precarious and contradictory sentiment, and so are willing to betray or disown each other any time. They have no illusions precisely because they believe in nothing but, in a completely new and original way, their cynicism stays this side of a peaceful self-fulfillment, of a solid, healthy and unique good sense.

Disconcerting modernity, we said, in the work of Petronius; but I intend to give the film a more varied composition, drawing episodes in a wholly arbitrary way, guided only by the choices of fantasy, from some of the other beautiful texts of classical antiquity: *The Golden Ass* of Apuleius for example, with its flair for the fabulous in the metamorphoses—the part where Lucius peeps through a keyhole and surprises the sorceress Pamphile in the act of changing herself into an owl, then hissing a strident lament she spreads her wings and flies off. *The Metamorphoses* of Ovid, the *Satires* of Horace. Horace himself would be a fascinating figure to portray, the hoary poet in exile, half-blind, his face disfigured by a granuloma in the eye.

And then that cruel, degenerate and crazy Roman world described by Suetonius in his lives of the twelve Caesars. A gallery of stars, fabulous figures, impudent and boastful, tyrannical and pleasure-loving, whose modern incarnations are no less numerous or crazy, even if more irrelevant, and giving performances of frank self-irony. Another very tempting aspect of this cinematic procedure is one of evoking this world not through the fruit of a bookish, scholastic documentation, a literal fidelity to the text, but rather in the way an archeologist reconstructs something alluding to the form of an amphora or a statue from a few potsherds. Our film, through the fragmentary recurrence of its episodes, should restore the image of a vanished world without completing it, as if those characters, those habits, those milieux were summoned for us in a trance, recalled from their silence by the mystic ritual of a séance.

What is important, it seems to us, is not descriptive precision, historical fidelity, the complacently erudite anecdote, or elegant narrative construction, but that the characters and their adventures live before our eyes as though caught unawares. They should be as free as the beasts of the jungle when they move about, wrestle with each other or tear each other to pieces, give birth and die, all without being aware of their observers.

Sometimes the customs of these characters must appear to us. as totally incomprehensible, some of their extravagant gestures are indecipherable: grimaces, winks and other codes whose meaning we have lost. We no longer know the allusions behind them, as if we were a foreigner gradually discovering the meanings and connotations of all those facial gymnastics the Neapolitans indulge in, or as if we were watching a documentary on some Amazon Basin tribe.

The film should suggest the idea of something disinterred: the images should evoke the texture of ashes, earth and dust. Thus the film will have to be made of unequal segments, with long, luminous episodes joined by far-out, blurred sequences, fragmentary to the point of never being reconstructed again—the potsherds, crumbs and dust of a vanished world.

Certainly it is difficult to wipe two thousand years of history and Christianity off the slate, and square up to the myths, attitudes and customs of peoples who came long before us, without judging them, without making them the object of a moralistic complacency, without critical reserves, without psychological inhibitions and prejudices; but I think the effort will be precisely one of evoking this world then knowing how to sit back, calm and detached, and watch it all unfold.

This it seems to us is the most honest and fascinating way of getting it together. Encolpius, Ascyltus, Eumolpus, Giton, Lichas, Tryphaena . . . make their fabulous adventures relive, without glamourizing them as sadistic or erotic. Even if their adventures were sometimes so cruel as to be revolting by our standards, if they were obscene in such a grand and total way as to become innocent again, yet beyond their ferocity, their eroticism, they embody the eternal myth; man standing alone before the fascinating mystery of life, all its terror, its beauty and its passion.

4. *Amarcord:* The Fascism within Us   *Federico Fellini*
An Interview with Valerio Riva

RIVA: Does the episode concerning the visit of the *federale*[1] have a special place in *Amarcord?*

FELLINI: This seems to me the central, irreplaceable, indispensable episode. The film is intended to be the portrait of the Italian provinces, not just at one time but also of today; and it is because of this that the element which characterizes the episode of the *federale* most succinctly—that is, the ridiculous conditioning, the theatricality, the infantilism, the subjection to a puppet-like power, to a ridiculous myth—this is really the center of the film, its fulcrum. Fascism was a way of looking at life, not from an impersonal but a collective point of view, and precisely in regard to this collective motif, the visit of the *federale* is, independently of its anecdotal and historical qualities, the veritable background of the whole story.

RIVA: How is fascism viewed by you?

FELLINI: Fascism is not viewed, as in most political films that are made today, from (how can I put it) a judgmental perspective. That is, from the outside. Detached judgments, aseptic diagnoses, complete and definitive formulae always seem to me (at least on the part of those of the generation to which I belong) a bit inhuman. The province of *Amarcord* is one in which we are all recognizable, the director first of all, in the ignorance which confounded us. A great ignorance and a great confusion. Not that I wish to minimize the economic and social causes of fascism. I only wish to say that today what is still most interesting is the psychological, emotional manner of being a fascist. What is this manner? It is a sort of blockage, an arrested development during the phase of adolescence. And I believe that such an arrest, such a repression of the natural development of an individual must, of necessity, unleash compensatory entanglements. It is perhaps because of this that

. . . .

From *Il film Amarcord di Federico Fellini,* eds. Gianfranco Angelucci and Liliana Betti (Bologna: Cappelli Editore, 1974), pp. 101-7. Copyright © 1976 by Diogenes Verlag AG Zurich. All rights reserved. Translated by Peter Bondanella.

when growth results in an evolution which is betrayed and deceived, fascism, in some of its aspects, can even seem to be an alternative to delusion, a kind of weak-willed and unhinged redemption.

RIVA: Does this evolution continue to be betrayed and deceived?

FELLINI: I don't wish to say that we Italians have not yet gone beyond adolescence and fascism. That would be an excessive and unjust affirmation. Things are certainly very much different from then, that is obvious. Even the fact that we are chatting here about the sequence of the visit of the *federale* for the festival of April 21st[2] and that I was able to shoot this sequence for the cinema and that it will be shown means that things have changed. And yet, if you withdraw from this entourage of one hundred thousand people that, more or less, know each other, and take a train (which we don't do any more) and climb into a second-class wagon and listen to the sounds that people exchange and almost succeed in referring these sounds to a concept, the impression is always not to know whether you are among your contemporaries or whether, on the other hand, you are a Martian, whether you have gone mad (but perhaps even our own talk will seem senseless to those travelers in second class . . .). In short, the feeling that one who travels across Italy in this way has, is that Italy, mentally, is still much the same. To say it in other terms, I have the impression that fascism and adolescence continue to be, in a certain measure, permanent historical seasons of our lives: adolescence of our individual lives, fascism of our national life. That is, this remaining children for eternity, this leaving responsibilities for others, this living with the comforting sensation that there is someone who thinks for you (and at one time it's mother, then it's father, then it's the mayor, another time Il Duce, another time the Madonna, another time the Bishop, in short, other people): and in the meanwhile you have this limited, time-wasting freedom which permits you only to cultivate absurd dreams—the dream of the American cinema, or the Oriental dream concerning women; in conclusion, the same old, monstrous, out-of-date myths that even today seem to me to form the most important conditioning of the average Italian. And, I believe, that even before fascism, the fault of this chronic insufficient development, this arrested development at a childlike stage, lies with the Catholic Church. Living in this kind of environment, each person develops not individual characteristics but only pathological defects. And just here lies the meaning of the scene of the *federale*'s visit. All the characters of the film are to be found there: the professors, the boys, the authorities, the lawyer, the whores, Gra-

disca, the son-in-law Pataca. All are present with their tics, their manias.
And up to that point they seemed to be manias, innocuous tics: and
yet, it is enough for the characters to gather together for an occasion
like this, and there, from apparently harmless eccentricities, their
manias take on a completely different meaning. The gathering of April
21st, just like the passing of the *Rex*, the burning of the great bonfire
at the beginning, and so on, are always occasions of total stupidity.
The pretext of being together is always a leveling process. People stay
together only to commit stupid acts. And when they are alone, there
is bewilderment, solitude, or the ridiculous dream of the Orient, of
Fred Astaire, or the myth of luxury and American ostentation. It is
only ritual which keeps them all together. Since no character has a real
sense of individual responsibility, or has only petty dreams, no one
has the strength not to take part in the ritual, to remain at home outside of it. The wake of the myth finds each one caught up in the midst
of this collectivity or strolling down the main street of the town, or
waiting at length on the high seas for the passing of the *Rex*, or
dancing, in a kind of medieval sand, around the "fogarazza" of St.
Joseph,[3] or looking at the carriage that passes with the new whores.

RIVA: Or looking at the television the RAI[4] prepares for us. . . .

FELLINI: Let's speak more clearly: fascism. I don't say this presum-
ing to come to any definitive conclusions. I only wish to suggest what
seems to me to be the most congenial point of view in order to answer
the question of how fascism is recounted in my film. *Amarcord* is a
story which unfolds in an Italian province, a province like any other,
and the film should thus be precisely the portrait of this province. I
seem to recognize the eternal premises of fascism precisely in being
provincial, therefore, in the lack of information, in the lack of awareness of problems which are concretely real, in the refusal to go deeper
into matters of life out of laziness, prejudice, convenience, and pre-
sumption. To brag about being ignorant, to seek to affirm ourselves or
our group not with the strength that comes from real skill, from experience, but instead with boastings, with affirmations of the self for
their own sake alone, the unfolding of feigned qualities rather than
true ones. For instance, sexual exhibitionism is also fascism. It should
be an emotion and, instead, it is in danger of becoming a show, something clownish and useless, an ugly thing which women endure passively and dumfoundedly. One cannot fight fascism without identifying
it as that aspect of us which is stupid, shabby, weak-willed: an aspect

which has no party affiliation, of which we should be ashamed, and for the repulsion of which it is not enough to declare, "I serve in an anti-fascist party," because that aspect is inside of us and, already once in the past, fascism has given it expression, authority, standing.

RIVA: But *Amarcord* is not only the revelation of the most shadowy archetypes of our collective psychology. I believe its main concern is the theme of power: the noble family who has someone search for their ring in the excrement;[5] the crazy uncle who is taken back to the mad-house by the intervention of the midget nun (who knows what she says to him, but it is authoritative to the point that not only does he obey but he even leaves smiling, voluntarily renouncing his ephemeral interval of liberty), then, the passing of the *Rex*, the gigantic symbol of power; and the puppet-like representations of this power—the prince, the generals, the *gerarchi*[6]—those more subtle and encompassing symbols—the great face of Mussolini made of pink and white flowers; and at the end, the fact that this power marries Gradisca, who represents everything in the film (sex, dreams, liberty, the conquest of adulthood) and has her carried away, and it is a power personified by a *carabiniere* who is absolutely of the same stock as the prince. . . .

FELLINI: More than that, it is almost simply the same actor. Or, more accurately, it is one who stands behind the prince in a tuxedo and bows; a little personal trick of mine, perhaps difficult to recognize but which precisely indicates a link between the two episodes. And then, as the *carabiniere* carries Gradisca away, he yells the words "Viva l'Italia!" Nevertheless, this discourse on power in *Amarcord* only ·continues an old argument. In *Roma* the sequence of the Jovinelli theater also intended to express the bewilderment of a consciousness profoundly wounded by power; and in the same film, yet another discourse on power was the scene of the ecclesiastical fashion parade with its pomp, the embarrassed nobility, the raving princess who dreams of the restoration of Pius XII, that scenography, that profound and continuously noticeable difference of caste. And also in *Satyricon* I believe I discussed power at length. . . . Perhaps here, in *Amarcord*, this argument is more pronounced because it is more personalized, recognizable: it is Italy, our own province, our own infancy, our own school, those were our professors, that was our priest; our own father, for better or worse, on different levels, was the same anguished neurotic, our own mother a kind of poor old woman who was always raving, damaged to the depths of her nervous system. . . . Even the dialects that are

Amarcord: The imaginary fascist marriage under the grotesque gaze of a bust of Il Duce. (Museum of Modern Art/Film Stills Archive)

present in the film make you feel that it is not merely an allusion or a symbol but something that directly concerns a past which is nearby and still very much present, at least in my opinion.

RIVA: And because of this, *Amarcord* seems to be your most detached, objective film rather than being an autobiographical film?

FELLINI: I'm always a bit offended when I hear that one of my films is "autobiographical": it seems like a reductionist definition to me, especially if then, as it often happens, "autobiographical" comes to be understood in the sense of anecdotal, like someone who tells old school stories. So much so that at the beginning, I felt a great reluctance in speaking about it. I continued to say: be careful, "Amarcord" doesn't mean "I remember" at all; instead, it is a kind of cabalistic word, a word of seduction, the brand of an aperitif: *Amarcord* . . . I felt that authorizing a viewing of the film with an autobiographical "key" would have been a grave error. So much so that at one moment I wanted to entitle it simply *Viva l'Italia!* Then, I thought that this would have been too mysterious or too didactic. Another title I wanted to give it was *Il borgo*, in the sense of a medieval enclosure, a lack of information, a lack of contact with the unheard of, the new . . . Then, finally, scribbling little sketches for the title, this word came to me—*Amarcord;* but you have to forget its origin. For, in its mystery, it means only the feeling that characterizes the whole film: a funereal feeling, one of isolation, dream, torpor, and of ignorance. As for the impression the film has given to many that it contains a greater detachment than in my other earlier films, this is perhaps derived, initially, from the preoccupation I felt not to have to repeat motifs overnarrated or enjoyed in other films; then, because in these last years, I have made films as if they were illnesses, as something from which to liberate myself as soon as possible and as something of which no longer to speak, both of us (the film and I) conditioned by a kind of reciprocal lack of esteem. I believe this sense of encumbrance, however, is an integral part of the creative process: a fantasy, even at a modest level, is always a kind of visitation which demands to be realized by you. The fact of being chosen and the feeling you cannot escape contain something authoritarian that you undergo unwillingly. And so, it happens that you enter hastily like a child, like an infant, into a state of mind in haste, in which you think you are inhabited by an enemy, by someone who wishes your ultimate ruin at the same time that he wants to be narrated, incarnated, rendered alive in the most complete fashion possible.

RIVA: This detachment is also, however, an involvement at various levels. . . .

FELLINI: Yes, but the more profound the levels are, the greater this resistance is, the greater this recalcitrance or this rebellion is noticed by you. The more this possesses you, the more you can release yourself from it and avoid the total and living envelopment that could have happened to you in the first stages. Then, in this film, there was the sensation of reaching bottom, of liquidating the storehouse of psychological residues. Probably all this gave a sense of detachment to the material. But psychologically, it would have been more accurate to speak of a kind of heartrending refusal of something which once belonged to you, of something which made you, of something which you still are. And in this refusal, there is always something sad, tortured, and torturous. You speak of that infamous school, of that stupid and dull life together, of ridiculous dreams, of the bruises that you have dragged along with you forever, of a complete refusal of that life. And, at the same time, you know very well that unfortunately you had no other life, you had only that one. During the few showings I have had until now, and only for friends whom I trust, besides the fun there has always been a great deal of agitation. Now, what is it that agitates if everything in the film is ridiculous? It is because you sense that it is your Italy, it is you, because you sense that if today you are able to look with an almost impious eye at this thing, at the same time it is your mirror. And then, notwithstanding that, you sense that there is no time left for another kind of life and that this thing from which you wish to detach yourself and which you judge without pity is the only life you have had. And the life others will have doesn't matter for you at all—let's say that to ourselves clearly for once. That is what leaves you touched, tortured, encumbered: for while you refuse, while you detach yourself from all this absurdity, you know very well that it is you who are cutting the ground from under your own feet, it is you who are cutting yourself off dangerously, definitively.

NOTES

1. A provincial secretary of the fascist party.—EDITOR
2. The mythical date of the foundation of the city of Rome and, therefore, a fascist national holiday because of Mussolini's desire to equate the fascist state with the Roman Empire.—EDITOR
3. The bonfire upon which the witch is burned in effigy to celebrate the coming of spring and the passing of winter on St. Joseph's Day, March 19.—EDITOR
4. The Italian television network, a state-owned corporation similar to the British BBC.—EDITOR
5. This scene is not included in the version of *Amarcord* distributed in America, although scenes depicting the family and their attempts to capture sparrows for food during the winter are retained.—EDITOR
6. Fascist party officials.—EDITOR

5. *Casanova:* An Interview with   *Federico Fellini*
Aldo Tassone

QUESTION: You have stated that you make films to free yourself, much like carrying out a hygienic operation on the memory. *Satyricon* in order to free yourself from high school and the ancient Romans, *The Clowns* to free yourself from the circus, *Roma* to free yourself from the capital city and "in order to shut out the capital, shameless with its baggage of nightmares," *Amarcord* to free yourself from the nightmare of Romagna, the fascists, and your schooling. With *Casanova* do you wish to settle accounts with the eighteenth century and the national Don Giovannis? How was this project born? How do you propose to bring it about?

FELLINI: To the question of why I am making this film, the answer is always the same: because I signed a contract. I read *The History of My Life* afterwards, and I was immediately overcome by a sense of dizziness and by the mortifying impression of having taken a false step.[1] Bernardino Zapponi, co-author of the scenario, gave me comfort by reminding me that with *Satyricon* almost the same thing occurred: I signed the contract and then I read Petronius. That is true, but with the substantial difference that there an emotion, a feeling for the film was immediately born. This time it did not happen that way, and the project continues to stand still because of the stubborn and hysterical reason of being forced to do it; as a consequence, even the film's point of view has been created by necessity, out of desperation, imposed completely extraneously to the book, to Casanova, to the eighteenth century, and to everything that has been written on the subject. Reading this kind of telephone book of artistically nonexistent and sometimes most boring occurrences, going ahead in the boundless, paperlike ocean of *The History of My Life*, the arid listing of a quantity of facts amassed without any selection, feeling, or amusement, where there appears a rigor of the statistical variety—like an inventoried list, pedantic,

· · · · · · · · · ·

From *Casanova rendez-vous con Federico Fellini*, eds. Liliana Betti and Gianfranco Angelucci (Milan: Bompiani Casa Editrice 6 C.S.p.A., 1975), pp. 138-45. Copyright © 1976 by Diogenes Verlag AG Zurich. All rights reserved. Translated by Peter Bondanella.

27

meticulous, petulant, not even untruthful—this has only produced in me a profound sense of irritation, estrangement, and disgust. It was this complete refusal, this total lack of the minimum of sympathy for the undertaking, it was this nausea, this aversion, that suggested to us the method of making the film, its only possible point of view. At least for me. A film on nothingness: there is no ideology, sensation, feeling; there are no emotions even of an aesthetic character; there is especially no eighteenth century and, consequently, no historical point of view of a historical-critical or sociological nature. A total absence of everything, a mortuary-like film, rendered without emotion—there are only forms that are outlined in masses, perspectives articulated in a frigid and hysterical repetition. In desperation, I grabbed on to this "vertigo of nothingness" as the sole point of reference to which to relate the story of Casanova and his nonexistent life. I thought I saw a very up-to-date existential attitude in that glassy eye which allows itself to slide over reality—and to pass through and to erase it—without intervening with a judgment, without interpreting it with a feeling. It is nonlife with its empty forms which are composed and decomposed, the charm of an aquarium, an absentmindedness of sealike profundity, where everything is completely hidden and unknown because there is no human penetration or intimacy.

QUESTION: All this was in you, as you read Casanova's *History of My Life*, or in the book?

FELLINI: Of course, if you approach the reading of *The History of My Life* according to the hallowed conventions, then you will discover nothing of all this. Casanova seems to be the example of the life of a man who has arrived, who has been realized: so many women, the courts, the voyages, the adventures, the encounters with important figures, with Rousseau, with Voltaire, and then he understood philosophy and mathematics and medicine and spoke and wrote about them. The ingredients are apparently those of authentic life; it is enough to project them on a life-giving desire and everything can become exemplary, a full, successful, enjoyable life. Many intellectual friends admire and love Casanova, they have beautified him as a matchless example of vitality, they see him as a man of transition, a great narrator, an enlightened spirit. In the fact that he may have passed through his whole life without judging it, in this absence of judgment and of an emotive personality, they see a great wisdom, an exemplary means of living in this world.

But it is not like that. Casanova for me does not exist. I have not

Casanova: Casanova (Donald Sutherland) emerges victorious from a love-making contest in Rome at the palace of the British Ambassador. (Federico Fellini and Produzioni Europee Associate, Rome)

recognized him, I have not discovered him in the pages that claim to reveal him to us, and—yes—there are thousands of them; Casanova is only the anagraphic enclosure of a mass of episodes, actions, persons, tumultuous but inert and often mute matter; Casanova is a completely external man without secrets and without shame (every so often he talks about Ariosto, declaims his verse and cries), a presumptuous man, a know-it-all, he is as cumbersome as a horse in the house, he has the health of a horse, he is a horse! There is nothing in *The History of My Life*, it recalls nothing to you, nothing! Only dust that rains all over you. There is no nature, no animals, no babies, no trees, no adjectives, no description of a moment in a day. He has gone all over the world, and it is as if he never got out of bed. He is really an Italian, *The* Italian: the indefiniteness, the indifference, the commonplaces, the conventional ways, the façade, the figure, the attitude. And, therefore, it is clear why he has become a myth, because he is really nothingness, a universality without meaning: Poetry, Woman, the Feminine Soul, Science, Arts . . . a complete lack of individuality, the indeterminant—that's it. In the indeterminant, there always resides a great fascination, because the indeterminant is the collectivity that gathers everything together, confirms everything, exalts everything, breaks up everything in a system of coercive and unalterable exchange. The film is aimed at being precisely this kind of portrait of nothingness: so many useless things that have no individual meaning because they are not penetrated, chosen, or selected; they are not defined, they are without limits in the sense of total bewilderment without delimitation, without true life.

QUESTION: But wasn't there at least a certain ingenuity in Casanova?

FELLINI: Who knows what Casanova was like? We are evaluating the character of a book. And the character is detached, he becomes a point of reference upon which people project themselves. To me, he seems like a boring writer who has spoken to us about a loud, annoying, despicable character, a courtier who calls himself Casanova, an ill-bred man bedecked with plumes who stinks of sweat and face powder, a man who possesses the stupidity, the arrogance, and the bumptiousness of the barracks and the church, a man who always wants to be right. And it even seems that he always was right, because he knows about everything. But in a manner that is so impersonal as to get on your nerves. He is a man who does not even allow you to be ignorant, he superimposes himself upon everything: he is also six feet four inches tall and recounts that he can make love eight times in succession so that competition even here becomes impossible; he translates from the Latin and Greek, knows mathematics, recites, acts, speaks French very well, and has known Louis XV and Madame Pompadour. So how does one go about being around a big turd like this? The character never suggests to you the minimum of interest, of curiosity, as undefined as he is, rhetorical, pompous, challenging, brave even—he fought duels. A fascist. A kind of anticipation of that crude and elementary self-satisfied classification of personality types which is outlined in fascism, that is— the collective, not individual, existence, the drunkenness in fireman-like, theatrical action, the manner of thinking according to a compulsory system of generic slogans without meaning, the debased emotion at a physiological and feverish temperature—in short, adolescence in its most declining phase; that is, arrogance, health, fanatic and hypocritical idealism. Fascism is a protracted adolescence beyond any immediate reality. Perhaps I exaggerate a bit, but the character that emerges is that one. There, you see, I could easily describe a character like that. The sad part is that he is without mystery or innocence, and his mediocrity is a shrewd mediocrity. Who knows, perhaps as an old man when the servants of the Count of Waldenstein mocked him and played atrocious jokes on him, and he—bedecked with plumes and powdered like an old clown—continued to act as he had before the French Revolution without realizing that the times had changed, that his muddled, completely bombastic life had been reduced to a tottering and sick carcass, there, then, he might perhaps have aroused a little bit of sympathy, of empathy—who knows? Everyone who has read the script likes it, and Zapponi is convinced that it is one of the most beautiful scenarios we have done. Anyway, the slightly hysterical operation of mysterious reevaluation that I want to undertake against that character is intellectualistic, rigid, strained. Above all, it is also anticinematic: a film wherein there is no story, there are no aesthetic seductions, an abstract and formless film on a nonlife. From the stylistic point of view, the experiment can be tempting. However, I am afraid that after the first five minutes. . . . Basically, cinema has, at any rate, its deep and indissoluble link with the romantic and with narrative, even in those works which seem the most disjointed. Here, instead, there is no narrative either in the romantic or the psychological sense. There are no characters, there are no situations, there are neither premises nor developments nor catharses—it is a mechanical, frenetic ballet like an electrified wax museum.

QUESTION: How is it that this film has seemed this way to you?

FELLINI: Because of the repulsion that it caused me, the bother, the vexation, the contract that I had signed, the mortification of hearing the misunderstanding—"Fellini is shooting Casanova!" "Casanova! Thousands of beautiful women!"—being obliged, after having bound myself to the contract, to encourage and to act as an accomplice to this operation. . . . Instinctively, because of the bit of Romagnol that exists in me, all this provoked such a rebellion in me as to render myself immediately intolerant of anything which concerned the project. Therefore, I read Casanova with a distrustfulness and a growing anger, ripping up the pages: every time I completed a page, I tore it up rather than turn it over. Bernardino Zapponi was demoralized at seeing

Casanova: Casanova (Donald Sutherland) and the mechanical ballerina (Adele Angela Lojodice) are instructed on how to play the final scene of the film. (Federico Fellini and Produzioni Europee Associate, Rome)

me rip to pieces the Mondadori edition of *The History of My Life*, which is impossible to find. The annoyance of being forced into a minimum of documentation, to leaf through books and documents, to look at hundreds of paintings, to dive into the eighteenth century, disinclined and unwilling, in short to lose a year's time, became by and by a form of total refusal. Because of this, I circled about the project, placing myself in a dark and ashen zone like an astronaut, in a place where there was no comfort whatsoever but only this foreign, vitreous fixedness. Because of this, I call it "hysterical." Besides the fact, then, that from the figurative point of view, the eighteenth century is the most worn-out century, exhausted and impoverished in every respect. To restore an originality, a new seductiveness, a new vision of this century is already, on the figurative level, a desperate undertaking. And then the film confuses me even more, it becomes ill also from these necessities and urgencies, and I—always more and more—feel like a person who does not know the reasons why he has been imprisoned and who is ensnared in a scheme which escapes him, like Kafka's "A Knock on the Manor Gate." Have you read it? (The man who is passing by gives a knock on a gate and continues to walk with his fiancée; and he is suddenly surrounded by arms bearers and is carried away only because he gave that knock). An irrelevant act that has set in motion a mysterious trial, an inevitable condemnation. The film as punishment, expiation . . .

QUESTION: And what do dreams tell you?

FELLINI: They help to confuse me.

QUESTION: Did something of the same nature happen with *The Voyage of Mastorna?*[2]

FELLINI: No, for Mastorna there was something else. . . . Mastorna, who then seemed like a frozen island lost in the cosmos, now appears to me a warm nest of comfort and protection. I tried, I proposed replacing the Casanova mess with that of Mastorna and was not successful, because as a result of a ridiculous misunderstanding—ridiculous when my state of mind is taken into account—Casanova is the film everyone wants to make. "Fellini Casanova!" "Casanova Fellini!"— there is not a producer in the world who has not greedily tried to grab this project. I even accepted a clause in the contract which adds confusion to confusion: shooting the film in English! [The reader should not overlook the subtle linguistic parallel between Fellini and Casanova. Casanova's autobiography was written not in his native Italian but in French in order to ensure it the widest possible audience, just as Fellini's financial backers urged upon him an English film to increase their chance of profits. The sense of alienation and estrangement Fellini describes was, therefore, already present to some extent in the autobiographical narrative which forms the nucleus of his film.—EDITOR.] A language that I know only in a crude, approximate fashion, and which represents a final estrangement of this material. Every so often I am also seized by hesitation of the moralistic variety, by ideological scruples. I think it should be time to put an end to the satisfying or anguishing representation of the "negative," alarming and alarmed mirrors of dissolution and disintegration. One ought to find the force to propose something—a character, an idea, a fantasy which recharges you with the energy of life.

QUESTION: But if you feel this way about the film . . .

FELLINI: I feel this way about it, but perhaps the task of anyone who pretends to speak to others must be, in these times, more concise, innocent, generous, and especially more unaware of the attractive privilege of skepticism, or of the gratifying but by now illusory tinsel of a solitary wisdom or salvation, in order to try, instead, to measure oneself by the very human risk of a more accessible solidarity and involvement. The "positive" emerges from the "negative," people are accustomed to say, but you know, people have spoken for so long and so uniquely of the "negative" that it has become an exclusive, diseased dimension. We must reflect upon and bear in mind the fact that the cinema is an instrument of vast, mass communication. This film of mine, instead, is extremely aristocratic, made for the initiate, and unpopular. Moreover, every so often this feeling of discouragement also seizes me: who knows? Perhaps it is a moment of fatigue, of personal entanglement in fear and separation. It would seem to me, however, that one ought to be able to shake off some of the "negative" with the representation of it. Beyond everything, no matter how gifted an author may be, when he attempts to communicate, the horror of the negative will never be that brutal, dull horror of our daily lives. There will always be a delight in the author—the same relief, the same euphoria of expressive liberation—that renders the affair domesticated, either because of aesthetic and ideological reasons, or because of the subliminal effect of every representation; in short, he will always create a spectacle, and as menacing or as admonitory as it may be, how can he ever achieve the terror provoked by the squalor, by the dissolution, and by the real chaos that we experience every day? There, moreover, is another reason which renders me unsteady in the face of such an undertaking: nostalgia, a certain allure, a kind of grief, the task of achieving a different kind of discourse. . . . But which one? In situations like this one, composed of intolerable elements, of unclear tensions, it is easy to fall into the misunderstanding—a completely visceral one—of speaking in a utopian manner of good feelings, of a paradise lost or of one to come . . . while, instead, it should be the moment to attempt in some way to . . .

QUESTION: . . . To achieve something like the latest Bergman of *Cries and Whispers* perhaps or to continue the argument of *La Strada* and *Cabiria* on communication between human beings. . . .

FELLINI: Yes, but an honest discourse on the necessity of projecting ourselves into something, a discourse on trust, on goodwill, on common objectives is still very dangerous. Whenever we hear a person who speaks in this manner, we immediately fall into an infantile state, there immediately arises the mortal danger of abandoning ourselves, of trusting ourselves, and there is always someone ready to exploit this abandon and to begin the whole affair from the beginning again with the same errors, the same misunderstandings, the same atrocities as always. It is evident that *unmasking the lie, identifying the inauthentic, and taking apart the indefinite or false absolutes* continues to be, for now, the only corrective resource—a mocking, inexhaustible safeguard—against our bankrupt history while we are waiting to be prepared to propose and to live under a new hypothesis of the truth.

NOTES

1. The *Mémoires* of Giacomo Girolamo Casanova (1725-1778) first appeared in 1821. The reader is reminded, however, that no edition or translation of this work in any language was complete or well edited until the publication of the entire original manuscript in 1960. In English, there is an excellent twelve-volume version of this complete manuscript translated by Willard R. Trask entitled *History of My Life* (New York: Harcourt, 1966).—EDITOR

2. This film, never completed by Fellini, is described in *Fellini: A Director's Notebook*.—EDITOR

2

. . . .

Perspectives on
Individual Films

La Strada

. . . .

6. *La Strada*   *Edward Murray*

. . . On one level, *La Strada* is a fable about Beauty and the Beast; in this case, however, Gelsomina's beauty is interior, not exterior, and it is Beauty who loves the Beast, not the other way round—at least for most of the picture. Before leaving the place of her birth, Gelsomina turns and kneels in the direction of the sea, in a silent farewell communion with those waters that throughout the film are identified with her. Revealing his usual sullen expression, the strongman watches the simple-minded girl on her knees. Then Gelsomina climbs in the back of Zampanò's motorcycle-driven trailer and the two depart on what is to become a spiritual odyssey for both of them.

Zampanò's main act consists of breaking an iron chain with the muscles of his chest, a performance that impresses not only the country people along the road but also Gelsomina. Over and over in the course of the picture, Zampanò utters the same words ("Sensitive souls are advised not to look. In Milan, Ettore Montagna lost his sight through this trick, since there is an enormous strain on the optic nerve . . ."), struts in a circle—stomach in, chest out—waving his chain in the air, prior to bursting its links by inflating his lungs. The repetition of this performance underlines Zampanò's monotonous, self-enclosed manner of existence. He is an animal, and he treats other people as though they were animals. On their first evening together, Gelsomina cooks soup that is so bad even she can't eat it; although Zampanò devours the soup—as he devours everything—he still calls it "slop for pigs." At the beginning of the film, Zampanò assures Gelsomina's mother that he "can even teach a dog to perform." Now he proceeds to teach Gelsomina. Her job is to announce his act by intoning: "Zam-pan-ò is here!" followed by drumbeats as the chain is broken. Unfortunately, Gelsomina is not a fast learner. The audience laughs at the attempts of
. . . .

Zampanò to make the girl understand the simple requirements of her role; but when the lout proceeds to strike Gelsomina on the leg with a switch in order to make her concentrate, the laughter dies. What starts like a kind of Abbott and Costello vaudeville turn, then, ends far from comedy. Just as Fellini juxtaposes beauty and bestiality, just so he alternates gaiety and sadness, the complex structure of his film moving from the seriocomic (up to about the middle of the picture) to the serious (there are few laughs in the second half of *La Strada*).

Fellini does not indulge in fancy camera work or bizarre compositions. Whenever he moves his camera, the movement is well motivated in terms of mood, action, and theme. For example, on their first night together Zampanò tells Gelsomina to sleep with him in the trailer. She wants to sleep outside. He repeats his order. The camera-eye has been recording the scene impassively in front of the motorcycle. The characters step out of sight and start around to the back of the trailer. Slowly, the camera glides forward, makes a turn to the left, and gazes downward at the mattress. Zampanò pushes Gelsomina roughly inside the trailer and closes the flap on the tarpaulin, causing the screen to go dark. This incident remains one of the few times in the film when the viewer becomes aware of the camera. Since Gelsomina is frightened, the camera seems hesitant, unwilling to look at what is to follow; the camera's eventual intrusion—with its serpentine downward motion—is both intimate and faintly ominous.

The structure of *La Strada* can be described as episodic. As Zampanò and Gelsomina journey from town to town, characters are introduced and then seen no more—which is lifelike, but unlike plotted films, where characters who appear at the beginning must also function in the middle and reappear at the end. The episodes are unified thematically; a scene that at first sight might strike the viewer as a digression later reveals its relevance to the overall design. Although Fellini structures his action vertically by concentrating on character development and idea, he also provides horizontal movement or story interest. Indeed, it is almost impossible to separate vertical and horizontal movement, or character exploration and story, so closely has Fellini woven together the various elements of his picture.

Like all his films, Fellini's *La Strada* is open in structure, thus reflecting his view of life as a mystery filled with unpredictable possibilities. Throughout the movie, Fellini alternates a day scene with a night scene, a rhythmic pattern that finds its musical parallel in the recurrence of Nino Rota's famous tune. A scene enacted in bleak, sometimes cold sunlight gives way to a scene involving an empty street or a market place at night, while the music comes and goes throughout; hence, the score not only augments the happy-sad thematic approach but also functions as a structural device for unifying the whole. The result is an exquisite blending of realism (the location shooting, the numerous nonprofessionals in the cast, the holes in Zampanò's sweater and pants) and a kind of "poetic," "lyrical" expressionism or surrealism (the numerous symbols, the fablelike quality of the action, the stylized conception of the three chief personages).

Fellini rarely puts his meaning into words; when he does, as we shall see, it is generally because certain ideas cannot be expressed in any other way. However, through his associational manner of linking scenes, Fellini not only gives his form continuity but he also supplies nonverbal commentary. After the screen goes black in the trailer, for instance, there is a scene in which Gelsomina wakes up in the night and begins to cry. Zampanò—his sexual appetite satisfied—is sleeping. Even though she has been taken against her will, even though her body has been used without respect for her person, Gelsomina stops weeping momentarily to gaze fondly at the unconscious male who has somehow, in spite of himself, aroused her love and inspired her hope. But the next shot makes clear how little Gelsomina can really expect from the future. It is the following day; and on the screen we see the strongman with a chain stretched across his chest: food, drink, breaking the chain, sex, sleep—Zampanò knows only these physical activities and needs.

Evening. The couple visit a café. Zampanò is in his customary surly mood, but Gelsomina remains delighted with the experience. When Zampanò, before eating, pokes a toothpick around in his mouth, Gelsomina imitates her hero; likewise, she mops her plate greedily with a crust of bread as he does, and she even tries to drink as much wine as the strongman. To no avail. Zampanò ignores the clownish little creature who shares his mean existence, constantly foiling her attempts at intimacy with disdain:

GELSOMINA: Where do you come from?
ZAMPANÒ: From my part of the country.
GELSOMINA: Where were you born?
ZAMPANÒ: (Sneering) In my father's house.

Drunk now, Zampanò notices a buxom, red-headed woman across the room and calls her over to their table. During this scene the strongman shows off his muscles and makes the woman laugh, treating her in a way he never treats the faithful wretch who assists him in his act. All the same, Gelsomina fails to understand what is happening, fails to grasp the fact that Zampanò intends to spend the night with the fat

La Strada: Gelsomina (Giulietta Masina) admires Zampanò (Anthony Quinn) at a restaurant. (Museum of Modern Art/Film Stills Archive)

redhead; so she naïvely laughs along with the other two, with no trace of jealousy apparent on her innocent countenance. However, in order for the viewer to see the scene from Gelsomina's perspective—or, rather, to see what Gelsomina would see if she had eyes to see—Fellini shoots the action partly from her viewpoint. The camera-eye does not actually "see" what Gelsomina sees; nevertheless, although her skull remains visible on the screen, the shot is clearly angled from her point of view, since the camera is situated just in back of her head. Outside the café, Zampanò helps the other woman onto his motorcycle and instructs the confused Gelsomina to wait behind for him. "But where are you going?" she cries. There is no reply, only the sound of the motorcycle fading into the night.

Dissolve. It is dark and quiet . . . and Gelsomina is still waiting for Zampanò. As she sits at the curb with a morose expression, a horse suddenly emerges and noisily clipclops past. The appearance of this stray, riderless animal has occasioned much comment. John Russell Taylor, for example, observes: "the effect is positively surrealistic: totally arbitrary, yet giving an instant visual reinforcement to the mood of the scene. The lost horse might well be a figment of Gelsomina's imagination, an image of her own state. But it is also a real horse, and its appearance here at this time is not impossible, only mildly peculiar." Is Fellini "saying" that Gelsomina is like a horse without a rider? Certainly the strongman treats her no better than he would a horse . . .

Morning. A child sits on the curb beside the petulant Gelsomina. Also beside her is a plate of food, which a compassionate woman has left for Gelsomina, but which she has not touched. When the woman returns, she informs Gelsomina that a man is sleeping in a field down the road, near a moto-trailer. Happily, Gelsomina returns to her brutal master. Dancing lightly across the desolate landscape, she suddenly pauses before a single bare tree. A child passes, watching her. With arms outstretched, a smile lighting up her small puffy face, Gelsomina imitates the tree. A boy approaches. "The dog died in there," he informs her, pointing to an area beyond a fence. Standing before the dog's burial ground, Gelsomina looks inside, wonderment evident in her expression. She listens for something. For what? Gelsomina communicates intuitively with the sea, with trees, even with the spirit of a dead dog. She is witness to a reality beyond the one that can be seen or touched. Yet, at the same time, she is very much a part of that natural world whose inner being she mysteriously apprehends. Because she longs to see the various manifestations of the Good—be it love or a tree—take root and grow, she plants tomato seeds by the side of the road, even though Zampanò plans to move on again. To her astonished question: "Are we leaving already?," Zampanò contemptuously replies: "Think we're going to stay here 'till your tomatoes come up? *Tomatoes!*" The brute's lack of understanding remains abysmal.

Fade in to a shot of an open area where a wedding celebration is taking place. On one side there is a long banquet table with happy people eating and drinking; on the other side Zampanò and Gelsomina are performing. Seated on the ground, Zampanò is beating a drum, while Gelsomina, wearing a bowler hat and a clown's makeup, goes through a simple dance number. Except for some children watching Gelsomina in the background, the act goes largely unnoticed. A man offers Gelsomina a glass of wine; she takes a sip, then unselfishly passes it along to Zampanò. During this scene, Fellini again moves his camera to advantage. There is a long tracking shot the length of the banquet table: faces of happy celebrants, a priest eating, wine glasses raised, confetti, the bride and groom; cut to a momentary shot of other celebrants again—followed by a shot of Gelsomina and Zampanò, set apart from the others. The visual juxtaposition of the bride and Gelsomina speaks for itself; the contrast between the boisterous fun along the table and the dreary routine of Gelsomina's life with Zampanò requires no verbal underlining. It tells us something about Fellini's tact that he does not starkly play off the image of the bride with a shot of Gelsomina, but instead separates the two images with a brief shot of a few guests in order to convey the relational nature of his editing in a more subtle manner.

Zampanò and Gelsomina are called by a woman to the farmhouse to eat. The children who have been watching Gelsomina perform intercept her, however, and lead her around to the side of the building and up a narrow flight of stairs. Skillfully employing a subjective camera, Fellini takes the audience (via identification with Gelsomina's field of vision) along a series of dimly lighted corridors. Shot of a tiny boy in a black cape; he looks made up to resemble a priest, or perhaps a magician. An air of the uncanny suffuses the scene. And when Gelsomina is led into a dark room, the subjective camera intensifies the viewer's sensation of entering the unknown. In a large bed, propped up on pillows, sits an idiot boy named Oswaldo; he stares at Gelsomina with a frightened gaze. The children want her to amuse the lad. Yet Gelsomina's imitation of a bird only seems to increase Oswaldo's fright. Tentatively, she steps closer to the bed, exchanging a silent, wide-eyed gaze with the strange boy opposite her. All at once, a nun enters the room and angrily chases Gelsomina and the children away.

As noted in an earlier chapter, the scene involving Oswaldo is based on an experience from Fellini's boyhood when he visited his grandmother in Gambettola. The film-maker has provided his own interpretation of the episode:

> I probably used it to give Gelsomina an exact awareness of solitude. There is a feast at the farm, and Gelsomina, who ultimately is a creature who likes to be in the company of other people, and who wants to take part in the singing and in the general gaiety, is led off by this host of children who, shouting, take her to see the sick boy. The apparition of this creature who is isolated, and a prey to delirium—and who thus has an extremely mysterious dimension—its seems to me that uniting him in a close-up with Gelsomina, who comes right next to him and who looks at him with curiosity, underlines with rather great suggestive power Gelsomina's own solitude.

While Gelsomina has been making her discovery of solitude, Zampanò has been making the acquaintance of the woman who called the performers to eat. Positioned outside the kitchen, Zampanò and the woman are discoursing on sex and swallowing their food ravenously. (This is the woman to whom Zampanò remarks: "Do you always eat standing up like a horse?") The woman has buried two husbands; she would now like to give Zampanò some suits and a hat left behind by her first mate, in exchange for some lovemaking on the part of the strongman. Gelsomina joins them; but when she tries to explain to Zampanò about Oswaldo, the brute ignores her. As he does so often, Fellini here makes use of contrast. Gelsomina's encounter with the mysterious boy represents a discovery of her own loneliness: she yearns for Zampanò to recognize her as a person, to genuinely share his life with her—not merely to exploit her in his act and to use her body for sexual purposes. To be sure, the farm woman also knows solitude; like Zampanò, however, all she thinks about are her physical needs (stuffing her face with macaroni, for example, she refers to sex as a "sweet"). Finally, Zampanò disappears with the woman, leaving Gelsomina to wait for him once more. . . .

Dusk. The wedding party is over, except for one last couple, still dancing to the accompaniment of a remaining musician. A lone tree is prominent in the composition. Next Fellini reveals Gelsomina, from within a barn, studying the scene we have just witnessed. The tree outside reminds the viewer of the single tree that Gelsomina imitated in the previous sequence; later in the film, as Zampanò's moto-trailer journeys down a road, a bare tree again appears in the distance. The lonely Gelsomina and the motif of a bare, isolated tree are what Kenneth Burke calls "equations." Humming the tune that is likewise associated throughout the film with her, Gelsomina asks Zampanò to teach her to play it on the trumpet. The strongman is too absorbed, however, in trying on his newly acquired clothes to reply. Preening himself in a pin-striped suit and snapping the brim down on his fedora, Zampanò mutters scornfully: "*Women!*" the way he had previously muttered: "*Tomatoes!*" Angry at Zampanò's refusal to respond, Gelsomina strides back and forth across the barn—until she falls into a deep hole. Zampanò is amused but Gelsomina obstinately decides to spend the night below. Although the scene is played in a seriocomic fashion, Gelsomina's confinement in the ground represents one of the numerous ways Fellini foreshadows her death.

Dissolve to morning. As though reborn, Gelsomina removes the clothes Zampanò had given her and proceeds to set off in her original garb on a journey by herself, thus leaving the sleeping brute (in the clothes the farm woman has given *him*) to seek another slave for his act. . . . Shot of Gelsomina sitting by the side of the road, examining a bug with curiosity and wonder. Suddenly three musicians appear out of nowhere, marching along in a single file, and Gelsomina, stirred by their spirited playing, jumps up and follows them. The procession involving the three musicians and Gelsomina gives way in the next scene to a conventional religious procession. Shots of a bishop coldly and mechanically blessing the enthusiastic faithful. Shots of the crowd. Shots of a huge cross and other traditional symbols. When Fellini shows us Gelsomina, who is thrilled by the event, he keeps his camera up close and moving with her; hence we tend to identify with Gelsomina, we experience her own emotions, we too are caught up in the excitement. In one long shot Fellini reveals the procession on the right-hand side of the screen, while on the left-hand side he presents a sign reading: BAR. The film-maker is fond of such polarities (consider, for example, the opening of *La Dolce Vita*, wherein the statue of Christ suspended from a helicopter remains juxtaposed to bikini-clad girls sunbathing on a rooftop). In *La Strada* "procession" equals "quest for love and spiritual meaning" (the Gelsomina motif), whereas "BAR" equals "drunkenness, brawling, and casual sex" (the Zampanò motif). When Gelsomina and the other members of the procession enter a church, Fellini again uses a subjective camera, a visual strategy that calls to mind the experience at the farm when the children led Gelsomina into the mysterious room of Oswaldo. By using the same kind of camera technique in both scenes, Fellini links up the two events thematically.

But if Gelsomina learned something about solitude from her meeting with Oswaldo, she is not blessed with a similar discovery upon stepping inside the church. From a low-angle subjective shot of the church interior, Fellini dissolves to the next scene: a shot of Il Matto (Richard Basehart), or The Fool, on a tightrope above a piazza at night. "In a moment," a woman working with the acrobat says into a loudspeaker, "Il Matto will perform the most dangerous of his stunts. Sitting forty meters above the earth, he will eat a dish of spaghetti." Gelsomina looks up to God, but the answer to her prayer comes in the next scene when she again looks up . . . this time at Il Matto. Fellini has said that The Fool is "Jesus." And not surprisingly, critics have managed to ferret out the "Christ symbolism": suspended high overhead, the acrobat is equipped with angel's wings; in one scene, he rides a donkey, just as Jesus did on Palm Sunday; also like Christ, The Fool predicts his own death; and when Zampanò finally kills the equilibrist, he drags the corpse over the ground in a cruciform manner. In religious art, Christ is never depicted with wings; still, one could argue that both Christ and angels are associated in a spiritual way.

Unlike Christ, The Fool does not willingly sacrifice his life for Zampanò; Gelsomina performs that function, though partly as a result of what she learns from The Fool. Christ provoked his executioners, and Il Matto torments Zampanò; however, Christ was motivated by the desire to show men how to live a more authentic existence, whereas The Fool taunts Zampanò out of irrational malice. The "Christ symbolism" is present, then, but it appears in an ambiguous way. Near the end of the film, just before his recognition scene, Zampanò shouts: *"Ho bisogno di nessuno"*; but twice in the picture, Il Matto repeats the same words to Gelsomina: "I don't need anyone." In short, Fellini avoids a too neat symbolic dovetailing of Christ and Il Matto. Yet, as noted, the link *is* there.

Fellini suggests that Jesus must be sought outside the Church, that in the present age Christ appears to men under different manifestations, even in the guise of a circus performer. (*"Today, we are finished with the Christian myth, and await a new one,"* Fellini observed to Tom Burke in 1970. "Maybe the myth is LSD? And the new Christ comes to us in this form?") As suggested previously, Il Matto is associated with another fool—namely Oswaldo—in that Gelsomina learns something from both of them. Of course, Gelsomina is a simpleton herself; and Il Matto is not really a fool—he merely plays the part of one. Furthermore, there is a sense in which Fellini's method of representation remains solidly traditional: individuals who have truly sought to live according to the teachings of Christ—that is to say, individuals who have taken seriously such injunctions as: "Thou shalt love thy neighbor as thyself"—have frequently been called "fools for Christ." And Fellini has always had a weakness for such people. Clearly, then, the symbolism involving Il Matto in *La Strada* cannot be reduced to a single pat explanation.

Following the scene in which Gelsomina sees The Fool for the first time, Fellini presents the gloomy square after the performers and the crowd have gone. Scraps of paper blow fitfully in front of an ancient fountain; looking feverish, Gelsomina pats a few drops of water on her brow. Some men, who are huddled nearby in the darkness, watch her; one of them grabs at her, muttering the word "balmy," but she slips away from him. Suddenly Zampanò appears. Descending from his motorcycle, he slaps Gelsomina several times and forces her into the back of his trailer. Then, gazing belligerently at the onlookers, he asks: "Any objections?" No reply. "That's what I thought," he growls. And off he goes, taking Gelsomina with him once more. . . .

Daylight. Zampanò and Gelsomina are discovered in the act of sign-

ing up for work in Colombaioni's Circus. Here Gelsomina also finds
The Fool again, for he too is now a member of the troupe. Gelsomina
is delighted with the acrobat (who plays a tiny violin with a cigarette
fastened to its end) but she remains dismayed by his habit of teasing
the vicious Zampanò. When Gelsomina asks the strongman what The
Fool has against him, he replies: "I don't know." Nor can his tormen-
tor offer a rational motive: "I can't help it," Il Matto confesses. "Zampanò's such a brute!" Unmindful of the danger, The Fool heckles
Zampanò during his performance with the chain, in an attempt to dis-
parage his strength; he also tries to use Gelsomina in his own act, much
against Zampanò's wishes; and once, he even throws a bucket of water
in the strongman's face. Finally, Zampanò pulls a knife on The Fool—
which results in his being jailed, and in both of them being fired by
Colombaioni.

While Zampanò is locked up, Gelsomina has a fateful conversation
with The Fool. It is night, and around the couple the circus tents are
half-dismantled, for Colombaioni has decided to leave town; Gelsomina, if she chooses, can remain with the circus. She asks The Fool for
advice. And it is here, because of the abstract nature of his theme, that
Fellini must rely on dialogue to carry the meaning:

> THE FOOL: So, go on, do it! It's a good chance to get rid of Zampanò,
> right? Can you imagine the look on his face tomorrow! He gets out and
> sees that you have gone off! . . . You want me to tell you whether or
> not you should stay with him. Isn't that so? . . . I can't tell you
> what to do.

Gelsomina explains how Zampanò, once before, had prevented her
from leaving him.

> THE FOOL: Why didn't he let you leave? No, no, all things considered I
> wouldn't take you with me, even if you wanted me to. Who knows
> . . . maybe he loves you?
> GELSOMINA: Me, Zampanò?
> THE FOOL: Inside, he's a dog. He looks like a man . . . but when he
> tries to talk, he barks! . . . If you didn't stay with him, who would? I
> am ignorant, but I've read some books; so, you are not going to make
> me believe . . . and yet everything in the world is good for something.
> Take . . . take this stone, for example.
> GELSOMINA: Which one?
> THE FOOL: Uh, this one—it doesn't matter which. Even this little stone
> has a purpose.
> GELSOMINA: What's it good for?

THE FOOL: Well, it's good for . . . How do I know? If I knew, you
know who I would be?
GELSOMINA: Who?
THE FOOL: God. He knows all. When you are born, when you die . . .
I don't know what it's good for, this pebble, but it certainly has its
use! If it were useless, then everything else would also be useless—even
the stars! That's the way things are, you know. You too—you have your
reason for being here. . . .

Convinced now that her purpose in life is to remain with Zampanò—
to teach him how to love, to teach him how to be a human being—
Gelsomina, the next morning, bids farewell to The Fool as she waits
outside the jail near the moto-trailer for the strongman. Separating
from Il Matto is painful for Gelsomina, inasmuch as a spiritual affinity
exists between the two (in some scenes Fellini visually suggests this
close relationship by matching Gelsomina's striped jersey with The
Fool's striped trousers), but she naïvely believes that Zampanò will
soon change in his attitude towards her. When the brute appears on
the sidewalk beside her again, however, he has little to say and the two
resume their travels.

At about the midpoint in the structure, Fellini shows Zampanò and
Gelsomina pausing by the sea. "Where's my home?" Gelsomina asks.
Wading into the water and nodding indifferently off to the right, Zampanò answers: "Over there." Gelsomina smiles warmly in the sun. "I
wanted to leave you once," she tells him. "But now *you're* my home."
Zampanò only laughs. "Sure," he says. "With me, at least you eat regularly." Gelsomina explodes.

This scene by the water reminds the viewer of the film's opening,
but it also prepares him for the ending.

Shot of Zampanò driving his motorcycle; behind him sit Gelsomina
and a beautiful nun. Dusk is closing in, fast. The strongman asks the
sister if he and his "wife" can stay at her convent for the night; once
there, the Mother Superior agrees and the nun brings food to her
guests. After eating, Zampanò tells Gelsomina to play something for
the sister on her trumpet. The simple, haunting tune—so expressive of
Gelsomina's soul—delights the nun. Close-up of Zampanò's face. Anthony Quinn's eminently plastic features reveal the complex feelings
suddenly experienced by this inarticulate boor. For the music seems to
touch something heretofore undiscovered in Zampanò: he looks uneasy, humble, softened, bashful, embarrassed. Positive forces appear to
be stirring inside him. However, perhaps Zampanò also feels threatened—not only by love, which would alter his whole personality, but

also by jealousy, for he has always mocked Gelsomina and here she is
playing in an admirable way. When the nun begins washing the dishes,
Zampanò offers to do them for her, but she won't let him. When an
elderly sister begins to split some wood, Zampanò jumps up and takes
the ax away from her. "Here, let me do that," he says. "That's a
man's work." Again, Zampanò's motivation would seem to be complex.
By offering his help, the strongman reveals an embryonic goodness in
his nature; yet, such physical activities as washing dishes and—especially—chopping wood also permit him to be the star of the show again.
It is hard for a man like Zampanò to change.

Night. Zampanò and Gelsomina are bedding down in the convent
granary. The composition—Zampanò in the foreground, lying on his
side with his back to his "wife"; Gelsomina in the background, facing
him across a space of ground—comprises a visual statement on the nature of the couple's relationship. Gelsomina yearns for Zampanò to
take an interest in her but he only wants to sleep. "If I died," she
asks, "would you be sorry?" He replies: "Why? You thinking of dying?" Exasperated, Gelsomina asks: "Don't you ever think?" He replies: "What's there to think about?" Perhaps hoping to stir him
again, as well as to give vent to her feelings, Gelsomina blows on her
trumpet; this time, however, Zampanò merely growls: "Knock it off!"

Later that night. As lightning flashes in the granary and thunder
booms outside the convent, Gelsomina wakes up. She discovers Zampanò trying to squeeze his hand through some narrow bars in an attempt to steal a few silver hearts from the wall of the adjacent chapel.
He tells her to help him. Shocked by his behavior, Gelsomina refuses.
The brute strikes his tiny companion, who slides down against a wall,
sobbing. The scene fades out.

Fade in on the following morning: Zampanò and Gelsomina are preparing to leave the convent. The strongman utters a pious, hypocritical
farewell; however, Gelsomina is reluctant to leave this place in which
women are happy because they feel useful. "Do you want to stay with
us?" the young nun asks. No reply . . . for Gelsomina knows her fate.
The nun attempts to console her:

> THE NUN: We change convents every two years, so as not to forget what's
> most important. I mean, God. You see, we both travel. You follow
> your husband and I mine.
> GELSOMINA: Yes, each one has her own.

And once more, Gelsomina drives off with Zampanò . . .
Bright sunlight. On an empty country road Zampanò and Gelso-

mina encounter The Fool, who is repairing a tire on his car. Still angry with the equilibrist, the strongman punches him several times, threatening him with more violence the next time they meet. Unknown to Zampanò, his blows snapped The Fool's head against the car, causing a fatal concussion. "He broke my watch" are the only words The Fool can say, as he staggers off and collapses on the ground, his fingers clawing spasmodically at the earth. Gelsomina becomes hysterical. Even Zampanò is frightened. "Now I've done it!" he says. "Now I'm in for it!" Dumping the body and the car down an embankment, Zampanò quickly drives off with Gelsomina.

Significantly, the next shots—showing the couple in flight—are enacted under a wintry sky, with bare trees shaking in the wind and snow falling on distant mountain tops. Zampanò attempts to continue with his act, but Gelsomina is unable to utter: "Zam-pan-ò is here!" or to beat the drum; instead, she constantly mutters: "The Fool is hurt! The Fool is hurt!" Gelsomina is distraught because she has seen the man she loves kill another man—the very man who had given her a reason for staying with the killer. Although her words attempt to belie the reality of The Fool's death (he is merely "hurt," not dead), deep down of course she knows the truth. At night, Gelsomina refuses to allow Zampanò to sleep with her in the trailer; and in a reversal of the earlier situation, Zampanò—who is not only afraid that Gelsomina will report his crime but who is also ashamed of the guilt he sees reflected in his companion's eyes—agrees to sleep outside on the ground. Ten days go by. On a cold, sunny afternoon, while the couple are sitting against a wall of rocks and cooking soup, Gelsomina appears to return to her old self. "It's about time," Zampanò sighs, with obvious relief. But then, off in the distance, very faintly, comes the sound of a dog barking. And suddenly, Gelsomina remembers the past: "The Fool is hurt!" she begins again. Frightened by her illness, Zampanò decides to go off alone. While Gelsomina sleeps, he gathers up his few belongings, stuffs some money beside the embers of their fire, and leaves her trumpet nearby. Pushing the moto-trailer down the road a distance, so as not to awaken Gelsomina, Zampanò vanishes from her life.

Five years pass. And we next find Zampanò working in a seaside town: his hair is gray; his stomach bulges. Although he has a new woman—a more attractive woman than Gelsomina—he doesn't seem to be happy with her. After one performance, he insists on going out for a walk, alone. On the street Zampanò hears someone humming the tune Gelsomina used to play on her trumpet; he stops, looks around

expectantly—but the humming suddenly ceases. Disappointed, he
moves on. Then, just as suddenly, the humming is resumed. Beyond
a fence, Zampanò discovers a young woman hanging sheets on a line in
the sun.

> ZAMPANÒ: Where did you learn that tune?
> THE WOMAN: From a little creature my father found on the beach one
> night. She was always playing it on her trumpet. We took her in for a
> time, but she was always crying, and she never ate.
> ZAMPANÒ: What happened to her?
> THE WOMAN: Oh, she died.

During this scene, Fellini's camera rarely shows us the woman. Either
we hear her words as we watch the wash flapping in the breeze, or we
watch a reaction close-up of Zampanò's face. For what is important
here is not what the woman looks like, but what she is saying and the
effect of what she is saying on Zampanò as he stands on the other side
of the fence.

Elsewhere in the film, as noted, Gelsomina stands by a fence to see
where a dog is buried. The reader will also recall that The Fool describes Zampanò as a dog who possibly loves Gelsomina, but who can't
express his love except by barking. And it was the sound of a dog
barking that made Gelsomina think of The Fool again, right before
Zampanò decided to desert her. It is impossible to wholly reduce the
associations just catalogued to the dimensions of rational understanding. Certainly love and death are common to the scenes and dialogue
involving fences, dogs, and Gelsomina; but Gelsomina communes with
the spirit of a dead beast, whereas Zampanò grieves over the loss of a
creature whom he had treated like a beast. (In one scene, Gelsomina
plays a quail who is shot to death by Zampanò, for the amusement of
the crowd.) On one level, Fellini seems to be "saying" that, ontologi-
cally, everything that has being should be regarded as holy. On another level, he appears to be "saying" that there is a chain of being,
and that animals must not be confounded with persons.

Long shot of a carnival, later that afternoon. The strongman enters
the arena and proceeds to plod listlessly through his routine with the
chain. Medium shot of Zampanò, as he treads in a circle, his posture
slack, his gaze turned inward. Long shot of the strongman, looking
small amid his surroundings. . . . Fade out.

That night. Zampanò is discovered in a cafe, drunk and belligerent.
The owner, with the help of some customers, succeeds in tossing the
strongman outside. Enraged, Zampanò heaves some barrels at his as-

sailants and, shouting "I don't need anyone," staggers down to the beach. What follows is surely one of the most powerful and cathartic moments in the history of the cinema. Zampanò wades into the water, reminiscent of the scene in the middle of the film when he stopped with Gelsomina at the sea. As observed in an earlier chapter, Fellini said: "In each of my films there is a character who goes through a crisis. It seems to me that the best atmosphere with which to underline this moment of crisis is a beach or a piazza at night; for silence, the emptiness of night, or the feeling that the sea is close by, brings the character into relief; this isolation allows him to be himself without any special effort." At the beginning of the film the children call Gelsomina, who is standing near the water, to come home. But isn't Gelsomina's real home the sea? And, by wading into the sea at the end of the film, isn't Zampanò trying to find Gelsomina again?

Turning, the strongman stumbles back up the beach and collapses on the sand, breathing heavily. Once more, Anthony Quinn's face portrays a number of reactions: Zampanò gazes out at the water, then up at the sky, and then—suddenly frightened by some thought—back out to the sea. What is going through his mind? Is he thinking of The Fool and Gelsomina, and the guilt he feels for having destroyed both of them? Is he afraid that God is looking down at him? Has the thought of committing suicide flashed through his consciousness? Pitching forward, Zampanò begins to weep, his hands clutching at the sand the way The Fool clutched at the earth when the strongman killed him. At last, Zampanò knows that he loved Gelsomina and needed her as much as she loved and needed him. Edouard de Laurot has remarked that Zampanò "is finally struck down by a cosmic terror and realizes, in his anguish, man's solitude in the face of Eternity."

Slowly, the camera recedes and rises, leaving Zampanò looking small and alone on the beach at night. The film begins and ends by the sea; but, though the structure is in one sense circular, the opening and closing are in sharp contrast. When we first meet Zampanò, he is standing tall and strong in the sunlight, arrogantly watching Gelsomina on her knees facing the water. When we take leave of Zampanò, however, he remains prostrate before the sea, no longer proud of his strength but humbly enduring his dark night of the soul.

Gilbert Salachas has declared that Zampanò's sorrow will be ephemeral, that "fleeting remorse is perhaps the furthest moral development a Fellini hero can make." Yet Fellini himself has said that La Strada is "the story of a man who discovers himself." One is free to speculate about the specific details of Zampanò's future (to the extent that it is

legitimate to raise such questions about a character in a work of art);
but the film-maker's own comments suggest that "enlightenment" and
"self-discovery" will lead to change. As Émile G. McAnany and Robert
Williams observe: "The cry of Zampanò as he claws the sand at the
end of the film is not that of a wounded beast but the anguish of a
human being in his birth pangs." What Zampanò has done to Gelsomina can be described as "tragic"; for no amount of tears will ever
bring back the love that she once offered him and which he blindly
trampled beneath his feet. Nonetheless, Gelsomina's "sacrifice" (as Fellini puts it) eventually becomes the means of Zampanò's "redemption," for man is useless and lonely before "Eternity" *only* if he does
not know how to love everyone and everything in the universe. Such is
the meaning of Gelsomina's life and death, and such is the lesson
Zampanò has begun to grasp at that final moment that Aristotle called
the *anagnorisis*. Of course, what helps to make *La Strada* so unforgettable is that Fellini subjects not only Zampanò but also the viewer to
the same recognition. . . .

.   .   .   .

7. *La Strada*   *André Bazin*

If Zampanò has a soul . . .
    The vitality of the Italian cinema is once more confirmed for us by
the admirable film of Federico Fellini. It is comforting to recognize
that the critics have been almost unanimous in praising it. Perhaps
without this support, which has placed snobbism on its side, *La Strada*
would have had some difficulty in imposing itself on an inattentive and
confused public.
    Federico Fellini has here achieved one of those very rare films, of
which we forget that they are movies and accept them simply as a
masterpiece. We remember the discovery of *La Strada* as a great esthetic emotion, an encounter with an unsuspected universe. I mean
that it is less a matter of a film's having known how to reach a certain
moral and intellectual level than a personal message, for which the

. . . .

From *Cross Currents*, Vol. 6, No. 3 (1956), pp. 200-203. Reprinted by permission of *Cross Currents*. Translated by Joseph E. Cunneen.

cinema certainly appears to be the necessary and natural interpreter, but which would virtually exist before it. It is not a movie which is called *La Strada*; it is *La Strada* which is called a movie. In this sense there comes to mind also the last film of Chaplin's, although in many ways it is quite different. Of *Limelight* too we could say that the cinema was its only adequate incarnation, that it was inconceivable in all other means of expression, and yet everything in it transcended the technique of a particular art form.

Thus *La Strada* confirms in its own way this critical probability, that the cinema has arrived at a stage of its evolution in which the form no longer determines anything, where its language no longer offers any resistance but suggests only as much as any effect of style that the artist might use. Surely it will be said that only the cinema could endow, for example, the extraordinary motor-cycle caravan of Zampanò with the force of concrete myth which this object, both unusual and banal, here attains; but we also see very clearly that the film is here neither transforming nor interpreting anything. No lyricism of image or montage attempts to orient our perception; I will even say that there is no *mise-en-scène*, at least not in cinematic terms. The screen limits itself to showing us the caravan, showing it better and more objectively than could the painter or novelist. I am not saying the camera has quite plainly photographed it—even the word photography is too much, it has simply shown it to us, or even better, has allowed us to see it. Surely it would be excessive to claim that nothing can be created in terms of the language of film, by its abrasive incidence on the real. Without even considering almost virgin areas like color and the large screen, the field of tension between technique and the subject treated depends in part on the personality of the director. Orson Welles, for example, always invents through technique. But what we can say with certainty is that from now on progress in the cinema will no longer be necessarily tied to originality of expression, or to the plastic organization of the image, or the images among themselves. More exactly, if there is any formal originality about *La Strada*, it consists in always remaining on this side of the cinema. Nothing that Fellini reveals to us owes any supplementary sense to its manner of being shown; nevertheless, this revelation exists only on the screen. It is here that the cinema attains its fullness, which consists in being the art of the real. Surely we understand that Fellini is a great director, but one who does not cheat with reality. Nothing is in the camera, nothing on the film, in any case, on which he has not previously conferred the fullness of being.

That is why *La Strada* does not at all seem to have departed from Italian neo-realism. But on this subject there is a misunderstanding that needs to be cleared up. In Italy *La Strada* has been received with some reserve by the critical guardians of neo-realist orthodoxy. This criticism is leftist, and in France would be called "Progressist," but these terms are equivocal for Italian criticism is both more Marxist and more independent. I am thinking of the group around Chiarini and Aristarco in *Cinema Nuovo*. This criticism has again taken up the concept of neo-realism, which was so scorned at one time, and is attempting to define it and orient it. The work of Zavattini is the concrete reference which most conforms to its ideal, although the neo-realism so conceived still remains only a *work in progress*, an investigation which starts out from *données* that have already been acquired and proceeds in a determined direction, but is not a static and already-conquered reality. I do not feel I have the necessary competence to clearly define the evolution of neo-realism, as seen by this Marxist group, but I do not believe I am falsifying its meaning by interpreting it as their substitution for "socialist realism," whose theoretical and practical barrenness unfortunately does not need to be demonstrated. In fact, as far as one can define it across the tactical changes of party line in esthetics, socialist realism has never produced anything convincing as such. In painting where its influence is easy to determine, since it opposed the whole modern evolution, the result is known. In literature and in the cinema, the situation is more confused since in these areas we are dealing with arts from which realism has never been eliminated. But if there are good films and good novels which do not contradict the canons of socialist neo-realism, it is still rather doubtful that these rules had any part in their success. On the other hand, we can easily see how they sterilized many other works.

It is true that theories have never given birth to masterpieces and that a creative flowering has a more profound source in history and in men. Italy has had the luck, like Russia around 1925, to find herself in a situation in which a certain cinematographic genius began to spring forth, and this genius was moving in the direction of social progress, and the liberation of men. It is normal and legitimate that the most conscious of the artisans and judges of this important phenomenon concern themselves to prevent it from being broken up; they would like to orient its direction towards the best of the revolutionary development whose cycle was inaugurated by the neo-realism of the immediate post-war period. In the cinema neo-realism can surely be advantageously substituted for socialist realism. The evidence of successful films and their coherence in variety furnish the Marxist esthetician with material for fruitful reflection. If the time comes when this reflection gets ahead of the creative output, then neo-realism will be in danger, but fortunately we have not yet reached that point.

That is why I nevertheless regret the intolerance which this critical group begins to exhibit towards the dissidents of neo-socialist-realism, Rossellini and Fellini (who was Rossellini's assistant and from many points of view remains his disciple). There are some things in Italy which are lamentably like the world of Don Camillo: whoever is anti-Communist has to be on the side of the priests. In the face of leftist criticism, the Italian Catholics try to revive neo-realism, whose very ambiguity lends itself to such an experiment. It is unnecessary to go into details in regard to the pitiful results of this Catholic effort. But Rossellini and Fellini are placed, because of this situation, in a very false light. It is true that their recent work could not be understood as social. Besides, as individual citizens, they neither flirt with Communism nor cooperate with the Christian Democrats. The result in Rossellini's case is that he is banned on all sides. As for Fellini, the jury is still out, and the success of La Strada gives him the advantage of a favorable reception from both sides, but mixed with uneasiness and a definite reticence on the part of the Marxists. Of course these political polarizations play only a complementary role, with greater or less importance depending on the personality of the individual critic. It may even happen that this aspect might be completely ignored, and we have seen Chiari, for example, defend Rossellini's The Little Flowers of St. Francis, whereas Cinema Nuovo was divided on the case of Senso made by the Communist Visconti. But this context certainly does not contribute to attenuate the hardening of theoretical positions when they lead in the same direction as political mistrust. Thus Fellini is threatened with being evicted from the neo-realist heaven, and cast in the outer darkness already haunted by Rossellini.

Obviously everything depends on the definition that we accept, at the very outset, of neo-realism. But it seems to me that La Strada does not contradict Paisan or Open City in any way, any more than The Bicycle Thief did. But it is true that Fellini has followed a different road than Zavattini. With Rossellini he has made a choice for a neo-realism of the person. Certainly the first films of Rossellini identified the moral and the social because this coincidence seemed to be the very experience of the Liberation. But Europe 51 in some sense crossed the social line in order to emerge in the area of a spiritual destiny. What in these works nevertheless remains neo-realism, and can be considered as one of its possible accomplishments, is the esthetic of the *mise-en-scène*, a direction of the elements of a film which Abbé Ayfre has judiciously described as phenomenological. We see very well that in *La Strada* nothing is ever revealed to us from the interior of the characters. The point of view of Fellini is the exact contrary of a psychological neo-realism which aims at analysis and ultimately at a description of feelings. Nevertheless, everything can occur in this quasi-Shakespearean world. Gelsomina and the Clown carry with them an aura of the marvelous, which baffles and annoys Zampanò, but this element of wonder is neither supernatural, nor gratuitous, nor even "poetic," it appears simply as a possible quality of nature. Moreover, to return to psychology, the very being of these characters is precisely not to have any, or at least to possess such a rough and primitive psychology that its description would have nothing but a pathological value. But they do have a soul. *La Strada* is nothing but the experience that they have of this fact, and its revelation to our eyes. Gelsomina learns from the Clown that she belongs in the world. She, the idiot, ugly and useless, learns one day from this vaudevillian that she is something besides an outcast; or rather, she learns that she is irreplaceable and that she has a destiny, which is—to be indispensable to Zampanò. The most overwhelming discovery in the film is surely Gelsomina's prostration after the assassination of the Clown by Zampanò. From then on she is haunted by her agony which dwells on that instant in which he, who had virtually given her being, suddenly ceased to exist. Little groans like the cries of mice irresistibly escape from her lips: "The clown is sick, the clown is sick." The stupid and stubborn brute who is Zampanò could not have discovered the need he had of Gelsomina through his conscience, and certainly could not sense the eminently spiritual nature of the tie which united them. Terrified by the suffering of the poor girl, at the end of his patience and afraid, he abandons her. But just as the death of the Clown had made life insupportable for Gelsomina, the abandonment and then the death of Gelsomina will little by little reduce this mass of muscles to its spiritual evidence, and Zampanò will end by being crushed by Gelsomina's absence. Not through remorse, or even by love, but through the overwhelming and incomprehensible sorrow which can be the only sensation of his soul, deprived of Gelsomina.

Thus we may consider *La Strada* as a phenomenology of the soul and perhaps even of the Communion of Saints, at least of the interdependence of salvation. With these people who are "poor of spirit" it is impossible to confuse ultimate spiritual realities with those of intelligence or passion, pleasure or beauty. The soul reveals itself there beyond psychological or esthetic categories, and much more clearly because we no longer know how to adorn it with the jewels of conscience. The salt of the tears that Zampanò sheds for the first time in his miserable life on the beach that Gelsomina loved, is the same as that of the infinite sea, which can no longer refresh its sadness here on earth.

La Strada
and the
Crisis of Neo-Realism

. . . .
8. Italian Cinema   *Guido Aristarco*

. . . In *La strada* of Federico Fellini we encounter an entirely different conception and understanding of art, an attitude towards it and
towards life similar to that prevalent in pre-war, and to some extent
in contemporary, literature. In this respect Fellini appears anachronistic, tied down as he is to problems and to human dimensions largely
already transcended (although they still persist in various domains of
culture and art). Along with some of our gifted writers (and Fellini is
beyond a doubt a gifted director), he has gathered up and jealously
preserved the subtlest poisons of that pre-war literature; he carries on
the tradition of the poetry of the solitary man, a poetry in which each
story, instead of being reflected, lived within the reality of the narrative,
is, through a process of individualization, reabsorbed into itself and
nullified as an historical entity only to be converted into a symbolic
diagram, a legend, a myth.[1]

"We started out with the intention of coming to know and understand reality more profoundly," Pavese once confessed, "and the result
is that we are closing ourselves up within a fictitious world inimical to
reality. So of course we suffer. In such a climate of unbalance, of moral
uncertainty there is bound to come a period of esthetic drought. We
remain in, or return to, our adolescence; and in our aimless struggles
we invent all sorts of theories, justifications and problems." Fellini, too,
tries to find justifications, struggles in his own way, and remains an
eternal adolescent, especially in *La strada*, which he himself describes
not by mere coincidence as his most juvenile, most lyrical, most con-
fessional film. He seeks out his own emotions along the treacherous
. . . .

From *Film Culture*, Vol. 1, No. 2 (1955), pp. 30-31. Reprinted by permission
of *Film Culture* and Guido Aristarco.

paths of suggestivism and autobiographism and mistakes agitation for an intense need for poetic expression; transcribing certain memories, contacts, moments, moods of his life—and on a sentimental level at that—is already in his view tantamount to the creation of poetry. His participation in reality is episodic, fragmentary, only sporadically enriched by realistic elements and attitudes; in Fellini we do not have the sense of our actual experiences. Somehow he seems to stop at the "evangelism," the "lyricism," the poetical experiments of war-time humoristic newspapers such as *Marc'Aurelio*, at certain of his own characters and vignettes of that period. . . .

NOTE

1. As editor of the major Marxist cinema journal, *Cinema nuovo*, Guido Aristarco naturally opposes the "poetry of the solitary man" (what more doctrinaire Marxist critics might have termed "bourgeois individualism") he detects in Fellini's works, not only because of the political implications of such a cinema but also because of the religious connotations in Fellini's early work underlined most especially by the criticism of André Bazin and Geneviève Agel. For a consideration of the ideological implications of criticism of neo-realist films, see Mario Cannella, "Ideology and Aesthetic Hypotheses in the Criticism of Neo-Realism," *Screen*, 14, No. 4 (1973-74), 5-60.—EDITOR

. . . .

9. An Interview with   *George Bluestone*
Federico Fellini

. . . INTERVIEWER: I have heard that an unofficial Vatican censor wanted to keep *Le notti di Cabiria* from going to Cannes, but that Cardinal Spira of Genoa was responsible for getting your film approved. Is this true?

FELLINI: Where did you hear this?

—I read it. In *Cinema Nuovo*, I think.

—Oh, well, if you want to understand my work, don't read *Cinema*
. . . .

From *Film Culture*, Vol. 3, No. 3 (1957), pp. 3-4. Reprinted by permission of *Film Culture* and George Bluestone.

Nuovo. They have called *La Strada*—called me—a traitor to neo-realism. In Italy, it is very difficult to find honest, objective criticism about directors. There are too many special interests.

—But there is some truth in the Cardinal Spira story?

—There are certain rumors. They . . . are unimportant.

—Do you find any problem of censorship over here?

—For the film-maker there has always been censorship. In every country. In Italy, if it has not come from the Church, it has come from the bureaucracy. If not from the bureaucracy, then from the Communists. But I do think that if a film is a good film, it will find its audience. The trouble with *La Strada* is that the Church seized on it, used it as a flag. The return to spirituality. So *Cinema Nuovo* turned against it. I assure you, if *Cinema Nuovo* had praised it first, the Church might very well have turned against it. It is very hard to see a work for what it is, without prejudice.

—What, then, would you consider a reputable critical analysis of your work?

—Geneviève Agel's book, in French, *Les Chemins de Fellini.*[1]

—We hear it said that neo-realism brought the Italian film to world attention, but that now the excitement of the immediate post-war years is over, that the innovations of neo-realism are over, that a vacuum has been created which has left the Italian film confused about where to go. What is your personal reaction to this?

—I don't think it is so confused. Remember, after the war our themes were ready-made. Primitive problems: how to survive, war, peace. These problems were topical, immediate, brutal. But today the problems are different. Surely the neo-realists would not hope for the continuation of war and poverty just because it gave them good material. I think the editors of *Cinema Nuovo* are partly responsible for what you call our uncertainty. Instead of realizing that neo-realism was a beginning, they assumed it was an end, a golden age. Some of the neo-realists seem to think that they cannot make a film unless they have a man in old clothes in front of the camera. That is not right. We have not even scratched the surface of Italian life. Who was it—Zavattini?— who said that the film-maker must not try to influence reality by telling a story, that his job is simply to record what passes in front of the camera? Well, no film was ever made that way. Not even by Zavattini.

—Then it is only fair to say that you are optimistic about the future of the Italian film?

—Yes. Neo-realism was only a beginning.

—You feel no uncertainty about the direction of your own work?

—No, not basically. One always has doubts, of course.

—How do the subjects of your films compare with those of the neo-realists, say?

—Well, so far, my films have been mostly autobiographical. They've been based on childhood experiences that made a profound impression on me. When I was twelve, I worked with a traveling circus. I remembered incidents, fragments, and these became *La Strada*. My films are my life. I had no "schools" in mind, no theories when I first began to work.

—Then you would say that essentially you begin with a story that has made some impression on you and work out your images and techniques from there?

—Yes, I would say so. . . .

NOTE

1. This remark represents one of the few instances in which Fellini has ever recommended a critical interpretation of his work. For Agel's analysis of *Il Bidone*, perhaps the section most typical of her book, see the selection reprinted in this anthology.—Editor

. . . .

10. Guido Aristarco Answers Fellini *Guido Aristarco*

I was surprised to read the interview Federico Fellini gave to George Bluestone (*Film Culture*, October 1957). First of all, the Cardinal Siri case was not, as Fellini states, merely a matter of unimportant "rumors." In Italy, the case provoked violent reaction, even polemics. *Cinema Nuovo* (No. 107) wrote on the subject: ". . . We take no part in the attack on Fellini which some papers began conducting—not altogether politely—after he, confronted with the perplexing issue of censorship, appealed to the eminent Genovese prelate. We limit ourselves to reporting an opinion expressed on the matter by Alberto Moravia in *Espresso*: 'It means, first of all, that the Italian state is gov-
. . . .

From *Film Culture*, Vol. 4, No. 2 (1958), pp. 20-21. Reprinted by permission of *Film Culture* and Guido Aristarco.

erned by men who, because they are Catholics first and citizens second, do not have the understanding of the State. It means that the real power now is no longer the State's, but is outside of it. It means, finally, that it is useless to have a censorship commission and many other such agencies, since the authorities which must decide on the last appeal are somewhere else. The story of Fellini does but confirm this.' "

What is the trouble between Fellini and *Cinema Nuovo?* We were among the few who defended Fellini; we backed him as far as *I Vitelloni.* But we expressed our doubts regarding *La Strada.* There is one viewpoint, that of Fellini's film, full of mystery, grace—that is, mysticism; then there is another viewpoint, that of *Cinema Nuovo,* holding forth a knowledge of and faith in man, his ability to dominate and modify his world, to solve problems within himself and outside himself —in a word, realism. Was it our purpose, in criticizing *La Strada,* to get Fellini to express a world that does not belong to him? events and persons that he could not naturally create? It doesn't seem so. But the critic, any critic, has his *ars poetica.* De Sanctis (the great historian of Italian literature) and the great realists are our teachers and inspirers, if we may use the term. In their names and in their teaching we have sought an internal development, a criticism which continues to demand explication—a methodology, a character not cold and self-centered, but militant. Is all this non-objectivity a "prejudice"? Objectivity is a myth, if we understand it as Fellini and others with him understand it. It is as misleading and false as any other myth. There are, of course, "particular interests," even "political ones," if you wish—but in a large and impartial sense, as in our case.

It is human and unavoidable that Fellini's poetry, which took shape with *La Strada,* should appear to us both limited and irritating, particularly since *Cabiria* and other films affirm the great and uncommon value of this talent. We must not, of course, impose our convictions on the personality of the director, and so we are forced to accept, for the moment, his logic, and comment on this or that isolated sequence as it reflects his talent and direction. Therefore, we don't say, nor have we ever said, that *La Strada* is a badly directed and acted film. We have declared, and do declare, that it is *wrong;* its perspective is wrong. (This personal classification is a relative one, derived from our refusal to support that film's perspective and solution.) Nor should one confuse, as Fellini confuses, the significance which we have attached to "neorealism" with realism, particularly as elaborated lately in *Cinema Nuovo* reviews. It might be that these reviews (especially of Fellini's films) are somewhat limited by a tone which is, on the whole, negative and perhaps polemic. The intention of these reviews, however, was to contribute to a wider understanding of the director and the overall neorealistic development, in which, it seems, Fellini takes only a fragmentary part (in his criticism of custom or his use of simple denunciation) but to which, in any case, he is not a "traitor." We have spoken of the vital trend of the Italian postwar cinema as a new civilizing force, a new humanism, but we have always considered it a starting point—not a point of arrival, an "end," a "golden era" beyond which it is not possible to go. We neither conceal nor reject our personal responsibility for the present uncertainty of the Italian cinema (we should have done more and better with greater clarity), but one cannot make us responsible, as Fellini does, for the specific fact that "some of the neorealists seem to think that they cannot make a film unless they have a man in old clothes in front of the camera." And among the "some," to judge from his films, we must put Fellini himself. It is evident that the flag, the pin-on-the-lapel, of neorealism is not the rags, at least in the external sense of the word. Fellini remarks, moreover, in his interview that we have not even scratched the surface of Italian life, and he is right. *Cinema Nuovo* has always stressed the need of a progress from chronicle to history, from short story to novel, that is—from neorealism to realism. From this came our public and private discussions with Zavattini, a genuine exchange of ideas.

We have not agreed with Zavattini—to take one example—on his insistence that the director must not try to influence reality in order to expose it, that his job is merely to register what goes on in front of the camera. This is chronicle, and not history. To this, let us say, Zola-esque method, we have preferred and insisted upon an approach like that of Balzac or Stendhal—a method which would lead us not to neorealism (naturalism in its various aspects) but to the great, the true and authentic realism.

Confronted with the scattered remnants of the postwar effort which was the crisis of Italian society, we must now understand the crisis of our cinema. We must perceive the reasons behind the decadent suggestions of loneliness, the return to the past, the search for style and expressive moods as seen in some of our "greats" (Visconti, Antonioni, Fellini, Castellani) as well as the simultaneous warmth and color that, in Fellini's case, have ascended into the clouds of mysticism.

But we would like to stress again here that an understanding and acknowledgment of stylistic (and in part, artistic) values do not necessarily indicate agreement and support. Today it is more necessary than ever to get out from under the autobiography, the restricted and subjective view of reality, and onto that road that has been traveled in the literary field in varying degrees by Pavese, Vittorini, and Pratolini.

I wanted to say this to readers of *Film Culture* because, in fact, Federico Fellini has not distinguished the negative critical judgment from the friendship and honesty of the critic, and because these casual accusations of dishonesty that he directs at Italian critics in general and *Cinema Nuovo* in particular are quite undeserved.

Il Bidone

. . . .

11. *Il Bidone*   *Geneviève Agel*

In a sense, *Il Bidone* is a Fellinian monument. While in *The White Sheik* there was a veritable festival of Fellinian style, Fellini adds all the constants of his message to the style of *Il Bidone*. What a joy for those who love the Fellinian universe to rediscover through *Il Bidone* the echoes, the signs of the preceding works, whether it is, as we shall see it, in a more detailed manner in the music of Nino Rota, in the actors or characters, in the locations or in the poetic and spiritual mythology. Again in this film we find the same Fellini—baroque, lyrical, and mystical—but with a refinement which recalls *I Vitelloni* and an audacity that surpasses even that of *La Strada*.

From the beginning, we rediscover that atmosphere so dear to us: abandonment in space, farce, pure neo-realism, the unexpected. It is introduced by the music of Rota, which resumes the musical theme of the desert of snow in *La Strada*. Then comes a long silence broken only by the chirping of birds; these introductory elements in the sound track find their visual illustration:

Farce
in the sense of comic ballet with three people who are amusing themselves by tossing hats around like children (Augusto, Roberto, and Picasso).
. . . .

From *Les chemins de Fellini* by Geneviève Agel (Paris: Les Éditions du Cerf, 1956), pp. 71-86. Reprinted by permission of Les Éditions du Cerf. Translated by Julia Conaway Bondanella.

The unexpected
the arrival of the three impostors, two of whom have donned ecclesiastical garb . . . the black car arrives in the courtyard of a farmhouse where silence and grayness hover; a woman who comes to meet them and another woman behind her become part of a disheveled and almost fantastic silhouette; in *La Strada* there is the same effect in the circus between performances. At one point, the Circus Master, Zampanò, and Gelsomina are speaking in the foreground; behind them, without actual importance and in a less assertive, indeed almost impalpable tonality, a strange woman is singing.

Abandonment in space
at the moment of their arrival at the farm, a long panoramic shot discovers space for us, natural space, but space to which Fellini, as we have already seen in *La Strada*, adds this intense feeling of desolation which erases any hope of ordinary living.

Neo-realism
the penetration into the kitchen where the furniture, the walls, the objects, the gestures of the guests are, for us, an admission into one instantaneous moment of reality.

But not one of these elements ever presents itself to us separately; they are entirely integrated, and that is without a doubt one of the reasons for the extraordinary richness of Fellini's work and that which causes each spectator to find in his work whatever most suits his own way of thinking and feeling. And the film continues thus, leaving us without enough eyesight to see everything and a heart far too small to embrace it all. In the middle of this space we find, in complete isolation, the tree shaped like a lightning bolt, both scrawny and majestic, and we cannot ever tell if it is a sign of the springtime to come or the lamentable vestige of a harsh winter. In any case, it bewilders us as much as the dog which passes across the screen like a sign of death when the impostors are on their way to unearth the "treasure," and they excavate the sacrilegious hole. All the characters dance a kind of frenetic ballet through the bad consciences of the thieves, who are in a hurry to end their confidence game, and through the curiosity of the women, a curiosity full of covetousness. Then the screen begins to clear; the silhouettes grow smaller to the advantage of space which becomes so pervasive that it becomes the essential character, that is, the desert. This desert will later on find its internal counterpart when, the treasure unearthed, all the characters find themselves once again in the kitchen, in a stifling, infernal atmosphere dominated by the fire. Around the treasure chest, the lustful, restless eyes of the women, the game so full of the malice, fear, and secret joy of the three confederates, and the contraction of the objects on the screen cause us to feel the same discomfort as the contrasting atmosphere of a minute before: on one hand, we see a world enclosed by space, and on the other, a world hemmed in by the rarefaction of space. At the moment when the old peasant women go to get their money for the impostors, Augusto walks to the threshold to see if anyone is coming. Simultaneously, the cart drawn by the donkey arrives and crosses the screen while in the distance a bell is heard. The donkey and the bells were also the companions of Gelsomina; the former echoes the scene of the first awakening of Gelsomina in the circus where a donkey attached to the gypsy wagon jostles her while it grazes and awakens her; the latter recalls the bells that toll far in the distance at the moment of the last encounter between Gelsomina and Zampanò. Both the one and the other are a mark of the more serene joy which Fellini creates for us here.

And while all these currents are evolving, others continue to cut through the film. In its composition and style, the departure from the farm strongly resembles the end of the wedding party in *La Strada*: the dull lighting is the same, the scene is built so that it tapers like a hillside, the mythological props are the same, the wind, the tree, the disjointed movements of the silhouettes. The entire beginning of the film undoubtedly puts us once again into the atmosphere of *La Strada*; the rest plunges us in a troubling way into that of *I Vitelloni*, to the extent that we have the impression that *Il Bidone* is a continuation of the earlier film. We find the same odor in the streets, the dilapidated walls, the shining macadam, the narrow blind alleys, the protracted, solitary, and fascinating street of *I Vitelloni*. Then, there is a cabaret where we rediscover Fellini's vast eroticism in the heavy, insistent, perverse, and disorderly atmosphere, in the latent despair of the lasciviousness of the women. This deliberate immersion in erotic waters constitutes the atmosphere of the cabaret in *Il Bidone*, since it had created the atmosphere of the little music-hall theater of Natali in *I Vitelloni*.

The second swindle of the film's heroes, in which they come to take the census of a shantytown posing as housing commissioners, gives rise to one of the greatest scenes in Fellini and to one of the strangest and most moving scenes in cinema. This scene alone provides an answer to all the unfounded objections concerning Fellini's neo-realist tendencies. The scene is presented to us as is the scene in *Miracle in Milan*,[1] in which we discover the Zone for the first time. And just as in *Miracle in Milan*, in which Totò is taken to see the end of a grand ball and is painfully dazzled by so much luxury and indifference before ending up in the poorhouse, so Fellini, upon leaving this shantytown, leads us right into the middle of the festivities of St. Sylvester's Eve through a joyous and triumphant street. Although the process is reversed, the shock is the same. We arrive among the poor behind the automobile of the impostors to the sound of this extraordinary march of the swindlers which Rota created for this film; our first vision is subjective, since it comes through the foggy windows of the automobile and since our faces mingle, so to speak, with those of the occupants of the car. It is reminiscent of the first encounter between Il Matto and Gelsomina; they look at each other through the windowpane, one ironic, the other blissful.

The children's faces appear to us first through the car windows; then we arrive in the heart of the Zone. It is not a question here of a ballet of sunlight or of sad fantasy; we confront the spectacle of brutish misery: starving silhouettes, cripples, empty, hostile faces. Dominating the background noise, the laments of children are first heard; then, we witness a movement toward equilibrium. When the automobile has advanced and stops and when the occupants finally get out, the group of poor people, rather reduced in size to begin with, becomes more and more compact, more and more menacing and imploring at the same time. As the camera glides from this group to the individual shapes remaining near the shanties, we become acquainted with a marvelous urchin perched on a roof, his legs dangling. If poetry is present, it is again, on Fellini's part, a concern for truth; poetry can even burst forth from a beautiful urchin both poor and sweet, sitting in the sun with the air of the insouciance of childhood. This impression is so much stronger when we turn our glance back toward the anguished, desperate faces of the adults. This scene could not be more authentically and honestly neo-realistic, and if Fellini goes beyond neo-realism in the limited sense of the term, it is when he lets his camera languish upon the dark, discordant, disjointed group, this veritable court of miracles, homeland of misery, this Wailing Wall. The sound accompanies this vision: the first laments of the little children are amplified and the voices of the adults are mingled with them in a long rising moan, a lamentation for all the miseries of men. The spectator is literally crushed by this long cry of pain and sorrow. This is a *Miracle in Milan* without music, without excuse, without moderation; this is the immodest excess of human suffering. With respect to the exploitation

of which these poor creatures are the victims, is it not even more unbearable when the exploiter is a false one? Here, Fellini spares us
nothing; with the gravest tone, he throws in our faces all the torment-
ing solitude, the cruel absurdity that the world could hold: this is his
ballad of hell.

At this very moment, the spectacle of indifference intensifies our
attack of conscience: the eve of St. Sylvester, with the illuminated
walls and trees, the town full of people, the festive streets, happy children, sidewalk displays with all the accessories of joyous celebration,
garlands, balloons, confetti. Full of wonder, Picasso buys presents for
his child and says: "This is nice. . . ." The air is full of soap bubbles
and the loud, clear sound of the bells; the music, which remained silent
during the visit to the Zone where it gave way to lamentations and
tears, now again takes on a festive air, accompanying the little games;
the ritornello is in the air. In this contrast, we believe we detect suffering more than rebellion in Fellini, and in this sense he is more Christian than specifically social, no doubt the source of certain unjustified
reproaches about his indifference toward social problems. Fellini profoundly loves the poor people whom he has shown to us with the terrible intensity of a Léon Bloy, but he also loves the privileged eve of
St. Sylvester; he becomes intoxicated and he intoxicates his viewers
with his own enchantment, but he cries over the outcasts. Is it not
basically this sympathy for the outcasts from society which inspires the
dramatic message of Fellini?

After this sequence, which is one of the crucial moments of the
film, Fellini continues to involve us in his symbolic universe. While the
two confederates (Picasso and Augusto) abandon themselves to the
excitement running through the streets during the celebration of St.
Sylvester's Eve, a long automobile slowly moves forward through the
middle of the crowd and the night and stops in front of them. The
driver makes them get in as if they are old acquaintances; the people in
the car appear to be "parvenus" by means of special effects. Nevertheless, there is one element repeated several times in this scene which
rather effectively gives the tone to the whole. On the front seat of the
car, a woman of questionable reputation on the verge of no longer
being equivocal remains immobile with a face that the abundance of
rouge could not succeed in reviving; each time a person enters through
the back of the automobile, another one must move the seat in front
toward the hood, and the woman in front moves with both the stiffness
and the docility of an automaton. An entire study could be done on
the women in Fellini's universe—the redeemer, the mannequin, the

flower, etc. A most suggestive musical background takes up the theme of the march of the swindlers in a key of languorous dissonance and accompanies this strange procession across town, introducing us into this new Fellinian celebration which could even be an anthology piece.

We arrive across town in a dim, moving, foggy, dark, bizarre atmosphere: someone offers to undress a model for Augusto, and all the men are excited by the idea of such a spectacle, when the wife of Picasso (Giulietta Masina, who continues here in a more normal and everyday manner, her role as Gelsomina, since she represents innocence, honesty, trusting love for her husband) looks with the frightened eyes of an innocent child upon the spectacle offered her; in another corner, a couple watch television with a profoundly sottish air; Roberto, the third confederate, courts an old coquette sitting on a divan in a self-seeking way; the mantel is full of glassware and ashtrays; on the television screen couples are dancing as they are in the living room. The atmosphere becomes more and more stifling, heavy, bitter, despairing; a somber vertigo runs through the scene in a balancing movement; silhouettes rise over the whole screen and fall back again from divan to divan; a discordant background noise drowns out the dance music and is soon dominated by a serious voice; in the middle of this visual and auditory confusion which comes over us and annoys us like pitch, the camera leads us to Giulietta who, fearful, bewildered, disgusted, clings to her husband's arm. We then return to the middle of this madness: a guest walks around with a lampshade on his head, his bizarre and vacillating form seen in the middle of this black, sticky multitude; with few objects present, decor has no place here; people jostle each other in this heap of bodies that roll their bored, corpulent forms to the sound of irritatingly monotonous music.

The choreography in the dance of *I Vitelloni* is pushed to its extreme, for in that film there was still a certain aeration in the dance, while everything here is willfully contracted. But in both films the camera, after having plunged into an infernal sea, stops on one single character: Augusto, who here does not join in the festivities. Near a sofa, we find him on his knees, half drunk, nearly unconscious; then, we pass again from his solitude into the surrounding frenzy: a drawing-room fireworks display, which both cheers and frightens the bystanders, bursts forth like an atmospheric paroxysm; someone fires a revolver into the air; the camera moves back to the fireplace where the empty cups and the bottles of champagne are placed next to the candelabra; again a rocket bursts forth. It is a moment of total exasperation, one of those moments when everything becomes possible: a man makes an exhibition of himself with a furpiece on his head, a rose in his hand, and then, behind the weary Giulietta, we see the end of the ball. It is the atmosphere of *I Vitelloni* after the carnival in its entirety: the street is deserted, the characters are disabused; there is the awakening of conscience in an atmosphere of internal misery, of self-disgust; there is the empty city square and the wind which rustles the pieces of paper in the street. It is at this moment that the discussion between Picasso and Iris, which strongly resembles the dialogue in *I Vitelloni* between Alberto and his mother, takes place. Like Alberto, Picasso sheds these tears which are both sincere and vain; Iris resumes her role as her husband's conscience.

At this moment, what we shall call the episode of the damned occurs as well. Fellini no doubt dreamed of Sordi to play the role of Franco Fabrizi, the swindlers' driver; here the role is that of a petty thief without scope, more amoral than immoral, who is not even able to keep himself from committing petty larceny at the home of his "friends" the evening of the festivities: he is the defective man who never asks himself a question, the weak man, the body without a soul. This role was completely in the tradition of the sheik and of Alberto in *I Vitelloni*, and it is evident that Sordi could have given the role its fullest meaning. At the end of the dance, when Augusto chases him and he runs off, unconscious and fearful, we really feel that Fellini has left him neither the right to redemption, as he had to Picasso, nor the right to remorse, as he had to Augusto. After this fantastic, infernal dance, what a pitiful and sumptuous vision of damnation Sordi would have given to this nocturnal flight!

After this descent into hell, we are returned to the light once again; the screen grows light, life revives, the sun shines, the bells mingle with the sounds of the day. Alone, the white car passes slowly across our field of vision like an ironic echo, something which could be the laughter of Satan; from this moment on, a sort of silent dialogue begins to be established between the forces of light and the forces of darkness. This secret struggle will be synthesized in the vacillating, uneasy attitude of Augusto. Let us follow the indecision of this dialogue. We witness the meeting between Augusto and his daughter on a city square bathed in sunlight, which is none other than the famous Piazza del Popolo in the center of Rome. Again, we enter into the intimacy of the household of Picasso and Iris, with its confidence, innocence, and light, a kind of redemptive light that bathes everything and everyone.

In Augusto's daughter, we find something of the Sandra in *I Vitelloni*. And then we come back again into the dubious wake of the im-

postors to the scene at the gas station around Picasso and again the
return to the nocturnal city, the riding school, the descent of the stairway, the dancing near the riding school, and again the stairway—this
world where drunkenness conceals the bad conscience acceptable to
Augusto and painful for Picasso which is expressed in a precise manner
at the moment of Picasso's drunken gesticulations. He wears a new
coat, put on for the needs of the imposture at the garage; he dances
while holding it like a robe and whirls around like a child at play.
Then the smiling game becomes unbearable for him, and the same
coat, the emblem of his casualness, becomes the symbol of his self-
disgust and of the profession which he has chosen. He begins to tear
off the buttons, to tear the coat apart in a rage while snickering: "Pure
wool . . . Made in England." The worthlessness of the coat thus revealed through its actual quality is the symbol of the life of the three
confederates, which is a miserable imitation in spite of the fleeting
riches which it can procure for them and the cunning which they
demonstrate in their confidence game.

After this moment of paroxysm that Fellini expresses in an atmosphere of fantastic symbolism, as he had expressed Alberto's departure
from the dance in *I Vitelloni*, Picasso, calm, downcast, stricken by the
smiling sottishness which always follows drunkenness or grief, finds
himself once again against a wall, recalling the importance of walls in
all of Fellini's films, the wall as snare, the wall as solitary haven. Behind Picasso, water is flowing all along the wall. Similarly, in *I Vitelloni*,
one recalls the fountain flowing behind Moraldo, the brother of Sandra, who, one evening in the deserted square, awaited his brother-in-
law, Fausto, who had been out with another woman until dawn. In
both films, the presence of water is like a prop, the sign of an awakening conscience. That night, Moraldo, who alone of the *vitelloni* was
reflective, who was not satisfied with his situation and who was afflicted
by his sister's problems, reaches the height of his self-awareness. In the
same way in *Il Bidone*, after the episode with the coat, Picasso experiences his most acute attack of conscience when he tells Augusto that
he cannot continue in their profession if his wife and child are to live
a safe and honest life. Augusto tells him that although one must stand
on his own, the essential thing is to be free. They are both going down
a flight of stairs; at the moment when Picasso confesses his remorse to
his friend, we hear the sound of a small child crying and we find ourselves again in the atmosphere of *I Vitelloni*; Picasso experiences the
same difficulty, left over from early youth, in becoming an adult, inasmuch as becoming an adult in the milieu of *Il Bidone* is to confirm

oneself in a life of confidence games with neither remorse nor scruples. During this discussion, Augusto is beside Picasso, sometimes appearing on the screen at his side, sometimes disappearing from the shooting angle or passing into the background, when Picasso's fate is played out most intensely through the stirrings of his conscience. But when Augusto pronounces the word "alone," he takes his place on the screen and it is then that we see the naked confusion in his face, a confusion so very profound that he does not know that he cannot release himself from the profession of his choice.

He denies this, however, and when Picasso says to him, "I admire you, you are never afraid," he answers, "Afraid of what?" They have arrived in the square, and Augusto obliges Picasso to refresh himself in a fountain, hoping that once sobered up, his young friend will be restored to him and will forget both his good resolutions and his remorse; he takes advantage of this moment to compliment him upon the indispensable and valuable nature of his collaboration; that takes only a moment and Picasso proclaims quite proudly: "I could swindle the whole world; I've got the face of an angel." It is possible here to imagine a dialogue opposite from that about the pebble between Gelsomina and Il Matto in *La Strada*. However, just at this moment, the little altar of the Madonna appears to Picasso who, first thinking he is the victim of a hallucination, then opens his eyes on reality. He seems both frightened and comforted by it; as he appears on the screen momentarily, tranquility, solitude, privation surround him while behind him, near the flight of stairs they have just descended, a horseman sleeps; in the background some little Fellinian lights appear. It begins to rain; and with the astonished expression which Picasso wears when he is not occupied by his profession as a thief, when he is at home, for example, he cries out, "Oh! it's raining!" Once again in Fellini's work, water assumes the significance of a symbol of deliverance.

Ending this sequence is the climb back up the stairs by the two confederates, each of whom now belongs to a different world. At the top of the staircase a woman of the night appears; it happens that the actress playing this role is the same actress who introduced Il Matto in *La Strada*, in which she was characterized as a relatively infernal creature. Augusto heckles her as he presents her to Picasso by introducing her as "Miss Frosinone," an ironic reference to the name of a very small, unimportant town. Then he rejoins her and leaves with her. Picasso, on the other hand, leaves by himself and we never see him again.

Henceforth, the film concentrates upon the destiny of Augusto: his struggle, his effort to redeem himself, his relapse, his death. When daylight returns to the screen, Augusto goes to find his daughter again and experiences a feeling which ranges between liberating tenderness and the constant feeling of oppression caused by a life which has become a veritable trap. The fluctuations in his mood, reflected in his face, are also portrayed on the screen by Fellini. At the beginning of their meeting during the festivities in the Piazza del Popolo, Augusto offers a white carnation to his daughter; a joyful breeze stirs the awnings of the little shops; at the end of the mass, the bells ring loud and clear. Up to now Fellini has scarcely accustomed us to this joyful breeze; only rarely in Fellini is the wind not dark and distressing. However, for a brief moment before Augusto's last days, the wind is light and happy. The scene in the movie house where Augusto takes his daughter is as heartrending in its way as the visit to the shantytown of the poverty-stricken; it is a moment of painful tenderness, a moment of fragile truce during which the music again takes up the theme of *The White Sheik*. It is a scene of glances; the father's is uneasy, while the girl's is steady. There is something both poignant and hopeless in the certainty of this impossible redemption. The impression is all the more intense because while the girl suspects nothing, we know Augusto's past and that he will not be able to extricate himself from it to this degree of compromise; on the one hand, we feel psychological suspense, and on the other, we anticipate the shock of his arrest, which is bound to come. Here we have exactly the same impression of the atmosphere, of the look on the daughter's face as we had of the bicycle thief and his child at the moment of their theft;[2] we perceive the same fright in the children, the same despondency and shame in the fathers.

When Augusto leaves his prison, we find once again the Fellinian street, its derisive shine in contrast with the dullness of the walls, and the ever present symbol. Shivering, bent, and uncertain, Augusto leaves the prison and at the end of the somber, dark street, we see a transversal avenue down which the white automobile from the celebration of St. Sylvester's Eve is passing. We have already hinted at its significance: Satan is keeping watch. Eventually, abandoned by all his former acolytes, Augusto goes back to the life of a *bidonista* with new confederates. Once again, we find ourselves behind the car that is starting off on another swindle; the spaces return, the wind, the desert, the rare tree. The ultimate comedy of the dishonest prelate is to be played out. We enter a farmyard where the scene at the beginning of the film will be re-enacted, but this time it will be modified in all its perspectives by Augusto's attitude. How clever he showed himself to be the

other times when he displayed deliberate calm which allowed no uneasiness, no worry, no impatience to show: it was a matter of great art.

Compared to his more fearful and eager accomplices, he formerly
had a certain nobility in confidence games which revealed him to be an
artful and adroit gambler. Now, on the contrary, one could not do
better than to compare him in all respects to Zampanò doing his act in
the circus overlooking the sea after having learned of Gelsomina's
death, a man visibly aged, out of breath, who no longer believes in
what he does, who scoffs at those who watch him or at those who do
not, who has lost any sense of life, who no longer wishes to act or to
perform. Augusto has the same look and uses the same monotonous
voice in making his pitch; and when he says, "We are not merchants,"
this phrase which once seemed so full of a savory humor now bothers
him, and he recoils upon pronouncing the words.

When he leaves the farm, the wind is violent and we can hear it
blowing. The climate of *La Strada* is renewed: the scene is revealed,
the characters are seen against a wall, there is some sunlight and a dialogue, which is reminiscent of the last scene between Gelsomina and
Zampanò, between the counterfeit bishop and the invalid begins. This
young invalid suddenly came into view inside the house in a manner as
bizarre as that in which the little invalid of *La Strada* appeared in the
house where the wedding took place. Nonetheless, this invalid comes
to take a preponderant place in the sequence once her mother has de-
tained the false bishop with the words, "Just say two words to my
daughter." As we have noted, the young actress is a dark complexioned
and reasoning Gelsomina, but she has that same inner radiance. A dialogue full of tenderness and delicacy takes place. Like Zampanò, Augusto, it seems, begins to take an interest in someone else. But what
was implicit, that work of spiritual transfusion which began to grow
silently between the two frustrated beings of *La Strada*, is explicit here.
We witness a real discussion: "Misfortune made me find God," says
the young invalid, and in this struggle we keenly feel discomfort when
the girl's evocation of God pushes Augusto's sacrilege to its limits; once
the invalid has accepted him as a real bishop, he is obliged to perform
all the duties of a bishop, to let her kiss his ring, to bless her. He cannot
bear her saintly confidence and everything becomes madly mocking to
him. He flees and would like to escape from himself as well; everything
around him is deserted, cold; the absence of music at this moment ac-
centuates once again the desolation of the scene which even lacks the
fluid and purifying counterbalance of the sea. We then come to the
scene of intolerable sacrilege, and we can never thank Fellini enough

Il Bidone: Disguised as a priest, Augusto (Broderick Crawford) comforts the crippled girl he is supposed to swindle. (Museum of Modern Art/Film Stills Archive)

for not having yielded to either commercial considerations or the producers. He wanted us to enter into a hell, and he has spared us in no way: total, monstrous, inconceivable sacrilege is committed here, the nadir of this infernal descent. Not only has Augusto robbed the invalid's family, not only has he decided to rob his "acolytes," but finally, and herein lies the supreme ignominy, he conceals his lie from his accomplices behind emotional blackmail: "This poor invalid—I could not bring myself to steal the money for her care."

And the hour of reckoning comes with the punishment of men . . . and of the Other. The moment of death has arrived; it is no longer possible to lie either to others or to oneself. How does Augusto die? His death, like his life, is inevitable, and this uncertainty, this latent fear which he has carried on his face and in his comportment, becomes concrete here: it is the presentiment which has become reality. All his accomplices, infuriated by his betrayal, rough him up and throw stones at him; as *La Strada* at the conclusion was placed under the sign of water, so *Il Bidone* is placed under the sign of the stone. Under the stones and among the stones, Augusto rolls to the bottom of a ravine and his comrades abandon him in this desert; this recalls the last sequences of *The Forbidden Christ*.[3] Now we find him entirely alone; in this supreme abandonment, he evokes the name of God. Suffering from a serious wound, panic comes over him: "I can't move." He finds his body paralyzed as if he were destined to experience in his turn the disease that afflicted the young paralytic whom he had swindled earlier.

Although Fellini portrays these infernal beings, his immense kindness never condemns them to absolute damnation: they recognize their own ignominy; yet, he conceives for them the terrible and slow road of atonement. Augusto must come to know a whole desert of suffering, solitude, hunger, and thirst in order to realize the true measure of his spiritual wasteland: "I was of no use to anyone; it is because of that that I am dying. . . ." At this moment, the bells reverberate in a distant echo as they did in the final scene between Gelsomina and Zampanò. Augusto, who can no longer hold himself upright, now begins to crawl up from the bottom of the ravine to the road. One thinks of Buñuel in this moment of epidermic cruelty during which this man, bloody and in pain, inches his way back up this rocky hillside, gripping the dry earth with his fingernails, and again in this nightmare incarnate, this exasperation in a face, in an event, in a sentiment, which for us opens on to a second reality, inconceivable and bearable only with great pain. When Augusto reaches the road, having lost the strength to cry out, a small group of young peasants has just passed by. There are some children, including one silhouette which strongly resembles Gelsomina with her cape and her bundle of twigs. This silhouette sings, and again in Rota's score, the human voice takes the place of the instruments. This human voice, these human beings move away, unfortunately, and it is really then that Augusto, whose call is in vain, sweats blood: impossible communication, intolerable and solitary suffering, physical and mental destitution. The child, joy, light cannot soften this calcination; Zampanò had to find Gelsomina again only after having earned her; perhaps Augusto had to go to the end of his own hell to have the right to escape from it to another plane. It is perhaps this hope that Rota's music ultimately leaves to us as it takes up the theme of the song of the peasants on the road, symbol of the hope on which Augusto will close his eyes in his solitary death.

Augusto also appears to us as an inverted Christ figure, arms crossed, face against the ground. The man-Christ rejoining the Christ-God and merging together in an intimate union: is this not the re-establishment of that order toward which the Christian, constantly jostled between his heaven and his earth, strives?

NOTES

1. *Miracolo a Milano* (1950), directed by Vittorio De Sica, parodies in many respects the canons of neo-realist cinematic style.—EDITOR
2. A reference to *Ladri di biciclette* (1948, *The Bicycle Thief*), directed by Vittorio De Sica. This is perhaps the most famous of all neo-realist films. —EDITOR
3. *Il Cristo proibito* (1950), a film directed by Curzio Malaparte. A fascist extremist during the early years of Mussolini's regime whose enthusiasm for the movement eventually cooled, Malaparte is best known for his important novel *Kaputt* (1944), a macabre picture of the horrors of war. —EDITOR

The Nights of Cabiria:
Music and Film History

. . . .

12. Music as Salvation: Notes   *Claudia Gorbman*
on Fellini and Rota

"The best film music is not heard." Why, then, does even the least
musically oriented spectator remark on the musical aura pervading the
films of Federico Fellini? Unlike films that accord a pre-eminence to
music with respect to the image,[1] Fellini's works focus only rarely on
musical performance as the center of filmic interest. What lingers
in the spectator's mind is the presence of the "background" music in
composer Nino Rota's characteristic style: lyrical, festive, contemporary, reminiscent of the fair-ground.

Speaking about the filmic image, Noel Burch makes the distinction
between looking—an intellectual activity—and seeing—a nonselective,
physiological activity. Similarly, we do not *hear* the sound track in its
entirety unless we selectively *listen* to it. Further, as the human ear has
proven a "lazier" receptor in the cinema than the eye, the spectator's
relationship to the sound track is even more complex, and to deal with
the theoretical and practical problems this poses becomes all the more
difficult. Of the sound track's three components, music, owing to its
abstract quality in contrast to dialogue and sound effects, has most successfully eluded systematic analysis. To begin with, what are the pertinent musical factors for a given film, and how should we go about describing them?

Examining a specific narrative film—in this case, *Le Notti di Cabiria*
—can elucidate some of the possible narrative roles that film music may
assume. We must of course study not only the music, but the music in

. . . .

From *Film Quarterly*, Vol. 28, No. 3 (1974–75), pp. 17-25. © 1974 by
The Regents of the University of California. Reprinted by permission of The
Regents and Claudia Gorbman.

its narrative context, and in its direct relation to the image. We will also consider thematic music: when, how, and why it may recur. The musical score can act to promote continuity or to punctuate, as well as to comment on emotional states in the dramatic action, as will be shown. By virtue of its own inherent structures—repetition and variations of melody, harmony, and rhythm, for example—it can play an essential part in creating and/or reinforcing broad structural patterns in the filmic text. Being a relatively abstract and subliminal entity, it has power to emphasize or render ambiguous the distinctions among various levels of narrativity.

Fellini's films are constantly preoccupied with mixing real life with a fictional universe. Most have frankly autobiographical scenarios, for example (whether as autobiographical fantasies or realities is irrelevant), and many take actors and only slightly fictionalize them (repeatedly with Giulietta Masina and Marcello Mastroianni). This tendency grows to such proportions by the post-*Satyricon* films that the cohesive strength of the plot gives way to a quasi-documentary effect, bigger-than-life and similarly disorganized. Fellini's use of music throughout his career is singular for it regularly participates in the ambiguities actor/character, narrator/narrated, subject/object, and reality/fiction. Not only does it participate: it often helps to create these ambiguities—by means of synchronic and diachronic variations in its placement in the fictional world and by the level of musical consciousness attributed to the fictional characters.

In *Le Notti di Cabiria* this idea is particularly at issue: we shall follow its development to appreciate fully that music is, in fact, *the* subject of the film. The complexity of its interaction with the film's other materials of expression ultimately resolves in a transcendental simplicity—a nonverbal moral statement. First we shall examine the role of recurrent music principally in *Cabiria*, and secondly, the opposition of diegetic and extra-diegetic music. (I use "diegetic" to refer, in the semiotic sense, to all that occurs within the apparent world of the narrative.)

THEMES

Cabiria has four themes, that is, recurring melodies, all of which are heard as the credits appear at the film's beginning. Here are the melodies in skeletal form:

In addition there are a few pieces of music occurring only once, such as on two occasions over a radio, two songs played by a nightclub orchestra, music performed at a variety show, and Beethoven's fifth symphony (which I will treat elsewhere at greater length).

A theme is not necessarily a leitmotif in the Wagnerian sense, namely, a readily distinguishable musical line that becomes associated with a specific character, locale, or idea in the global text. In *La Strada* Fellini and Rota demonstrate the poetic power of the leitmotif in film, in its full role not only as a static or redundant identifying tag, but as a true signifier that accumulates and communicates meaning not explicit in the images or dialogue. *La Strada* has three leitmotifs: the theme of the road itself ("la strada"); that of Zampanò, Gelsomina's brutish keeper and spouse; and that of the Fool, Gelsomina's saving angel. Let us briefly, and necessarily schematically, examine the fate of this third leitmotif. Once the Fool has shown Gelsomina that she has an essential place in the universe, that her life has meaning and value, she some-how acquires his song; from time to time she plays it, and the extra-diegetic sound track also assigns it to her. Even after her angel is gone, she has interiorized his lesson. We know this solely from the musical line which has now been transferred to her. Originally played by the Fool on a small trumpet, the theme is destined to undergo several per-mutations in instrumentation and accompanying orchestration, but al-ways remains easily identifiable through the basic clarity of the melody, just as the idea it represents retains its simplicity despite its continual reapplication to new situations. Its final transmutation is perhaps the most moving: what started as the Fool's theme, then Gelsomina's, ulti-mately becomes the broken and remorseful Zampanò's, years after he has abandoned Gelsomina to her death. Hearing the leitmotif, this time sung unaccompanied by an anonymous woman, is enough to stir in him, and in us, the memory of Gelsomina and what she came to represent in the moral realm of *La Strada*. The Wagnerian leitmotif, then, forms an essential part of the action as a nonredundant signifier which undergoes changes in meaning as the story develops.

But a search for a strict system in *Le Notti di Cabiria*, grouping scenes or persons according to musical themes, proves relatively unin-teresting. There does seem to be a principal theme for prostitution ("D"), and Fellini capitalizes on our increasing awareness of its asso-ciation with the prostitutes and their street. On the first occasion it comes to us *via* a car radio in the scene. Another night, on the same street and with the same characters, we hear it on the sound track, harking back to our original acquaintance with it and Cabiria's com-panions. Finally, after Cabiria has met her prospective husband, we see her alone on the habitual street at night; theme "D" plays in the back-ground, as if to remind us that the ever-innocent protagonist is still really a prostitute. A car passes to pick her up but in her reverie she does not respond. The music comments quasi-ironically on the action, or rather the lack of it. Cabiria should be seeking clients, but is not keeping her mind on the job. She is not listening to the music.

In general, however, the four themes are used rather loosely, not ap-plied to specific characters, places, or ideas. Theme "A," for example, occurs several times throughout *Cabiria*, but twice particularly effec-tively on an emotional level. When the actor Lazzari reconciles with his girlfriend, it swells romantically in reinforcement; likewise when Cabiria runs to tell her friend Wanda of her engagement, the same orchestral theme warmly accompanies her happy cries. It is a melody line which, largely depending on the instrumentation in each instance, is appropriate for the reinforcement of a certain range of emotions elicited by the dramatic action. It could be argued that the very presence of theme "A" in these two seemingly disparate situations sets up a connection, a comparison, nonredundant albeit nonexplicit in meaning. However, the use of "A" differs so dramatically from the treatment even of "D," its significance so "floating" in contrast, that it eludes any conscientious inquiry as to its meaning other than a generalized emotional one. Fellini exploits each of the themes primarily in this second manner—as mood setters, and not leitmotifs.

The fifth theme is silence. Music prevails so much in *Cabiria* that its absence is quite noticeable. Take for example the film's beginning and end, each of whose musical silence reinforces the other structurally. The very first shot, a long pan, shows Giorgio and Cabiria running toward the river; he grabs her purse and pushes her into the water. This and the rest of the segment depicting Cabiria's rescue has no musical accompaniment. In the final segment, equally devoid of music, Oscar walks with Cabiria toward the river, about to take all her money and push her to her death. The stakes are much higher now; so is the distance from the cliff down to the river; and the protagonist has in the meantime become a fully developed character with whom the spectator identifies. The silence, then, is all the more terrible. The ever-present music is not there to comfort Cabiria; a part of her reality is threatened or missing. But again we cannot attribute a specific meaning to the silence "theme" except in each particular context, because music is also absent on other occasions in the film, and without the least reference to these two segments.

DIEGETIC AND EXTRA-DIEGETIC MUSIC

The interplay of diegetic and extra-diegetic music emerges as an important dialectic in the text. Kracauer in his *Theory of Film* requires that the source be explicit in the image,[2] though the music "may be alternately synchronized with images of its source and other images." His definition is erroneous, or at least becomes problematic, in numerous obvious instances. If a character in a film exits from an opera performance we need not see the performance inside, though it is certainly reasonable for us to hear a few strains of music before the door closes behind him. Likewise, in *Cabiria*, a guitarist plays somewhere at an outdoor restaurant though his presence is never visually rendered explicit.

Opposed to this is music that is outside the diegesis. We hear it on the sound track, but like a commentary or an internal voice, it could not conceivably be heard by the characters. This kind of music has traditionally had as its function to reinforce the emotional content of the images, whether it conveys a certain eerie tension like Bernard Herrmann's score for *Vertigo*, or a galloping pace as for countless chases in westerns, or the peace and tranquillity of a Mozart woodwind quintet in Varda's *Le Bonheur*. Note that music as reinforcement can work in either "positive" or "negative" terms: it can suggest emotional states parallel or in counterpoint to the action. A shot of a sleeping baby accompanied by ominous rumbling music will produce quite a different effect than the same shot accompanied by a music box playing a lullaby.[3]

We will get a clearer idea of the importance of the dialectical parameters of the diegetic vs. extra-diegetic in film music by going through instances of each in *Cabiria* to determine how each is treated, whether intended for the sake of realism, ambiguity, dramatic irony, etc.

(1) Music appears diegetically for the first time on the radio in Cabiria's one-room house. This is, in fact, the first appearance of any music whatsoever after the credits (the river segment being voice/noise only)—a point worth remembering, for the last occurrence of music in the film will also be diegetic, and also associated directly with Cabiria as the listener. The importance of diegetic music in both the first and last segments is emphasized by the ominous musical silences before each, as I have already mentioned.

Cabiria seeks consolation in the radio music—something she certainly needs, just having not only been nearly drowned by her boyfriend, robbed of her purse, and locked out of her own house, but consequently having been proven naive in her trust for him. Wanda comes to comfort her but has a less soothing effect than the radio. The radio plays a role of convenience in supplying the scene's background music; but further, it already helps to establish the inseparability of Cabiria and music, a certain type of music—unsophisticated, rhythmic, jazzy. The segment ends with a shot of Cabiria outside the house; Wanda has walked off angrily. A new melody (theme "A") is heard on the sound track. Should we assume it to be another tune on the radio, or external to the characters' universe? The film provides no clear answer: it has set up the diegetic/extra-diegetic ambiguity with the first music.

(2) We hear music ("C") along with our introduction to the prostitutes' place of work, a street in the outskirts of Rome. It becomes evi-

dent that it issues from the radio of a car belonging to a pimp. When the mambo ("D") starts, everyone joins in a dance out on the street. Strictly speaking the theme on the sound track sounds too loud and too clear to be coming from the car's meager radio speaker, but we will nevertheless call it diegetic with qualifications.

The same theme plays later on the Via Veneto where the pimp and his girlfriend have dropped Cabiria. It accompanies the image of the small, awkward heroine visually imprisoned between two threateningly looming hookers whose rightful territory it is. Can the music be issuing from the nearby café? There is no reason to assume so, but on the other hand the text has already made an issue of weak or ambiguous diegetization of music, suggesting its pervasiveness in Cabiria's world.

(3) Theme "C" is heard again on a darkened street later the same night, as Cabiria still attempts to find a client. We have no basis for believing the music to be diegetic this time either, until Cabiria looks into a ground-level window, apparently that of a nightclub, and starts moving her hips in rhythm. Her response, then, indicates her awareness of the music as well as ours. Its source—probably a band or a record player—does not need to appear in the image. We note also how this retrospectively places into further doubt the "non-diegeticity" of the Via Veneto music.

(4) The next possible case of diegetic music arises shortly thereafter, with the appearance of the aging movie star Alberto Lazzari (played by an aging movie star named Amedeo Nazzari—a fact that contributes to Fellini's characteristic clouding of distinctions between the real and the fictional). After a tiff with his mistress outside the nightclub, he motions Cabiria to get into his car. Theme "C" plays once more; its source, though not indicated, could easily be his car radio.

(5) The diegesis provides the music for the entire sequence in the nightclub with Lazzari. Cabiria enters to the sound of a clarinet which plays an exotic melody to accompany two long-legged Negresses in their dance. Cabiria listens and looks on in a sort of tentative and unsophisticated approval. The show finished, the band switches to sedate mood music to which all including Cabiria and Lazzari dance. The following song, a fast-paced number, inspires Cabiria. She dances uninhibitedly (as she and her companions dance to a similar kind of music at their regular night location), to the abashed amusement of those present—a reversal of all musical stimuli and responses at the sequence's beginning. Her identification with rhythmic, contemporary popular music

is once again reinforced, this time by means of a contrast with the society of the rich, pretentious, and decadent. Finally, as she and Lazzari leave, theme "C" is in the air. Is the orchestra "inside" the sound track, outside the characters' earshot?

(6) One of the most striking scenes involving diegetic music—in which music virtually "orchestrates" for a while the dramatic action— occurs at Lazzari's residence. In his bedroom, Alberto sits down on the bed next to the record player (which indicates the immanent possibility of a diegetic music source). The second movement of Beethoven's fifth symphony is heard: a shot of Lazzari and the phonograph comes shortly after the music starts. When asked about Beethoven, Cabiria admits that it is not her type of music but that she enjoys it (as the first nightclub music, and indeed, Lazzari himself, are not her types). And for the rest of the duration of the piece, or until Lazzari removes it from the turntable, Fellini paces the action to match exactly the movement of the symphony. At the point of a great crescendo and modulation,[4] as the music swells on the sound track to improbable volume, a servant brings in a majestic tray loaded with food in silver serving dishes. The synchronization of music and action does not stop there; for a full two or three minutes they continue to indulge in spectacular interplay. During a quiet, pensive moment in the Beethoven, Lazzari, having inspected the champagne and its vintage, repeats the year 1949 nostalgically, *as if directed by the music* to do so at that time and no other.

Note 1: Can we by this time consider a third category lying somewhere between the diegetic and extra-diegetic? Is the music we hear exactly the same as that which the characters hear? And if not, may we justifiably speak of music heard by the "narrator,"[5] a sort of music which, though one single signifier, has more than one signification?

There is a degree of stylization achieved by manipulating the characters' action so that they submit to *musical* division of time rather than dramatic or realistic time. The characters in the narrative film, whom we *conventionally* accept as subjects, unquestionably become objects when their movements and speech coincide strictly with the music: for we can consider musical rhythm— an abstract, mathematical, highly organized disposition of time—to be the opposite of spontaneous, "real" time. We sense that the characters have been *created*, and they do not inspire us to identify with them. The resulting stylization, then, necessarily constitutes a definite departure from concern for psychological realism within the diegesis. Consequently the music employed acts ironically as a much stronger narrative intrusion, even though "diegetic," than extra-diegetic music.

Note 2: Fellini enthusiastically uses the idea of the "orchestrated" scene in other films. Near the beginning of *Otto e mezzo* (8½) occurs a magnificent descriptive panorama of the health resort where Guido (Marcello Mastroianni) is staying. As Wagner's "Ride of the Walkyries" plays, the camera obeys its rhythm: the shots we see seem to (ironically) fit the music, and not vice versa. Fellini weakly renders the music diegetic, providing visual indices of an open-air orchestra at the spa. Again the diegetization of the music lies somewhere in between the two parameters, simply because an on-location orchestra would not be performing the piece with such perfection, and with such clarity and volume exclusive of any background noise.

(7) Music plays a central role in the picnic sequence following the pilgrimage. We have witnessed Cabiria's naive expectation of some message of salvation, and the subsequent crushing of that expectation achieved filmically by showing the failure of the cripple to walk, and by expressive close-ups of Cabiria herself. Now Cabiria, drunk, has reached her lowest point of despair and bitterly shouts her hopelessness to those near her, to herself, and to us. In more exact terms, her speech is directed to the rest of the set of diegetic characters, to herself as the protagonist and as voice of a point of view partially shared by the narrator, and to (from) that same metafilmic level that participates in the paradoxically diegetic music (see above, Note 1) which makes Fellini such a non-"realist." Three distinct witnesses to her despair, hence three levels of interpretation. Wanda and the other prostitutes attribute Cabiria's outbreak to her drunkenness and do not listen to the content of her ravings. Cabiria herself, a tough character who believes she has learned to handle life's misfortunes, is angry at the world, in the most concrete of terms (shouting, staggering, violently throwing a soccer ball), in physical actions and in verbal content as well. The metafilmic level, the narrator's point of view, allows us to perceive the spiritual implications of the scene. The filmic text presents Cabiria's life as an almost unbearable series of vulnerable/hurt, hope/despair progressions; and we see the picnic as a demonstration of her deepest psycho-spiritual pain.

At the beginning of the picnic the music appears extra-diegetic, until the introduction of the group playing instruments (accordion, guitar, drum) in a shot with Wanda in the foreground gently chastising Cabiria for her drunken behavior. They play all the film's major themes as Cabiria shouts. A musical crisis, and outpouring, accompanies and contributes to her crisis. Diegesis and that which is external to it lose their meaning as separate entities.[6] The music acts as a recapitulation and compression of what has come before—and what will follow—and as a background continuum, both aural and visual, against which Cabiria's release of agony, correspondingly verbal and physical, acquires remarkable force. The culmination of the scene is achieved when, having staggered over toward some parked cars, Cabiria leans against the side of a bus. The accordion music dissolves magically into the monodic melody of a line of choirboys making their way across Cabiria's field of vision beyond a stream. Framed by pure, fresh water, the stream and the arc of a water sprinkler, they sing an *ora pro nobis* that brings a simple purity to image as well as sound track. Cabiria's expression changes with this dissolve from anger into serenity (her head lies under the bus gas cap which looks unmistakably halo-like). The scene thus executes a transformation: it progresses from considerable movement/society of prostitutes and boyfriends/polyphonic, rhythmic music, theme after theme/Cabiria's physical and verbal violence—to relative stillness/children in religious dress/monophonic, arhythmic, "pure" music/Cabiria's silence and truer perception of her surrounding universe. Movement also from verbal violence to a complete, if brief, peace independent of verbal communication.

(8) A live orchestra plays in the "Lux" theater: first as plain vaude-. ville entertainment, as in Fellini's first feature film, *Luci del Varietà,* but then much more artfully and subtly as Cabiria, hypnotized to believe in "Oscar," a pure and simple love, dances gracefully on the stage. Many of the musical examples already cited can cause us to doubt the care or sincerity with which Fellini diegetizes them. The quiet, hypnotic melody heard during Cabiria's romantic trance at the Lux does not really suit the somewhat seedy instrumentalists shown in the orchestra pit. The handy presence elsewhere of portable and car radios suggests this same syndrome. It might be tempting to take to heart the rather uncharitable view of Hanns Eisler and Theodor Adorno in *Composing for the Film,* that diegetic music is a cheap excuse for realism at points where the director wants to fill in gaps of silence on the sound track.

But the music in *Cabiria* does more than fill in spaces in the dramatic action. It is a force that works to erase distinctions between the diegetic framework, narrative framework, and spectator's framework. Maurice Jaubert, whose understanding of the possibilities of music in cinema as early as the first sound films (his scores for Jean Vigo's *Zéro de conduite* and *L'Atalante* have yet to be equalled) deserves the utmost attention, had this to say:

> Into the raw materials of cinema—which acquire artistic meaning only from their relations to one another—music brings an *unreal* element which

is bound to break the rules of objective realism. Is there no place for it in the film?

Certainly there is. For just as the novelist sometimes interrupts the telling of a story with an expression of his feelings, argumentative or lyrical, or with the subjective reactions of his characters, so does the director sometimes move away from the strict representation of reality in order to add to his work those touches of comment or of poetry which give a film its individual quality, descriptions, movements from one point to another in space or time, recalling of earlier scenes, dreams, imaging of the thoughts of some character, etc. Here the music has something to say: its presence will warn the spectator that the style of the film is changing temporarily for dramatic reasons. All its power of suggestion will serve to intensify and prolong that impression of strangeness, of departure from photographic truth, which the director is seeking.[7]

Though Jaubert does not specifically discuss diegetic music in this passage, we have already seen in Fellini how the diegetic–extra-diegetic dialectic, with all its possible ambiguities, surprises, and stylization, is rich territory for narrative intrusion or dramatic irony, for the director's "departure from photographic truth."

(9) Cabiria, thinking happily about the "real" Oscar—the man who introduces himself to her after her hypnosis/disillusionment and who will capitalize on her trust and vulnerability in order to take all her money—lies on her bed as some soothing music plays. Her radio is nearby. If we assume the music comes from the radio, we set up a parallel between this scene and the end of sequence 1, that is, when Cabiria comforts herself with radio music following Giorgio's betrayal. The correspondences between the two scenes in terms of their diegetic music situation, the visual elements of decor and the radio itself, and similarities of plot (Giorgio's betrayal foreshadowing Oscar's) touch off a series of structural resonances that reverberate consistently throughout the film.[8]

(10) At the outdoor restaurant where Cabiria and Oscar embark on their honeymoon, a guitarist sings and plays (theme "B"). Though he does not appear on the screen at all, I consider this music diegetic in the context. The deliberate ambiguity already set up between diegetic reality and narrative musical comment, combined with the fact that this music is sufficiently localizable and appropriate to the action, support this view.

(11) The final segment finds the resolution of conflicts, profilmic and metafilmic, in music. It begins as Cabiria walks despondently through the forest after Oscar's ultimate betrayal; strains of an accordion are heard on the sound track. Until she reaches the musicians

on the road, the film gives no indication that (a) she has been walking toward a destination, the road, and that (b) once again, the music is diegetic. Thus this scene participates in the situation already established on numerous occasions, the situation of retrospectively indicating music's presence in Cabiria's world. Why? Unlike the attractive mysteries of religion or magic, and more realistically (in the film's pessimistic point of view) than the possibility of a prostitute marrying a "good" man, music as a source of peace has been there all the time, in all its simplicity and availability.

The very fact of the protagonist's deep despondency, accompanied by seemingly extra-diegetic music, recalls the beginning of the pivotal picnic scene. Indeed, the parallels multiply to such an extent as to confirm the structural and thematic pre-eminence of the two scenes in the global text. First, the diegetic source of the background music turns out to be a group of young people playing the same assortment of instruments: accordion, guitar, and various rhythm instruments. Theme "B" had appeared briefly in the picnic scene (and at the restaurant) as if in anticipation of its full expression at this point, for the walking musicians now adopt the song. Two different types of music played during the picnic, though, and the film's final scene acts as sort of a *combinatoire* at the same time as a simplification (reducing the number of songs to theme "B" exclusively). The musicians play the same genre of music, but it is harmonically simpler, and in contrast to the other themes, flowingly melodic, with no interval jumps between notes in the theme itself. In fact, we notice an uncanny resemblance between the choirboys' *ora pro nobis* and the stepwise rise and fall of theme "B":

Having suggested the idea of a musical *combinatoire*—the picnic musicians' rhythmic accordion style and the flow and direction of the choirboys' melody—we note the same principle operating in the depiction of the groups of performers themselves. Though the musicians in the final scene appear at first to share most of the visual characteristics of the instrumentalists at the picnic, they participate also—markedly so—in the choirboys' *youth* (they are teenagers at best) and in their *movement*. The picnic musicians were static, standing or sitting on the lawn as they played. The choirboys in contrast moved across the visual field as they sang. The musicians now move forward on the road, not in the choirboys' orderly lines, but in circles, at angles, and with pauses—with spontaneity. (One of the group rides a motorcycle— a detail to be classed with the men at the picnic, who associate themselves with cars, motorcycles, and the spatial realm of the parking lot.) In general the idea of the procession takes on a quasimythical dimension in the work of Fellini. It appears often: a patriotic marching band in *Lo Sceicco bianco*, a pilgrimage and a trio of musicians in *La Strada*, an orgiastic line dance in *La Dolce vita*, the grand finale of *Otto e mezzo*. And the road itself is a strong theme with Fellini, obviously central in *La Strada*, for example, with its own musical leit- motif.[9] At the end of *Il Bidone* the dying protagonist sees a small pro- cession of children and their mothers, singing and walking up the road in the mountainous countryside where he has been abandoned. An even more pessimistic film than *Cabiria*, *Il Bidone* does not allow Au- gusto to reach the road and his possible salvation from death.

Salvation: the text of *Cabiria* has demonstrated a search for it in every way—through plot, imagery, thematic structures, character con- figuration, Fellini's own symbolic structures, and the disposition of music. The text has presented the agonized faces of the pilgrims, on their knees before relics of the Virgin Mary, calling out for her grace and for salvation from their spiritual drowning. It has shown the hyp- notized subjects in the Lux theater fall to their knees also, praying and begging to be saved from the physical drowning they think is their fate. Twice, at the film's opening and just before the final segment, Cabiria has almost been pushed to her death by drowning. As the priest and the hypnotist guide the illusions of their subjects, Cabiria tries repeatedly to believe in Giorgio, in Lazzari to a lesser extent, and finally in Oscar.

The quest, then, may terminate filmically in the final musical pro- cession. Music *is* salvation: unmotivated, gratuitous, ubiquitous. It is everywhere in the text spatially, temporally, and on all narrative levels as I have demonstrated. Its effect in the final segment owes to the fact that it provides answers to the film's conflict in "form" and in "con- tent," in the profilmic and metafilmic contexts. Let us note once more the transformation achieved in the picnic sequence via the oppositions it had articulated (see 7 above): Cabiria's violent movement vs. her peaceful immobilization, stillness of first set of performers vs. movement of the second, social rank of prostitutes vs. church choir-boys, adulthood vs. childhood, harmonic rhythmic music vs. monodic arhythmic music, anguish vs. peace. The final scene arrives at a resolu-tion of these oppositions. Cabiria, neither violent nor immobilized, walks on the road *along with the musicians;* they move, though not in a strict linear fashion; the choirboys have been secularized and/or the picnic musicians have been purified; and the music has undergone an equally complete reconciliation of differences. Attained entirely by means other than verbal, Cabiria's salvation does not leave her as it did halfway through the film. This time the music acts as the agent of *communication* between her and the youths. She joins the procession with a mixture of grief and joy, aware of herself, of those around her, and of the renewed possibility of life. The text closes not only with a close-up of Cabiria's face filling the screen, but also with a transfer to extra-diegetic instrumentation of theme "A" as an ultimate statement of the narrator's presence. The two presences, the protagonist's and the narrator's, are thus reconciled on an absolute and final plane.

NOTES

1. E.g., the *musical* proper, or more experimental forms such as in Jean Mitry's *Pacific 231,* Walt Disney's *Fantasia,* and Jean-Marie Straub's *Chronicle of Anna Magdalena Bach.*
2. His rudimentary distinction of "actual" vs. "commentative" corresponds to diegetic and extra-diegetic.
3. An elaborated discussion of any music's emotive effect *a priori* is too com-plex to be included within the aims of this study.
4.

5. *narrator:* the force through whom/which the story is viewed and re-counted. The intermediary, explicit or not, between the characters in the diegesis and the spectator.
6. In the context of the diegesis, why should they play those four particular tunes in such well-organized succession? Perhaps the "prostitute theme" and theme "C" have been in the diegetic air long enough to justify the musicians' familiarity with them. But especially in playing theme "B" they are acting as a musical oracle for the narrator.
7. As quoted in E. Lindgren, *The Art of the Film* (London, 1948), pp.

192-3. Jaubert's original article in French is "Petite école du spectateur," *Esprit*, 1/4/36.

8. For instance, I find music's relationships to two pervasive thematic structures of prime importance. The first is the set of Cabiria's relationships with men: primarily the trio Giorgio, Lazzari, and Oscar, and secondarily the friar and the hypnotist. The other set of interrelationships has to do with three hopes of salvation: marriage, religion, and music itself.

9.

. . . .

13. *Cabiria:* The Voyage to the   *André Bazin*
End of Neorealism

As I sit down to write this article, I have no idea what kind of reception Fellini's latest film will have. I hope it is as enthusiastic as I think it should be, but I do not conceal from myself the fact that there are two categories of viewers who may have reservations about the film. The first is that segment of the general public likely to be put off by the way the story mixes the strange with what seems to be an almost melodramatic naïveté. These people can accept the theme of the whore with a heart of gold only if it is spiced with crime. The second belongs, albeit reluctantly, to that part of the "elite" which supports Fellini almost in spite of itself. Constrained to admire *La Strada* and under even more constraint from its austerity and its "outcast" status to admire *Il Bidone*, I expect these viewers now to criticize *Le Notti di Cabiria* for being "too well made"—a film in which practically nothing is left to chance, a film that is clever—artful, even. Let's forget the first objection; it is important only in the effect it may have at the box office. The second, however, is worth refuting.

The least surprising thing about *Le Notti di Cabiria* is not that this is the first time Fellini has succeeded in putting together a masterly script, with an action that cannot be faulted—unmarred by clichés or missing links, one in which there could be no place for the unhappy

. . . .

From *What Is Cinema?* (Vol. II) by André Bazin, trans. Hugh Gray (Berkeley: University of California Press, 1971), pp. 83-92. Copyright © 1971 by the Regents of the University of California. Reprinted by permission of the University of California Press.

cuts and the corrections in editing from which *La Strada* and *Il Bidone* suffered.[1] Of course, *Lo Sceicco bianco* and even *I Vitelloni* were not clumsy in their construction, but chiefly because, though their themes were specifically Fellinian, they were still being expressed within a framework provided by relatively traditional scenarios. Fellini has finally cast these crutches aside with *La Strada*: theme and character alone are the final determinants in the story now, to the exclusion of all else; story has nothing now to do with what one calls plot; I even have doubts that it is proper here to speak of "action." The same is true of *Il Bidone*.

It is not that Fellini would like to return to the excuses which drama affords him in his earlier films. Quite the contrary. *Le Notti di Cabiria* goes even beyond *Il Bidone*, but here the contradictions between what I will call the "verticality" of its author's themes and the "horizontality" of the requirements of narrative have been reconciled. It is within the Fellinian system that he now finds his solutions. This does not prevent the viewer from possibly mistaking brilliant perfection for mere facility, if not indeed for betrayal. All the same, on one score at least Fellini has deceived himself a little: is he not counting on the character played by François Périer (who to me seems miscast) to have a surprise effect? Now it is clear that any effect of "suspense" or even of "drama" is essentially alien to the Fellinian system, in which it is impossible for time ever to serve as an abstract or dynamic support—as an *a priori* framework for narrative structure. In *La Strada* as in *Il Bidone*, time is nothing more than the shapeless framework modified by fortuitous events which affect the fate of his heroes, though never in consequence of external necessity. Events do not "happen" in Fellini's world; they "befall" its inhabitants; that is to say, they occur as an effect of "vertical" gravity, not in conformity to the laws of "horizontal" causality. As for the characters themselves, they exist and change only in reference to a purely internal kind of time—which I cannot qualify even as Bergsonian, insofar as Bergson's theory of the *Données immédiates de la conscience* contains a strong element of psychologism. Let us avoid the vague terms of a "spiritualizing" vocabulary. Let us not say that the transformation of the characters takes place at the level of the "soul." But it has at least to occur at that depth of their being into which consciousness only occasionally reaches down. This does not mean at the level of the unconscious or the subconscious but rather the level on which what Jean-Paul Sartre calls the "basic project" obtains, the level of ontology. Thus the Fellinian character does not evolve; he ripens or at the most becomes transformed (whence the metaphor of the angel's wings, to which I will shortly return).

A SPURIOUS MELODRAMA

But let us confine ourselves, for the moment, to the structure of the script. I totally reject, then, the *coup de théâtre* in *Le Notti di Cabiria* which belatedly reveals Oscar a swindler. Fellini must have been aware of what he was doing because, as if to compound his sin, he makes François Périer wear dark glasses when he is about to turn "wicked." What of it? This is a minor concession indeed and I find it easy to pardon in view of the care Fellini now takes to avoid in this film the grave danger to which a complicated and much too facile shooting script exposed him in *Il Bidone*.

I find it all the more easy to pardon when it is the only concession he makes in this film; for the rest Fellini communicates the tension and the rigor of tragedy to it without ever having to fall back on devices alien to his universe. Cabiria, the little prostitute whose simple soul is rooted in hope, is not a character out of melodrama, because her desire to "get out" is not motivated by the ideals of bourgeois morality or a strictly bourgeois sociology. She does not hold her trade in contempt. As a matter of fact, if there were such creatures as pure-hearted pimps capable of understanding her and of embodying not love indeed but just a belief in life, she would doubtless see no incompatibility between her secret hopes and her nighttime activities. Does she not owe one of her greatest moments of happiness—happiness followed consequently by an even more bitter deception—to her chance meeting with a famous film star who because he is drunk and feeling embittered against love proposes to take her home to his luxurious apartment. There was something to make the other girls just die of envy! But the incident is fated to come to a pitiful end, because after all a prostitute's trade commonly destines her only to disappointments; this is why she longs, more or less consciously, to get out of it through the impossible love of some stalwart fellow who will make no demands of her. If we seem now to have reached an outcome typical of bourgeois melodrama, it is in any case by a very different route.

Le Notti di Cabiria—like *La Strada*, like *Il Bidone*, and, in the final analysis, like *I Vitelloni*—is the story of *ascesis*, of renunciation, and, (however you choose to interpret the term) of salvation. The beauty and the rigor of its construction proceed this time from the perfect

The Nights of Cabiria: The hypnotist (Aldo Silvani) performs his act with Cabiria (Giulietta Masina). (Museum of Modern Art/Film Stills Archive)

economy of its constituent episodes. Each of them, as I have said earlier, exists by and for itself, unique and colorful as an event, but now each belongs to an order of things that never fails to reveal itself in retrospect as having been absolutely necessary. As she goes from hope to hope, plumbing enroute the depths of betrayal, contempt, and poverty, Cabiria follows a path on which every halt readies her for the stage ahead. When one stops and reflects, one realizes that there is nothing in the film, before the meeting with the benefactor of the tramps (whose irruption into the film seems at first sight to be no more than a characteristic piece of Fellinian bravura), which is not proved subsequently to be necessary to trick Cabiria into making an act of ill-placed faith; for if such men do exist, then every miracle is possible and we, too, will be without mistrust when Périer appears.

I do not intend to repeat what has been written about Fellini's message. It has, anyway, been noticeably the same since *I Vitelloni.* This is not to be taken as a sign of sterility. On the contrary, while variety is the mark of a "director," it is unity of inspiration that connotes the true "author." But in the light of this new masterpiece maybe I can still attempt to throw a little more light on what in essence is Fellini's style.

A REALISM OF APPEARANCES

It is absurd, preposterous even, to deny him a place among the neo-realists. Such a judgment could only be possible on ideological grounds. It is true that Fellini's realism though social in origin is not social in intent. This remains as individual as it is in Chekhov or Dostoievsky. Realism, let me repeat, is to be defined not in terms of ends but of means, and neorealism by a specific kind of relationship of means to ends. What De Sica has in common with Rossellini and Fellini is obviously not the deep meaning of their films—even if, as it happens, these more or less coincide—but the pride of place they all give to the representation of reality at the expense of dramatic structures. To put it more precisely, the Italian cinema has replaced a "realism" deriving in point of content from the naturalism of novels and structurally from theater with what, for brevity's sake, we shall call "phenomeno-logical" realism which never "adjusts" reality to meet the needs imposed by psychology or drama. The relation between meaning and appearance having been in a sense inverted, appearance is always presented as a unique discovery, an almost documentary revelation that retains its full force of vividness and detail. Whence the director's art lies in the skill with which he compels the event to reveal its meaning—or at least the meaning he lends it—without removing any of its ambiguity. Thus defined, neorealism is not the exclusive property of any one ideology nor even of any one ideal, no more than it excludes any other ideal—no more, in point of fact, than reality excludes anything.

I even tend to view Fellini as the director who goes the farthest of any to date in this neorealist aesthetic, who goes even so far that he goes all the way through it and finds himself on the other side.

Let us consider how free Fellini's direction is from the encumbrances of psychological after-effects. His characters are never defined by their "character" but exclusively by their appearance. I deliberately avoid the word "behavior" because its meaning has become too restricted; the way people behave is only one element in the knowledge we have of them. We know them by many other signs, not only their faces, of course, but by the way they move, by everything that makes the body the outer shell of the inner man—even more, perhaps, by things still more external than these, things on the frontier between the individual and the world, things such as haircut, moustache, clothing, eye glasses (the one prop that Fellini has used to a point where it has become a gimmick). Then, beyond that again, setting, too, has a role to play—not, of course, in an expressionistic sense but rather as establishing a harmony or a disharmony between setting and character. I am thinking in particular of the extraordinary relationship established between Cabiria and the unaccustomed settings into which Nazzari inveigles her, the nightclub and the luxurious apartment.

ON THE OTHER SIDE OF THINGS

But it is here that we reach the boundaries of realism, here, too, that Fellini, who drives on further still, takes us beyond them. It is a little as if, having been led to this degree of interest in appearances, we were now to see the characters no longer *among* the objects but, as if these had become transparent, *through* them. I mean by this that without our noticing the world has moved from meaning to analogy, then from analogy to identification with the supernatural. I apologize for this equivocal word; the reader may replace it with whatever he will—"poetry" or "surrealism" or "magic"—whatever the term that expresses the hidden accord which things maintain with an invisible counterpart of which they are, so to speak, merely the adumbration.

Let us take one example from among many others of this process of "supernaturalization," which is to be found in the metaphor of the angel. From his first films, Fellini has been haunted by the angelizing of his characters, as if the angelic state were the ultimate referent in his universe, the final measure of being. One can trace this tendency in its explicit development at least from *I Vitelloni* on: Sordi dresses up for the carnival as a guardian angel; a little later on what Fabrizi steals, as if by chance, is the carved wooden statue of an angel. But these allusions are direct and concrete. Subtler still, and all the more interesting because it seems unconscious, is the shot in which the monk who has come down from working in a tree loads a long string of little branches on his back. This detail is nothing more than a nice "realistic" touch for us, perhaps even for Fellini himself, until at the end of *Il Bidone* we see Antonio dying at the side of the road: in the white light of dawn he sees a procession of children and women bearing bundles of sticks on their backs: angels pass! I must note, too, how in the same film Picasso races down a street and the tails of his raincoat spread out behind him like little wings. It is that same Richard Basehart again who appears before Gelsomina as if he were weightless, a dazzling sight on his high wire under the spotlights. There is no end to Fellini's symbolism. Certainly, it would be possible to study the whole body of his work from this one angle.[2] What needed to be done was simply to place it within the context of the logic of neorealism, for it is evident that these associations of objects and characters which constitute Fellini's universe derive their value and their importance from realism alone—or, to put it a better way, perhaps, from the objectivity with which they are recorded. It is not in order to look like an angel that the friar carries his bundles of sticks on his back, but it is enough to see the wing in the twigs for the old monk to be transformed into one. One might say that Fellini is not opposed to realism, any more than he is to neorealism, but rather that he achieves it surpassingly in a poetic reordering of the world.

A REVOLUTION IN NARRATIVE

Fellini creates a similar revolution at the narrative level. From this point of view, to be sure, neorealism is also a revolution in form which comes to bear on content. For example, the priority which they accord incident over plot has led De Sica and Zavattini to replace plot as such with a microaction based on an infinitely divisible attention to the complexities in even the most ordinary of events. This in itself rules out the slightest hierarchy, whether psychological, dramatic, or ideological, among the incidents that are portrayed. This does not mean, of course, that the director is obliged to renounce all choice over what he is to show us, but it does mean that he no longer makes the choice in reference to some pre-existing dramatic organization. In this new perspective, the important sequence can just as well be the long scene that "serves no purpose" by traditional screenplay standards.[3]

Nonetheless—this is true even of *Umberto D*, which perhaps represents the limits of experimentation in this new dramaturgy—the evolution of film follows an invisible thread. Fellini, I think, brings the neorealist revolution to its point of perfection when he introduces a new kind of script, the scenario lacking any dramatic linking, based as it is, to the exclusion of all else, on the phenomenological description of the characters. In the films of Fellini, the scenes that establish the logical relations, the significant changes of fortune, the major points of dramatic articulation, only provide the continuity links, while the long descriptive sequences, seeming to exercise no effect on the unfolding of the "action" proper, constitute the truly important and revealing scenes. In *I Vitelloni*, these are the nocturnal walks, the senseless strolls on the beach; in *La Strada*, the visit to the convent; in *Il Bidone*, the evening at the nightclub or the New Year's celebration. It is not when they are doing something specific that Fellini's characters best reveal themselves to the viewer but by their endless milling around.

If there are, still, tensions and climaxes in the films of Fellini which leave nothing to be desired as regards drama or tragedy, it is because, in the absence of traditional dramatic causality, the incidents in his films develop effects of analogy and echo. Fellini's hero never reaches the final crisis (which destroys him and saves him) by a progressive dramatic linking but because the circumstances somehow or other affect him, build up inside him like the vibrant energy in a resonating body. He does not develop; he is transformed; overturning finally like an iceberg whose center of buoyancy has shifted unseen.

EYE TO EYE

By way of conclusion, and to compress the disturbing perfection of *Le Notti di Cabiria* into a single phrase, I would like to analyze the final shot of the film, which strikes me, when everything else is taken into account, as the boldest and the most powerful shot in the whole of Fellini's work. Cabiria, stripped of everything—her money, her love, her faith—emptied now of herself, stands on a road without hope. A group of boys and girls swarm into the scene singing and dancing as they go, and from the depths of her nothingness Cabiria slowly returns to life; she starts to smile again; soon she is dancing, too. It is easy to imagine how artificial and symbolic this ending would have been, casting aside as it does all the objections of verisimilitude, if Fellini had not succeeded in projecting his film onto a higher plane by a single detail of direction, a stroke of real genius that forces us suddenly to identify with his heroine. Chaplin's name is often mentioned in connection with *La Strada*, but I have never thought the comparison between Gelsomina and Charlie (which I find hard to take in itself) very convincing. The first shot which is not only up to Chaplin's level but the true equal of his best inventions is the final shot of *Le Notti di Cabiria*, when Giulietta Masina turns toward the camera and her glance crosses ours. As far as I know, Chaplin is the only man in the history of film who made successful systematic use of this gesture, which the books about filmmaking are unanimous in condemning. Nor would it be in place if when she looked us in the eye Cabiria seemed to come bearing some ultimate truth. But the finishing touch to this stroke of directorial genius is this, that Cabiria's glance falls several times on the camera without ever quite coming to rest there. The lights go up on this marvel of ambiguity. Cabiria is doubtless still the heroine of the adventures which she has been living out before us, somewhere behind that screen, but here she is now inviting us, too, with her glance to follow her on the road to which she is about to return. The invitation is chaste, discreet, and indefinite enough that we can pretend to think that she means to be looking at somebody else. At the same time, though, it is definite and direct enough, too, to remove us quite finally from our role of spectator.

NOTES

1. Alas, the facts give me the lie: the original-language version shown in Paris reveals the deletion of at least one long scene that was still in the film when it was shown at Cannes, namely the scene of "the visitor of Saint Vincent de Paul" to which I allude below. But then we have seen how easy it has been in the past to convince Fellini—if it is indeed he who is responsible for this cut—that a truly remarkable sequence is "useless." [The "visitor" is a member of the Society of Saint Vincent de Paul founded in France in 1833 to care for the sick, the aged, the poor, and what were then known as "fallen women."—TRANSLATOR]
2. See the article by Dominique Aubier in *Cahiers du Cinéma*, No. 49.
3. This is true of the sequence that has been deleted from the film.

La Dolce Vita:
Fellini and T. S. Eliot

. . . .

14. Waste Lands: The Breakdown of Order

. . . In the film one can also find a steady concern with this loss of order. From *The Cabinet of Dr. Caligari,* and *Un Chien Andalou,* and *L'Age d'Or* to *La Dolce Vita, L'Avventura, Mondo Cane,* and *Dr. Strangelove,* the film has borne consistent witness to a world in which entropy rules, order dissolves, and the grotesque becomes the normal. It can be argued that this relaxation of order has reached even further, undermining the design and pattern of the work of art itself. Ezra Pound's great work, *The Cantos,* has apparently foundered because of the absence of a sufficiently large organizing principle. The same can be said for William Carlos Williams' *Paterson,* a long poem which went on and on, like life itself, unable to find or to fulfill its pattern. So Hart Crane's *The Bridge,* a deliberate attempt to bridge gaps and perceive order, failed even to order itself as a poem. Yeats' late poem "The Circus Animals' Desertion" chronicles the successive failures of Yeats' various masks and designs, and one might even claim that Eliot's "The Waste Land" and Robert Lowell's "The Quaker Graveyard in Nantucket" are triumphs of the attempt to write significant poetry without resorting to any sort of clear order, pattern, or design. So in the film, from *Intolerance* and *Greed* to *Ivan the Terrible,* 8½, *Eclipse,* and *The 400 Blows,* one can find innumerable films which are undeniably fine works and which seem deliberately to have avoided or submerged any visible or obvious order or pattern.

. . . .

From *Film and Literature* by Robert Richardson (Bloomington: Indiana University Press, 1969), pp. 105-16. Copyright © 1969 by Indiana University Press. Reprinted by permission of Indiana University Press. Excerpts from "The Love Song of J. Alfred Prufrock" and "The Waste Land" by T. S. Eliot are from his volume *Collected Poems 1909–1962* and are reprinted by permission of Harcourt Brace Jovanovich, Inc.; copyright, 1936, by Harcourt Brace Jovanovich, Inc.; copyright © 1963, 1964, by T. S. Eliot.

This sense of a lost order has been so strong and has had such a pervasive effect on the arts that one of the commonest images for our times is the image of the wasteland. From the ash heaps in *The Great Gatsby* to the desolations of Ravenna in *The Red Desert*, modern narrative art has maintained that this is a dry time, a barren and sterile place, and that we lead empty and futile lives. And two of the artists who have dealt most honestly and most thoroughly with this theme or image are T. S. Eliot and Federico Fellini. Though working at different times, in different countries, and in different mediums, they have still a surprising number of things in common. Indeed some of their work is so similar in theme, approach, and even technique that the work of each can to some extent illuminate that of the other. To put it simply, Fellini's films depend heavily on what are usually thought to be solely poetic techniques, while Eliot's poetry makes frequent use of certain cinematic techniques. We have already seen Eliot describing Perse's *Anabasis* as a verbal montage. It takes little insight to see that this also applies to Eliot's own poems, especially to "The Waste Land." Fellini, on the other hand, has been quoted as saying, "Movies now [1965] have gone past the phase of prose narrative and are coming nearer and nearer to poetry. I am trying to free my work from certain constrictions—a story with a beginning, a development, an ending. It should be more like a poem with metre and cadence."[1] Eliot's poetic practice thus leans toward cinema style, Fellini's toward poetic style, and it is not, therefore, surprising that there are numerous suggestive parallels to be found in their work.

Both "The Waste Land" and *La Dolce Vita*, for example, have been unusually successful in that each has seized the imagination of a large audience, and each has become almost an epitome of the outlook of a generation. Critics continue to complain that they are poorly structured, chaotic, difficult, and even private or idiosyncratic, but despite these objections, there is a quality in each work which has made it popular or available. Each has been widely quoted and imitated; the title of each has entered common speech. And if one thinks of "The Waste Land" as a poem written as a film-like sequence of images and of *La Dolce Vita* as a filmic poem, a film designed with the complexity, structure, and texture of a modern poem, each work will seem less difficult or capricious. Each is episodic, "The Waste Land" being made up of five detached and individually titled sections, "The Burial of the Dead," "A Game of Chess," "The Fire Sermon," "Death by Water," and "What the Thunder Said." *La Dolce Vita* is also composed of semidetached sequences, long scenes which are not always clearly related to one another. There is the encounter with Maddalena, the Field of the Miracle, the Steiner episode, the sequence centered on Sylvia, the scene with Marcello's father and Fanny, and the two contrasted and final parties, one at the home of the desiccated aristocrats, the other at a modern seaside villa. There is little strict narrative continuity in either work. Indeed neither is really narrative in any important sense. Each is a continuous succession of scenes and images which build up impressions only cumulatively, impressions which are neither complete nor fully comprehensible until the end.

Both the film and the poem are twentieth-century versions of Ecclesiastes, visions of the hollowness of contemporary life. The hero or central figure of each is a suitably ambiguous figure. Tiresias, in "The Waste Land," is called by Eliot, in a note appended to the poem, a "mere spectator and not indeed a 'character,' . . . yet the most important personage in the poem, uniting all the rest. . . . What Tiresias *sees*, in fact, is the substance of the poem."[2] In *La Dolce Vita*, the central character fulfills much of the same role. What Marcello, the reporter, sees, is the substance of the film. He, too, is more a spectator than a character, though he is also the latter, and he, too, is the personage who unites the other characters. Everything that the others act out is somehow a part of Marcello's personal world. (The figure of Tiresias in "The Waste Land" is also paralleled, in other respects, by the strange prophet named Bhishma, who is half-man and half-woman, and who plays an important part in Fellini's later *Juliet of the Spirits*). Tiresias in "The Waste Land" and Marcello in *La Dolce Vita* stand at the center of and preside over a series of incidents, encounters, and memories, having largely to do with religion and sex. Eliot's poem ranges from the affair between Elizabeth and Leicester to a scene which relies on Shakespeare's *Antony and Cleopatra* and Pope's *The Rape of the Lock*, to a tawdry assignation in a flat, to the sex-centered pub scene between Albert's wife and her "friend," to the hyacinth girl and her earlier innocence and youth, all united in and seen by the androgynous figure of Tiresias. So Marcello, in the film, witnesses or takes part in a variety of sexual encounters or attempts. There is the scene with Maddalena in the prostitute's flat; several scenes between Marcello and his cloying maternal mistress, Emma; his infatuation with Sylvia the American movie star; the pathetic encounter between Marcello's father and Fanny; and Marcello's increasingly desperate sexual forays in the closing scenes. The cumulative effect of all this is as wearisome and as meaningless for Marcello as it was for Tiresias, whose description of himself is also a decent description of Marcello:

His vanity requires no response,
And makes a welcome of indifference.
(And I Tiresias have foresuffered all
Enacted on this same divan or bed;
I who have sat by Thebes below the wall
And walked among the lowest of the dead.)
Bestows one final patronising kiss,
And gropes his way, finding the stairs unlit. . . .[3]

As each work accumulates a range of sexual encounters but finds it all less than satisfying or fulfilling, so each explores a like variety of religious scenes and concerns. Eliot takes a different tone on this subject from Fellini, and does not insist, as does Fellini, on the total poverty and emptiness of religion. From the Ascension by helicopter at the start of the film to the scene in which Anita Ekberg, dressed in parody of a priest, skylarks to the top of St. Peter's, from the long sequence on the Field of the Miracle to the sequence in which Steiner's great religious organ music serves as a prelude to his ugly suicide and the killing of his children, Fellini is, in what is probably the heaviest handed and least balanced aspect of the film, attacking the worn out religiosity of Rome. One possible exception to this might be the breaking up by thunderstorm of the elaborate, phony, and infinitely seamy and corrupt exploitation of the "miracle." There is poetic and natural, if not explicitly divine, justice in this. But in general, Fellini concentrates on one religion only and on the external features of that religion. "The Waste Land," by contrast, ranges from St. Augustine's arrival at Carthage to the subject of Buddhism, from the stoic resignation of "Death by Water" to the solemn almost hopeful closing chant from the *Upanishads.* Eliot does not mock belief, in this poem, unless in the section on Mme. Sosostris, the fortune telling clairvoyante, yet even this is treated without obvious scorn.

Both "The Waste Land" and *La Dolce Vita* tell a modern story, or better, they reveal modern conditions against an older and supposedly richer background. Fellini draws on Rome's aqueducts, fountains, churches, palaces, monuments, and ruins, and this gives the film a rich, heavy setting, much like Hawthorne's setting for *The Marble Faun.* Fellini's background is redolent of antiquity, of the Renaissance, of nobler, more spacious and cultured ages piled upon ages. Against this setting, the thinness of modern life appears all the more dramatically. The Steiner episode is typical. The splendid church in which Steiner plays and the flooding organ music of Bach are contrasted with the bare gauze-filled room in which we later see the children Steiner has killed. Inner poverty and outward magnificence form a steady contrast all the way through the film. The episodes in which Sylvia appears contrast the Baths of Caracalla, the Fountain of Trevi, and St. Peter's itself, with the vacuous vivacity of Anita Ekberg, while the party in the aristocratic and decaying villa sets modern enervation in pointed opposition to Renaissance splendor. In "The Waste Land," Eliot has managed a similar effect with different means. The poem is richly suffused with references to and quotations from western and eastern literature of all genres and ages. Passages from the Greeks, Ecclesiastes, Ovid, Augustine, Dante, Shakespeare, Marvell, Kyd, Webster, Spenser, *Tristan and Isolde*, Baudelaire, Verlaine, and Buddha are all worked into the fabric of the poem. The modern moments and experiences of the poem are given depth, significance, and a strange quality of timelessness by Eliot's continual weaving in of the older and more familiar material. In both Fellini's film and Eliot's poem, this background material from the historical and literary past serves to extend the significance of the present, to place the present in some relation to the past, to provide a richness and fullness of texture which the present moment continually lacks, falls short of, or openly mocks.

Fellini and Eliot also share a gift and a taste for witty and elaborate images much like those associated with John Donne and the so-called Metaphysical Poets. And while Fellini's taste runs more to Baroque while Eliot's could be called Mannerist, there is a considerable likeness between say, the opening image of "The Love Song of J. Alfred Prufrock" and the opening image of *La Dolce Vita*. The poem begins:

> Let us go then, you and I,
> When the evening is spread out against the sky
> Like a patient etherised upon a table;
> Let us go, through certain half-deserted streets,
> The muttering retreats
> Of restless nights in one-night cheap hotels
> And sawdust restaurants with oyster-shells:
> Streets that follow like a tedious argument
> Of insidious intent
> To lead you to an overwhelming question. . . .[4]

The bold and arresting image of the patient, while it startles one, also manages to cast over the entire ensuing poem a sense of illness, paralysis, even narcosis which ends by enveloping the title figure himself. The opening of *La Dolce Vita* also gives us an arresting image which casts its shadow over the whole film.

A vast panorama of the Roman countryside. To one side are the ruins of the San Felice aqueduct, towering arches that come striding across the land. Two thousand years ago, these arches brought water to the city, but now there are many gaps where whole sections of the aqueduct have fallen in. Directly in front is a soccer field, the goal posts dwarfed by the height of the aqueduct. In the distance the sound of motors is heard. A speck in the sky grows rapidly larger. It is a helicopter, and beneath it is a hanging figure. A second helicopter follows close behind. As the 'copters pass over the field the figure suspended below can be clearly seen. A large statue of Christ the Laborer swings from a cable. The shadow of the 'copter and this incongruous figure flashes across the walls of the aqueduct. The helicopters pass on.[5]

This opening shot, besides being quite as witty and as bold as Eliot's image, is also just as complex as the opening of the poem, and its relation to what follows is just as well worked out.

One finds also in the work of both men similar images of innocence. For example, in the opening section of "The Waste Land" there is a quick tender moment of memory:

> *"You gave me hyacinths first a year ago;*
> *They called me the hyacinth girl."*
> *—Yet when we came back, late, from the Hyacinth garden,*
> *Your arms full, and your hair wet, I could not*
> *Speak, and my eyes failed, I was neither*
> *Living nor dead, and I knew nothing,*
> *Looking into the heart of light, the silence.*[6]

This scene is much like the one in which Marcello meets the young girl waiting on table at the empty seaside restaurant, when he experiences a moment of peace, but a moment half marred by the knowledge that it is already too late. Even so, in both poem and film, innocence is a magic moment when things seem a little better, if only for a moment.

And for images of the opposite of innocence both men turn to vague but powerful evocations of the monstrous. Prufrock ruefully speculates, "I should have been a pair of ragged claws/Scuttling across the floors of silent seas." Marcello comes, at the end of *La Dolce Vita*, to the horrible monster the fishermen have caught. Down on the beach, he gazes at the ugly shapeless thing, which with "A lustreless protrusive eye / Stares from the protozoic slime." The lines are from Eliot's "Burbank with a Baedeker: Bleistein with a Cigar," but they describe perfectly the hideous aquatic throwback that lies on the beach and stares at the dawn-exhausted partygoers in the film.[7]

La Dolce Vita: The helicopter carrying the statue of Christ over the Roman ruins which opens the film. (Museum of Modern Art/Film Stills Archive)

Further, both Eliot and Fellini have hit upon a like way of describing the confusion between the classical and the popular. The distance between classic and jazz is ironically put by Eliot:

> O O O O *that Shakespeherian Rag—*
> *It's so elegant*
> *So intelligent. . . .*[8]

And in *La Dolce Vita,* almost exactly the same technique is used to make the same point when Steiner, sitting down at the great church organ, breaks first into jazz, then into Bach.

One can also find both men concerned and in similar ways with the problem of aging. Prufrock and Guido—the protagonist of *8½*—or Juliet and the title character of "Portrait of a Lady" are close in this respect. These works are also close to one another because they deal with the relations between fantasy and whatever one calls the other part of life. Juliet's world and that of Prufrock, and indeed the whole image-haunted world of "The Waste Land," seem peopled by many of the same figures. There are saints, and barbarians, clowns, monsters, religious and sexual fanatics, apparitions, supported by a rich baroque texture. One thinks of the wildly opulent and sleekly glossy sensuality of the scenes in Susy's villa in *Juliet of the Spirits* and of the opening of Section Two of "The Waste Land":

> *The Chair she sat in, like a burnished throne,*
> *Glowed on the marble, where the glass*
> *Held up by standards wrought with fruited vines*
> *From which a golden Cupidon peeped out. . . .*[9]

As one might expect, if the above similarities are not indeed exaggerated beyond usefulness, the endings of some of Eliot's poems are remarkably close to the final sequences of some of Fellini's films. *La Strada* and "The Hollow Men" share a terrible bleakness. "The Love Song of J. Alfred Prufrock" ends with Prufrock's failure becoming apparent just as he has his final and most touching moment of vision.

> *I have heard the mermaids singing, each to each.*
>
> *I do not think that they will sing to me.*
>
> *I have seen them riding seaward on the waves*
> *Combing the white hair of the waves blown back*
> *When the wind blows the water white and black.*
>
> *We have lingered in the chambers of the sea*
> *By sea-girls wreathed with seaweed red and brown*
> *Till human voices wake us, and we drown.*[10]

At the end of *La Dolce Vita*, Marcello wanders down to the beach in the early morning, sees the horrible shapeless one-eyed monster, then becomes aware of the girl from the restaurant, clean, lovely, untouched by the tawdriness of the party, calling to him from across an estuary. They cannot hear one another, and soon Marcello turns away, tugged back into the world he can neither live in nor leave. Marcello, like Prufrock, can neither reach nor be reached by whatever it is that the girl and the mermaids represent. Both turn back from the sea to drown in human life.

So too in some ways, the ending of "The Waste Land" is rather like the ending of 8½. Each concludes by remembering and forcing into use what Eliot calls the "fragments I have shored against my ruins." Such as it is, life must be accepted, must indeed be celebrated. So all the figures from Guido's life join in the circle gravely dancing to the brave, tinny music of the little band of circus people, the *saltimbanques* so loved by Picasso and Rilke too, and the night falls; Eliot's poem ends with the stately and circular chanting from the *Upanishads* in a final muted celebration of life ending in the injunction to give, sympathize, and control.

The work of Fellini and Eliot is similar in ways that range from the fortuitous to the important, but beyond particular likenesses of theme, image, tone, or technique, there is, I think, an overriding similarity that has significance not only for their work but for a great deal of twentieth-century poetry and film. This crucial similarity I would describe as an aesthetic of disparity. Both Fellini and Eliot have made highly sophisticated, perfectly deliberate attempts to work out a modern narrative form that does not emphasize narrative smoothness or continuity. Each suppresses "links in the chain," each tries to avoid analyzing, giving reasons or explanations. Each is concerned to show, to project an image of modern life as shallow, silly, and sterile, and each uses a technique of juxtaposing images in such a way as to continually insist on disparity without ever saying so in so many words. And indeed, this technique of using simple sequences of images, carefully juxtaposed one against the next in place of a narrative or logical technique, which I have claimed is a technique common to film and modern poetry, is in fact a variety of montage. And montage, whether of pictures or of words, is a technique almost ideally suited to handle the theme of disparity. One image plays against the next, the old can be pushed up against the new, the tender with the harsh, the lovely with the sordid. And as Eliot and Fellini both use the technique, each achieves for his work that overpowering sense of the disparity between what life has been or could be, and what it actually is.

And if this is finally the central theme of the work of both these men, then perhaps their success is in some measure due to the fact that montage provides an excellent form for this subject. Through juxtapositions, Fellini dramatizes the disintegration of modern life against the massive and orderly scenery of Rome, and Eliot shows the triviality of modern life by setting the sordid scenes of the present against the dignity and beauty of a fabric woven of literary reference. Each work is, in its own way, a lament for a nonexistent, or at least, a lost order. Each finds modern life characterized by disparity and lopsidedness, consisting essentially of a "heap of broken images." And the waste land may be, at last, the shadow that lies between the good life and all the endless inequities and disparities, a waste land which Fellini showed in *La Strada* as well as in *La Dolce Vita*, and which Eliot showed in "The Hollow Men" as well as in "The Waste Land."

> *Between the idea*
> *And the reality*
> *Between the motion*
> *And the act*
> *Falls the Shadow* . . .[11]

This sense of disparity, disequilibrium, or unbalance, which I have called the main theme of Eliot's poetry and Fellini's films, is one of the most important ways in which modern art has voiced its troubled awareness of the disorder of our times. And it is significant that the expression of this sense of disorder should be the poetically and filmically formed technique of montage, developed in western countries to emphasize disparity, while its Russian form emphasized conflict.

Thus the sort of montage that one can find in the work of Eliot and Fellini and, of course, in a great many other poems and films, and in other genres and media as well, may be considered one of the most typical and impressive of the ways the modern artist has evolved of looking at his material. Montage as the aesthetic of disparity provides both a way to see one's subject and a way to organize one's work. Properly understood, it may even lend eyes to criticism. For the sort of montage I have been trying to describe is after all a fairly orderly way of coping with the disorders of modern life, and thus may come to be a welcome and powerful force for some sort of viable noncoercive order. . . .

NOTES

1. Quoted by Lillian Ross in *The New Yorker*, Oct. 30, 1965, p. 66.
2. T. S. Eliot, *The Complete Poems and Plays*, New York, Harcourt, Brace, 1952, p. 52.
3. Ibid., p. 44.
4. Ibid., p. 3.
5. Federico Fellini, *La Dolce Vita*, New York, Ballantine Books, 1961, p. 1.
6. Eliot, p. 38.
7. Ibid., pp. 5, 24.
8. Ibid., p. 41.
9. Ibid., p. 39.
10. Ibid., p. 7.
11. Ibid., p. 58.

8 1/2:
The Perspectives of Literature, Psychology, and Semiotics

. . . .

15. Federico Fellini's *Purgatorio*   *Barbara K. Lewalski*

Fellini's film 8½ has occasioned much comment and interpretation in autobiographical-psychological terms. It may be argued that Fellini has invited this, using as he does the process of movie-making as the framework of the action, and choosing as his hero a bored, somewhat dissipated, still comparatively young film director who has reached a crisis of emotional sterility in his life and of stymied creativity in his art. Criticism of the film has accordingly examined in detail the parallels to Fellini's own life and probed the various Freudian complexes he supposedly reveals. But Fellini has also invited (though he has not received) another kind of analysis, one that will recognize and do justice to his conscious, carefully controlled, structural use of medieval themes and imagery, and his skillful and subtle transposition of them into a modern idiom. For example, his contribution to *Boccaccio 70*, "The Temptation of Dr. Antonio," obviously reworks the popular medieval saint's legend, *The Temptations of St. Anthony the Hermit*, whose hero was continually tempted by Satan in the shape of beautiful women. So pervasive is the Dantean influence in *La Dolce Vita* and 8½, and so explicit are Fellini's efforts to call attention to the Dantean elements especially in the imagery and language of the latter work, as to suggest that Fellini has consciously undertaken in these two films a contemporary *Divine Comedy* in a modern medium, for modern times.

In *La Dolce Vita* the characters and situations make fairly obvious allusions to their Dantean prototypes in the *Inferno*. As the character

. . . .

From *The Massachusetts Review*, Vol. 5, No. 3 (1964), pp. 567-73. © 1964 by The Massachusetts Review, Inc. Reprinted by permission of *The Massachusetts Review*.

Dante undertakes a journey through the various circles of Hell, observing and discussing but not taking part in the entire range of damnable evil and perversion, the hero of *La Dolce Vita*, Marcello, observes and only passively participates in the various evils and perversions of modern life. As in Dante, the scale of evil extends downward from the natural sins of the flesh (Anita Ekberg as Sex-Goddess and Nature-Girl) to the much more reprehensible perversions of intellect (Steiner's prostitution of his noble gifts so as to be able to afford the life and the possessions of an aesthete; Steiner's effete, pseudo-intellectual circle of friends, exemplifying the intellect turned parasitically inward upon itself, completely divorced from nature, society, and reality). Also, as Dante has in Virgil a guide whose province is the realm of the intellect and who is at once a fellow-poet and a tremendous formative influence upon him, so Marcello has a guide for a part of his journey in Steiner, a fellow writer and idol of his youth who had first introduced him to the life of art and of the mind. Virgil, however, is a true guide, however inadequate in the realms of the Spirit, but Steiner by his prostitution of intellect has become a false guide, tempting Marcello to a similar degradation. Also, as Beatrice is for Dante a means to salvation and a symbol of his transcendent spiritual goal, so Marcello has a Beatrice-figure in the young waitress in white at the country restaurant who brings him temporary peace and repose and who in the final scene with the dead fish calls out to him across a narrow stream, though he cannot then recognize her or hear her voice.

The imagery too is transposed from Dante. The film begins with a huge statue of Christ, its arms ironically extended in benediction, being carried, it seems, away from the city by airplane; it ends with a shocking inversion of a traditional Christ symbol in the monstrous, hideous dead fish holding in its mouth a swarm of smaller dead fish—a transposition of the Satan figure at the pit of Dante's hell, his three heads mocking the Trinity and his three mouths gnawing on the heads of the notorious damned. The omnipresent news photographers who are at once ludicrous and horrible as they swoop down like harpies on any likely prey, and who show themselves to be intellectual panderers exploiting all that is sacred or human for their own vile purposes, are reminiscent of the faintly comic demons with pitchforks in Dante's circle of the panderers and seducers (Canto xviii) who are both projections and persecutors of the sinners they torment. As Dante's *Inferno* is a place of darkness illuminated by fire, so the film has principally night scenes lit by glaring artificial light and false glitter. And as Dante progresses from locale to locale—the various circles, the City of Dis, the Bolgias, the Pit—so Marcello visits the various houses and cafes at which his assorted circles of acquaintances congregate and manifest their various corruptions.

Some of these features are retained in 8½, in clear indication of the continuity intended. The title itself suggests that this film builds upon and progresses from its predecessor. The same actor, Marcello Mastroianni, is used as hero, but he is now a different character, Guido Anselmi, a hero more suited to the changed focus of the new film. The essence of Purgatory, as Dante conceived it, is that it is an interior pilgrimage, a transformation of the self. In the *Inferno* the character Dante is a detached observer, for the *Inferno* was not his destined realm, but in the *Purgatorio* he relates himself closely to and even imitates the penitential actions of the persons punished for sins of which he convicts himself. So Fellini's new hero—like the character Dante a projection of his creator in some but not all respects—is a movie-maker endeavoring to make a film based upon his own life, a film which will put together, will organize coherently the persons and the elements which make up that life. Making the film is thus a symbol for remaking a life (the proper activity of Purgatory) as well as a study in the problems of artistic creation. Guido clarifies this point by his often reiterated declaration that he desires to make an honest, uncompromising film that will finally bury everything dead within us. And Daumier's statement that Guido is attempting to make a film about the Catholic conscience in Italy at the present time indicates that, as in Dante, the hero is not merely a projection of the author but also a figure of his nation, an Everyman.

Again there is a Virgilian guide, Daumier, this time more obviously identified and present throughout the entire action: he joins Guido just as Guido begins the cure and accompanies him until the end; his standards for the film are those of strict logic and perfect classical order; and he is symbolically hanged in Guido's fantasy just before the arrival of Claudia, the Beatrice-figure (as Virgil disappears at the end of the *Purgatorio*). Again the Virgil-figure is an inadequate and in some sense a false guide since with him as collaborator Guido cannot make the film. Again there is a Beatrice, and her significance is made even more explicit than in the earlier film: she appears to Guido's fantasy first as a nurse in white offering the curative mineral waters; in the course of the film Guido defines her as a symbol of purity and sincerity, young yet ancient; in another fantasy she promises to stay with him always, declaring, "I want to create order, I want to create cleanliness"; at length she arrives in person after Daumier's symbolic slaying and drives away with Guido from the unsuccessful casting session.

In addition to the Dantean elements repeated and reworked from *La Dolce Vita*, the new film adapts other sequences of action and methods of presentation from the *Commedia* and especially from the *Purgatorio*. The opening dream sequence—the massive traffic jam with the corpse-like multitudes waiting in their stalled cars; Guido's frantic escape and flight through the air arrested by two curious figures who pull him down by a cord attached to his leg and pronounce judgment upon him, "Down, definitely down"; Guido's awakening in the bed at the fashionable Bath, ready to undergo a "cure"—clearly invites a Dantean explication: Guido escapes from among the dreary multitudes in the antechambers of hell awaiting transportation by Charon, endeavors to "soar" but is found unfit to do so, and is sent to the place of purgation or cure, where the doctors immediately prescribe a course of treatment. At the end of the film Guido's symbolic "death" by suicide after he finds that he cannot give an account of his film to the newsmen, and his subsequent rebirth to a new life, suggest Dante's swooning under the reprimand of Beatrice (Cantos xxx-xxxi) who demands that he realize and account for his failures, and his subsequent immersion in Lethe from which he awakens purged of his sense of guilt.

Furthermore, Dante's allegorical method, wherein some of the characters such as Virgil and Beatrice have their own external reality but also represent qualities of the hero (Reason and Faith), provides a model for Fellini's subtle use of Guido's Mistress, Wife, and Dream-Woman to present the old trope of the conflict of Flesh, Mind, and Spirit within man. The mistress Carla (The Flesh) is voluptuous, bosomy, overdressed, constantly concerned with clothes, food, and sex, and symbolically clad in black with white fur accessories; she has play-acted with Guido a vast range of sexual roles and adventures, and she is made ill by drinking too much of the curative mineral water. The wife Luisa (The Mind) has a slender, flat-chested body, an ascetic, intellectual face whose quality is emphasized by prominent black-rimmed glasses, and simple, elegant, predominantly white clothing always highlighted with black; she bitterly resents, derides, and passes moral judgment upon Guido's sexual adventures and self-delusions. The ideal woman Claudia (The Spirit) is always clothed entirely in white, her face and skin radiant; throughout the film Guido catches only fleeting glimpses of her and at the end identifies her as a means of salvation but one which would necessitate his turning aside from all the other involvements of his life.

Another striking feature of the *Purgatorio*, its pervasive communal rituals which contrast sharply with the individualism and isolation of Hell, is reflected in several important scenes of the film: (1) The impressive, highly stylized procession to the mineral water springs at the beginning, with all manner of people participating, young and old, nuns and society ladies, artists and business-men. Though obviously imperfect and sometimes foolish (e.g., the coquettish nun), the cure-seekers are not reprehensible and the use of the stirring *Ride of the Valkyrie* music for their procession is only partly ironic; the function of the Valkyrie is to transport heroes to Valhalla, and though these are manifestly unheroic they are undertaking a cure which signifies their salvation. (2) The slow, formal procession of the entire clientele, clothed in white garments, down to the steam baths where all are given treatments in accordance with the prescriptions on their charts. (As with Dante who questioned and sought to learn from the various eminent men he met in Purgatory, Guido has an important conversation with the Cardinal in the steam bath.) (3) The several scenes of persons walking up and down Guido's massive tower or "launching pad" (one of the sets for his movie) clearly suggest the groups of souls climbing up the Mount of Purgatory. (4) The final group dance in which the Magician leads a procession of all the characters in Guido's film and life, now clad symbolically in white robes and with hands joined, is Fellini's transformation of Dante's great pageant of the Church throughout history from Eden to the Last Judgment which concludes the *Purgatorio*.

Several of the recurring images are also Dantesque. A number of scenes of the film, outdoor scenes often following upon purgation sequences, are bathed in excessively bright sunlight, just as in the *Purgatorio* the Sun is a symbol of grace which makes ascent possible, and the alternation of dark and bright emphasizes the "middle state" of the place of purgation. Such brightness illumines the first ritual march to the fountain, and again the garden scene after the steam bath when Guido first sees Luisa, and also the encounter between Carla and Luisa at the sidewalk cafe, when Guido daydreams of their reconciliation and friendship. The film also shows constant perspectives up and down stairs, and ascents and descents in elevators, reinforcing the Tower-climbing sequences as reflections of Dante's pervasive imagery of ascent. Finally, the film resounds with music used in ritualistic ways as in the *Commedia*, especially the *Ride of the Valkyrie* which recurs on several occasions.

The Dantean allusions and images function in the film to develop a Dantean theme, and also in some important respects to repudiate the Dantean resolution of the human predicament as impossible in the modern world. The essential problem in the *Purgatorio*, as Virgil makes clear to Dante in several discourses (notably in Cantos xvii and xviii), is the right ordering of man's loves; the seven capital sins punished on its cornices are all effects of perverted, defective, or excessive love. In Fellini this is also the problem: Guido is constantly berated, or berates himself, as one who does not know how to love. He is upbraided that he cannot make a love story; Luisa insists that his whole life with her has been a lie; Daumier denounces him as self-centered; Claudia reiterates as a kind of refrain, "You don't know how to love."

However, Dante's vision is that of man purging his impure loves, and ordering his life so as to give absolute predominance to Beatrice, the realm of the spirit. Fellini's Guido has as his goal not purgation but integration—in life and in the film—of all the aspects of his nature, all the loves of his life. Two false resolutions are attempted before the final integration is attained. The first is the pattern which everyone tries to force upon Guido and which he tries at times to force upon himself—a bringing of order·out of the chaos of life by giving an absolute predominance or exclusive interest to some one element. Guido is pressured incessantly to do just this: Luisa scornfully denounces his affairs with other women; the several actresses whom he is considering for roles in the film vie for his exclusive attention; the producer insists that he "choose" the cast for his film; Daumier demands that he cast out his nostalgic childhood reveries and disconnected images, in order to build his film on strict logical and philosophical principles; the Cardinal pronounces repeatedly, "Outside the Church there is no salvation"; the young Guido is told that Saraghina is the devil. Even Claudia demands an absolute predominance: during their final ride Guido rejects the promise of salvation that she holds for him since it would entail setting aside all the other relations of his life.

Guido rightly resists these efforts but he also cooperates with them to the extent that he tries to put his film together with Daumier's collaboration, tries to weigh and choose which element should have priority in his life. But it is a dead end; the film cannot be made in the modern world on Daumier's principles. Daumier can only recommend that it not be made at all, that where strict order is not possible one should

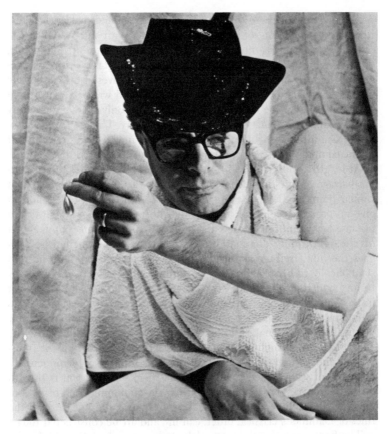

8½: Guido Anselmi (Marcello Mastroianni) in the harem sequence. (Museum of Modern Art/Film Stills Archive)

decide not to contribute further to Chaos, and should make a Declaration of Silence. This is, of course, a total defeat in art and in life. Reacting against a life based upon exclusion and predominance, Guido daydreams of an easy, immature, false integration through egocentric domination. In the harem fantasy all the loves of his life, all the aspects of his nature live together in humble and willing service upon him. But the ménage based on domination can only be maintained by violence and the reduction of intellect to slavery. Unable to find a solution Guido retreats further and further into inaction and rejection of all the competing forces: he cannot choose a cast for his film.

At length Guido is forced to a place of no escape under the shattering barrage of questions from the newsmen (as Dante was forced to a similar point by Beatrice's tirade) and is forced to admit that he can give no orderly account of himself, that he cannot make a logical film because he cannot give some one element an absolute predominance in his life, and cannot dominate them all. At the point wherein he foregoes the film itself as an image of an ordered, coherent life, he dies symbolically to his old egoism and sterility and is reborn to a capacity to love and to create. The Magician is the new guide who takes over just as Daumier has recommended the Dedication to Silence: he shows Guido in procession all the characters of his life and his film in a new perspective which enables Guido to accept and to love them. In the Magician's earlier nightclub acts, he had served as an instrument transmitting indiscriminantly the thoughts of the mind, past or present, to his assistant who then read and revealed them; his function is thus to open the mind up to itself and to further the communication of its contents, whatever they may be. Only by his "grace" and not through the rules of Daumier's classical order, can life and art be constructed today.

The final processional dance celebrates a new integration. Guido invites all the characters to come *down* from the tower and he joins hands with them on level ground—accepting all, rejecting none. He explicitly refuses to define priorities among them or to impose a final ordering upon them, but says all that a modern man is capable of saying about ordering his loves and the aspects of himself: he will live with them, and attempt to learn more. In some sense the dance is Dante's great symbol of the Church as *Communio Sanctorum* transposed to a *Communio Humanorum*, and is thus an appropriate close for the modern *Purgatorio*.

What, one may well wonder, will Fellini's *Paradiso* be?

16. *8½* as an Anatomy of Melancholy

Timothy Hyman

Unlike Truffaut's *Day for Night*, 8½ is not centrally about film-making, any more than it is about the Artist, or even about Fellini himself: it is about much more general processes of experience. The key concept with which this essay will be concerned is that of temperament, and the way the awareness of an inner world affects the language of film. 8½ demonstrated how a film could be about a temperament: the events it dealt with were interior events, and its most important episodes happened outside time, in fantasy, dream and vision. In 8½, Fellini renounced the political or social emphasis of neo-realism, and the new relation between the artist and the outer world that resulted has since become fundamental to much Italian cinema. Guido, groping blindly from within toward his millennial vision, is the blueprint for a new kind of film director, whose ideology originates not in any analysis of society, but in the artist's own constitution. Yet 8½ stands apart from all that has followed, even from Fellini's own subsequent work; and an understanding of 8½ can help us to pinpoint the change in orientation, which has generally been felt to be a "falling off," not only in Fellini but in Pasolini, Antonioni and Visconti also.

Everyone would perhaps agree that each one of us has a fundamental and recurrent "pattern," to which his experience largely conforms. I take 8½ to be the description of one such pattern, the mapping-out or "anatomising" of a particular constitution. In every way, Guido's pattern defines the film; both its structure, since in the course of the film Guido works through one complete cycle of experience; and its subject, because Guido's predicament is shown to be caused by a conflict between his pattern and his conscious self.

8½ is about an inner process which takes place in Guido on several levels, his reaching for artistic potency, for intellectual consistency and for spiritual purity. But Fellini shows Guido's development as occurring, not through his conscious will or intellect, but rather as springing directly from some interior bodily rhythm, to which Guido remains al-

From *Sight and Sound*, Vol. 43, No. 3 (1974), pp. 172-75. Reprinted by permission of *Sight and Sound*.

most passive. His experience is given. While, on the one hand, this view brings us close to a religious or mystical philosophy, with Grace as the key to experience, it also approaches the mechanistic; and this dichotomy is reflected in the language of 8½, which is very direct and physical yet which also tends towards an abstract language, of pattern and interval. The riddling title, *Fellini 8½*, goes far to clarify the film's problem; it points, beyond the opus number, to a fusion of the film's conflicting polarities, not only Life and Art, but physical and abstract, person and pattern—that is to the "solution," the state of integration momentarily achieved at the end of the film.

Film is the ideal vehicle for the kind of experience Fellini wants to convey here—the sense that every event is subordinate to a prevailing inner rhythm. Film photographs the actual world, yet can present it to us shaped like music. And in film it is a potentially very internal, visceral relation that exists between spectator and artist. As we sit in the darkened space of the cinema, it is as though we were watching images projected upon the dream-screens of our own minds (the mechanism of the shutter echoing our life-pulse). Nietzsche defined art as the "code tapped out by our nervous systems"; and watching 8½, one is peculiarly aware of film as a "total art," harnessing enormous and diverse powers so as to bring the spectator into the fullest possible relation with the director's most personal experience.

But in an interview with Gideon Bachmann in 1964, a year after completing 8½, Fellini contended that this power in cinema—the tour de force inseparable from the medium—can only be validated in the context of a clear moral intention:

> In the hands of traditional film-makers, the cinema has become a form of art which allows no space for meditation. . . . Films made after a formula, factory films, are of course the maximum point of degradation. But cinema contains in its nature the danger of psychological suggestiveness. It isn't just a meditative form: it is potently naturalistic. A pistol shot in a film is a pistol shot that you hear—boom!—with your ears. All representations of reality in film appear to be objective, but in fact they are coordinated to assail the spectator from a definite point of view. It is much more difficult for a film-maker to be sincere than for a writer or painter, because the means he uses are extremely dangerous. They are means—camera, editing, sound, movement—which tend to function directly on the plane of intellectual and psychological aggression. . . . Now, when this fantastic power is used for the liberation of the spectator, in other words when it is white magic, it is all right. But when it is used as black magic, it can lead to terrible results.

Of all Fellini's films, 8½ is the one in which the cathartic intention—the use of the "white magic" of cinema to "liberate the spectator"—is most explicit. The earlier part of the film is an intentional oppression of the spectator, a kind of "black" magic that is only justified as the necessary preparation for the literally white, liberating vision (the sequence which, as Fellini has emphasised, constituted his "whole reason for making the film").

Correspondingly, the language in 8½ has an urgency unique in Fellini's work. In *La Strada* or *La Dolce Vita* the script, in *Giulietta* and his subsequent films the sets and costumes, have the central role, which here belongs to the exclusively cinematic means of sequential juxtaposition and rhythm. It is the oscillation of light and dark, the precise length of their duration, which finally shapes 8½; and this music of interval is combined to maximum effect with the actual music of Nino Rota, whose theme tune, an extrovert braying march, transforming into a wistful circling melody, itself incorporates the double rhythm of Guido's experience. The syntax of the film becomes the embodiment of Fellini's doctrine: that our experience is cyclic, that pleasure comes out of pain, true out of false, comedy out of tragedy.

The cyclic structure of Guido's experience is announced at the outset of 8½, in the Crisis, Liberation and Fall, archetypally enacted in Guido's dream. In the sequence immediately following, the cycle is reenacted in the real world. First, Guido wakes to find himself in a hotel bed, surrounded by intrusive and alien people, a situation which obviously recalls the traffic jam in the dream; then, in the hotel bathroom, at last alone, he experiences a self-awakening, corresponding to his dream flight; and then, exactly as in the dream a rope had tugged him down, so here the buzzing of the telephone intrudes, making him sag into alienation. This sense of a succession of "corresponding" sequences, with a common pattern, is maintained throughout the film. When Guido entered the hotel bathroom, fluorescent lighting suddenly flickered on, flooding the screen; and the recurrence of this motif, the sudden welling up of light, will give the film its overall continuity.

This pattern, of crisis, liberation and fall, is the key to Guido's behaviour. Just as the necessity of waiting on liberation forces on him his indecisive and conditional manner of action, so the mysteriousness and unreasonableness of his experience enforces his ambiguous ideological stance. He is caught in a machine, yet his moments of liberation seem evidence of a *deus ex machina*. The bleached and dazzling light which floods the screen at moments throughout the film conveys to us not simply Guido's heightened consciousness, but also his sense of an over-whelming but totally mysterious force, at work in an unstable world.

I think that Fellini is being no less than precise when he defines "this business of making a film" as "giving an account of his melancholy." For the pattern of 8½ is that of melancholy; the ambiguous commerce between archetypal and real is typical of that state; and Fellini has himself described the mood of 8½ as "melancholy, almost funereal, but also resolutely comic." The tradition surrounding the melancholic is very relevant to Guido.[1] The melancholic is to be seen, on the one hand, as a sick man, afflicted with a cyclic madness; but on the other, as one singled out to be vouchsafed, at the expense of suffering meanwhile, moments of vision or exceptional power. There is a "double potentiality in melancholy, for Good or for Evil."

Now it seems to me that this double potentiality provides the structure of 8½: we are made to see Guido first as a sick man, then as a visionary artist. Guido's crisis, his inability to begin his film, results from his own interpretation of his experience as being fundamentally diseased, false: doubting its validity, he cannot express or reflect it in his art. And because the white episodes (the moments of liberation that are clearly also the inspirations given to Guido as an artist) are inextricably bound up with, are even the product of, his moments of sickness and crisis, he refuses his inspiration as tainted. Fellini's theme can be summed up, that liberation consists in our acceptance of the interdependence of contrary states within our experience; only his failure to accept distinguishes the impotent from the creative individual.

First, as a sick man. Fellini makes us not only observe Guido's descent, but also participate in it. The pattern of crisis endlessly repeated soon becomes as alienating for the spectator as it is for Guido. And that initial ambiguity of dimension, of our entering in the middle of the traffic jam of Guido's dream, which we assumed to be reality, persists. Not only do memory and dream, fantasy and reality, slide into one another, but there is also a threat that we are watching, not Guido's immediate experience at all, but merely episodes from the film he hopes to make. What is put before us is not to be trusted; and in such a context Fellini's splendid formal compositions appear grandiose, self-parodying, false. Everything works to confirm the spectator in this view of Guido, as an artist who has lost his way and whose labyrinthine experience will never lead him to the reality he is looking for.

The white episodes continue to well up, like coherent messages from the unconscious, and with their slower rhythm and narrative unity, each offers a momentary respite against a present world where consciousness is staccato and fragmented. Each presents Guido with some variant of a visionary reality. First, in a mock vision: Guido's walk in the spa is presented as a burlesque parnassus (to be paralleled later by the burlesque Hades of the underground baths). But in the ASANISIMASA sequence, the most serious of the film, Guido seems to find the authentic "ANIMA" or soul he has looked for; it is in the sensations of early childhood, the image of a communal society in a condition of love. The intimation is drained of much of its talismanic significance, however, when Guido's fantasy of the Harem takes place in the same primitive or tribal farmhouse, and the child's sacred rituals are knowingly perverted and trivialised by the adult's infantile self-love.

The central part of the film focuses on Guido's attitude to the Church. He first encounters the Cardinal in the hotel lift, and the alternation of darkness and light, as the lift descends past each floor, marvellously conveys Guido's fluctuating faith. Guido's key memory-inspiration proves to be ambivalent. If, at the seminary, the child turned from the saints to Saraghina, yet the dance of the prostitute beside the glittering sea provides an intuition of some primitive or natural worship, leaving him closer to the Church than to her materialist opponents. Inevitably, such ambiguity is condemned, first by the Marxist critic ("You begin intending to renounce, but you end as an accomplice"); then by the Cardinal's attendant, who has read Guido's script and complains that it "mingles sacred and profane love far too freely." These sequences end in Guido's fantasy of Hades where, as a shutter comes down, the Cardinal pronounces "*extra ecclesiam nemo salvatur*—outside the Church, no one shall be saved."

As each alternative fails him, Guido's hope of redeeming his experience comes to reside more and more exclusively in the film he intends to make. Allusions to it were present in his dream, for the film will concern a corrupt and exhausted mankind (that of the traffic jam), and the effort of a few to escape (via the rocket-launching tower, glimpsed by the dreamer in his flight through the clouds) so as to begin a new life on some new planet. Clearly, then, Guido's film is an allegory of his own predicament. His wish to commit his will to the Church, or to his marriage, or to ideal love, is a wish to escape to so many "new planets," to be liberated once and for all from the wheel of his temperament. This wish is what has defined him, and the making of the film itself is the last remaining hope of its fulfillment; so that his abandonment of it at the press conference really does constitute his personal extinction, the "suicide" shown us.

Then, as visionary artist. For it is only here, when Guido, in losing

each of his alternatives, has been stripped of his ego, that the real protagonist of the film, not the personality of Guido but the fatality of his
temperament, is able to assert itself. These final minutes entirely alter
our view of what has gone before. Unfurling out of Guido's extinction,
the emergence of the vision unifies the film's interior oscillation into a
single cathartic motion of crisis transformed to liberation. It is as
though the movement of the whole film were to trace out this transformation as a kind of graphological curve; to define the rhythm by
which sickness becomes vision.

"But from whence comes this joy of life"? asks Guido, as the white
figures first appear. The vision is an affirmation of the temperament, as
a creative centre beyond the personality. The white smiling figures
walking across the plain; the unveiling of the rocket-launching steps,
on which the entire cast of the film are assembled as though they are
indeed that remnant, just arrived on that fresh new planet; and the
final ritual, by which all these figures form a dancing circle: each of
these sequences has its dramatic rightness, in resolving the conflicts established earlier, within a new dispensation.

Once the vision has reaffirmed Guido's integrity, we see that his
sliding from dimension to dimension may have been not evasion or
confusion, but the necessary completion of a journey towards a view of
life that must include several distinct worlds, a "multiverse." Saturn
was identified with melancholy because its orbit, wider than any other
in our system, included all the rest; and it is the principle of inclusive-
ness that is upheld by Guido. The condition of love embodied in the
vision (and confirming the paradisiac experience of childhood) will indeed "mingle sacred and profane," just as within its circle Communist
and Christian, wife, mistress and Ideal, the Cardinal and Saraghina,
can link hands. It is in this sense that Guido is right when he declares
to Rosella that "at bottom, I have nothing to say." It is an experience
where meaning is not particular but resides in the unfolding of life
itself.

William James, in *Varieties of Religious Experience*, names Melancholy as (with conversion) "one of the two main phenomena of religion." The essentially religious nature of 8½ is seen in its structure,
which may be likened to the Eucharistic Mass, processing us through
various levels of descent, into a realisation of spiritual death; the state
where we are most ready to receive Grace, and to partake of the communion (to which the vision clearly corresponds). Guido's spiritual
development is shown as fused with the creative process. "Unless the
seed die, it shall not be born again." At the beginning of 8½, Guido

has his seed, his idea of a film; but it is only when he has accepted its extinction that the flowering, the vision which is the true film he has to make, is able to appear. And in this affirmation Fellini's monumental fresco imagery at last finds a content fitting to its epic scale.

Thus 8½ is the "simple thought" promised to Rosella, a "film which would help us to bury every dead thing that we carry around in ourselves." There is an interesting account in Laing's *The Divided Self* of a girl patient whose identification with Gelsomina in *La Strada* was decisive in her recovery of reality. 8½ achieves a similar liberation, but it does so by far more direct and astonishing means; it takes us bodily up in a rhythm, which carries us through catharsis to peace and self-acceptance.

8½ is pivotal in Fellini's work. What had remained implicit in the earlier films, a core of the personality, a certain rhythm of experience, here becomes explicit. In exposing this core Fellini may have said in 8½ all that he urgently had to say. But in subsequent works he has dared to pass so to speak inside this core, into the stifling enclosed world of his temperamental archetypes.[2]

It is a reversal common to much Italian cinema, the transition from neo-realism to what might be called "neo-symbolism." The critic in 8½ is the voice of neo-realism, who regards the subjectivity of Guido's script as evidence that "cinema is fifty years behind the other arts." One can see what he means; the film works by symbols (whiteness, clowns, tower, etc.), and together with the episodic form by which Guido, like Peer Gynt or Baal, enacts a quest for self through various dimensions, it must have seemed to point back to 1910, or beyond.

But in the event, of course, the critic was wrong; the discarded aesthetic has become the new, and the last ten years have seen a general movement in the arts away from the idea that an "objective" or purist aesthetic alone represents progress. If it affirms anything, our present culture affirms the right to private worlds. The revival of Art Nouveau can be taken with the popularity of writers such as Hesse and Tolkien, and with drug-taking and the art associated with it, as related phenomena; and, whether we like it or not, Italian cinema, which once stood for an art of social realities, is now a key disseminator of this art of the Fantastic.

In varying degrees, films like *Pigsty, The Spider's Stratagem, Death in Venice, Juliet of the Spirits* or *Blow-Up* explicitly reflect a vision personal to the director. But while the neo-realist aesthetic entailed conflict between documentary and myth, between reality and the director's temperament, the resolution of this conflict in these later films has involved some loss of urgency. To what extent *should* the artist's temperament dominate his material? In an interview given in 1962, the year before 8½ was made, Pasolini admitted that Fellini and he shared a basic affinity of temperament, although his own view was "societal," whereas Fellini's was "personalist." He went on to define this affinity as: ". . . a kind of emotivity, a tendency to see reality always in a fabulous or distorted way. There is a difficulty in submitting to real empirical contact with objects, with what they are, personalities, facts of life. A tendency always to look behind objects . . ."[3]

At the time that this was written, however, Fellini and Pasolini were still making very different films; and when we compare *Accattone* (1960) with *La Dolce Vita* (1961) this difference is exactly defined by the director's world view, respectively the societal and the personalist. It is only now, many years later, their temperaments fully indulged, that their affinity has become obvious (and not only theirs; Pasolini's words can serve as a description of almost all recent Italian cinema). To indulge the temperament has meant to blur distinctions which may be not more fundamental, but more interesting.

I feel it is significant that these recent films have employed lush colour. It was Fellini himself who had earlier declared that "colour in film is like breathing under water," and that "film is motion, colour is immobility." The kind of imagery we have come to expect from the masters of cinema, where each frame is individually meaningful, tends in colour to effects of dissociation, which narrow the range of emotion. As in 19th-century symbolism, the artist's sense of unreality threatens to become the sole subject of the work. The static tableaux of *Fellini-Satyricon*, unfolding in a dream space, point towards a completely "anti-real" cinema. But while, in its incorporation of many modes, *Fellini-Satyricon* can be seen as developing from the "multiverse" implicit at the end of 8½, what it significantly does not do is to create a structure to reconcile all these modes, or to give them meaning, to close the circle, or to achieve catharsis. And without that catharsis, are we not perilously close to "black" cinematic magic? By contrast, Guido's vision, although it does assert the triumph of the temperament against any objective "reality," gains conviction from its difficult emergence out of conflict. It retains some of the tensions of neo-realism; just as it employs the absolute polarities of black and white.

8½ is, in the phrase P. W. Martin coined for Jung and Eliot, an "Experiment in Depth"; like *The Waste Land*, it descends into a Jungian inner world, seeking some primary contact with experience, so as to return renewed to the outer. In a wider view, it may be that the main movement of Italian cinema will come to be seen in these terms; that finding, like Guido, an impasse in the external world, Italian directors embarked on a "return inward." The question then is, when will they re-emerge? What we have to accept meanwhile is the lack of any glimmer, in a work like *Satyricon*, of wholesome reality. It exists solely, as Fellini says, to "realise his fantasy"; the inner world is presented not, as in 8½, as part of a process, but as though it were sufficient in itself. The distinction is close to Coleridge's "Imagination" and "Fancy." It was the additional dimension, by which Guido and Fellini were separate, that helped to give 8½ its vitality; as the objectivisation of a temperament, the film could draw on deep levels of dream and fantasy, while remaining still an examination of the external, "real" world.

Yet while 8½ defines the moment of perfect balance in Italian cinema, the subsequent descent into self, into archetypal realms, has resulted in a kind of profundity. The obvious parallel is with Mannerism; it arouses the same ambiguous responses, and it may, like Mannerism, become more fascinating to future generations, less starved of an art of above ground, and less nostalgic for the achievements of the High Renaissance of cinema that the years of 8½ now seem to represent. Do we see Mannerism positively, as an experiment, a "return inwards" which initiated the modern era; or do we see it negatively, as the decline of the Italian tradition, a "failure of nerve"? Do we see Mannerism's concern with the "dangerous" areas of subject matter as morally courageous (Fellini hoped that even *Satyricon* would be "liberating"); or do we suspect a search for the bizarre or troubling as a substitute for a less superficial kind of originality?

NOTES

1. See *Saturn and Melancholy*, Saxl, Klibansky, Panofsky. (Nelson, 1947). Artists are traditionally melancholic, being "born under Saturn," the star of melancholy.
2. Fellini at this time was undergoing analysis by the Jungian, Dr. Bernard.
3. In *Entretiens avec Federico Fellini*, Les Cahiers R. T. B. Série Télécinéma, 1962.

17. Mirror Construction in Fellini's *8½*   *Christian Metz*

Like those paintings that show a second painting within, or those novels written about a novel, *8½* with its "film within the film" belongs to the category of works of art that are divided and doubled, thus reflecting on themselves. To define the structure peculiar to this type of work the term *"construction en abŷme"* (literally, "inescutcheon construction"), borrowed from the language of heraldic science,* has been proposed,[1] and indeed it lends itself quite well to that structure permitting all the effects of a mirror. [At the risk of losing some of the accuracy of the original term, the translator has preferred to substitute the term "mirror construction," which is less unfamiliar, certainly less awkward-sounding, and therefore perhaps more suggestive than "inescutcheon construction." The image is that of a double mirror, reflecting itself.]

In a very interesting study devoted to Fellini's film, Alain Virmaux[2] has shown that, although mirror construction in the cinematographic domain is not an invention of Fellini's, since it is found already in various earlier films—*La Fête à Henriette*, by Jeanson and Duvivier, René Clair's *Le Silence est d'or*, Bergman's *The Devil's Wanton*†—the author of *8½* is nevertheless the first to construct his *whole* film, and to order *all* his elements, according to the repeating mirror image. In fact the precursors of *8½* only partially deserve to be called "mirror-construction" works, because in them the "film within the film" was only a marginal or picturesque device (*Le Silence est d'or*), at times a simple "trick" of the script-writer's (*La Fête à Henriette*), at best a fragmentary construction (*The Devil's Wanton*) lending perspective to only part of the film's substance, the rest being presented directly, and not through reflection. Moreover, Alain Virmaux,[3] Raymond Bel-

* In heraldry the term "inescutcheon" refers to a smaller shield placed at the center of a larger shield, and reproducing it in every detail, but on a smaller scale.—TRANSLATOR

† One might add Roger Leenhardt's *Le Rendez-vous de minuit*, in which the "film within the film" already played a more central and complex role.

From *Film Language: A Semiotics of the Cinema* by Christian Metz, trans. Michael Taylor (New York: Oxford University Press, 1974), pp. 228-34. Copyright © 1974 by Oxford University Press, Inc. Reprinted by permission.

lour,[4] Christian Jacotey,[5] and Pierre Kast[6] have all emphasized the fact that the content of the entire film, and its deepest thematic structure, are inseparable from its reflecting construction: the character of the director, Guido, Fellini's representative in the film, resembles his creator like a twin, with his narcissistic complacency, his immense sincerity, his disorderly existence, his inability to make a choice, his persistent hope in some kind of "salvation" that will suddenly resolve all his problems, his erotic and religious obsessions, his open desire to "put everything" into the film (just as Fellini puts all of himself into his films, and especially into 8½, which is like a pause in his career, a general viewing of the past, an aesthetic and effective summing up).* As Pierre Kast observes, the criticisms one might address to the style of the film, or to the style of Fellini's work in general (that it is confused, disparate, complacent, has no real conclusion) are already present in the film, whether they are expressed by Guido himself or by his scenario-writer, Daumier, his inseparable companion, a companion Guido curses but whom he needs as he needs his bad conscience; thus, again it is the mirror construction alone that has allowed Fellini to integrate into his film a whole series of ambiguous reflections on whatever his own film might be accused of.

There is however a point that, I believe, has never been emphasized as much as it deserves to be: for, if 8½ differs from other films that are doubled in on themselves, it is not only because this "doubling in" is more systematic or more central, but also and above all because it functions differently. For 8½, one should be careful to realize, is a film that is *doubly doubled*—and, when one speaks of it as having a mirror construction, it is really a double mirror construction one should be talking about.† It is not only a film about the cinema, it is a film about

· · · · · · · · ·

* As Alain Virmaux observes, the title 8½ designates the film less in terms of its own characteristics than in terms of a sort of retrospective reference to all of Fellini's previous work. [Since it was, literally, his eighth-and-a-half film. —TRANSLATOR]

† One might also say—it is essentially a question of vocabulary—that the expression "mirror construction" refers *only* to those works defined here as "doubly self-reflecting," and not to the majority of cases where a film appears within a film or a book within a book or a play within a play. A shield is not said to be "inescutcheon" everytime it contains some other shield, but only when the other shield is, except in size, identical to the first. [Metz is, of course, referring to the heraldic term "construction en abŷme," which I have changed to "mirror construction." A double mirror reflects itself into infinity— and this captures something of the suggestiveness of "en abîme," "abîme" meaning "abyss" or "chasm"—each reflection being identical to, though one

a film that is presumably itself about the cinema; it is not only a film about a director, but a film about a director who is reflecting himself onto his film. It is one thing in a film to show us a second film whose subject has no relationship, or very little relationship, to the subject of the first film (*Le Silence est d'or*); it is entirely another matter to tell us in a film about *that very film* being made. It is one thing to present us with a character who is a director and who recalls only slightly, and only in some parts of the film, the maker of the real film (*The Devil's Wanton*); it is another matter for the director to make his hero into a director who is thinking of making a very similar film. And, if it is true that the autobiographical and "Fellinian" richness of 8½ is inseparable from its mirror construction, it is nevertheless only explained in its opulent, baroque entirety by the self-reflecting of that construction.

Guido's problems, it has been said, are those of Fellini reflecting on his art: was it enough, then, for Guido to be a film-maker, like Fellini? The similarity would have remained very general. But Guido is a director reflecting on his art, and by a curious irony these two successive reflections end by canceling each other out to a certain extent, so that 8½ is finally a film of perfect coincidence; extremely complex, its structure nonetheless attains a lucid simplicity, an immediate legibility. It is because Guido is thinking of his film, and reflecting on himself, that he merges—at least temporarily*—with Fellini; it is because the film that Guido wanted to make would have been a study of himself, a film-maker's summing up, that it becomes confused with the film that Fellini has made.† The ordinary interplay of reflection would never have yielded such a wealth of echoes and relationships between

---

degree smaller, than what it reflects.—Translator] If one agrees to this acceptation, one will have to say *Le Silence est d'or* contains nothing resembling mirror construction, and that in *The Devil's Wanton* or in *Le Rendez-vous de minuit*, mirror construction remains partial and fragmentary.

* Taken as a whole, the relationships between Guido and Fellini are obviously more complex; among other things, Guido's character is not entirely identical to Fellini's. However, I am not concerned with psychology here, but simply with identity (in the sense that one speaks of identity cards). *For the duration of the film*, Guido fully represents the person of Fellini.

† Must I point out that I am speaking here of the film Guido dreamed of making, not the film that outside pressures (his producer, etc.) might perhaps have imposed on him had he finally decided to start filming? For Fellini's film, although it tells us only very little about the exact state of his working plans, or the intentions of his producers, is on the other hand extremely precise about Guido's deepest wishes concerning his film.

Fellini and his character had it not been reflected by the reflecting of that character himself; film-maker and reflecting film-maker, Guido is doubly close to the man who brought him to life, doubly his creator's double.

It is even in the concrete details of its handling that the device of "the film within a film" diverges here from its more common use. For *we never see* the film that Guido is to make; we do not even see extracts from it, and thus any distance between the film Guido dreamt of making and the film Fellini made is abolished: Fellini's film is composed of all that Guido would have liked to have put into his film—and that is precisely why Guido's film is never shown separately. The reader can judge for himself the extent of the difference between this structure and the structure in *Le Rendez-vous de minuit*, for example, where large extracts of the "film within the film" are explicitly shown at several specific points in the first film, which suffices to create a distance between the two films. In 8½ we do not *even* see Guido shooting his film or working on it—and here it differs from *The Devil's Wanton*, for example; we see him, simply, in the period when the film is being prepared, living or dreaming, accumulating in the very stream of his own chaotic existence all the material that, without ever succeeding, he would like to place in his film and that Fellini is able to put into *his* film. It is, therefore, because the "film within the film" never appears separately within the first film that it can coincide with it so completely.

All that we see of this film Guido is dreaming about are the screen tests of the actresses; but it is here that the *tripling* of the film most clearly manifests itself. Guido has an actress to play the role of his wife in the film; the latter is played, in 8½, by Anouk Aimée; and she in turn can only be an incarnation—very much interpreted, it goes without saying—of the problems Fellini encounters in his own life.* It is during the sequence of the screen tests that a character in 8½, watching the private screening and thinking of Guido, whispers, "Why, that's his own life," making a reflection that one can only reflect on by applying it to Fellini himself.

It is therefore not enough to speak of a "film within the film": 8½
. . . .

* If one reflects that the actress in the screen test was herself played, in Fellini's film, by another actress—and that, at the other end of the chain, Fellini's wife (Giulietta Masina) is also an actress—one will become positively dizzy. More seriously, one can observe that, following 8½, Fellini shot *Juliet of the Spirits*, which is, as we know, a sort of feminine version of the preceding film; the woman's role is played by Giulietta Masina. This confirms the tripling process that appears in the screen-test sequence in 8½.

is the film of 8½ being made; *the "film in the film" is, in this case, the film itself.* And of all the literary or cinematographic antecedents that have been mentioned in connection with Fellini's work, by far the most convincing—as critics have often pointed out,[7] but perhaps without ever entirely explaining why—is André Gide's *Paludes,* since it is about a novelist writing *Paludes.**

This triple-action construction gives the ending of the film, which has been variously interpreted, its true meaning. The version Fellini finally retained† contains not one but three successive denouements. In a first resolution, Guido abandons his film because it would have been confused, disorderly, too close to his life to become a work; because it would have been reduced to a disparate series of echoes and resonances; because it would have carried no central message capable of unifying it; and finally, and above all, because it would not have changed his life. That is the meaning of Guido's symbolic suicide at the end of his stormy press conference, as well as of the last words of Daumier. In a second movement—the allegory of the fantastic rondo—the abandonment of the film returns Guido to his life, as he sees all those who have peopled it parading in front of him; he asks his wife to accept things as they are; he has given up, at the same time he has given up his film, that rather messianic hope of a "salvation" that would suddenly bring order to all the elements of his chaos and thus modify their profound meaning and lend them the perspective of the future. But it is at this moment that Guido—who is no longer a director but is again a man like other men—once more takes up his director's megaphone to direct the audience of his memories. Therefore the film will be made; it will have no central message, and it will not alter life, since it will be made out of the very confusion of life; but out of that

· · · · · · · · · ·

* One thinks of course also of *Les Caves du Vatican* and *Les Faux-monnayeurs.* Alain Virmaux, Raymond Bellour, Pierre Kast, and Max Milner (articles already quoted) have all emphasized the Gidian aspects of Fellini's work. Alain Virmaux quotes this sentence from Gide's *Journal* (1899–1939): "J'aime assez qu'en une oeuvre d'art on retrouve ainsi transposé à l'échelle des personnages, *le sujêt même* de cette oeuvre." ("I rather like the idea that in a work of art one finds, transposed in this way to the scale of the characters, *the very subject* of the work.") I have underlined *"le sujêt même"* (*"the very subject"*): Gide, one sees, was thinking less of ordinary "doubling in" than of the peculiar variety of "doubling in" I am discussing in these few pages. Similarly, one should remember that Gide was one of those who have used the term *"construction en abŷme."*

† Fellini had first planned another resolution. See Camilla Cederna, *8½ de Fellini: Histoire d'un film* (Paris: Julliard, 1963).

8½: Guido Anselmi (Marcello Mastroianni) organizes the magic circle that closes the film. (Museum of Modern Art/Film Stills Archive)

very confusion *it will be made.* Notice that this second phase of the film's resolution heralds not only the existence of 8½ itself, but also the principle of its creation: it will be a film woven from the life of its author and possessing the disorder of his life. Things, however, do not stop there: having organized his fantastic dance, Guido, holding his wife by her hand, *himself now enters the circle.* Is this merely the symbol of that complacent tenderness—Fellini's as well—that ties Guido to his own memories and to his own dreams, and of which he has accused himself (not without some complacency and some tenderness) in earlier sequences? Are we not at last witnessing the final casting off of this great vehicle of a film, which, like a rocket freed from its various supports, will be able to soar on its true flight? Having entered the circle, Guido has also come to order; this author who dreamed of making 8½ is now one of the characters of 8½; he can give his hand to the maid, the producer, the cardinal, his mistress; he no longer needs his megaphone, for it is now Fellini's film that will commence. No longer is Guido at the center of the magic circle; now it is only the small child dressed in white, and blowing his pipe, the ultimate, and first, inspirer of the whole fantasy—Guido as a child has become the symbol of Fellini as a child, since, in any case, *the place of the director, which is now empty*, can only be occupied by a character external to the action of the film: by Fellini himself.

And so Fellini's film begins. And though one is right to underline the paradoxical and startling thing about 8½—that it is a powerfully creative meditation on the inability to create—the fact remains that this theme takes us back, beyond any possible affectation on Fellini's part, to a situation more fundamental and less paradoxical than it is occasionally said to be. Out of all the confusion we have witnessed in the film, an admirably constructed film and one that is as little confused as possible will, it is true, be born; but is this not simply because the last stage of creation—that voluntary awakening that *stops* the undefined course of things in order to *establish* the work—can never be described in the created work, which owes its creation only to that ultimate step back, to that infinitesimal yet gigantic instant that is all that separates Guido from Fellini?

NOTES

1. With regard to the cinema: Alain Virmaux, "Les limites d'une conquête," *Études cinématographiques*, no. 28-29, 4th quarter, 1963, pp. 31-39. For the term "*construction en abŷme*," see p. 33.
2. Ibid.
3. Ibid.
4. R. Bellour, "La splendeur de soi-même," *Études cinématographiques*, pp. 27-30.
5. C. Jacotey, "Bilan critique," *Études cinématographiques*, pp. 62-68.
6. P. Kast, "Les petits potamogetons," *Cahiers du cinéma*, no. 145, July 1963, pp. 49-52.
7. Pierre Kast (p. 52), Alain Virmaux (p. 33), Raymond Bellour (p. 28): previously mentioned articles. Also Max Milner, "8½," *Études*, Sept. 1963.

Juliet of the Spirits:
Fellini and Jung

. . . .

18. *Juliet of the Spirits:*   *Carolyn Geduld*
Guido's Anima

Juliet of the Spirits is frequently interpreted as 8½ from a female view-point. The character of Juliet seems to correspond closely with that of Luisa, Guido's wife in 8½, and this correspondence is particularly compelling if 8½ is viewed as an autobiographical film. Guido is, like Fellini, a director directing a film called "8½." Mario Pisu, Guido's alter ego who deserts his wife for a younger woman, physically resembles Fellini, which is possibly why he was cast as the husband of Fellini's real wife, Giulietta Masina, in *Juliet*. Together, *Juliet* and 8½ seem to be a composite of the Fellini marriage, with *Juliet* representing Giulietta Masina's or Mrs. Fellini's side of the story. Rumors about the director's marital difficulties at the time of the filming of *Juliet* lend support to this assumption.

Juliet and Luisa do have much in common. Both are relatively asexual, cloaking their femininity with loose-fitting Oriental clothing. Luisa wears a white Nehru jacket, and Juliet frequently wears a white Chinese "coolie" outfit. In their marriages, both take the role of the offended moral force. Both are attended by unaggressive male admirers—Luisa's Enrico and Juliet's José; and by women friends interested in spiritualism—Luisa's Rosella and Juliet's Val. Insofar as Luisa and Juliet (as well as Guido and Giorgio) are perceived as the same character, however, each film sees that character differently, and often unfairly. The wife of Guido is a threatening woman, critical and aloof, whose accusations make him chew his nails with guilt or feign sleep. Juliet's husband is a refined, nonviolent Zampanò—dominant, selfish, unsympathetic—whose feigned sleep and evasions are signs of neglect and abandonment. As Guido is never aware of his wife's secret sen-
. . . .

This work is published here for the first time by arrangement with the author.

suality, so Juliet is never aware of her husband's secret fear and uncertainty.

The conflict between Guido–Giorgio and Juliet–Luisa may reflect the nature of the Fellini marriage, but it also reflects Fellini's indebtedness to Jung. During the filming of 8½, Fellini actually underwent therapy with a Jungian psychoanalyst. Guido may be recognized as one of Jung's "extraverted"[1] types, whose orientation is toward objective reality, and specifically, toward his profession as film director. His depression, inability to act, and retreat into fantasy are typical reactions of the extravert who fails to adapt to external conditions. Nevertheless, because his conscious perceptions are focused on the "real" objective world, they are filmed "realistically" in black-and-white. Despite its subjective techniques, 8½ may be considered from a Jungian perspective the last Fellini film to contain remnants of the neo-realist tradition.

Juliet is one of Jung's "introverted" types, oriented toward subjective or internal reality. Unlike her husband, who is a man of the world, traveling, multilingual, with a wide circle of friends and clients, Juliet's primary orientation is toward her home and her marriage. As is typical of the introverted type, she perceives her husband as a superior external being over whom she has no influence or control. Although her basic impulse is to cling desperately to her husband and to try to control him, a contrary impulse to free herself is also present, as the American psychoanalyst, Dr. Miller, suggests to Juliet in the pine woods. Her conflict drives her deep into the purely subjective world of unconscious fantasy. The surreal or "unreal" content of her perceptions is appropriately filmed in color because, as Fellini states in "The Long Interview,"[2] color is a personal and subjective factor, closely connected with dream concepts.

Jung considered the introverted role normal for women in marriage. In "Marriage as a Psychological Relationship" (1926), Jung used the terms "container" for the extraverted male role and "contained" for the introverted female role. The contained, like Juliet, who lives totally within the context of marriage, achieves a sense of completion through identity with—and absorption into—her husband. The container, like Guido, who has interests beyond marriage, feels suffocated by the contained, yet envies her sense of completion. In the second half of marriage in particular, when the process of aging is felt as a disintegrating force, the container will often seek completion himself through infidelity. His desire at this point is to become a contained, like his wife. Sometimes, during the breakup of the marriage following the act or period of infidelity, both the container and the contained realize that psychic unity is not achieved through marriage, but only through a process occurring within the individual. Both Guido and Juliet discover their completion as individuals at the end of their films. Guido's culminating fantasy of everyone dancing in a circle creates an inner psychic unity of all the disparate external elements that had entered his life and shattered his sense of self. The phantasmagoria that occurs after Juliet's abandonment by Giorgio forces her to face and resolve all the disparate internal elements that had frightened her into seeking shelter in the shadow of her husband.

According to Jung, the conscious extravert is an unconscious introvert and the conscious introvert is an unconscious extravert. Similarly, every male has an unconscious female identity (anima) and every female an unconscious male identity (animus). In marriage, a man will tend to choose a woman who resembles his anima, and a woman will choose a man who resembles her animus. Thus, Juliet is both an individual woman and the unconscious feminine side of Guido–Giorgio. Indeed, the most striking correspondence between 8½ and *Juliet* is not between Luisa and Juliet or between Guido and Giorgio, but between Guido and Juliet. In this sense, *Juliet of the Spirits* is not simply 8½ from Luisa's point of view, although the female viewpoint is what is represented.

Fellini emphasizes this correspondence between Guido and Juliet in the casting of the two films, in which some of the same actors who appear in equivalent roles have equivalent relationships with the two protagonists. As mentioned previously, Mario Pisu is Giorgio in *Juliet* and Mario Mezzabotta, Guido's friend in 8½. Sandra Milo, Susy/Iris/Fanny in *Juliet*, plays Guido's mistress Carla in 8½. Caterina Boratto appears as Juliet's mother and as the mysterious woman who reminds Guido of *his* mother, whereas Mario Conocchia is the lawyer Juliet rejects and also Guido's neglected production collaborator.[3]

This correspondence between Guido and Juliet is built into the structure of both films, as a comparison of the following outlines indicates:

8½	JULIET OF THE SPIRITS
1. Guido dreams he is pulled from the sky into the sea by a rope tied to his foot. [cf. *Juliet* #2]	1. Juliet, seen mostly from the back of her head and in mirrors, is helped to dress by her maids. She is disturbed by an unwelcome group of friends who invade her home. [cf. 8½ #2]

2. Guido, seen mostly from the back of his head and in mirrors, is examined by nurses and doctors. He is disturbed by the unwelcomed visit of Daumier. [cf. *Juliet* #1]

3. Guido sees what is evidently an apparition of Claudia, who offers him water. [cf. *Juliet* #3]

4. Guido is criticized by Daumier and shown an alternative—for a man his age—by Mezzabotta, who has a young mistress. [cf. *Juliet* #4]

5. Guido spends the night with his mistress, Carla. [cf. *Juliet* #5]

6. Guido attends a mind reading demonstration. [cf. *Juliet* #6]

7. Guido's childhood memories of the farmhouse. [cf. *Juliet* #8]

8. Guido has an unsatisfactory private audience with the Cardinal. [cf. *Juliet* #7]

9. Guido's childhood memory of La Saraghina. [cf. *Juliet* #11]

10. Guido meets Luisa. [cf. *Juliet* #9]

11. Guido's harem. [cf. *Juliet* #12]

12. Guido screens film of actress portraying Luisa. [cf. *Juliet* #10]

13. Luisa abandons Guido. [cf. *Juliet* #15]

14. Guido rejects Claudia. [cf. *Juliet* #13]

15. Press conference: a summation of all the pressures on Guido. [cf. *Juliet* #14]

16. Guido considers suicide. [cf. *Juliet* #16]

17. Guido cancels the film. [cf. *Juliet* #17]

18. Resolution: Guido "directs" his own fantasy (unconscious)—entire cast dances in circle and departs. The boy Guido is the last to leave. [cf. *Juliet* #18]

2. Juliet dreams she pulls a barge out of the sea by a rope. [cf. *8½* #1]

3. Juliet sees what is evidently an apparition of Susy, who swims in the sea. [cf. *8½* #3]

4. Juliet is criticized by her mother and sisters and shown the alternative—for a woman of her age—of remaining sexually attractive. [cf. *8½* #4]

5. Juliet overhears Giorgio in his sleep say "Gabriella," the name of his mistress. [cf. *8½* #5]

6. Juliet attends Bhishma's lecture. [cf. *8½* #6]

7. Juliet has an unsatisfactory private audience with Bhishma. [cf. *8½* #8]

8. Juliet's childhood memory of the circus. [cf. *8½* #7]

9. Juliet meets José. [cf. *8½* #10]

10. Juliet hires Lynx-Eyes to film Giorgio. [cf. *8½* #12]

11. Juliet's childhood memory of the school play. [cf. *8½* #9]

12. Susy's villa and tree house. [cf. *8½* #11]

13. Susy's party: Juliet rejects Susy's teachings. [cf. *8½* #14]

14. Lawn party: a summation of all the pressures on Juliet. [cf. *8½* #15]

15. Giorgio abandons Juliet. [cf. *8½* #13]

16. Phantasmagoria: Juliet considers suicide. [cf. *8½* #16]

17. Juliet rejects her mother and frees the girl Juliet from the grill. [cf. *8½* #17]

18. Resolution: Juliet learns to "control" her fantasies (unconscious); entire cast invades and departs from her house. The girl Juliet is the last apparition to leave. Juliet leaves her house and walks toward the pine woods. [cf. *8½* #18]

Within these narrative structures, Guido and Juliet are also associated by the subjective techniques Fellini uses in both films, including such nonlinear material as memories, fantasies, apparitions, and dreams. It is often impossible to separate the fantasy elements from the real elements, especially as the two films progress and the unconscious perceptions of both characters are heightened. Juliet's perceptions are more difficult to distinguish from the "real" than Guido's, since she is, by nature, closer to the subjective. Although we know that Claudia is sometimes an apparition and sometimes real, it is not easy to determine when, if ever, Susy ceases to be an apparition. Similarly, although people in 8½ generally look and dress realistically, although their sexuality is overemphasized, there are characters in *Juliet* whose exaggerated dress or appearance raises doubts as to their objective existence. Is Juliet's mother, for instance, "really" as outrageously glamorous as she appears, or is her beauty grossly overestimated by Juliet's subjective impression of her? Is she "really" taller than Juliet, or is this the distorted impression of the child Juliet once was?

Guido and Juliet share a conflict, the source of which is the mother archetype. For Guido, the reproachful—yet dangerously sexual—woman who is his biological mother (and in later life, his wife Luisa) is an unpleasant synthesis of the two types of motherly women he knew in childhood. One type is the nurse, an image generated by the female relatives who bathed and swaddled him in the farmhouse. The other is the prostitute, an image originating from his boyhood experiences with La Saraghina and possibly with his grandmother, whose mutterings about his grandfather have sexual overtones. The adult Guido is still obsessed with this division between Claudia, the nurse and healer, and his mistress, Carla, who plays the prostitute to stimulate Guido sexually.

Juliet's splitting of the mother archetype into whore—nun is perhaps the strongest evidence of her correspondence with Guido. If she were simply a correspondent of Luisa, the film would emphasize her struggle with the animus—the father or male archetype. In fact, there *is* a conflict of male types that originates in the difference between the puritanical headmaster and Juliet's hedonistic grandfather. Juliet's choice of Giorgio as husband is an attempt to resolve the conflict between the two male (im)possibilities. But the problem of the animus is less striking in *Juliet* than the problem of the anima (i.e., Susy), which is, after all, Guido's problem.

Juliet's biological mother's combination of sensuality and propriety is the ultimate source of Juliet's own disturbed femininity. Her two childhood memories of the circus and the school play offer a key to the nature of this disturbance. Like the two childhood memories of Guido in 8½, one memory (the circus) deals with Juliet's sexual development and the other (the school play) deals with the suppression of this development. There are, however, strong visual links between the two memories. In the center of each is a female on a swing (Fanny on the trapeze in the circus, the girl Juliet on a raised grid in the play) surrounded by horses and strong men (circus attendants, Roman soldiers) on the stage below. This composition is repeated in Juliet's adult life in, for instance, the tree house scene (Juliet in the raised basket, two young men waiting below) and in Susy's bedroom (Juliet on the round bed in the middle of the room, statues of horses around the bed, Susy's godson in attendance, a mirror on the ceiling reminiscent of the trapdoor on the ceiling of the school play).

The circus memory is the psychic equivalent of Guido's memory of La Saraghina. Both recall the wonder and terror of sexual awakening. For Juliet, there are two sexual objects discovered at the circus. One is the strong man, surreptitiously ogled by her mother, whose menace is reinforced by the half-clad caged African dancers. The other is Fanny, who represents the unsuppressed lust of Juliet's mother. Like Gabriella, Fanny robs Juliet of her protector—in this case, her grandfather. When Grandfather and Fanny take off in the circus airplane, Juliet is left behind and exposed to the double threat of first, her mother, who appears in one flashback as an evil queen, and second, the strong man. (In an earlier script of *Juliet*, the father is a Nazi officer, a terrifying strong man who forces his daughters to do gymnastics near an open window in the winter. Giorgio's goose-stepping during the séance and the Nazi officers who appear in the phantasmagoria—in the released version of the film—remain to associate the circus strong man with fascism.)

The school play is the psychic equivalent of Guido's farmhouse memory in 8½. Both the child Juliet and the child Guido are in the care of warm female figures—Guido's aunts and Juliet's nuns—although the aunts are, admittedly, more sensual and human than the faceless, hooded nuns. Both memories involve frightening rituals. Guido is bathed in a wine vat so that he may become a strong man like his grandfather. Juliet, chosen for the role of martyred saint, is burned to death on a flaming grill. Guido is told that if he recites the magic words "Asi Nisi Masa" (an anagram for anima), the eyes in a portrait of his grandfather will move to reveal a hidden treasure. Juliet believes

Juliet of the Spirits: The school play depicting the death of the sainted martyr, a central part of Juliet's past. (Museum of Modern Art/Film Stills Archive)

that after reciting the line "I wish only to save my soul" (a word interpreted by Jung to mean anima or animus), the door of the stage ceiling will open to reveal God.

Juliet's memory is complicated by the action of her grandfather, who stops the show and more or less accuses the audience of cannibalism: of roasting the girl like a beefsteak. This greatly confuses Juliet's concept of sexuality, a confusion previously generated at the circus by her grandfather's claim that "a beautiful woman always makes me feel more religious." Juliet martyrs herself to avoid making a sacrifice to the Emperor (i.e., sacrificing her virginity to the Roman strong man). Yet, if her grandfather's accusations are taken literally, her act of martyrdom involves her with the naked circus Africans, who dance like "cannibals." Either choice is a threat to her sexuality. For Juliet, sex is as dangerous as celibacy, and this is why images of both are increasingly confused in her fantasies and hallucination.

The dreams of Juliet and Guido share several elements, although Guido's dream is simpler. His struggle to escape suffocation in the tunnel where he is trapped by traffic and people corresponds to his struggle as a "container" in marriage and to his struggle against the subjective as an extravert as well as to his struggle against his "real" pressures as a film maker. In Jungian terms, his drift over the sea can be interpreted as a desire to become godlike, free from human conflict. (His flight may also be associated with the trapeze and circus airplane of Juliet's childhood.) But he is connected to Earth by a rope tied to his foot, a familiar Freudian and Jungian phallic symbol suggesting the binding quality of both his sexual needs and his masculine identity. Mezzabotta pulls him into the water (a Jungian symbol for the unconscious) upon the orders of Claudia's manager, who wears a medallion on his forehead and rides a black horse—a typical incarnation of the magician archetype who acts as a guide to the unconscious in Jungian dream mythology. The message is clearly that Guido cannot escape the unconscious material released during his current crisis.

Juliet's dream occurs after she has rejected her lawyer and after she has been rejected by Giorgio, who forgets their anniversary and leaves before she awakens the next morning. As a result, she again unconsciously faces the double menace of sexuality and celibacy—as well as the real possibility of Giorgio's abandonment. The morning brings another renewal of this menace. Her maid, Teresina, is caught embracing one of her townsmen, and then the gardener (a strong man) arises half-naked from the garden pool, singing a song associated with both sex and her grandfather's airplane ("I'll fly, I'll fly to the arms of my beautiful love. . . ."). The gardener's remark about the pool's clogged drain suggests the troubled relationship Juliet has with water—her unconscious. For Juliet, water is connected with Laura's drowning. This is in sharp contrast to Gelsomina, Claudia, La Saraghina, and Susy, who have mystical relationships with water. Juliet and Guido are only comfortable with water in small, controllable quantities, such as the water from Juliet's garden sprinkler or the glasses of mineral water offered to Guido at the spa. Juliet fails to appreciate the advice of José, another magician or guide, who tells her water is trustworthy, one of the "simple things, things which don't hide something else."

At the beach, but well away from the sea, Juliet's doctor recommends that she buy a horse (a vehicle to the unconscious associated with Guido's dream) just before a barge lands with Susy (Fanny's double), several strong men, and several Asians (exotics, like the circus Africans). But the dream that follows concerns the horrific underside of these same elements. Like Guido, Juliet believes she is protected from the sea, until she is handed a rope attached to a barge containing all that she unconsciously fears or represses. Emaciated, half-naked people (her repressed sexuality), three emaciated horses (her refusal to be "guided"), invaders or strong men brandishing swords, and a huge Turkish strong man (Olaf or the gardener) who rises from the sea[4] at the sound of a jet (a modern equivalent of Grandfather's plane). The dream suggests the consequences of repression at a time when she is losing the protection of Giorgio. Giorgio does not appear in the dream, but Juliet is denied the protection of his substitutes—the doctor, Lynx-Eyes, and (by association with the jet) her grandfather.

After his dream, Guido reacts to the crisis brought on by his age and by the renewal of childhood memories with depression and chronic indecision. He is unable to continue his film and, more specifically, fails to choose between Carla and Luisa—between the image of Woman the Prostitute and Woman the Nurse. His harem fantasy is not a desire simply to possess both kinds of women, but to avoid the necessity of choosing between them at all, to lapse into passivity while appearing to "direct" the household.

Juliet also takes the passive, most retiring role rather than choose from the possibilities confronting her. Her indecision is evident in the first scene, when she fails to choose between wigs. Juliet's failure, like Guido's, springs from an earlier inability, as a child, to choose between the teachings of the circus and those of the church. As an adult, Juliet's world is also filled with antithetical options. Upon analysis, these options may actually be marked more for their similarities than their differences, like the wigs or Juliet's twin nieces. But there again is precisely the source of Juliet's confusion. Among the antithetical models offered her are, for instance, her two maids, the saintly Elisabetta and the sensual Teresina; her two sisters, the righteous Adele and the narcissistic Sylva; her two friends, the childish Val and the lusty Dolores; and two spirits (representatives of the unconscious in Jungian theory): Iris, the saintly one who promises a Christian "love for everyone" (but who later betrays this promise by turning into Susy) and Olaf, the heathen who embarrasses Juliet with his coarse remarks.

In the middle section of both 8½ and *Juliet*, the tension between images and choices is heightened by the events that initiate the resurgence of childhood memories. Guido's memories are sparked by his visit to Carla's hotel and by his encounter with Maurice and Maya, the mind readers in the spa nightclub. Juliet's memories occur after her visit to Bhishma's hotel, where the separate images of saint and whore are hopelessly intertwined. The hotel itself was once a brothel, although it is now open to religious functions: a wedding (an equivalent in tone of the school play) and Bhishma's lecture on Buddhism (the

equivalent of the circus and of the mind reading demonstration in
8½).

Bhishma is an enigma combining and confusing everything Juliet has
feared from childhood. Her sex is indeterminate, as was the nuns'.
Yet, she has Fanny's exaggerated sensuality. Her fraudulent association
with Eastern (non-European) religion recalls the fraudulent dance of
the circus Africans. Bhishma is attended by an Indian woman and a
modified strong man type wearing an undershirt. She is accompanied
by the sound of wind—from the fan and from the "storm" of Juliet's
hallucinations—a reminder of Grandfather's plane. Her suite is part
hospital (associated with martyrdom) and part bordello. The furniture is covered with medicinal items and wine; Bhishma reclines on a
clinical table and later on a bed with a deep red canopy. She is much
like Juliet's mother *after* Juliet's refusal to obey her: old, ugly, witch-
like. This negative image of the mother archetype—and of female sexuality—is corrected by Susy in the second half of the film.

Bhishma's violent fit, which occurs after Juliet rejects her advice, is a
kind of grotesque orgasm. It is precisely because Juliet rejects her own
sexual side that female sexuality is so distorted in the film.[5] Juliet perceives a progressive exaggeration of sensual women from Teresina to
Dolores to Sylva, the culmination of which is Susy. Like Bhishma, Susy
sexualizes the image of the saint, confounding Juliet's compulsive
separation of the two. Fellini, however, does not allow tape recorders,
electric fans, and medical paraphernalia to undercut Susy's power. Unlike Bhishma, she is an authentic guide. Her villa, which is decorated
like a brothel, is right next door to Juliet's house. Her wardrobe, consisting of hoods and wings, recalls both the circus and the school play.
Whereas Bhishma can speak only of bird sounds and bird bites from
the confinement of a bathtub, Susy is truly a creature of the air. She
takes off in Grandfather's plane, swings on a trapeze, rises to the top of
a tree, and decorates her villa with white peacocks, statues of eagle-
women, and an extravagant curved staircase. She surrounds herself
with the usual assortment of strong men and non-Europeans. Her
fiancé, Momy (a Turk like Olaf), is approximately the age of Grandfather when he flew off with Fanny.

The most significant member of Susy's household is the catatonic,
Arlette. She is reminiscent of Oswaldo, the speechless, bedridden boy
in *La Strada*. Both the boy and Arlette appear to be object lessons for
Gelsomina and Juliet: what they could become if they fail to compro-
mise with reality (in Gelsomina's case) or with the unconscious (in
Juliet's case). Arlette is the culmination of a number of "saintly"

women who balance the sexual women in *Juliet:* Elisabetta; Val, who wears a confirmation dress; Adele; and Laura, the schoolgirl who committed suicide (an act Arlette attempts several times) when abandoned by her boyfriend.

Arlette and Laura illustrate the most dangerous options left to Juliet if she cannot "take" Giorgio's desertion. Laura drowned herself at age fifteen; Juliet will be abandoned by Giorgio and plagued by thoughts of Laura's suicide shortly after their fifteenth anniversary. Arlette's room is filled with the same kind of leaves that cover the window of Juliet's bathroom, where Juliet sees an apparition of Laura turn into Susy. Arlette is attended by a Spanish chauffeur whom she later seduces; Juliet is attended by José, who waits so long for seduction that he is "frozen" in a stop-frame during a phantasmagoria.

The ultimate choice for Juliet *seems* to be between becoming a Susy or an Arlette, as it once was becoming Fanny or a nun. Yet, Juliet cannot simply model herself after one at the expense of the other because Susy contains Arlette. (Arlette lives in Susy's villa.) For Guido as well, the final answer does not come from giving up one of his women or images of Woman. He does not stop Luisa from leaving him by ignoring Carla. Juliet's attempt to participate in the orgy with Susy's godson does not instantly grant her sexual release. Instead, it heightens her sense of guilt, which brings on the terrifying apparition of Laura on the burning grill.

The final answer for Juliet and Guido is to assimilate the two female images. The polar opposites among the female characters in both films represent the splitting of the mother archetype. These must not be projected separately, but be brought to consciousness, where they can be dealt with.

This occurs in 8½ after Guido has been disappointed by his father and the Cardinal, and after Luisa deserts him. It is then that he confronts both an apparition of Claudia and the real Claudia in a piazza. While the apparition continues to act like a nurse, the real Claudia shares Luisa's and Guido's mother's critical attitude toward Guido. For the first time, Guido perceives the split image of femininity in the figure of a single woman. Guido rejects Claudia, recognizing that no woman or projected image of woman can save him, and admitting for the first time that he cannot make his film.

He must still face a final assault from the external world at the press conference, after he has given up the persona of film director in the piazza. Juliet faces this sort of assault at and after the lawn party, which is held after she has given up the attempted persona of prostitute at Susy's party and at a time when her loss of persona as wife is imminent—since Giorgio is about to leave. Both Guido and Juliet react to the loss of their personae by regressing, which, for Jung, is a means of activating the archaic, collective level of the unconscious in order to achieve wisdom and balance. Both risk psychosis in a final effort to gain integration. Guido, for instance, crawls under the conference table, regressing to the time when he attempted to escape his bath by crawling under the farmhouse table. By reliving this experience, he attains the inner unity represented by the concluding dance of all characters in 8½.

Juliet experiences a similar regression in a more complicated way at the lawn party, where she appears in public with Giorgio for the last time. Both the séance and the lawn party, the two events that frame the end of Juliet's marriage, evoke the memories that frame Juliet's childhood, reinforcing her basic fear of abandonment. The séance is visually constructed like the primal memories of the circus and school play. While strong men (Dolores's and Val's lovers) lounge on the periphery, the spirit Iris/Fanny is borne on the air above a round table that is the focal point of the scene. Just as Juliet's childhood experiences concerned sex and the suppression of sex, Giorgio's conversation with Cesarino in the garden, during which they agree "it is better to lie" about extramarital affairs, provides an ironic commentary to the sexual "truth" of the spirits' messages.

The spirit Iris reassures Juliet. Her message, "love for everyone," seems to suggest that Juliet is still loved by Giorgio. It also dimly recalls the compassion of the nun who, unlike Juliet's mother, recognized something special and precious in the child Juliet's innocent look. The nun implied that Juliet was like a saint, the recipient of God's—and everyone's—love. The intent of Iris's message, however, is sexualized by the passionate gesture of Juliet's lawyer, who interrupts the ritual. This invokes the coarse spirit of Olaf, who replaces Iris's gentle message with insults. Olaf, the spiritual strong man, now attempts to shock the women at the séance by indicating that they are all whores. His insults are similar to Grandfather's insinuations about the nuns: "You go up on that grill—or are you afraid to show your legs?" Olaf's message for Juliet—"You're no one to anybody. You don't count, you wretched thing"—refers not only to Juliet's impending loss of Giorgio, but also to the loss of saintliness that made her "count" in the school play before Grandfather's outburst. This was perhaps the one moment when she "counted" more than her two sisters.[6]

Juliet responds to Olaf as her mother responded to Grandfather, by fainting. The difference, of course, is that Juliet's mother's collapse earned her the sympathy of the headmaster and exonerated her from Grandfather's behavior, whereas Juliet's collapse seems to confirm Olaf's message and encourages the smugness of her friends.

The lawn party is close in structure to the séance, although it is also the converse of Susy's party, which directly precedes it. In fact, the lawn party is a suppressed, daytime version of the nighttime orgy in Susy's villa; the two sets of guests are characterized by their boredom and dissipation. Familiar types attend both parties: the man with the goatee and Genius, the Goddess of Vice and Dolores, the woman with feathers and Sylva, the fetishist Alyosha and Juliet's love-sick lawyer, Grandmother Olga (described as a witch) and Juliet's mother, Susy's godson and José. All three parties include rites and rituals that recall the school play: the séance, the Egyptian rite for the passage from life to death (evoking the Christian rite of martyrdom), and the psychodrama at the lawn party.

Dr. Miller, the American psychoanalyst who conducts the psychodrama, is the last and the wisest of the doctor-guides who have appeared. These have included Juliet's doctor, Bhishma's doctor, and Dr. Valli. Essentially, the psychodrama has the same function as the séance. As Dr. Miller notes, "Each participant must be a vehicle for truth." In both cases, the nature of this truth refers to the discovery of the shadowy side of the personality. During the lawn party, Juliet's shadowy side is revealed through regression, when she is asked to join the drama. As if she were back in the school theater, she appears to answer the questions originally asked by the Emperor, although with a resentment that may be contrasted with the child Juliet's acquiescence.

EMPEROR: Will you sacrifice before your Emperor?
CHILD: No, never. JULIET: Life is all sacrifice.
EMPEROR: You are willing to accept martyrdom?
CHILD: Yes, I accept it. JULIET: Take your revenge!

Increasingly, she mimics Grandfather's response to the play.

GRANDFATHER:What are you teaching these poor little girls? What are you trying to do to them, you crazy women!
JULIET: Be more feminine, we'll teach you. My life is full of people who talk, talk, talk.
GRANDFATHER: Go home girls. Away with you, away, away!
JULIET: Get out! All of you! Go away!

Juliet's anger seems to mount, perhaps in a long delayed response to Grandfather's words while he was removing her from the grill: "Don't you rebel? You let them do anything they want with you? You like being burned alive, eh? Aren't you the stupid one!"

Meanwhile, advice from the guests at the lawn party contradicts that of her grandfather. José's desire that she find peace within herself, the lawyer's plea for a divorce, Dr. Miller's suggestion that she enjoy her freedom—all fail to stem her anger. Still in the grip of Grandfather's spirit (her animus), she attempts a confrontation in Gabriella's apartment. Giorgio's mistress, however, proves to be as distant (and as sexual) as Juliet's mother, refusing any closer contact with Juliet than a brief conversation.

Juliet's abortive attempt at a confrontation is finally achieved, significantly, when Giorgio leaves. During the phantasmagoria that occurs when Juliet is alone in the house, she refuses her mother's demand for obedience (as Grandfather had refused the headmaster's similar demands). By now, Juliet is fully in touch with her animus and can take over his role. This time *she* frees the child Juliet from the grill, symbolically releasing the martyr whose image she has constantly re-created. This act, like Guido's crawl under the table, reverses the effect of her nightmare on the beach, in which an assemblage of characters and horses personifying her neurosis had landed by barge. Now, the same figures, and others collected in the course of the film, depart on an enormous, ungainly wagon. The wagon does not go back to the sea (unconscious) where it may simply be repressed, but departs from Juliet's whole environment, disappearing across the field where Susy's villa once stood. This scene is the equivalent of the dance that ends 8½, a resolution of all the elements—collective and personal—that had been disrupting Juliet's consciousness.

Juliet also includes an additional scene that does not match anything in 8½: a shot of the now integrated Juliet walking away from her house toward the pine wood. It is notable that she walks with, rather than against, the direction of the most prominent camera movement used in the film, the pan from left to right. Her movement conforms to the conventional film sign for progress: moving on and ahead. Presumably, the subjective problems connected with her childhood and marriage no longer overwhelm her. She is prepared to accommodate the objective world, a difficult task for an introvert. By contrast, the adult Guido does not appear in the last shot of 8½. Presumably, he is absorbed by elements from the past, accommodating the subjective world he had previously ignored (before his breakdown). This is a healthy activity for an extravert.

It was, perhaps, a similarly therapeutic impulse to explore the world of the introvert that inspired Fellini's conception of *Juliet*, as he notes in "The Long Interview":

> More than the desire to make another picture with Giulietta, I felt that my desire to use the cinema to penetrate certain areas of reality could find the perfect guide in Giulietta. The germination of the idea was lost in the last years, in my search for a theme that—even more than the story of Gelsomina—would lend itself to describing a different reality.[7]

After *Juliet*, Fellini apparently found this kind of subjective exploration unprofitable. To date, he has not made another film representing his anima. The clearest indication of his rejection of Jung occurs in *Roma*, in which the ancient frescoes discovered in the evacuation are destroyed as soon as they are exposed. Evidently, for Fellini, the past can no longer be called upon to heal the present in quite the same way as it could in *8½* and in *Juliet of the Spirits*. .

NOTES

1. Jung's spelling.
2. Published with the script of *Juliet of the Spirits*, ed. Tullio Kezich (New York: Ballantine, 1966), p. 27.
3. It might also be noted that Cesarino Miceli Picardi plays Giorgio's confidant and Guido's production manager, who keeps two "nieces" in his bed. One of the nieces, Dina de Santis, reappears as Elisabetta, Juliet's maid. Yvonne Casadei plays Teresina, Juliet's other maid, as well as Jacqueline Bonbon, the member of Guido's harem too old to remain downstairs.
4. On the collective level, the figure of the giant rising from the sea is Poseidon, the god of the sea who claimed to have created the horse.
5. The sexual failure of Juliet's marriage may be inferred from the red-fringed shawl lying on the marriage bed, a reminder of the red streamers representing fire on the grill. This visual clue suggests that Juliet thinks of herself as a martyr in bed. Her sexual martyrdom is also indicated during the mock bullfight, when Giorgio "attacks" her while she is playing with the shawl.
6. In an earlier script, Juliet's "Cinderella complex" is mentioned: her feeling in childhood that she was the ugly, unwanted sister. Her underestimation of her role in her family might be contrasted with Guido's overestimation of his role, derived from a privileged childhood. He, for instance, is the only child in the farmhouse who does not have to share a bed.
7. Ibid., p. 57.

Fellini: A Director's Notebook

. . . .

19. The Director as Superstar   *Joseph McBride*

You'd think that an autobiographical film by the director of 8½ would attract considerable critical attention, but *Fellini: A Director's Notebook* has been almost completely ignored since it appeared in 1969. Evidently the reason for this is that it was made for American television (NBC) and, unlike Fellini's second television film, *The Clowns*, not shown in theatres. But with some of our most important directors turning to TV for backing these days (Renoir, Welles, Rossellini, Godard, *et al.*), critics are going to have to lose some of their snobbishness about the medium.

The notebook has long been an accepted literary form, but Fellini's is the first of its kind in the commercial cinema, despite the recent proliferation of films about directors, including two about Fellini himself. It was made at the end of a very difficult period in his life, when he had given up a project which had occupied him for three years, *The Voyage of Mastorna*, had suffered a total physical collapse, and had just returned to work with a short exercise film, the *Never Bet the Devil Your Head* episode of the three-part Edgar Allan Poe film *Spirits of the Dead (Histoires Extraordinaires)*, a feverish tale about a film star whose hallucinations on a trip to Cinecittà finally lead him to his death. It was not hard to draw a connection between the character and Fellini himself. Andrew Sarris made a perceptive comment on what it revealed of Fellini's artistic dilemma: "If Fellini can trot out the same old satirical routines at the drop of a hat or an option, what possible personal meaning could they ever have had? At what point, therefore, does a personal cinematic language become a tired cliché? . . . Fellini has spent a whole decade on this theme, and we are now moving into the Seventies. Perhaps his *Satyricon* will be a source of artistic renewal

. . . .

From *Sight and Sound*, Vol. 41, No. 2 (1972), pp. 78-81. Reprinted by permission of *Sight and Sound*.

or, in some ultimate way, an occasion for artistic release of his more repetitious mannerisms."

The Satyricon's theme was, in both its historical and personal senses, the clearing away of dead conventions and obsessions in a new spirit of moral freedom. Its marvellous ending, with the young men climbing into the boat as the old men sit on shore eating the poet's corpse, made this surreally explicit. And I think the reason why *The Satyricon* was the kind of renewal Sarris hoped for, rather than just an occasion for the release of obsessions, was that Fellini was able to take stock of himself on film in *A Director's Notebook* before shooting it.

Although the film may seem at first glance to be a disconnected grab bag of gags, skits and memorabilia, it is actually a rigorous development of the theme of artistic stasis which Fellini pursued in 8½. A development, not a regression: this is a film about how a man breaks loose from his artistic inhibitions and finds the moral strength to move forward and work again. Why did Fellini turn to documentary? Perhaps because he felt that he had gone so far into the fantasy mode that he became barren and stultified (*Giulietta of the Spirits* is a dead end in many ways) and needed to re-establish contact with the real world. This has happened before in Fellini's career. He began, after all, as a scriptwriter in the neo-realist movement, and his first decade of directing was marked by a constant flux between theatrical fantasy and neo-realism, often within the same film. *La Dolce Vita* was a grand attempt to impose his fantasy life on to the reality of modern Rome (as his new film, *Roma*, evidently is), and from there Fellini veered completely into the interior world.

A Director's Notebook, admittedly, is fully accessible only to those familiar with Fellini's *oeuvre*; but this should not be an excuse for keeping it in obscurity. If I would not presume to put it in the first rank of Fellini's work (even though I enjoy it more than, say, 8½, though less than *The Nights of Cabiria*), this is because the limitations of the notebook form are inherent in its virtues. There are parts of *A Director's Notebook* which are frankly awful, notably a scene of a bunch of whores and truck drivers cavorting in ancient Roman dress along the Appian Way which is about on the level of those Fellini pastiches that disfigure every student film festival. There are also parts of the film which rank with his best work; the long concluding sequence, a series of bizarre characters auditioning for roles in *The Satyricon*, moved me more than anything else he has done. But the special charm of *A Director's Notebook* comes from its inclusion of the bad along with the good, the silly with the sublime. If Fellini had exercised conventional artistic discretion and retained only the most "presentable" sequences, we would have lost much of the insight into his personality; which, in the end, is what we hope to find in a notebook.

Fellini's preparations for filming his *Satyricon* form the running thread of the narrative. And since he is still in the free-associative stage of preparation (we don't see him actually shooting it until the very end, under the credits), the format is loose enough to let him go off on tangents only vaguely related to the central thread. The film divides into ten segments:

(1)   A visit to a group of hippies living in an abandoned set for *Mastorna*; a look at some of the props and set designs in a warehouse; and a brief glimpse of what the film would have been like.

(2)   A visit to the freaky night people who inhabit the Colosseum, as part of Fellini's attempt to seek parallels between modern and ancient Rome for *The Satyricon* (and for *Roma?*).

(3)   Fellini's wife Giulietta Masina introducing a sequence cut from *Nights of Cabiria* about a Santa Claus character known as "the man with the sack" whom Fellini found in the Colosseum.

(4)   Fellini's reminiscence of his childhood moviegoing, including a parodistic recreation of a silent movie about ancient Rome.

(5)   Genius, the medium who appears in *Giulietta of the Spirits*, conducting a séance along the Appian Way in an attempt to communicate with the old Romans.

(6)   A tongue-in-cheek journey through the Roman subways, with a silly "professor" who is dumbfounded when the subway suddenly turns into the catacombs.

(7).   A visit to Marcello Mastroianni, who is too busy being lionised by journalists, fashion photographers, and a busload of matronly fans to talk with Fellini; a hectic screen test for *Mastorna*; and a brief discussion between director and actor about Fellini's inhibitions.

(8)   A search for old Roman types in a slaughterhouse.

(9)   The audition.

(10)   The beginning of shooting on Fellini's *Satyricon*.

The opening sequence, with the camera making spooky combination tracking and zooming movements through the field around a moored airplane and a cardboard church, invokes the same feeling of death in the midst of life as the opening tunnel sequence of 8½. The airplane, winglessly suspended in scaffolding, bears a marked resemblance to the rocket of the science-fiction movie which the director Guido was unable to "get off the ground" in 8½, and Guido's entrapment in the automobile is echoed when we see a black-hatted figure sitting in the window of the airplane. But more than a purely psychic stasis is involved here, for the presence of the hippies—whose brightly painted car has no wheels—puts the *Mastorna* movie into a generalised context of cultural dissolution.

When Fellini came to make *The Satyricon*, he said he thought of the three young central characters as figures out of time, divorced from history and convention, and compared them to the hippies of the (then) present day: "They have no illusions about anything, because they do not believe in anything, but theirs is a new form of cynicism, a sort of peaceful disengagement, a healthy, concrete common sense, a singular realism." What made *The Satyricon* seem so healthy next to Fellini's previous work, and also so disturbing, was that the young characters were totally amoral; their utter liberation, in Fellini's eyes, is both a mysteriously beautiful and a dangerous thing. Ever the Catholic moralist, he was not content to end the film on the face of young Encolpius, as he had originally planned, but cut from the living face to its frozen image on a crumbling, ruined fresco mired next to the sea, a *memento mori* symbolising the ultimate failure of any attempt at total liberation.

The pre-*Satyricon* hippies in *A Director's Notebook* seem to find Fellini in two minds. On the one hand, he identifies their rootlessness and lack of direction with his own and that of Guido/Mastorna: there is a shot of a girl sitting silently in the automobile, just like Guido, as the wind blows and a jet flies into a brilliant setting sun. But on the other hand, Fellini is exploring the possibility that these hippies, like his projected *Satyricon* characters, might provide an alternative to the myths of Western culture. They are, after all, finding a new use for his abandoned set, just as their culture in general attempts to find a new way of life in the shards of modern civilisation. A "priest" has just united a couple in marriage, and another hippie has made art out of Fellini's failure—he wanders around the set reciting a poem contemptuously entitled "Mastorna Blows." Like them, Fellini is unable to speculate on the future (the science-fiction world of *Mastorna*), so he decides that the best way of reaching the future is to return to primitivism . . . via *The Satyricon*, which he later described as a "science-fiction film set in the past." But Fellini also indicates, as he does in the ending of *The Satyricon*, that the rebellious young may be making a fetish of rebellion, that they may have no alternative to offer except a return to zero and a pathetic defiance whose hollowness is defined in the childishness of the poem's title.

The hippies disappear from view, and Fellini's images become apocalyptic. The wind howls, the sky darkens, and snow begins to fall as we see Mastorna, in the black cape and hat from 8½, walking from the airplane with a suitcase and a cello case. He leaves the cello behind just as Fellini leaves the film behind. But the director, now seen walking in a bright vernal landscape, declares that he will do the film in the future "because it is the story I prefer the most." He is walking toward what he jocularly calls "the *Mastorna* cemetery," the warehouse which contains, among other things, a pile of rubber heads which were to be used for a scene in which "people kill themselves by jumping out of a window." Fellini playfully pops one of the heads apart, and his script girl Marina Boratto (daughter of the mother-figure Caterina Boratto from *Giulietta*, who appears as a depraved matron in the slaughterhouse episode) gingerly touches it and squeals with delight. It has all become rather a silly joke. What remains, he confides, is "a kind of remorse . . . as if a million eyes were staring out at me, waiting."

Fellini goes from the ruins of *Mastorna* to another set of ruins, the Colosseum. But he realises that the sickness of the modern world has extended even there, infecting our view of the past; what he finds in the Colosseum is a collection of pimps, whores, transvestites, tramps and cripples, alternately hiding from his camera and screaming into it. The tracking shots along the walls and crevices of the labyrinth seem to have inspired (or to have been a first draft of) the opening sewer sequence of *The Satyricon*, which is a metaphor for the decadence of the culture the young heroes are leaving behind. (Fellini points out that Petronius visited the Colosseum while preparing to write his *Satyricon*, so things haven't changed that much.)

In his article on the making of *The Satyricon* published in the May 1970 *Playboy*, Fellini confessed that his research was very difficult. "There existed no models, no aesthetic canons to copy; each conventionally expressive perspective was confused, upset; and if, perchance, I let myself be tempted by it, the result could be unexpected or catastrophic. The Appian Way? The ruins of the Colosseum? Picture postcards. Nothing was coming to me. . . . Then one night, in the Colosseum, I saw that horrendous lunar catastrophe of stone, that immense skull devoured by time, as the testimony of a civilisation with a different destiny. . . ." By thinking of his central characters as hippies, Fellini was able to "regard pagan Rome with eyes unclouded by the myths and ideologies that have followed in these 2000 years of Christianity."

What gives Fellini his kinship with the hippies is reflected in the opening shot of the Colosseum segment, a view of the ruins through bustling modern traffic, repulsively overlaid with a red filter. Orson Welles defined Fellini best when he observed in 1967 that his "limitation—which is also the source of his charm—is that he's fundamentally very provincial. His films are a small-town boy's dream of the big city. His sophistication works because it's the creation of someone who doesn't have it. But he shows dangerous signs of being a superlative artist with little to say."

Welles undoubtedly picked up that last line from Guido's declaration that he has nothing to say, but he is going to say it anyway. The whole of *A Director's Notebook* is that search for "something to say." The morbidity of the first two episodes is dispelled by the introduction of a character who is both real and a lost fragment of Fellini's cinematic past: the "man with the sack" who brings charity and compassion into the foul world of the Colosseum and into the miserable life of Cabiria (who, when the meeting was to have occurred, had just been abandoned by a client after leaving the ghastly "procession of Divine Love"). Fellini has explained that the sequence was cut from *Cabiria* because the producer thought the film was too long; but it seems appropriate that it *was* cut so that it can be resurrected now at a time of renewal.

Fellini returns to his innocent childhood dreams of wickedness in the cinema memory which ends with himself, as a little boy in his father's arms, staring rapt at the screen as the camera zooms through the midst of the crowd. "For me," Fellini has said, "a movie house is a room bubbling with noises and odours; chestnuts, the urine of children; that feeling of the end of the world, of disaster." The orange-tinted film the little Fellini is watching, like the circus the little Fellini enters at the beginning of *The Clowns*, is a grotesque vision of lechery and violence which looks merely droll to us but which is appalling to the child. The film has unsettling correspondences to the fantasies of childhood: a grossly fat, baby-faced Roman is eating grapes out of a woman's hand when his mother comes to pull him away by the ear. Without warning, she stabs him in the back, and then leers into the camera with her tongue hanging out in the patented Fellini image for female lust. As we stare into the flashing blue lamp of the projector, we are made to feel the hypnotic effect the experience is having on the little boy.

This childlike view of the world's nonsensical wickedness is debased into childishness in the next three segments (Genius, the subway, the whores and the truck drivers), which are on an even lower level of sophistication than the silent movie Fellini parodies. This is the Fellini who would be in control if, as in *Never Bet the Devil Your Head*, he couldn't find "something to say." It is reported that Fellini takes, or used to take, Genius seriously as a medium, but if his appearance here is any indication (Genius, who looks and acts like Liberace, scorns the ancient Romans as "very vulgar people"), the director has been barking up a very wrong tree.

The segment with Mastroianni, who was to have been Mastorna, is a merciless guying of his post-*Dolce Vita* image as a "Latin lover." It proves Mastroianni to be a remarkably good sport, and it also allows him to reciprocate the insult by criticising Fellini, in an eerily Pirandellian scene, for not having the "faith" to let him play Mastorna. Fellini hovers around the edges of Mastroianni's adulators with the look of a man who has created a Frankenstein monster. It is as if the narcissistic character he created in 8½ has actually taken possession of the actor, who, in fact, dons his Guido hat at one point. Mastroianni wears the same look of bemused submission as the actor in *Never Bet the Devil Your Head*. When the busload of women pulls up outside his villa, there is a pan along the row of obscenely excited old faces; seen through the green glass of the windows, they look like zombies, and again we are reminded of the opening of 8½, with Guido suffocating in his automobile. Fellini cryptically remarks that Mastroianni has "all the virtues and all the faults of the ancient Romans"; but this sequence has less to do with his research for *The Satyricon* than with a reminder, lest he weaken, of the stasis of the *Mastorna* period.

In the screen test, we see Mastroianni idly drawing a bow across Mastorna's cello, making a moaning sound, as a horde of sycophants scurry around preparing him for the role and the camera tracks aimlessly back and forth in front of him, conveying a palpable feeling of tension and imprisonment. "When you made *La Dolce Vita*, wasn't I your character?" Mastroianni asks the director while sitting at a make-up table. "In 8½, wasn't I you?" Yes, says Fellini impatiently, but that was in the past. Mastroianni replies, "You are scared," adding that he would become Mastorna if only Fellini *believed* that he was Mastorna.

After this we take the plunge into the frighteningly real world of *The Satyricon*, the camera tracking through the empty slaughterhouse from the viewpoint of an animal being led to the cutting tables, with animal bellowing on the soundtrack. Fellini is dragging himself kicking and screaming into his new film.

It is his practice, when preparing a film, to put an advertisement in the Roman papers announcing an open audition. As he has explained: "For me, working on a film is a journey—I've said this so often that I hardly believe it any more. You don't take a journey in the abstract, but consider the exigences that come up from hour to hour, your own mood, things that are impossible to predict . . . you must put yourself in the hands of the thing that is to be born. . . . I call in people; I have hundreds of faces pass before me. It's a kind of ceremony to create an atmosphere. . . . I see a hundred in order to get two for the film; I compare clothing, dialects, whiskers, tics, postures. Some poor man may be so happy because I insist on having him photographed—and the only thing that interests me is a picture of his eye-glasses. At a certain point, I've had enough of the office and of the people passing in front of me, and then I begin the tests. This is the definite phase of the ceremony. At this point, I know that in a short time I have to begin the film." What is needed, then, is the courage to let the real world take over and put a definite shape to the chaotic, ultimately sterile world of the imagination. Fellini's audition may seem chaotic to the casual observer, but to him this is a process of discovery.

When Fellini/Guido claims that he had "nothing to say," he is actually defining the role of the artist to be less an arbiter of reality than a passionate *interpreter* of reality (or, to use Fellini's favourite metaphor, a ring-master). Leonardo-like, Fellini takes sustenance from faces and from the physical, even clinical, detail of the human body. He will always be a neo-realist at heart, even when his researchers take him into the realm of the surreal. This is why it is absurd to take Fellini's work with too much solemnity; as exaggerated as it may seem, it is too close to life. And this is why Andrew Sarris' characterisation of Fellini as "the Busby Berkeley of metaphysics" is not as damning as it might sound.

With uncharacteristic humility, Fellini avoids showing us his own face during the audition sequence, although we once see his hands putting a woman's photograph into a filing envelope. We watch the procession of faces from a vantage point behind his desk, next to his own chair, as if we were doing the research with him. His voice ranges from affection to amusement to condescension to vexation as the people flow past: a frumpy woman (later to appear as his "script girl" in *The Clowns*) reading one of her poems; a businessman type reading from a Balkan newspaper; an aging dressmaker giving him a youthful pin-up of herself; a sluttish-looking girl asking him, "Tell me what you really think about women—should I be a virgin or not"? (his reply is tacitly revealed when we realise that she played one of the whores along the Appian Way); a man touting his son, who looks like a pin-head and whistles like a blackbird (the boy is the "sound man" in *The Clowns*); a con-man who tries to sell Fellini a painting by "an artist greater than Raphael" whose name, unfortunately, slips his mind; a balding man who says, "If I had a wig, it would change my whole life," and gives Fellini a sample of his hair; a *really* sluttish-looking girl who says she played Joan of Arc, twice, in Sunday school; an effeminate drama student who gives an hysterical rendition of Chekhov; a pretty girl; an exotic woman who says she dances with trained snakes (and suddenly appears in a sexy costume, as if Fellini is daydreaming); and a fat matron with her two muscle-bound sons, who strip off their shirts and strike beefcake poses.

Finally a woman in black with a ravaged face tells Fellini that his films "express exactly the same thing as my music," and pulls out an accordion. "Is it very long"? he asks wearily. As she starts playing her "Fortune, Where Art Thou"? in the manner of Nino Rota, the camera zooms all the way out to make her look small and pathetic against the wall of the office. Marina Boratto enters, looks towards Fellini and stifles a smile. But the camera slowly zooms in to a large close-up of the woman passionately belting out the song, and Fellini muses, "Yes, I know it must seem sinful, cruel, but no, I am very fond of all these characters who are always chasing after me, following me from one film to another. They are all a little mad, I know that. They say they need me, but the truth is that I need them more. Their human qualities are rich, comic, and sometimes very moving."

Under these words, the camera pans rapidly from face to face of a new group of characters, with the accordion playing underneath. All of them are talking at once and smiling, from a monstrously fat bespectacled man with his arm around his little boy to a vain curly-haired girl spinning around the office in a little dance. It is a fresco of human absurdity and loveliness, and it is all Fellini has to say. At the end of *A Director's Notebook*, we see him back in action on the set, brash, jovial, and liberated.

Fellini Satyricon:
Color and the Classics

. . . .

20. Dreaming up Petronius   *Alberto Moravia*

The *Satyricon* of Petronius, as everyone knows, is an "open" novel, like
the novels of Henry Miller and Louis Ferdinand Céline, and unlike the
closed, tightly closed novels of Flaubert and Manzoni. An open novel—
a series of events and adventures without a beginning, middle, or end;
without a story, an internal structure. One could add whole chapters to
the *Satyricon*, as to the novels of Miller and Céline, and not damage it
at all. Unfortunately, in the *Satyricon's* case, whole chapters have disappeared, to its serious impairment, so that today we have only the
conclusion of a long, saga-like novel of antiquity. Yet the fact is that
even with these amputations the meaning of the work is not lost. But
just try to amputate part of a novel by Flaubert and see what you
have left.

What is the reason, though, for this open, serial construction, that
is, a novel told in episodes or segments barely tied together? We believe
that it was that Petronius, like Miller and Céline, reflects in his work a
world that is also "open"—the world of the Roman decadence, bereft
of rigorous social structures, respected moral conventions, reigning intellectual patterns; but, in recompense, rich in the unexpected, in novelties, absurdities, incongruences, and surprises. Closed novels reflect
closed milieux: salons, houses, palaces; open novels, like that of Petronius, the open milieu par excellence—the street. In the salons,
houses, and palaces we encounter the castes, classes, professional
groups; in the street, the crowd.

It is obvious that Petronius was only partly aware of all this. As the
refined and cultivated man of letters, he was in his novel simply using
. . . .

From *The New York Review of Books*, Vol. 14 (March 26, 1970), pp. 40-42.
Copyright © 1970 by NYREV, Inc. Reprinted by permission of the author
and his Agent, James Brown Associates, Inc. Translated from the Italian by
Raymond Rosenthal.

a genre that had by then most likely attained a definitive maturity: the satire or picaresque novel of ancient times; which in fact demanded that the narration pass with ease and agility, without order or logic, from episode to episode, from subject to subject, with the sole apparent aim of amusing the reader.

Of course, such a novel can only be comic. The scale of values lies shattered on the ground; not only does the writer not believe in anything but he also does not feel any yearning or desire to believe. Standing just above his contemptible characters, he establishes a distance of derision between himself and them, in the very way that the people in certain groups or, better, certain cliques mock each other, even cruelly and harshly, without the mockery implying any real moral differences.

Petronius is superior to his characters in only one respect: that of culture or, more precisely, good literature. It is understood that Petronius, even in his cynicism, always preserves his detached and scintillating gentility; but this aristocratic trait is chiefly expressed in the dazzling stylistic virtuosity which ranges with an incomparable adroitness and freedom from low tones to high, from the courtly to the dialectal, from dialogue to description, from magniloquence to realism, and so on. Hand in hand with this stylistic skill so ingrained in Petronius, the elegant rhetorician, goes a vast knowledge of life; and so we have psychological nuances set down with unerring aplomb. And, finally, Petronius is amusing because he is amused; this too is the quality of a great storyteller, and among all the most gracious.

There is no obscurity in the *Satyricon*, not in the personality of its author, its characters or events. There is so little that at least two of its main characters have become proverbial: Giton, the lewd and inconstant young man, and Trimalchio, the crude and vital host. To these two characters who have, so to speak, broken away from the novel's orbit and now roam the world, we must add Eumolpus, the pseudo-philosopher and small-time street *littérateur*, Encolpius and Ascyltus, Giton's two reckless and cynical vagabond lovers, and a mob of pimps, prostitutes, ladies of good society, tavern wenches, merchants, actors, and jugglers. Encolpius, Ascyltus, Giton, and Eumolpus proceed from one place to another, from one adventure to the next, just as happens in everyday life.

The sole connecting thread of all these comings and goings is Encolpius' sexual prowess, which, after having been above average for a good part of the novel, is suddenly destroyed by the enraged and vindictive God, Priapus. Which, if one thinks about it, is just and meaningful—in the absence of other values, sex obviously provides the most suitable ground for keeping an action going and giving it a dramatic appearance.

As we have already said, even though mutilated and incomplete, the *Satyricon* is a very clear novel not only in its plot and characters but also in respect to its author and his intentions. In short, we are not at all sure that certain famous contemporary novels will be equally clear some twenty centuries from now. As for the antiquity that forms the novel's background, this too is clear and well known. Indeed, no period of history has been so minutely studied, analyzed, and sounded to its depths as that of Latin classicism. So much so that the sum of these studies, researches, and analyses in the end exploded in that imposing cultural phenomenon, the Renaissance. But the renaissance or rebirth or resurrection of classical culture did not take place only once. It might be said that as a stone skips over the water producing at each contact ever smaller circles, there were several rebirths. Of course, always less profound, less committed, less trenchant. And the last Renaissance is precisely the one on which Federico Fellini draws in his movie version of Petronius' novel.

What is the nature of this last rebirth of antiquity? Here we find the explanation for the definition Fellini offered some time ago for his film—"the documentary of a dream." The last Renaissance is somewhat like a farewell. The contemporary world, by now definitively "projected" out of the humanistic orbit and definitely "entered" (in this case the space-age terms are appropriate) into the technological orbit, bids farewell to antiquity, which, if appearances can be trusted, will progressively fade away, so that in a few centuries it will be nothing but a shadow, like the archaic and prehistoric cultures today.

In what way does this very last of the Renaissances bid farewell to antiquity? That is, in what way does Fellini, in his movie, bid farewell to Petronius' world? He does so by finding it obscure, incomprehensible, half-obliterated, absurd, mysterious. In short, as one might say psychoanalytically, dreamlike. After having been many different things in turn, antiquity has become a dream from which we feel we might awaken at any moment, so that at any moment it could be transformed from a dream to the memory of a dream. Do dreams have a meaning as do the events of one's waking life? Yes and no. In waking events the meaning is, finally, always accessible to our intuition; in the dream it is there but irretrievable. For Fellini antiquity is a dream whose meaning has been lost, while still being there and making its presence felt at all times.

But how does Fellini avoid, indeed ignore, the rich knowledge we have of antiquity? By one of the simplest of operations, to which more-over, he is led by the specific nature of his craft: by overlooking all that has been "written" about antiquity and adhering to what has been "depicted." And he does this, first of all, because very little re-mains of ancient painting and that little fragmentary, incomplete, and therefore mysterious. In the second place, because in painting the legi-ble margin is, in contrast to literature, very limited; and so, basically, painting is by its nature an obscure and enigmatic art. Indeed one says, or rather used to say, of certain portraits: all that it lacks is the power of speech; but one has never said of a biography: all that it lacks are the colors. So Fellini, a perhaps unwitting participant in the last Renaissance, the one that bid farewell to antiquity, has shown a re-markable intuition, discarding what has been written and sticking to what has been painted.

All the qualities and the limitations, the very character of his film, derive from this intuition, which finds its confirmation in the last scene of *Satyricon*, when, according to the words of the scenario, the plot "fills with cracks, is blurred by the dust of the centuries, is trans-formed into an ancient faded fresco in Pompeian colors, where Encol-pius is only one of the many ambiguously smiling faces which adorn the fresco."

So, through his film, Fellini takes leave of antiquity, treating it as a dream, documentable and documented but inexplicable. Fellini's intui-tion finds expression in various stylistic and technical procedures which it is worthwhile to trace and mention: To begin with, a strong aestheti-cism or, if one prefers, a marked aesthetic contemplation. The ancient world is not reconstructed in accordance with naturalistic convention, as, for example, in D'Annunzio's movie *Cabiria*; but rather contem-plated in those pictorial representations of itself which it has left be-hind. On the other hand, Fellinian aestheticism is packed with cultural references, ranging from surrealism to functional modernism, from cubism to abstract expressionism, from expressionism to pop. Without, of course, forgetting Pompeian art, Byzantine art, barbarian art, *l'art nègre*, and the archaics and primitives in general.

Fellini has never read a thing; we take him at his word; but he has seen and examined many things and from all of them he has drawn some inspiration. To use a generic term, it must finally be said that his *Satyricon* is an expressionist film. Less in the sense of historical expres-sionism than in that of a representation where subjectivity pushed to the borders of the unconscious signally prevails over objectivity.

Besides aestheticism, one of the most frequent devices which Fellini makes use of to create the atmosphere of the dream is that of dissociation, or an alienated and incoherent simultaneity. As the scenario says apropos of the theater of the actor Vernacchio: "The audience must not give a feeling of compactness but rather of disunion; in fact, each person behaves in a different way from the next . . . in short, somewhat the atmosphere of a lunatic asylum." Moreover, this dissociative process has been inspired by painting. Greek and Roman painting, first of all, but also Italian classic painting, from Giotto to Piero della Francesca, Paolo Uccello, Masaccio, and Giorgione.

In these models, the violence of the depicted episodes creates a mysterious contrast to the serenity and indifference of many of the characters witnessing them. Fellini has pushed this procedure, which in classical painting was motivated by a quest for harmony and contemplative calm, in a romantic, surrealistic direction, halfway between de Chirico's metaphysics and Magritte's surrealism. But above all he has exasperated it to the utmost. The alienating dissociation which in classical painting is a marginal element, in *Satyricon* invades the representation. There is no longer a distinction between the drama and the dream. All is dream.

But if *Satyricon* were only, as Fellini has said, the documentary of a dream, it would merely amount to the modern illustration of an ancient text. Yet we have said that this is a basically expressionist film. By this we mean that *Satyricon* has a specific content, that Fellini has expressed in it not only his own taste but also the least explicit part of himself. Now what is this content which makes *Satyricon* a movie in which imagination is so much more significant than illustration?

The content, obviously, is the usual one in Fellini, which he has already expressed in his "realistic" movies; but precisely because his *Satyricon* is not a realistic movie, this time Fellini seems to have drawn more directly and profoundly on his unconscious. This content is, broadly speaking, religious. In the sense that Fellini, at the very moment that he pronounces an elegiac farewell to antiquity, situates and defines in it, almost despite himself, all of his nostalgia and metaphysical terrors. In an interview we had with him not long ago we said that Fellini's conception of antiquity was essentially not so different from that of the epoch immediately following antiquity, i.e., the high Christian and barbaric Middle Ages. An age which, fearing antiquity and having just issued out of it, was compelled to view it from a distance.

We also said that, whereas for the humanists of the Renaissance antiquity was the ideal age of luminous and perfect forms, for Fellini, as for the primitives of the not yet humanistic Middle Ages, antiquity was the era of a fallen and corrupt nature, teeming with physical and moral monsters, not yet redeemed and saved. Now having seen the completed film, we can only confirm that first judgment. Antiquity is seen by Fellini as the decadence and death of the life of the senses, a period which was perhaps at one time happy, innocent, and pure; but today is unhappy, corrupt, impure, ugly, and saturated with death.

To understand Fellini's special kind of religiosity, we believe that the greatest importance must be attributed to his manifest preference for the monstrous and impure. In *Satyricon* the monstrous and impure regularly take the place of the ugly and beautiful. The monsters are the old, the sick, the infirm, the unattractive; the impure, the young and the beautiful. Monsters populate the fantastic backgrounds of the brothels, the Subbura, Trimalchio's house, the garden of delights (we cite at random three important episodes); against these backgrounds are set the "impure" beauties of Giton, Encolpius, Ascyltus, and many other "beautiful" characters.

The hermaphrodite is not by chance both monstrous and young, beautiful and impure. One does not have to make a great effort of the imagination to trace back this preference for the monstrous and impure to a fascinated and funereal moralism. Fellini is attracted by antiquity precisely because he sees it as corrupt and moribund. There is in him a decadent who is magnetized by the most celebrated and most historic of all decadences. And Fellini's double and triple decadence is punctually confirmed by the film's images. Nights, twilights, dawns, never full day; dark, inflamed, or murky air, never clear and bright; hallways, blind alleys, caves, courtyards, cells, never open spaces; natural settings that are deserted, squalid, arid, craggy, denuded, never inviting; clothes in washed-out colors that go from black to brown and red and suggest dust and mud, never luminous, sharp tints; finally, even the water transformed into something sordid: the subterranean flow of a sewer.

This theatrical representation varies in quality from episode to episode. It runs from picturesque, decorative, stagy backgrounds to subtle suggestions typical of the art of painting. Fellini seems freer and more capricious in the parts where he gets further away from Petronius' novel; this defines quite adequately both Fellini and Petronius.

To sum up, the difference between the author of the novel and that of the film is that the first, with all of his Gadda-like linguistic and stylistic refinement, is nevertheless always a realist; while the second is not and above all, at least in this movie, does not want to be one.

Fellini's invention flows freely in the episode of the death of the emperor and in that of the labyrinth; whereas it appears more circumspect and restrained in the scene of Trimalchio's banquet. But all in all Fellini seems, in this his most recent movie, to have completely surmounted the personal crisis which, objectified and transformed into a subject in 8½, almost got out of hand in *Juliet of the Spirits*. This is eloquently proven by his dilation of Petronius' text. In fact, not only has Fellini succeeded in interpreting the Latin text in his own fashion but he has expanded it to include his own ideas about life and death.

At this point, to indicate the movie's limitations would not be very difficult. As always happens in the work of mature artists such as Fellini, they are to be found in the very character of the work. The rhetoric of the original text has been transformed into an aesthetic contemplation and this produces a static quality in the film. Versatile and raffish realism, wavering between satire and parody, has been supplanted by a monumental and mortuary epic tone. With the oars of his galleys suspended in the air, Fellini revives for us the lances of the battle in Eisenstein's *Alexander Nevsky*; but he does not recapture the real homosexual passion of Encolpius and Ascyltus for Giton that lives beneath the fiction. In Petronius there is psychology, even when changed into eloquence; in the movie it is sacrificed to the dreamlike effect.

Is there a psychology of dreams? Yes, there is, but it is not that of the characters who appear in the dream but rather that of us who dream about them. Only in two episodes does Fellini show himself intent on representing a reality that is not dreamlike: the episode of Trimalchio and that of the villa of the suicides. These are two contrasting and equally significant situations. The rich man who vulgarly and unrestrainedly enjoys his wealth; and the rich man who not only rejects wealth but also life—in this contrast one might say the ultimate meaning of the film is expressed. That is, a feral attachment to life which, at any moment, can change into disgust, denial, and a desire for death.

This account of *Satyricon* would not be complete without some mention not so much of the art of the actors as of the use that has been made of their art. It is clear that in order to make the documentary of a dream it is crucial that the actors should not become characters but must remain apparitions; and this is what happens through much of the film. Martin Potter as Encolpius, Hiram Keller as Ascyltus, Salvo Randone as Eumolpus, Max Born as Giton, Mario Romagnoli as Trimalchio, Magali Noël as Trimalchio's wife, together with all the other

actors who appear in the film, have been fundamentally changed by
Fellini into strongly expressive and ambiguous images, precisely as if
they were figures in a fresco. So one might say that their task as inter-
preters consists principally in pretending to be just that—painted images. And that this is extremely difficult, indeed an authentic feat on
the part of the actors, can be seen when we compare the truly
"painted" apparition of Salvo Randone, for example, with the realistic
and not at all "painted" interpretations of some of the minor actors.

. . . .

21. Color, Growth, and Evolution   *Stephen Snyder*
in *Fellini Satyricon*

There is a sequence of frames in *Satyricon*'s sub-story of the Widow of
Ephesus whose metaphoric implications reach beyond the immediate
context. As a guard attempts to seduce the Widow from her husband's
corpse to his own living body, a pronounced contrast in the skin complexions of guard and Widow becomes apparent. Against the ruddy,
life-like hues of the guard's skin, the Widow's face manifests a chalky,
stark whiteness. Yet as we watch, a miracle of pigmentation occurs. The
Widow and the guard embrace, and when her image next appears on
the screen, the whiteness has been converted to a chromatic radiance,
bearing all the tones of a living human complexion. As the Widow
chooses to wed herself to life rather than death, her transition is marked
by a process of pigmentation. The significance of this process lies in
its relationship to the story of Encolpio. Like the Widow, he will
leave a rotting corpse (Eumolpus) and evolve from a state of whiteness into coloration—i.e., from an indistinct shadow on a white wall
at film's inception, to a brilliantly colored portrait at film's end.

If the parallel between the two stories had no more significance
than this, it would still represent a substantial artistic achievement.
But the parallel is important for much deeper reasons, specifically for
. . . .

From 1976 *Film Studies Annual*, eds. B. Lawton and J. Staiger (West Lafay-
ette, Indiana, Purdue Research Foundation, 1976), pp. 272-87. Copyright ©
1976 by Purdue Research Foundation. Reprinted by permission.

its suggestions that Fellini is dealing with the possibilities of color
usage in *Fellini Satyricon*, that he is exploiting color metaphorically to
tell Encolpio's story, and that in the most "cinematic" sense, he is
creating a film about the story of color. To the trained literary mind or
the cinematic initiate, this last claim may ring with all the irrelevance
often accorded the movies by academia. The story of color seems far
removed from the accepted concerns of narrative endeavor, human suffering and self-knowledge. Such in fact are the criticisms of the film
by such basically "literary" critics as Pauline Kael.[1] But the problem
with such criticisms is that they emerge from the assumption that the
main province of cinema is "character." My own study works from a
different assumption, that an equally valuable province of the movies
is movement and change; that, as such, one of the greatest stories they
have to tell is the story of possibility.[2] While "character" deals with
what is permanent in man, possibility deals with what is fluid: man's
ability to grow, to annihilate character, to actualize potentiality and,
in an existential sense, to continually create essence from existence.[3]
To move in time is to confront experience, and to assimilate this is to
grow and respond creatively to the challenge of living.

It is in terms of expanding possibility that the story of color finds
its significance in *Fellini Satyricon*. In the Widow's story, the relationship of color and possibility is easily seen; she chooses to continue
living by uniting with another life. Her choice bears with it the possibility of further creative activity and is rewarded with the restoration
of color to her complexion. In Encolpio's story the relationship of
color and possibility is more complex and is obscured because his choice
at film's end (to refuse the inheritance of Eumolpus in order to ven-
ture into the unknown) involves no explicit union with his sexual opposite. The viewer may recall that an interesting facet of the film's inception is the lack of the protagonist in the opening frame. What we
see is a rather whitish wall,[4] marked with indecipherable graffiti. As
the camera moves slowly down this wall, we hear the voice of Encolpio,
although we cannot see him. Taken by itself, of course, this image
means nothing; but in the context of the entire film, especially the
end in which a colored portrait of Encolpio stands forth on a whitish
wall, it can be seen as posing a cinematic and moral problem: the
transformation of shadow and disembodied "word" into a concrete
life-supporting system. More explicitly, this opening scene is a visual
statement of Encolpio's emptiness and dissociation from the concrete
world of nature, the closeness of the wall suggesting self-confinement

and restriction. Encolpio's own speech subtly suggests his very displacement: "The earth has not succeeded in dragging me down into the abyss and swallowing me! Nor has the sea swallowed me up, ready as she is to take even the innocent for herself."[5] Thus, the scene defines the nature of Encolpio's quest in the film as an acquisition of color and form and a restoration (particularly in light of his homosexuality) to a procreative, liberating process of nature. It can be seen that there is a dual requirement for Encolpio in actualizing life potential: the need for assimilating physicality and the need for releasing his procreative capacity, especially in the sense of his capacity for self-impelled growth.

Fellini has chosen to portray this dual life adventure in terms of two color patterns. The first, because it translates Encolpio's story into a process of assimilating nature, will be referred to as the "assimilative pattern." The second, because it reveals Encolpio's adventure to be, as well, one of self-impelled growth, will be termed the "generative pattern." The assimilative scheme works by an associative symbolism in which each of the four symbolic elements of nature is associated with a particular color: blue with water, red with fire, white with air, and brown with earth. Each of these colors is allowed a domination of the screen image for a certain span of the film, thus imposing a four-part division upon the story.

The generative scheme operates in a more "internal" way. Its significance results not from any color-concept association, but from the way in which its colors interact. This interaction involves the visual illusion of infinite color being generated from a basic three, the pigment primaries red, blue, and yellow. The process of generation, here, creates a metaphor of Encolpio's emerging power of imagination, the power to actualize possibility and thus provide a release from the restrictions of a sterile, immobile world. The primary complication with this generative scheme is that it is repeated three times during the film, thus imposing a three-part division upon the narrative. As these divisions have their own thematic coherence, they should not be confused with those in the four-part assimilative scheme. Each system maintains its integrity in operating in contingency with the other. The assimilative pattern works by imposing a single color dominance over large sections of the movie; the generative scheme operates within this framework, occasionally exploiting the assimilative colors, but usually in a position of visual subordination. The diagram below provides a rough picture of how the two patterns overlap.

	blue	red	white air	brown	
	water	fire	Licha to	earth	
	Vernacchio	Trimalchio	Hermaphro-	Festival to	
Assimilative	/	/	/ dite	/ Oenothea	/
Generative	/ opening to Widow's story.		/ Color process /	Color process /	
	primaries to all color.		repeated.	repeated.	

Because the assimilative scheme is easier to see and requires less introduction, it is taken up first. A description of the generative pattern follows this discussion and afterward an attempt to clarify the rationale of the three-part division it provides the narrative.

I

The first section of clear color dominance begins with Encolpio's entry into the public baths in search of Ascyltus. Here, and more spectacularly in Vernacchio's theatre, the screen image is suffused with a bluish, aquamarine tint. While the means of achieving this suffusion is beyond the pale of the discussion here, we may note that there are several possible methods: the use of a color filter, a particular color film stock, or special lights on the set. Eileen Hughes, in her book on the making of the film, notes on several occasions Fellini's concern with set lighting to achieve special color effects.[6] Whatever the method, the resulting effect is a bluish cast on the frames in this portion of the film. This dominion of blueness does not mean that no other colors can be distinguished on the screen. Indeed, the fire in front of Vernacchio's stage is a brilliant red. But these other colors never achieve hegemony; they always appear in a predominantly blue field.

The most conclusive key to the element coordinate for this bluish cast occurs in the soundtrack. The viewer may recall that as Encolpio leads Gitone out of Vernacchio's theatre, unusual sound-effects may be heard which simulate the sound of drops falling into a pool of water. In fact, this portion of the soundtrack, combined with the aquamarine tint of the image, produces the fleeting sensation of the scene's submersion in water. In accordance with this sensation, we may recall that this "blue" section opens in the public baths, where water is, of course, of pronounced importance, and ends with the collapse of the

Satyricon: Vernacchio (Fanfulla) plays the lyre in the Roman theater sequence. (United Artists)

Insula Felicles, featuring the striking shot of a white horse lifting itself from a pool of water, possibly suggesting an aquatic birth.

At this point in the movie the bluish prominence of the visual field is lifted and for a few moments, while Eumolpus guides Encolpio around an art museum, there is no single color dominating the screen. But as the two begin their journey toward Trimalchio's villa, a new color-element association emerges. Their path is marked by parallel lines of brilliantly burning bonfires, and the first appearance of Trimalchio occurs as an image of his head against a background of red haze and hundreds of burning candles. The viewer soon discovers the ascendancy of the element "fire" and the color "red" in Trimalchio's villa. The walls in this mansion are entirely red, the shade varying from crimson to darker rose. At the same time, the pervasive energies of fire are manifested in the steaming foods, the roasted pig, the perspiring faces, the huge oven fire in front of which Eumolpus wrestles with

some slaves, and, finally, the torches which light the path to Trimalchio's tomb.

As the story moves from Trimalchio's estate to Licha's ship, the red-
ness characteristic of the former world is replaced by a whiteness, which
at times becomes a lack of pigment entirely. The clothing worn by
Licha and Encolpio is essentially white, as is that of many crew members. All naturally occurring colors, like those of the ocean or the ship,
are kept at a low intensity both by apparent overexposures, which cause
two momentary bleachings of the screen image, and by a simulated
snow storm, which effects a literal white-out on the screen. The suicide
of Caesar, which follows Licha's own death, occurs against a stark white
cliff, and the first shot of the Villa of the Suicides is photographed
through a patch of white flowers. The whiteness extends to the clothing
of the inhabitants, their complexions and the pony which carries away
the children. There is a definite interruption in the pattern with the
entrance of Encolpio and Ascyltus, then a return to it in the desert
scene in which the nymphomaniac is encountered. Another interruption occurs at the shrine of the hermaphrodite (although "it" itself is
albino), but the pervasive whiteness returns as Encolpio and Ascyltus
fight for their lives with the thief, the scene which brings to a close
the "white" section. While these interruptions in the pattern are
prominent, they do not inhibit the general dominance of whiteness on
the visual field during this section of the story. They do, however, play
significant roles in the second "generative" color pattern and will be
treated in that discussion.

The symbolic element one would most logically expect to find associated with whiteness (or colorlessness) is air. Each of the four elements appears somewhere in this section of the film, but it is air, as
the perpetual sound of the wind, which is most pervasive. It is present
on Licha's ship as one of the major forces of propulsion and as the
power which brings the snow. It tears at the tent and clothes of the
travelers in the desert of the nymphomaniac. Its sound, in fact, obliter-
ates the dialogue at points. The presence of air is emphasized at the
Villa of the Suicides by the toy of the young child, a glider "airplane"
(see screenplay), and by the solemn, unearthly, "airy" behavior of the
patricians in their act of suicide. There is intermittent wind present as
the three thieves flee with the hermaphrodite, and "its" loss of breath
marks the end of this air/white section of the narrative.

The final color-element association in the assimilative color pattern
appears in the scene immediately following the slaying of the thief.
The initial image in this scene is that of Encolpio being driven down

a long dirt trough (see screenplay), literally into the earth. In the labyrinth scene which follows, some method of color control seems to be in
operation again, for the screen image is pervaded by a definite brown
hue, thus drawing the element earth and the color brown into association. The gear and complexion of the minotaur are brown, and, of
course, the prize waiting for Encolpio is a brown, symbolic, "earth
mother"; later, another brown earth mother awaits Encolpio in the
form of Oenothea's mountain of flesh.

In his encounter with Oenothea, Encolpio is brought into rapid contact with the four symbolic elements. He journeys across a lake for copu-
lation with an earth mother beside a roaring fire, and leaves on the
tail of a wind which threatens to tear him from the corpse of his dead
friend, Ascyltus. In Oenothea's "womb-like" house, he has experienced
a birth; in the symbolism of the assimilative color pattern, Encolpio
has been made whole, given substance, and united with natural processes of change. Accordingly, he chooses to follow the promptings of
these processes, as suggested by the moving clouds and water, and to
push out into the unexplored world, rather than consume the corpse
and inheritance of Eumolpus which would tie him to an immobile,
dying world.

II

In moving to a discussion of the generative color pattern, it must be
stressed that this pattern, unlike the assimilative, is not based on a color
allegory, that is, a symbolism in which each color stands for a value
outside itself. Indeed, the metaphoric quality of this pattern arises
from its activity, which I refer to as color generation, or the production
of color from color. The overlapping of the two patterns invites confusion insofar as two of the colors of the assimilative pattern, red and
blue, figure also in the generative pattern. What the reader must understand is simply that these two colors operate in two ways (at least) at
the same time. The appearance of one in the generative pattern does
not negate its value in the assimilative scheme. As I hope to make
clear, this double symbolism of red and blue can occur primarily because the generative process functions, with two exceptions, within the
assimilative. That is, while certain portions of the film are dominated
by a particular shade, like brown, other colors occur subordinately
within the visual field which work toward metaphoric ends.

The generative color scheme operates as a result of the very nature of color pigments. The three pigments which form the basis of the generative scheme are red, yellow, and blue. These are called subtractive colors, or pigment primaries, and should not be confused with the so-called additive primaries (green, red, and blue). While the result of combining the subtractive primaries is black (the color of Encolpio's tunic at the film's end), the result of combining the additives is white. As I have argued elsewhere, the use of these additive primaries is part of the color scheme in Fellini's first major color production, *Juliet of the Spirits*, a film which might be seen as the quest for light.[7] In a sense, *Satyricon*, Fellini's first movie after *Juliet*, begins where the latter leaves off: in liberated "white" light. But in *Satyricon*, as the transformation from white wall to colored image suggests, Fellini is concerned not with the story of light so much as he is with the story of color pigments.

In such a story the three subtractive primaries—red, blue, and yellow—must play an important role, for they not only combine to produce the all-absorbing pigment, black, but are the ultimate derivatives of all natural color in the world. The human eye, in fact, has receptors only for these basic three.[8] It creates the colors we see by combining the pigment primaries. To possess these primaries is to possess all color. Hence, on a literal level, color production is requisite for the human pigmentation which is one end of the film's overall quest. But on a more symbolic level, the ability of the basic three pigments to generate countless others provides a willing director with a natural metaphor of "possibility," the concept, as I stated earlier, which seems the most central to the film. To manipulate the occurrence of color on the screen so as to suggest a process of growth and generative activity is, for Fellini, to solve what he has noted, in a famous statement, as the essential problem in the use of color: "Making films in color, is, I believe, an impossible operation; cinema is movement, color immobility; to try to blend these two artistic expressions is a desperate ambition."[9]

In *Satyricon*, however, Fellini's particular formula for "mobilizing" color is to open the film in black and white, introduce the three subtractive primaries, allow a slow flowering of those colors capable of being generated from the interaction of the three subtractives, then conclude the process at some point in the film with an image of harmonized natural color. Color thus begets color and in the process metaphorically begets Encolpio, portraying his growth as an increasing actualization of potential.

The complications in perceiving this "formula" of color generation are its contingency to the assimilative pattern and the fact that Fellini has chosen to enact this process three times in the film. Hence, the film has a three-part generative pattern whose sections overlap those of the assimilative pattern. These sections may be denoted as follows: first, the episodes from the opening through Trimalchio's party; second, those from the adventure on Licha's ship through the theft of the hermaphrodite; and third, those from the Festival of Mirth through Encolpio's departure. While each of these sections in the generative trinary scheme has a thematic differentiation from the others, I would like to leave the discussion of this thematic significance until the patterns themselves have been documented. The reader will find the photographs contained in the screenplay helpful in following the descriptions.[10]

As noted in the discussion of the assimilative scheme, *Fellini Satyricon* begins in black and white rather than color. The credits are given thusly, and the first screen image is Encolpio's shadow on a chalky wall. Encolpio's entrance into the visual field (by a self-generated leap) signals the introduction of color in the easily discernible yellow of his tunic. His shawl is black and his skin, due to whatever lighting effect, has a pallid cast. Much less obviously, there is a minute amount of red present in his lips and a trace of blue in his eyes. While this "chromatic birth" is not ostensibly propitious, it contains infinite potential by virtue of the presence of the three subtractive primaries.

Although this "primary" color scheme might seem unintentional at such an early point in the film, its significance becomes clear as the adventure proceeds. Encolpio, wearing his yellow tunic, enters the public bath in search of Ascyltus. At this point the bluish quality of the image, discussed in the assimilative pattern, becomes pronounced. Since the loin cloth of Ascyltus is dull red, the only colors as yet distinct are the pigment primaries red, blue, and yellow.

As the story moves to Vernacchio's theatre, these three pigments are intensified, while other colors are still unpronounced. Vernacchio's costume features a muted blue shirt with a brighter yellow tail. The garments of the audience, however, are much brighter than those of Vernacchio. As Encolpio pleads for the return of Gitone, the camera focuses on three patricians whose togas are, respectively, solid red, solid yellow, and solid blue. As the camera pans the cavernous theatre, it discovers repetitions of this same color pattern in the clothes of the audience, the only exceptions being an occasional "colorless" white or black garment. The magistrate who chides Vernacchio wears a bright red scarf (over a black toga), while his immediate neighbors wear robes of solid red, blue, or yellow. The fire in front of Vernacchio's stage is an intense pure red, as is the blood which flows from the stump of the amputee. The false hand placed over that stump, in a parody of regeneration, is a gold-yellow color.

The relatively weak intensity of the pale blue and yellow of Vernacchio's costume suggests a dissipation rather than expansion of life potential. As much is borne out when he removes his head covering. Revealed beneath his mask is an anemic face and a shock of black hair. For Vernacchio the black-white opposition is not a demarcation point for growth, as it is for Encolpio, but a permanent condition. Confined by his materialism and total subservience to codified thought, he is incapable of growth. Hence, he quails before the chastisements of a magistrate, following a crude display of power: "Vernacchio crumbles . . . he holds out his arms to the magistrate like a poor beggar" (p. 110).

As the narrative proceeds out of Vernacchio's theatre, its colors become more diverse and plentiful. The particular colors being added to the screen in this process of expansion are precisely those produced by the interaction of the pigment primaries: orange (from yellow and red), green (from yellow and blue) and purple (from blue and red). While each of these added colors could conceivably have an allegorical or symbolic significance of its own, its importance in the generative scheme inheres in the image of increasing possibility to which it contributes.

As Encolpio and Gitone flee the theatre and enter a brothel, not only are the three pigment primaries visible—the wall is red, the doorframe yellow, the interior partially blue—but a secondary pigment as well, in the green staircase leading to the main room (see screenplay). This marks the first pronounced occurrence of a secondary color in the film, for until the collapse of the Insula Felicles such colors appear sparsely. While occasional traces of orange, green, or purple appear in the gallery of prostitutes, thieves, patricians, and diners which Encolpio and Gitone pass en route to Encolpio's room in the first scene, the predominant colors are still the pigment primaries and they tend to occur in balanced, obvious patterns (as for example in the solid red, blue, or yellow robes of the three prostitutes who call out to the youths). But after the collapse of the Insula and the departure of Gitone, the screen registers a momentary burst of the secondary colors, in balance with the primaries, during the scene at the art museum. Some tourists wear purple, several paintings are predominantly orange, and several frames are green.

As the story proceeds to the feast of Trimalchio these secondary colors are allowed greater prominence and intensity; near the end of the episode some of the tertiary colors of brown and maroon become visible in traces. As we enter Trimalchio's villa we discover first, of course, a predominance of red (in accordance with its "fire" symbolism in the assimilative scheme). But within the red framework there is a garish intensification of orange, purple, and green. The screenplay provides a convenient reference here; in one photograph, for example, we can see several of the guests bedecked in orange and green against the background of a red wall. Trimalchio himself wears a deep purple tunic and his two "boys" wear shades of orange, green, and yellow. Interspersed among these secondary colors are the pigment primaries. Encolpio's tunic is now blue as is the dress of Tryphaena, the woman who will soon aid in his capture. To sense the degree to which color has been intensified and generated in the film, one need only compare these latter images with those of the beginning part of the film. The "color story" has progressed from a near lack of color, through a stage of predominant blue, to a flowering (under the aegis of the dominant red) of pigment primaries and secondaries.

On a literal level, this chromatic expansion is an increase of realized possibility; on a metaphoric level, it provides a reflection of Encolpio's own growing potential. This sense of greater potential is thematically enhanced by the art gallery episode in which, for the first time, the viewer is offered a vision of real artistic achievement. To move from the banal parodies of drama enacted on Vernacchio's stage to the mythical representations in the gallery is to enter a world of greater imaginative potency. Even Trimalchio's world, though greatly taken up with plagiarism and vulgarity, contains elements of artistic achievement, as in the classical Greek poetry recited during supper. While all these poems and artifacts are achievements of the past, they have the power to provoke Encolpio's imagination: "Ganymede . . . Narcissus: Apollo turned the young man's spirit into a flower. . . . All the myths speak to us of love, of unparalleled couplings" (p. 124).

The first pattern of color generation reaches a climax in the story of the Widow of Ephesus. Here a natural, living human tonality is achieved, providing not only a perfect end to the first segment of generation but a metaphor of the color story of the movie. Following this scene the film recedes into its primal black and white, where it remains for some time before repeating the process of color generation again.

Encolpio leaves Trimalchio's villa in the dead of night. He awakens in the glare of a sun whose intensity bleaches most of the color from the image. He is shuttled into the dark hold of Licha's ship, in which color is undeterminable, and appears on deck, sometime later, in a white garment decorated with one black stripe. Licha's world is characterized by its polarization of light and dark. His own clothes tend to be either white or black, and when color does make an appearance its quality is drastically inhibited by the intensity of the light or by the apparent overexposures. Licha's decapitation is followed by a montage series in which color is still nearly absent. A youthful Caesar in a white gown commits suicide against a white cliff (there is some primary red from his blood), a new Caesar is proclaimed, and at a quiet, white villa a patrician and his wife begin to commit suicide.

The only discernible colors at the Villa of the Suicides are those of the utensils of the last meal which husband and wife share. These are, in their faintness, the basic pigment primaries. Encolpio and Ascyltus soon enter the mansion, but between the pervasive whiteness and the scenes shot in the dark corridors, there is little discernible color until a large geometrical design becomes visible on the wall behind the action. With the exception of some black lines on the design, its principle colors are the pigment primaries: red, blue, and yellow.

During this episode and the one that follows with the nymphomaniac the colors on the screen are by and large limited to the red loin cloths worn by Encolpio and Ascyltus, an occasional patch of blue sky, and an occasional patch of yellow in a garment. However, as the story moves into the shrine of the hermaphrodite, a flowering of secondary colors occurs not unlike that at Trimalchio's Villa (see the screenplay). Brilliant shades of orange, green, and purple flourish alongside the pigment primaries. In answer to the question of how Encolpio's own life embodies a growing realization of possibility, we may note, first, that the very concept of stealing the hermaphrodite, unsavory as it is, represents a real attempt to capitalize on "its" money-earning potential, and second, that it is in this section of the movie that Encolpio's erotic instincts have found an object of attraction in a member of the opposite sex, the African girl at the Villa of the Suicides.

As Encolpio, Ascyltus, and the thief attempt to flee with the hermaphrodite, the background against which they move flourishes with non-abstract, natural colors: olive, brown, beige, and azure. Once again, we arrive at harmonized natural color through a process of self-impelled color generation.

The third and final section of the generative pattern begins with Encolpio's fall down the dirt trough into the labyrinth of the Minotaur.

In this section the pattern is partially marred by the omnipresence of the brownish hue (in the "earth" section of the assimilative pattern) over the image. Nevertheless, within this framework we find the same process in operation. Instead of beginning from a black-white reduction as in the other cases, the generative pattern here begins from a brown-white basis.

There are practically no colors discernible in this episode (except brown and white) until Encolpio has passed through the labyrinth, when the red of his torn cloth again becomes visible and the pool of water surrounding Ariadne reveals a deep blue. The final pigment primary is introduced with the entrance of Eumolpus, but here a strange visual trick occurs. The other color in his robe is primary blue, but as Eumolpus moves and causes the colors to receive the light differently, the blue and yellow combine in flashes of green. Another secondary color, purple, is discovered as the camera focuses on the departing master of ceremonies.

Essentially, as in the previous two patterns of generation, the colors intensify and multiply as the story continues. At the Garden of Delights, where Encolpio has gone for treatment of impotency, both the subtractive primaries and the secondary colors are garishly exhibited in the stylized figures on the wall and in the clothing of the cavorting girls. The final state of harmonized color is achieved only after Encolpio emerges from the hovel of Oenothea. He has been not only sexually restored but, in effect, transformed into a free agent, no longer in subjugation to figures of spiritual or political authority.

The colors of Encolpio's own clothing during *Fellini Satyricon* have been, variously, the subtractive primaries. His initial garment is a yellow tunic, which is replaced by a blue one at Trimalchio's Villa; after wearing a black and white tunic on Licha's ship, he dons a reddish loin cloth which serves him until his trip to Oenothea's hovel. When he emerges, his tunic is a dark, heavily pigmented color, not necessarily black, but something suggesting the integration of the subtractive pigments, something capable of absorbing light. In the assimilative pattern, the garment suggests the completion of his quest of assimilation; in the generative pattern, it suggests his possession of all the primary pigments and thereby the possibility of infinite creation. By contrast, Encolpio's friends wear no more than two colors in the course of the film. Ascyltus is limited only to red, Gitone to white, and Eumolpus, perhaps indicative of his partial creative power, yellow and blue. Although he wears a blackish robe at Trimalchio's villa, Eumolpus never acquires the third essential primary, red.

III

While the very existence of the three-part division in the generative pattern is intriguing from a technical standpoint, it invites questions and explorations of its rationale. It will be helpful, in order to clarify the operation of the pattern, to consider *Fellini Satyricon* in the light of another film completed and released in the same year, Kubrick's *2001: A Space Odyssey.*

Misunderstood at first, *2001* has now become generally recognized as a story of human evolution, an evolution consisting of three phases.[11] The interpretation of the first two phases has troubled no one. Man begins as an animal at the mercy of anything more physically powerful than himself. This situation is altered by the ingression of the reflective, abstract powers of thought into his life. One ape connects the potential of a bone to smash a dead skull to its ability to destroy a living one. Abstract logic is born, and, as a mark of its entry into history, a rectangular cobalt slab appears.

Phase Two of the movie begins at the point where man's adventure with abstract thought has reached its limit. The environment is characterized by a certain sterility and the ascension of the word over the visual powers. No one is particularly interested in seeing but Dave Bowman, the one crewman who will carry man's evolutionary adventure beyond the bounds of reason. The perfect rational mind, of course, is the computer Hal, whose destructive actions demonstrate the relationship between abstract throught and egoism. Dave Bowman's feat is the dismemberment of this rational machine in order to go beyond the bounds marked by the Cobalt Slab on an adventure which ends with a birth of the eye, a symbol of human imagination. Thus, in Kubrick's vision, human growth involves a trinary system of physicality, intellect, and imagination.

While Fellini's concern with the trinary scheme of evolution is not as overt or exclusive as Kubrick's, it nevertheless informs the narrative structure of the film as divided by the generative color scheme. If indeed the film presents a story of the compounding actualization of possibility, it necessarily portrays individual growth as an evolutionary process. And, in fact, this sort of critical perception is not new in Fellini criticism.[12] Fellini's own views on human growth are helpful here:

> Thought encloses itself within limits, which are its negation, and beyond
> which it has a hard time going. One should use thought as a point of de-

parture for going beyond thought . . . To get out of a prison without inventing another prison.

But morals, the conventions of morality, the order that flows from them, all that is of another time.

It seems to me that freedom . . . is a conquest to be made, not a gift to be received.[13]

The novelty of this discussion is the analysis of the growth process into the three divisions more obviously seen in *2001*. And, of course, I have discussed *2001* not to imply its influence on *Fellini Satyricon*, but to provide a simplistic account of *one* dimension of *Fellini Satyricon*, a dimension which, because of the greater complicity of its content, is less salient than the similar dimension of *2001*.[14] Essentially, the divisions imposed upon the narrative by the generative process are the exact points of general transition in the evolutionary pattern.

If I am correct, then we would expect to find the first portion of the film defined by the generative pattern to be more exclusively concerned with man's sensual instincts than the latter two sections. And this is what we find—a great concern with man's digestive, bodily, animal functions and far less concern with his rational or imaginative potential. Trimalchio's world revolves around the unbounded consumption of food. While he allows Greek poetry to be read during dinner, he neither comprehends it nor listens to it. His concern, as reflected in his sprawling body, is the acquisition of material substance in the forms of food, land, and slaves. His own corpulence is such that he is practically immobile, requiring two stretcher-bearers to move him from place to place. The concerns of Vernacchio are likewise bodily. His performance is a mélange of fly-eating, farting, and bodily assault. As his insect-like costume suggests, he operates primarily on the level of man's animal powers. The thrust of his obsession is a separation of the bodily from the intellectual functions. This is, I think, what is dramatized in Vernacchio's severance of the slave's hand. In a later section this act will be replaced by a decapitation, the reverse act of separating the center of intellect from the body. The one time in this "primal" section that a representative of man's reflective powers, the magistrate, rears his head, Vernacchio becomes totally submissive.

Encolpio's own motivation in this section is primarily the possession of an object of sexual attraction. Even the incipient ignition of his imagination in the art gallery is expressed verbally in sexual terms ("unparalleled couplings"). And in the largest sense, his pursuit of Gitone is the pursuit of an image of childhood, a resistance to natural change, the desire to live only in a childhood world of undifferentiated sensual activity. In addition, many of the scenes registered in the background as Encolpio and Gitone meander toward Encolpio's room, depict people performing their bodily acts. One man defecates, others offer their bodies, a family is shown eating dinner, a group of pederasts pass by (see screenplay, p. 112) and pigs and chickens are everpresent, much as they are at Trimalchio's. One of the many symbols of this vegetative physicality is the huge whore offered to the two youths on their tour of this area (see screenplay).

To move from the worlds of Vernacchio and Trimalchio into that of Licha is to move into a world in which the bodily functions have been integrated into a more complex scheme and subordinated to man's abstractive powers. Licha, of course, is a physically powerful man, but his physicality is far different from the sprawling, unchecked corpulence of Trimalchio or Vernacchio. Licha's physicality is outstanding precisely because it is the result of a controlling intellectual will. More important, for all its salience, it exists at the beck and call of the chief political functionary, Caesar. While Licha is certainly not an intellectual in the sense that Steiner is in *La Dolce Vita*, he operates as an extension of the law of the state, the product of man's rational, abstractive powers. And as the unavoidable feature of the law is the polarization of man's behavior into the realms of good and evil, light and dark, so there exists on his ship the most extreme polarization of light in the film. Each scene is either flooded with whiteness and light or obscured in darkness. The scenes on deck are literally light-saturated (as seen in the discussions of the assimilative color pattern), while those in the hold are submerged in darkness. One of the scenes in the screenplay, but cut from the film version distributed in the United States, shows Licha winning a wrestling match with a bear. While the scene is absent from our version of the film, its message, the triumph of abstract man over his animal nature, is still applicable to Licha. In our version he defeats, instead, a bestial-looking man. Licha's intellectual bias is revealed as well in his relationship with Encolpio. Unlike the homosexuals in the first section of the film, Licha is not content with the mere pleasure and possession of Encolpio; he desires a public wedding. His drive is to have their relationship formalized in law and word. If indeed, Encolpio can be seen as undergoing changes of growth and personal evolution, his wedding to Licha suggests, allegorically, his union with man's adult, reflective powers. In this regard it is significant that he becomes irreparably separated from Gitone at this wedding (the latter person drops entirely out of the film). It is also important that he not remain in this limited catagorized role. Unchecked by a greater unifying force, the thrust of the abstractive powers leads to a dissociation of intellectual from bodily power. This severance is the essential symbolic feature of Licha's decapitation. While the symbolic division inherent in Vernacchio's materialism is the separation of the body (as represented by the hand) from the head, the division inherent in the abstractive sphere is the separation of the head from the body. In regard to head orientation we may note that one of the bizarre features on his ship is a giant head suspended on deck (see screenplay).

Just as in the middle portion of *2001*, the powers of thought, principle, and codified action rule over this portion of *Fellini Satyricon*. No less than Licha, the family at the Villa of the Suicides is trapped in the divisive net of intellectualism. Their suicides dramatize, even more than Licha's life, the veneration of the intellect and the scorn of the body. They choose to negate life in favor of a principle of honorable action. While the scene may well be a tribute to Petronius, its more pathetic dimension is made abundantly clear by the immediate entry of Encolpio and Ascyltus into the house, two people whose healthy interest is not in assuming intellectual positions but in surviving, not in death but life. The whiteness of the death scene is fitting not only for its place in the assimilative pattern, but for its reminder of the Widow's story. Her choice was life over death, her reward a pigmentation.

Like the stories of the Suicides and Licha, each of the episodes in this "intellectual" section dramatizes a formalization of, or control over bodily instincts. Whereas the human libido was viewed in the "physical" portion of the trinary structure in its unrestrained tendency, it is now seen as something to be contained. Hence the nymphomaniac, unlike the sexual deviates of the earlier portion, must be tied down and restrained. This circumstance only seems to aggravate her condition; it certainly does not cure it. The aggressive tendency of the abstractive powers is suppression.

Encolpio's own imagination is somewhat in tow to the power of abstractions, as made manifest in the final episode in this "intellectual" section by a quest for a pristine source of "the word," a hermaphroditic oracle. The word is, after all, both an abstraction and an essential tool in abstract thinking. While the powers of the word have reached an apex in the figure of the oracle, those of the body are on the verge of disintegration. Though he contains two sexes, the hermaphrodite contains no capacity for life. He stands as the end of man's intellectual quest, if unrelieved by any higher unitive power: an immobile ghost-like figure who dies upon exposure to the sun. It is significant that this section of the film ends with a blow to the head, that which kills the thief whose idea it was to steal the hermaphrodite. In the allegory of the section, the intellectual powers, which have resulted in a certain degree of growth (Encolpio's ever greater freedom) must be dismantled in order for the life adventure to proceed.

The episode of the Festival of Mirth initiates the third phase of the trinary scene: the mythological, imaginative one. It coincides with the third repetition of the generative color pattern. Appropriately, the first image of Encolpio shows him being driven downward into the natural world rather than outward (where the tendencies of the disembodied intellect would carry him). It is not his power of strategic thought which helps him negotiate the labyrinth of Theseus, but his unpretentious will to live. His plea of being a student places him not in the class of intellectual men of abstractions but in that interested in learning. The Festival of Mirth is a fertility rite in which man's spiritual and sexual powers are supposed to be harmonized. But the imaginative power of this rite has been amputated and lost, and with it man's sexual powers. Hence the problem posed in this episode of the film is the regeneration not merely of Encolpio's sexual vitality but of human creative potential in general. Significantly, this regeneration can occur not in the conventional and rational Garden of Delights (the suggestion of the word-oriented Eumolpus) but only in a location where the powers of magic and imagination are sovereign. To reach the hut of Oenothea one must leave the known world behind. Ultimately even Ascyltus, who has certainly embodied two phases of the trinary scheme, sensuality and wit, must be left behind. In a sense, he is ostracized from the mythical experience of Encolpio precisely because of his inability to comprehend it. By Encolpio's humble acceptance of the demands of the creative forces in Oenothea's hovel, and by his submission to an essentially optical experience (the various mirages), he is made whole and is reborn into the world. As the shrunken skulls in Oenothea's hut indicate, this transformation is not accomplished through the agency of reason, but through something more powerful and more comprehensive. As her hands-on-head posture indicates, that power unifies the mental and physical poles of existence separated in the other phases of growth.[15]

The huge phallic symbol Encolpio encounters upon leaving Oenothea's hovel suggests not merely the restoration of his sexual powers but a quantum actualization of life potential. He has no interest in the inheritance of Eumolpus which could only tie him to a decayed, word-oriented, land culture. He moves instead toward the open sea and the wing-like ship, and represents, as he walks between the baffled intellectual Greek and the dark instinctual African, the myth-informed vitality of imagination capable of integrating the opposed powers represented by his companions into a new generative system.

NOTES

1. Pauline Kael, "Fellini's Mondo Trasho," in *Deeper Into Movies* (N.Y.: Bantam, 1973), pp. 160-66.
   "One gets the feeling that more excitement and energy go into casting than with what he does with his cast . . . there was little depth in *Juliet of the Spirits*, and there is none in this *Satyricon*. Perhaps Fellini thinks Christ had to come back before people could have souls, but, lacking emotional depth, the movie is so transient that elaborate episodes . . . barely leave a trace in the memory . . . and one hardly knows or cares who the leads are."
2. See W. R. Robinson, "The Movies as a Revolutionary Moral Force," *Contempora*, 6(1971), 15-20.
   "As a tool of the human imagination, their province is the creative act and creative possibility: it is in a word value. The stories told through them are not merely reflections of the human condition in our time but change in the making" (15).
3. Not in every Existentialist's sense, perhaps, but in Nietzsche's "man must overcome himself," or Sartre's "existence precedes essense." William Barrett's *Irrational Man* (N.Y.: Doubleday & Co., 1958) directs itself to these concerns.
4. There are two different prints of *Fellini Satyricon* at large in this country, one entirely in Italian with subtitles, the other partly in English. Moreover, there are some differences in color tones in each film. My sense of the wall's whiteness comes from the all-Italian version; in the other print one can detect more red. In either case, the color is of low enough intensity to suggest visual and moral anemia. In the published screenplay, *Fellini's Satyricon* (N.Y.: Ballantine, 1970), from which much has been altered in the prints released in the U.S., the wall is denoted as being red.
5. As quoted in the screenplay (see above), p. 93. All quotations from the dialogue are taken from the screenplay. [Note: some names cited in this article employ the Italian spellings, not the English translations; thus Encolpio or Licha refer to Encolpius and Lichas.—EDITOR]
6. Eileen Lanouette Hughes, *On the Set of "Fellini Satyricon,"* (N.Y.: William Morrow & Co., 1971), pp. 12-13.
7. "Color and Light in *Juliet of the Spirits*," an unpublished paper delivered at a Fellini seminar, March 15, 1975, at the University of Florida. The film begins at nighttime with the camera moving between two trees, one red, one green, toward a source of light. Throughout the film the light derivatives red, green, blue are emphasized, along with such abstractions as

orange and purple, in the clothing or the background of the characters. The film moves toward a unification of these fragments, which occurs when Juliet passes through the light saturated door near the end of the film into the realm of her psyche. When she re-emerges the world around her pulses with natural color and non-refracted light. Fellini says of this film, "color is part of the ideas, the concepts, in the same fashion as, in dream, red or green have this or that significance. The color participates not only in the language, but in the plot, itself, of the film." From *Interviews with Directors*, ed. by Andrew Sarris (N.Y.: Avon, 1967), p. 180.

8. Rudolf Arnheim, *Visual Thinking* (Berkeley: University of California Press, 1969), p. 30.

9. From *Interviews with Directors*, ed. Sarris (N.Y.: Avon, 1969), p. 179.

10. *Fellini's Satyricon*, ed. by Dario Zanelli (N.Y.: Ballantine, 1970).

11. See, for example, W. R. Robinson and Mary McDermott, "*2001* and the Literary Sensibility," *Georgia Review*, 26(1972), 21-37.

12. Armand J. Cauliez in speaking of *La Strada* says, "The film is like a chain of examples that all refer back to an underlying rule (the rule of the game; the rule of life). It is this rule that ultimately gives unity to Fellini's baroque creations; man must continually strive to master himself, to go beyond himself, to evolve. . . ." As quoted in Gilbert Salachas, *Federico Fellini* (Paris: Seghers, 1963), trans. Rosalie Siegel (N.Y.: Crown, 1969), p. 183.

Charles Pozzo di Borgo, in the same volume, notes, "Fellini's heroes live out their drama in a universe that seems to be summed up by the words *mobility* and *volubility*. Everything is in flux; nothing agrees to remain as it is; everything is in the act of becoming, especially the characters. . . ." p. 196.

See also, Roger Ortmayer, "Fellini's Journey: an Essay in Seeing," in *Three Directors*, ed. by James Wall (Grand Rapids, Michigan: Eerdmans, 1973), pp. 67-107.

13. *Interviews with Directors*, pp. 189, 190.

14. Fellini, himself, has compared his own film to Kubrick's: "The young, they just love and feel . . . and if there is a new cinema, pictures such as *2001*—and yes *Satyricon*—it is for them." As quoted in Pauline Kael's *Deeper Into Movies*, p. 165.

15. I am indebted for this observation to Philip Sawyer, "Hand and Head Imagery in *Fellini Satyricon*," an unpublished paper delivered at a Fellini seminar at the University of Florida, April 15, 1976.

22. Fellini's *I Clowns* and the Grotesque

William J. Free

Federico Fellini, discussing his film *I Clowns* in the French periodical *L'Arc*, attributes the disappearance of the clown to the sense of absurdity and disorder which pervades modern life. "The clown," he says, "was always the caricature of a well-established, ordered, peaceful society. But today all is temporary, disordered, grotesque. Who can still laugh at clowns? Hippies, politicians, the man in the street, all the world plays the clown, now."[1]

Fellini's explanation of the disappearance of clowns is appealing in its simplicity and stimulating in its suggestiveness, but it is hardly an adequate accounting for either the phenomenon of clowns or for the film which his remarks intend to illuminate. His instincts as an artist were surer when later in the same interview he proclaimed his distrust for logic and definitions and his "horror at the words of order by which we explain reality. . . ." The grotesque little man with the red nose epitomizes a reality which cannot be explicated in terms of the logical schemes, definitions, and labels which Fellini so distrusts. In that sense, the clown represents the modern world most of our literature describes—absurd, grotesque, meaningless, chaotic, suited only for the blackest of comedies or the most ironic of tragedies.

Yet Fellini is also right when he says that the clown has all but disappeared. The great circuses of Europe are closed or have become museums, and Fellini's film *I Clowns* has met with misunderstanding and solemn condemnation in many quarters. Paradoxically, the absurd clown may be an alien in the age of absurdity.

This paradox, central to Fellini's lifelong involvement with the clown, goes deep into his own work and into modern art. Baudelaire said that one of the artist's tasks is to expose those qualities of life lack-

From *Journal of Modern Literature*, Vol. 3 (1973), pp. 214-27. Reprinted by permission of *Journal of Modern Literature*.

ing in his age so that it might recover a sense of wholeness. To this purpose, he must be alienated from his society to gain perspective.[2] No one would seriously contend that the sense of the grotesque is lacking in the twentieth century. Kafka, Beckett, Genet, Ionesco, Albee, Flannery O'Connor, de Chirico, Ernst, Klee, Dali—to extend the list or belabor the point would be foolish. But, I contend, a major difference distinguishes Fellini's artistic vision and that of most twentieth-century artists. The grotesque, Modernist, or absurdist artists of our century almost unanimously find in the grotesque dark visions of the evil times upon which we have fallen. If their attitude is comic, theirs is the ironic laughter of despair—the laugh of a condemned man, of Meursault before the guillotine. Such laughter is the result of an art which, as J. L. Styan has pointed out, "is self-analytical and self-conscious. . . . At its worst, this may appear as a novelty for the sake of shocking us, an attempt to cover a deficiency by taking the audience off guard; at its best, it is a shaking of the bottle before the dose is administered, a skillfully controlled dramatic irony."[3]

Fellini's world is no less grotesque than that of his contemporaries. But, unlike most modern artists, he does not see a dialectic of despair. He administers no doses. His reaction to the absurd world is joyous, his laughter optimistic. It is a laughter much closer to the origins and original functions of the grotesque than is Beckett's or Kafka's decidedly post-Romantic vision.

The fallacy of Fellini's statement about clowns with which this paper began is that the clown functions not to parody a specific ordering of society but a more universal human need that changes superficially through the evolution of societies and their languages but not fundamentally. The clown is not the same thing as a hippie, and his relationship to the hippie can still be as fresh and revealing as it was to the more stable, ordered, and peaceful times of Fellini's nostalgia. The emptiness in modern life which Fellini the artist uncovers in *I Clowns* is its inability to see the clown and the world comically rather than solemnly and dialectically.

To trace in a paper of this length Fellini's concern with clowns in the corpus of his work would be impossible, for that concern is not only explicit in films such as *Variety Lights* and *Il Bidone*, but implicit in his characterization of Gelsomina in *La Strada*, Guido in *8½*, and Giulietta in *Juliet of the Spirits*. To say that the structure of clown shows is at the heart of most of his films would hardly be an exaggeration.

I will concentrate on his film *I Clowns* because it seems central to an understanding of his other works and because its apparent simplicity has misled many reviewers and viewers to misunderstand its form and tone. But before discussing the film, I shall trace the outline of a theory of the grotesque within which I think Fellini is working and which provides an alternative to the language of the grotesque as dark absurdity which dominates much of the art of our century.

The word *grotesque* originally designated a style of decorative art which flourished at the beginning of the Christian era and which came by the Renaissance to suggest, as Wolfgang Keyser states, "not only something playfully gay and carelessly fantastic, but also something ominous and sinister in the face of a world totally different from the familiar one—a world in which the reality of inanimate things is no longer separated from those of plants, animals, and human beings, and where the laws of statics, symmetry, and proportion are no longer valid."[4] The grotesque work of art evokes an estranged world which defies our powers to explain its coherence and order, one which disobeys the common sense laws of cause and effect which we have come to expect of reality. Wolfgang Keyser explains the popularity of grotesque art in the late middle ages and early Renaissance by claiming that it provides a third alternative to the two prevailing views of peasant life in art—the comic, as exemplified by the fabliau tradition, and the allegorical, as exemplified by the field of folk in *Piers Plowman*. The grotesque romanticizes common life by finding in it traces of the most extreme demonisms or manifestations of the disorder which contradicts the elaborate sense of orderliness which the medieval church and social structure fostered.[5] Thus the grotesque in art was originally a mode of rebellion in almost the same sense Baudelaire used in describing the alienated artist of his time as standing apart from the established explanation of life and pointing to an incompleteness of vision which was to him intolerable. The medieval world order failed to accept the chaotic and the inexplicable; rather, it integrated their manifestations into the order and in the process may have made the grotesque style necessary as a counterbalance.

But the grotesque was not a single vision. It had two faces, the fanciful and the sinister, perhaps best represented visually by the works of Pieter Brueghel and Hieronymus Bosch.

The grotesqueness of Brueghel's paintings comes about chiefly through two techniques, the amassing of detail and the distortion of the human face and figure. Many of his best-known paintings—*The Fall of Icarus*, *The Numbering of the People of Bethlehem*, most of the peasant paintings—teem with such an abundance of detail that the central action is lost amid the other figures or is relegated to an insignificant corner. The effect is to achieve a comic disproportion between the solemnity of the announced subject of the painting and the actual facts of the canvas. In *The Numbering of the People of Bethlehem*, Mary on the donkey is almost unnoticed amid the peasant activities of ice cutting, hog butchering, snow shoveling, and the crowd pressing around the census table. One of the central events of Christian history becomes lost in the everyday welter of life.

This irreverent attitude toward subject, combined with the distortion of perspective and the caricature of faces, gives Brueghel's canvases a comically grotesque look which conveys the artist's joy at contemplating the hurly-burly confusion of life which swallows up any attempt of history to impose meaning on it.

Bosch, on the other hand, presents a terrifying grotesque which expresses demonic forces through the mixing of distorted human, animal, and vegetable forms. In his series on the deadly sins, he represents lust by a horrifying collection of animals and humans—toads having intercourse with female lechers; lizards, dogs, and winged black figures torturing the genitals of various human figures. The effect of images such as these is to show an insanely demonic world peeping from beneath the order of life and threatening to destroy it in disgusting violence.

There is clearly an apocalyptic element in Bosch which is missing in Brueghel. The grotesqueness of Bosch arouses our fear and disgust much as does the plight of Gregor Samsa in Kafka's *Metamorphosis*. We feel powerless in a world bereft of all "reality," a world which we evoke in order to be awed at life's potential for chaos. We respond thoughtfully to Bosch's grotesques, not laughingly.

The clown belongs to Brueghel's world. The rapid multiplicity of his actions, the broad caricature of his mask, and his parody of human conduct seem analogous to the detail and comic emphasis of Brueghel's canvases. He is also, like most of Brueghel's subjects, a peasant. The word *clown* according to Pierre Bost, "signifies, in English, peasant or rustic. The clown, in the plays of the old English theatre, was a comic character analogous to the *gracioso* of Spanish comedy, to the Harlequin of Venetian farces, to the Neapolitan Pulcinello, to the German lout or fool or trickster who provoked the hearty laughter of our medieval ancestors. He portrays the rascal, the churl, always beaten, always the ridiculous, pigheaded fool, but not without a witty and astute companion."[6] In each of these traditions, stretching from the middle ages and beyond, the comic figure is a rustic, a member of the common class of men from whom grotesque art sprang.

The clown, wherever he appears, has three identifying traits: his mask and costume, his comic actions, and his rebellion. The mask and costume set him apart from the rest of mankind by making his physical appearance grotesque. The red, white, and black facial make-up and the exaggerated costume are the mark of his aesthetic distance from reality. They identify the style of comedy in which he is privileged to act.

The nature of his privilege lies in his ability to destroy our usual concept of reality by creating a world in which there exists a grotesque disparity between cause and effect. Willson Disher contends that the clown's jokes have in common the presence of "effort without result and result without effort—or, more generally, between much effort with little result and little effort with much result."[7]

The clown's actions defy either the cause and effect relationships which we have come to expect of reality or a special fictional sequence of cause and effect which the clown establishes in his act for the purpose of defying it at the climax. We see the first in the clown's enormous gun which shoots water or powder rather than bullets; the second, in Grock's trick of being repeatedly unable to catch his violin bow only to catch it absentmindedly when distracted by something else. In both cases, the clown rebels against the limitations of his reality in an action in which the disparity between his effort and its results is grotesquely exaggerated. The greater the distance between the effect and the effort, the more effective the comedy. When the context of the comic action involves a fundamental instinct or emotion, the effect is further enforced. This fact explains the popularity of violence in clown acts. When one clown plants an axe in the skull of another with no visible effect, the act is a rebellion against violent death, which all of us fear. The clown's action thus satisfies one of Wolfgang Keyser's definitions: "THE GROTESQUE IS A PLAY WITH THE ABSURD."[8]

The circus has captivated Fellini's imagination throughout his life, and from this fascination has come much of the reckless abandon and comic optimism which characterize both his fictional world and his method as a director. "Clowns," he says, "are the ambassadors of my profession. In my childhood they were the premiere image of disrespect."[9] *I Clowns* champions the need for disrespect in a solemn and all-too-respectable world.

Fellini has talked a great deal about *I Clowns* and has, consequently, planted many mistaken expectations. Most of the comments concern a White Clown-Auguste[10] game which Fellini likes to play with contemporary figures: "The white clown is the symbol of authority. He is your mother, or your teacher, or the nun who was always right. . . .

The *augusto* is yourself, doing all the things you'd like to do: making faces, shouting, rolling on the ground, throwing water at people."[11] This oversimplified dichotomizing of the two clown figures leads irresistably to the pairing of modern celebrities: white clowns are Pope Pius XII, Hitler, Freud, Visconti; Augustos are Pope John, Mussolini, Jung, Antonioni, Picasso, Einstein, and, one would assume, Fellini. The game is amusing, but it has caused many reviewers to condemn the film because it does not consistently develop the theme of Clown *vs.* Auguste and has even caused as astute a critic as Andrew Sarris, who sees through the game, to lament that "Fellini does not pursue the power implications of the Pierrot-Auguste relationship. Nor does he indicate the inner stress of Pierrot-Auguste on the artist. . . ."[12]

Two irrelevancies are involved here. First, the Clown-Auguste contrast does not necessarily imply as neat a psychological dialectic as Fellini's statements indicate, a fact that Fellini's own use of clown figures attests to. Adrian's *Ce rire qui vient du cirque* says merely that "the clown has for his principal role to make the most of the outrageous buffooneries of the Auguste by becoming the antithesis of his dress and his behavior."[13] The Clown and the Auguste are a contrasting pair. This contrast, to operate successfully, needs some sense of the normal against which the grotesque image appears aberrant. In caricature, the norm is our perceptual experience with the human face; we perceive the caricature as a distortion of recognizable features, but a distortion still. In the contrast of Clown and Auguste, the same perceptual structure operates. Clown becomes the norm against which Auguste is a comic contrast. A happy Auguste would be balanced by a sad Clown; a bungling Auguste by superior efficiency. But since both are clowns, *i.e.* masked and performing clownish actions, both are distortions of the norm of natural human conduct which the audience brings to the performance. A double vision is at work: Clown *vs.* Auguste, both against reality.

Fellini may have derived his psychological game from the historical development of the Clown-Auguste contrast which Adrian describes as epitomized by the team of Foottit and Chocolat: "the one, haughty, sarcastic, quick witted; the other, stupid looking, perpetually surprised and flabbergasted, always the loser. . . ."[14] Thus the Auguste has in a sense taken over the traditional role of the Clown as bungling and bewildered country bumpkin and the Clown, descendant of the mild-mannered Pierrot and the English rustic, has assumed a new identity as haughty, elegant, and somewhat effeminate. However, this seems to be a functional contrast for the purposes of the comedy, not the kind of psychological sheep and goats game which Fellini the thinker made of it.

The second irrelevancy comes from the assumption that Fellini the artist set out to make a documentary illustrating the Clown-Auguste contrast, a mistake which most reviewers seem to make. The mistake is understandable. *I Clowns* began as a documentary for Italian television, and Fellini has remarked that he researched the film rather than trusting to his own memory. But there the resemblance to the documentary stops. Fellini said in *L'Arc* that the film has the form "of the documentary of a dream. . . ." He further said that he did not pose questions about clowns as a journalist might, but "I have made the parody of an enquiry."[15] The form, rather than being documentary, is that of the personal essay. The subject is the imagination of Federico Fellini.

Two sets of clowns are involved in the film. The first consists of the famous European clowns of the past seventy years—Grock, Foottit and Chocolat, the Fratellinis, Rhum, Jim Guillon, Antonet, Charlie Rivel, Bario—most of them played by lesser clowns or by amateurs as is Fellini's custom in casting. The second set consists of Fellini's film crew engaged in the project of filming a documentary about clowns. The two sets of clowns perform a series of relationships to each other, one being Auguste to the other's Clown, then reversing roles and playing Clown to the other's Auguste. Through these relationships Fellini develops a set of interlocking themes which are central to his concerns as an artist.

Fellini's first theme is the ambiguity of the clown and the average man in our time. The film opens with Fellini as a boy being awakened by the raising of a circus tent. He goes the next day to the circus to witness a grotesque variety of comic acts—fire eaters, midgets, a knife thrower, two Amazonian wrestlers who comically perform to the "Flight of the Valkyries," a mermaid who swallows a goldfish and is loved by a moony-eyed midget, fetal Siamese twins pickled in a jar of brine, and clowns parodying the actions of the other performers, being cooked over a fire, clapping, hitting, clubbing, shooting, and abusing each other. When the boy cries, he is taken out.

Fellini explains that he was afraid because the clowns too much resembled the people of his village. There follows a remarkable sequence in which the clowns whom we have just been watching reappear as the residents of the village—an obscene giant named Big John; a crazy midget nun who spends half of her time in the convent, half in the asylum; the village idiot; a comic and self-important little stationmaster

who is the butt of everyone's practical jokes; a disabled war veteran who
faces the sea and listens to a woman recite Mussolini's speeches; a Fascist officer who absurdly goes round and round in his motorcycle side-
car; a crowd of village loafers. All are grotesque versions of humanity;
all are caricatures.

The structure of the episode, and of the film, involves a complex set
of multiple Clown-Auguste relationships (understood as just such a
functional contrast as described above). The villagers of Fellini's youth
and the clowns of the circus ring which open the film exist in a shifting
Clown-Auguste contrast. In one sense, the villagers provide the norm
of human conduct which the clowns parody. But in another sense the
clowns are a norm by which we recognize the grotesqueness of the villagers. The sinister and haughty Fascist officer is reduced to being
comic partly because we recognize him as the haughty clown who had
been the giver and receiver of blows in the circus ring. The stylized grotesque of the clown's performance in the ring becomes the norm
against which we can see the officer's absurdity, and the effect is to
render him laughable and no longer sinister. The same is true of the
Amazon wrestlers in the ring and the equally Amazonian wife who re-
trieves her husband from a tavern in a wheelbarrow. The village woman
becomes the model for the Amazon just as the Amazon becomes a
measure by which we can recognize the same grotesque masculine quality in the woman.

Beyond both levels, functioning as the eye of "reality," is Fellini.
The villagers are stylized and grotesque in their own right. The village
of Fellini's youth resembles a film version of an Italian village, a parody
of the world created at Cinecittà, and even of Fellini's own films.
There is certainly at least a superficial resemblance between Big John,
the obscene giant of the village, and Zampanò of *La Strada*. The insane antics of the village idiot Giudizio attacking the village is a parody
of every war movie ever made dealing with street fighting.

But the most obviously and broadly comic parody is the poolroom
scene. When the village loafers are shooting pool at the rear of a tavern, a middle-aged man dressed in 1920s driving coat, gloves, and gog-
gles enters with an overdressed blonde à la Marilyn Monroe to the
background music, "Fascination." The village dandy, every-woman's vision of Ramon Navarro in his youth, and the woman exchange soulful
looks, broken only by the obscene suggestion and gesture of Giudizio.
In this scene, the silent film, itself a grotesque measured against our
standard of reality and against the films of our time, becomes the
ground against which the actions of the villagers and the idea of the

film itself become comic. The villagers and the film parody each other. Neither is real—both are clowns.

At this point we become acutely aware of a third clown, Fellini himself, manipulating the act in the ring and emerging as the ultimate grotesque of the performance, the creator who rebels against absurdity by creating the ultimately absurd performance in which he himself is the star clown; for, if, as is frequently contended, the face of reality in the modern world is grotesque and absurd, and if that grotesqueness stems from man's alienation from himself, to rebel against the grotesqueness of reality is to attempt to create a unified and meaningful self. But the nature of the world makes such an attempt the act of a clown.

A second theme of the film records Fellini's quest for the clown—an abortive attempt to find reality and to film it. From the blank expressions of the camera man and sound man to the fumbling incompetence of the script girl Maya, the film crew is as clownly a collection of bumpkins as was ever assembled. Fellini also indulges in a luxurious series of self-parodies. He, the crew, and a half-dozen others emerge solemnly from a tiny Mini-Mote. The crew goes to the Fratellini home to see a rare documentary of the three Fratellinis only to discover that no one knows how to operate the projector. They bump heads and stumble over the machinery. The film falls on the floor rather than winding up on the takeup reel. It gets stuck in the projector and burns before our eyes in the helpless presence of the crew of famous filmmakers. Fellini goes to the French television studios to see the only film of Rhum's performance. The woman curator at the network calls him "Bellini." The Rhum film is so short and so technically unsatisfactory that we are left with a sense of having watched an illusion. Rhum is more ghostly and mysterious than ever. The film cannot capture reality. Posing Anita Ekberg before a cage of tigers at the Cirque Orfre parodies Fellini's use of Ekberg to parody the grotesque modern obsession with sex in *La Dolce Vita* and *Boccaccio 70*. The faces of the aged clowns visited in their mausoleum homes recall similar faces in 8½.

The parody also has its serious side. Fellini is a fool to attempt such a film. Seeking reality (the clown), he finds only old men, memories, faded photographs, and legends. No one cares any more. People have forgotten how to laugh. The question keeps recurring: why make a film about clowns? The circus no longer exists; the clown deserves to die. The attitude is best represented by the cab driver who never heard of Rhum: he doesn't go to the circus; he has other things to do. After the fiasco at the television station, Fellini concludes that perhaps the clown is indeed dead.

The third theme of the film presents the consequences of that conclusion. If the clown is dead, Fellini will resurrect him in a bizarre and fantastically imagined funeral played in the circus ring. Here is the creator at his most arrogant and clownish.

The funeral is an orgy of clown tricks. The eyes of one mourner spout water like a fountain. The widow has her bosom deflated with a pin. The white-bearded son of the deceased arrives joyfully to receive his legacy. The activity grows more and more frantic in an indescribable anthology of clown acts, as Fellini recreates some of the greatest moments of clowning in what seems to be the triumph of the artist's imagination over death.

But three ideas undercut and finally destroy the funeral. First, there is age. As the funeral procession starts to exit, it circles the ring more and more rapidly until it becomes a breakneck chase. Then, one by one, the aged clowns begin to drop out—one breathing hard and staring accusingly at the camera, another protesting sickness and unable to go on. Fellini can drive them only so far for the sake of his spectacle. They are old men; their day has really passed.

Secondly, there is the continued comic reminder that Fellini's clownish crew is making a film. This comes particularly in two bits of comedy. In one, an elaborate piece of special effects machinery repeatedly fails to work, to the growing irritation of the clowns, and then explodes unexpectedly, setting fire to the equipment around it. The structure of this action duplicates that of Grock's famous violin bow act. It parallels another fire set by the clowns in the ring to bring on the traditional clown fire company. In this way, the reality of film making and the fictional action being filmed are intermixed. The machine becomes the Auguste.

The second bit of comedy comes at the height of the mayhem. We cut to a shot of Fellini and a reporter sitting behind the lights. The reporter asks Fellini, what is the meaning of all this? Before Fellini can answer, a bucket thrown from the ring where it is part of the clown show falls over his head. Another falls over the reporter, silencing them both. The author of the spectacle is thus mocked by his own creation. The idea of "meaning" in the sense of an explication of the comic action into ideas is ridiculed.

But the most serious undercutting comes from the idea of death itself. The funeral reaches its most joyous climax with the resurrection of the deceased Auguste. The entire company of clowns breaks into a waltz as the reborn clown is lofted above the ring and swung back and forth through a sea of paper streamers which have descended from the ceiling. Then the tall, gaunt white clown dressed in tails and top hat who has been the driver of the hearse bows to the camera. In a series of quick cuts the clowns disappear. The reborn clown swinging above the ring becomes ensnarled in the streamers in a slow-motion shot which gives the impression of a clock running down.

The white clown in tails clearly represents death and order. He is the driver of the hearse, and in that role he has urged the funeral to its completion and has become the dignified foil of much of the clowning, particularly that of the horses. The six clown horses who pull the hearse are rebellious and lazy. In a vicious English accent he is constantly forcing them back into their places. His refrain, "Go back to your places," is directed not only to the horses but ultimately to Fellini and the whole spectacle. "Your place" is the solemn orderliness of the real world where the clown and all he represents are dead to the majority of people. His horses defy him, fart at him; but in the end his bow ends the show. The clowns have gone and Fellini's crew shuts down the lights and packs up its equipment.

All but one elderly clown. "I liked it," he tells us. He can't go home. Then he tells of his act with his partner Frou Frou. Frou Frou has pretended to be dead. The clown protests, searches for him in vain. Then he calls him on a trumpet.

Fellini concludes the film by reproducing this clown's act and in the process summarizes the film. In the empty circus, the two clowns, each at the top row on opposite sides of the arena, call to each other on the trumpet, playing in alternation phrases from "Ebb Tide." As they play, they descend the steps until they are in the ring. With a full orchestra playing behind them, they walk to the center of the ring in the spotlight and exit together. Just as they reach the door of the arena, they fade from the picture, leaving only the empty circus, all life gone from it now.

This ending is clearly reminiscent of the conclusion of 8½ in which Guido, having decided to try again to make order of his life and to make another film, assembles the people from his past, who are also characters in the film he is to make, in a circus ring, and leads them through a dance around the ring and out, leaving only the uniformed child version of himself in the spotlight to exit into the darkness playing a piccolo. Both scenes appear almost as codas. Both are grotesques verging on sentimentality. Both record the triumph of the creative imagination over the absurdity of the world.

In each of four feature films—8½, *Juliet of the Spirits*, *Satyricon*, *I Clowns*—Fellini has shown us characters almost destroyed by the gro-

The Clowns: The white clown and the Auguste clown are reconciled in the final sequence of the film. (Museum of Modern Art/Film Stills Archive)

tesqueness of their times but at the end saved by acceptance or exuberance. Guido, harried by the grotesqueness of the film business and by his own weakness, resolves to try again and turns the world into his private circus ring. Juliet, torn between the equally grotesque poles of her repressive childhood memories and the parodies of sexuality in Susy and in her own mother and sisters, learns to accept herself and both extremes and makes an optimistic new start. Encolpio's exuberance drives him through the grotesque violence and deformity of first-century Rome and, at the end, beyond to new adventures. Fellini the film maker triumphs over the death of the clown by accepting the absurd conditions of his own artistry.

In these films, I think, Fellini has widened the dimensions of the grotesque vision in contemporary art. He has rebelled against the darkness which is so pervasive that it is the established view of life for the modern artist. In this sense, Fellini functions as does Baudelaire's artist as the rebel who shows the deficiences of his time. Surveying the critical reaction to *I Clowns* makes that fact clear.

Vincent Canby has accused Fellini of creating in *I Clowns* another "too easy" metaphor for the breakdown and collapse of our culture.[16] Richard Schickel admits that an indifference to clowns and what they represent clouds his ability to criticize Fellini's film accurately.[17] Sylvie Pierre attacks the film because it does not create a meaningful dialectic study of the sociology of its subject and because it deteriorates into a thinly veiled revelation of Fellini's castration complex.[18]

These three critics, not the film, are metaphors of cultural failure. Each of them wants a film that treats life with deadly seriousness, that probes into the darker "meanings" of it all. Canby is particularly revealing. He condescends to admit that, if viewed on the medium of television, *I Clowns* might be entertaining enough; but on the movie screen it invites comparisons to Fellini's more serious films, or, less relevantly, to *Lear*, where the breakdown of one man is meaningful and powerful, in contrast to what he imagines is Fellini's metaphor for the collapse of our society. Canby's attitude resembles that of Fellini's taxi driver; he has more important things to do. He is paid to review serious movies.

The failure of these critics to understand what Fellini is about is an interesting commentary on the rigid consciousness of our time. Obsessed by seriousness and intellectualizing, we forget that the grotesque and the absurd can be a joy as well as a terror. If our culture is breaking down, it might be because we have forgotten how to laugh at ourselves. Such laughter is Fellini's strength.

Fellini's films function like Brueghel's paintings. Reality and the grotesque become completely merged in the illogicality and detail of the work of art, so that rather than being frightening or apocalyptic, as are the works of Bosch and most twentieth-century artists, the grotesque seems natural and acceptable. Acceptance is essential to a true

comic vision. In *I Clowns* Fellini accepts the comic grotesqueness of
his own obsession with clowns in a world in which the clown is dead
and the grotesqueness of the artist's attempt to create a meaningful
vision amid a grotesque and humorless reality. In the process of laughing at his own and the world's absurdity, he accomplishes the creative
task which he has accepted as impossible. At the end of the film, the
clown becomes apotheosized in a world beyond reality.

NOTES

1. "Fellini," *L'Arc*, No. 45, p. 69. This and subsequent translations from
   the French are mine.
2. "New Notes on Edgar Allan Poe," *Modern Continental Literary Criticism*, ed. O. B. Hardison, Jr. (New York, 1962), pp. 166-7.
3. *The Dark Comedy*, Second Edition (Cambridge, 1968), p. 289.
4. Wolfgang Keyser, *The Grotesque in Art and Literature*, tr. Ulrich
   Weisstein (Bloomington, Ind., 1963), p. 21.
5. Keyser, p. 35.
6. *Le Cirque et le Music Hall* (Paris, 1931), p. 81.
7. *Clowns and Pantomimes* (Boston, 1925), p. 22.
8. Keyser, p. 187.
9. *L'Arc*, No. 45, p. 68.
10. Quoted in *Life*, July 30, 1971, p. 60.
11. "Films in Focus," *The Village Voice*, July 1, 1971, p. 47.
12. (Bourg-la-Reine, 1969), p. 12.
13. *Ibid.*, p. 23.
14. The White Clown is historically the earliest of the clown figures, with
    roots in the Pierrot of Commedia dell'Arte and beyond. He is distinguished
    by his white powdered face and his ornate white costume. The Auguste
    came into being during the eighteenth century in England. He is the
    invention of the famous English clown Grimaldi. Twentieth-century
    Augustes are distinguished by the red nose, blackened face, large white
    eyes, and baggy, often trampish, costume.
15. *L'Arc*, No. 45, p. 69.
16. "Everybody Wants to Breakdown," New York *Times*, Sunday, June 20,
    1971, II. 1.
17. "Pagliacci plays Fellini," *Life*, July 9, 1971, p. 9.
18. "L'homme aux clowns," *Cahiers du cinéma*, No. 229 (May-June 1971),
    pp. 48-51.

3

. . . .

Themes and Techniques

23. Fellini's Imagery from *Variety* Lights to *Juliet of the Spirits* — *Gilbert Salachas*

THE POET

. . . It is frequently debated whether Fellini brought a valid or a suspect change to the Italian neorealist movement. Unfortunately, this discussion, tied as it is to many other social and esthetic considerations, has degenerated into a quarrel, and the quarrel into a polemic. An artist will never lack for attendant theorists to show him the way he must follow if he is not to lose his immortal soul. Whether Fellini was loyal to or a betrayer of neorealism is a very minor problem, neorealism itself being but an infinitely variable abstraction, a label encompassing contradictory definitions whose meaning depends on who uses the term. Like all creators, Fellini treats reality in his own fashion, that is, according to his heart. In Fellini's films human nature, and simply nature itself, intertwine with an imagination that remolds reality in terms of Fellini's secret rapport with the nature of things, and it is through this rapport that we recognize the originality of his inspiration.

At this point, it is appropriate to review the key elements in the Fellini landscape—a cinematographic landscape held to the dimensions of the screen, but made fertile by the incorporation of a sumptuous internal landscape. The realism of Fellini is the world recorded in black and white, together with certain haunting leitmotivs (not perforce extravagant ones) that rise up from the natural scene like so many incongruous landmarks. The experts find many adjectives to describe this particular realism: poetic, fantastic, expressionistic, lyrical, baroque, strange. . . . To simplify matters we shall call on only the vaguest of them all—poetic.

If Fellini's friends (and even his enemies) call him, although with a certain irony, *il poeta*, it is because they acknowledge in him a singular quality, unavailable to logical analysis, which an inspired artist, master

. . . .

From *Federico Fellini* by Gilbert Salachas, trans. Rosalie Siegel (New York: Crown Publishers, 1969), pp. 39-60. © 1963 by Éditions Seghers, Paris. Reprinted by permission of Crown Publishers, Inc. and Georges Borchardt, Inc. The material here reprinted (editor's title) is from the sections entitled "The Poet" and "The Human Comedy."

of his personal universe, possesses. This "universe" (a word that is over-employed and frequently misused, but for which I can find no substitute) is apparent, first of all, in the presence of certain special images. They run through all the films, call and answer to one another, intertwine and assume order; they are the visual rhymes of the "poet." It is difficult to list them according to any hierarchy of ascending values. Everything is important in this forest of repetitions, the flashing detail as well as the long, modulated sequence. Would it not be a betrayal of the exuberant quality of Fellini's disorder—the effect of art—to regroup the various elements according to a supposed hierarchy of importance?

There follows below, then, in random order, a list of the recurring images that cohere into the permanent fundament of his films, luminous signal lights through an unbroken creation: the procession is unquestionably a constant, found under varying poetic necessities in all his films, from *Variety Lights* to *Juliet of the Spirits*. In the first of these films, the roving actors parade, one holiday evening, along the deserted paths of a country village. The troupe ascends the hill, breaks apart and then regroups, moved by an aching, nocturnal, troubling enchantment. The promenade of the pathetic actors of the photo-novel in *The White Sheik* is no less moving under the dismal, heavy twilight. And the never-ending *ronde* in *I vitelloni* represents the gregarious advance of an indolent procession, bereft of any goal of which one could possibly conceive. In *La strada* three joyful musicians materialize out of nowhere, and gambol at daybreak, playing their instruments. These three capering silhouettes lead us to another, more compact, more solemn procession, both pagan and Christian in nature, where the circus people more or less merge with the cohorts of the Lord. In a more intense atmosphere of collective participation, the crowd of penitents invades the screen for a long and remarkable sequence in *The Nights of Cabiria*. In response to this spectacular, psychopathological-mystical release, a graver procession, headed by a priest bearing a banner, crosses the wasteland where the remainder of this monstrous pilgrimage has split apart, as if in a muted echo. In this same film, in the very last moments, there is another procession, also very Fellinian, and more strangely poetic. A group of young revelers parades and dances in the heart of the forest, accompanied by a guitar, an accordion, and song.

After a long night of anguish and pain, Augusto (the old swindler in *Il bidone*) believes he sees a strange procession at the end of the tunnel: a few villagers winding along their path in a sort of cheerful spontaneous dance.

The sound and fury of *La dolce vita* are appropriately punctuated by a great variety of parades, farandoles, processions. There are columns of cars on the congested highways serving the airport. Here, the procession is motorized. In the ruins of the Baths of Caracalla, transformed into a nightclub, the lavish, indefatigable Anita Ekberg stirs up another saraband; it is sinewy, cacophonic, and dizzying. Finally, the most beautiful and most fascinating of all the processions in this film comes in the sequence that ends the orgy among the nobility. It is a sinister promenade of sleepwalkers harassed by a night of disorder but to whom the air and the light of morning suddenly give an ambiguous and subtle charm.

In *Juliet of the Spirits,* Juliet sees a completely different defile pass by near the sea. It seems, at first sight, an effect of her reverie. There is a chariot preceded and followed by an altogether eccentric equipage dedicated to the cult of a fascinating goddess.

But the most fantastical, the most exalting, and the most moving farandole of all is that which concludes 8½. All the protagonists of the film, together with some strangers who add to their number, are gathered together pellmell into a sort of fanfare of adieu. More than a stylistic device or a recall of a beloved idea, this joyous *ronde* invites, with its gaiety and vigor, a general reconciliation. It is the circle of friendship.

Thus Fellini's universe is sown with trailing processions that often partake of the fantastical, of mythic odyssey. His universe is punctuated as well by public squares and crossroads that favor encounters and conversation: the famous plazas that are preferably shown by night, and embellished by a fountain. The itinerary of the Fellini hero is dotted with such places. They are an ideal setting for repose, meditation, and the confidences exchanged, thanks to the complicity of the calming, deserted, silent atmosphere.

As early as *The White Sheik,* the little harassed husband is gently picked up in one of these piazzas by a passing prostitute. There also comes to mind the short and magnificent sequence in *Variety Lights* when picturesque creatures of the night serenade one another in a square at an hour when all good people are in their beds. The ballad of public squares runs through Fellini's entire work; its throbbing couplets mingle harmoniously in *La strada, Il bidone, I vitelloni, La dolce vita,* and 8½, and become refrains.

In the enclosure of a theatre in the round the abandoned Gelsomina wanders like an animal who has lost her master; it is in the same sort of space that the *vitelloni* arrest the passage of time with their hollow reflections; that Moraldo addresses a few timid reproaches to his pitiful brother-in-law; that the swindlers let themselves be upbraided by provincial prostitutes, that Marcello receives the weary confidences of Maddalena, the unhappy millionairess; that he contemplates the spectacular whims of Sylvia, the monumental star with the brain of a sparrow; and that Guido confides his doubts to the beautiful and laughing Claudia. Thus in each successive film, the public squares that encircle their fountains lead to other such squares via narrow streets carved in the stone of the urban labyrinth. And there is always this enormous contrast in lighting, ranging from very dark to very brilliant, silhouetting the contours of the solitary strollers in the black light.

Black light, white light: the nocturnal scenes receive contrast from big bare panoramas across which the eye sweeps, coming to rest on some unexpected natural or artificial accident in the landscape. The pallid gray horizons of the Fellini landscape do not really follow any symbolic or Manicheistic concept of lighting. It is simply that Fellini's poetic and visual universe is always based upon the refined, striking alternation between dark and light, between the open sky and the dense culture medium. The unrestricted views, the fields, the immense bare spaces, the beaches and unlimited stretches aerate the filmic landscape like so many esoteric compositions.[1] If the swarming masses of the city call to mind Hieronymus Bosch, the desolate open spaces evoke instead the paintings of a Salvador Dali.

The natural, soothing harmony of empty space is almost always invaded by some solitary piece of architecture, as preposterous in this emptiness as a steel pipe standing in the middle of a field would be; there is often no other justification for the presence of these objects than their plastic effect. In *I vitelloni* the gray beaches of the Adriatic are broken up by a series of enormous stakes arbitrarily stuck in the sand. The denuded countryside welcomes the quasi-surrealistic visit of a stucco angel. In *La strada*, as the motorcycle proceeds along the road, a bare tree looms far off on the horizon, like the one that rises near the farm where the country wedding takes place. Geneviève Agel refers to a "tree of lightning" in her interesting work,[2] and several examples of it can be found in *Il bidone*. Similar "sentinels" also crop up along the way in this same film: enormous gaping pipes that lie on the ground; the bent pole with a flag silhouetted against the open sky like a bird caught in a snare. In *The Nights of Cabiria* we see a metallic scaffold erected on the banks of the Tiber, the square-shaped house of the heroine, and so on; in *La dolce vita* there are the pylon buzzing at the side of the road and the ivory tower of the lady novelist;[3] and in *Boccaccio 70,* the towering billboard perched on its pipes in the midst of a wasteland; without forgetting the greasy pole in *Juliet.*

Springing from the same poetic inspiration but even more strange are the human or mechanical objects absurdly suspended between sky and earth: the swing in *The White Sheik,* the Christ-carrying helicopter in *La dolce vita,* tightrope walker in *La strada;* the human kite and the spaceship of *8½;* the prehistoric aeroplane, the cockpit elevator, and the suspended grill of *Juliet.*

Another invariable is the fiesta. Collective celebrations occur in all Fellini films: carousing and cabaret sequences in *Variety Lights;* wedding banquets, traveling performances in *La strada;* the costume ball and theatrical performances in *I vitelloni;* the re-creation of a historical setting in *The White Sheik;* the New Year's Eve celebration in *Il bidone;* orgies of every sort in *La dolce vita* (which orchestrates all the festivities of earlier films into an exhaustive and exhausting synthesis). The fête goes on in the white nights of *8½* (which ends, moreover, with an authentic street parade) and in the sumptuous festivities of *Juliet,* awakened from the Thousand and One Nights.

The atmosphere is frenzied, agitated, chaotic, and filled with real or make-believe gaiety. The intoxication of the ball and its consequences reach a culminating point of exaltation, after which there can only be a dizzy fall. At the heart of the wildest abandon there inevitably appears the sneering specter of solitude and disarray—the despair of the pale dawn.

The themes of the fiesta and theatrical performance naturally give birth to two other invariables: the taste for masquerade and the world of the travesty. Fellini's characters are quick to adopt a disguise, either for advantage (the fake priests in *Il bidone*) or professional calling (the white sheik and in general all the actors who haunt the various films) or as a sort of game: in *La strada* the secondhand clownlike costume worn by Gelsomina[4] and the little wings worn by Il Matto; the exotic pajamas of Cabiria; the costume ball where each character in *I vitelloni* more or less selects that disguise that corresponds to his or her ideal; the priestly habit worn by Anita Ekberg in *La dolce vita* and the helmet that adorns a lady walk-on in the same film; Guido's false nose in *8½,* and the curious costume parties of *Juliet.*

Furthermore, Fellini personally shares this pleasure in disguise. Somewhere at random in each of his films he himself appears dressed as a bishop or a monk or in knight's armor. . . .

But there are disguises and disguises. Many of Fellini's characters

The Vitelloni: Alberto (Alberto Sordi) dances with a huge papier-mâché head at the costume ball. (Museum of Modern Art/Film Stills Archive)

also seek to hide psychologically or morally behind borrowed poses. The theme of imposture can be seen in the journalist's lie in *The Marriage Bureau,* the braggadocio of the *vitelloni,* of Checco in *Variety Lights,* or the white sheik, or the respectable mask that Augusto assumes for the benefit of his daughter and the crippled girl, or even for his accomplices in *Il bidone;* there are also the false sincerity of Oscar in *The Nights of Cabiria* and the lamentable lies of the unfaithful husbands in *8½* and *Juliet.* Literally and figuratively, the carnival (masks, costumes, poses) becomes a kind of ritual ceremony. The desire to change one's life, one's skin, to escape the burden of man's fate, is exposed through the most basic and superstitious response of all: to make-believe, to deceive the gallery in the half-avowed hope of deceiving one's self.

This leads us to examine further the crew of comedians, clowns, and performers of every size and shape who inhabit the luxuriant world of the poet. In title and content, *Variety Lights* heralds the theme of the professional performer, a subject used again, rearranged, and expanded in successive films and which has the most spectacular effect in 8½. The troupe of strolling performers, which inspired some of the greatest painters of the nineteenth and twentieth centuries, has found its most inspired cinematic bard in Fellini. Cruel and compassionate at the same time, he contemplates the animators of the stage with lucid sympathy, with a complicity that is not without bitterness.

In *Variety Lights*, the troupe with their gaudy, soiled costumes, their grotesque numbers, and all their wretched hopes, seems condemned to wander from place to place, and they reappear, hardly changed, in the famous sequence from *I vitelloni*. They show no hint of talent, but exhibit a lot of bad acting and touching insincerity. The old-fashioned cabaret in *La dolce vita* gathers together a few worn-out ballerinas and a moving clown to distract the loitering clients. A single hypnotist exercises his profession in movie theatres in the poorer neighborhoods of Rome, and brings Cabiria the illusion she so craves. This same power of enchantment is possessed by the white sheik, who dispenses it to naïve souls with all the conceit and arrogance he believes to be the mark of a great artist.

Zampanò, the fairground athlete, flanked by his assistant, Gelsomina, in her rags and tatters, form a still more modest team of wandering performers.

The bitter "bidonist," Augusto, finds ephemeral comfort in the companionship of a little nightclub dancer, a sad and humble call girl.

But the theatre, circus, vaudeville, and photo-novel are all supplanted by the cinema and its equally delirious universe. The shoddy spangles and dusty plumes give way to the prestige of haute couture. The clown with his empty money box becomes a star with a checkbook. The era of the nouveau riche is upon us in all its glorious neon folklore. Fellini has witnessed this transformation, and his latest films introduce the opulence and ostentation of that status symbol—the private city house. The young Lazzari (*The Nights of Cabiria*) lives in a kind of thousand-and-one-nights castle of modern gadgets. Poor Cabiria feels lost in it, as if she were in a cathedral, and is dazzled and dismayed by such magnificence. The new-style entertainment world also includes the sophisticated liturgy of publicity, orchestrated by the trumpets of the press; it is futility elevated into dogma—the servile, in a certain sense comical, whirlpool of the priests appointed to maintain the cult of the monstrous superstar. I am referring, in other words, to *La dolce vita*, to Sylvia and her court, to this monument of tempting flesh that overflows with physical health. The cinema and its folklore reappear in 8½;

absurd, fantastic, black comedy playing on both sides of the camera. They are marginal fauna, picturesque and worldly, extravagant and pitiable, sad and joyous. The same milieus animate (although in a more allusive fashion) the entourage of Juliet: her husband is in "public relations," and her beautiful neighbor keeps a fabulous caravanserai rivaling in vulgar splendor a superproduction from Hollywood or Cinecittà.

But where are the clowns of yesteryear? They stand by in the heart of the poet, ready to surge forth all in a rush, as in 8½.

Added together, these elements form a composite that is not easily defined or classified. If a historical reference is required (something Fellini in no way denies), it must be sought in the French school of the 1930's best known as "poetic realism." To this particular influence were joined the crucial experience of neorealism and above all the pulsating obsessions of the impenitent dreamer—Fellini himself.

Is the "poet" aware of the symbolic significance of his own dreams? Does he see the hidden meaning in the imaginative images that he so spontaneously elaborates? Perhaps not. But fortunately for those who love these games, exegetes of sharp and penetrating gaze exist, capable of interpreting (frequently in contradiction to one another) the intuitions of the artist. Thus, trees, fire, water (public fountain or sea), costumes, the paradox of the performer, the desert—all become so many symbols to be deciphered according to the psychoanalytical or cabalist grid forged by the few great initiates. Geneviève Agel[5] and Dominique Aubier[6] have reflected at great length upon the secret significance of these symbols. Moreover it is natural that the special atmosphere that permeates Fellini's films—films regularly visited by the dark angels of the baroque, the bizarre, and the surreal—should prove a boon to those who enjoy deciphering hieroglyphics. Oh, what wealth of unintentional allegory!

THE HUMAN COMEDY

The numerous characters winding through the Fellinian labyrinth are so integral a part of their setting that is it a shame to lift them out of their natural surroundings in order to analyze them more closely. Gelsomina exists, certainly, and with exceptional force, but she is nourished by everything around her—trees, air, sea, and people. Separating the characters in this way from their setting is both a painful and slightly arbitrary intellectual operation. Still, we must nevertheless resolve to do so, for Fellini did, after all, choose to bestow privilege upon certain individuals out of the multitude that invades his frescoes. The destiny of each is completely his own, and if certain characters bear definite spiritual resemblances to one another, each shines with his own individual, irreplaceable radiance.

The impression they give of all belonging to one family derives, first of all, from their common position in society, or rather, I should say, lack of social position. Their job, when they have one, is connected to some marginal, hazy sort of operation. It is a job that can be exercised intermittently, and never constrains in the least; its very irregularity constitutes both its charm and its servitude. Hence the permanent disequilibrium that encourages the spectacular ups and downs of Fellini characters, all of whom are manic-depressives either by nature or vocation.

At first sight this little inorganic world constitutes a picturesque, turbulent fauna, free of routine obligation, and jealous in guarding this freedom. Color and motion are born spontaneously from their social nonconformity and the strange adventures this gives rise to.

Such a conglomeration of characters makes up a fantastic, ageless bestiary: from the sinister, hulking reptile to the slender bird who can take flight and dominate the mud pit. In Fellini's world the laws of evolution are none too orthodox. Still, it is clear that his species do evolve, that a caterpillar represents a potential butterfly and that the most monstrous mythological pairings (Zampanò and Gelsomina) can bear fruit.

But under the more conventional light of direct observation, one sees that the heroes that spring from Fellini's imagination have definite affinities with their creator and, above all, with each other. Certainly they live in the contemporary world, but they prudently remain on the sidelines of the institutions that govern it. At best, they are journalists. This is the profession, let us recall, that first tempted Fellini. The journalist-hero in *The Marriage Bureau* adopts the weary, indifferent pose of a reporter doing a story on assignment; it is the same attitude that, much later, causes Marcello in *La dolce vita* to be such a weak figure. But if this latter appears "immune," the former was still vulnerable, that is, able to respond to the revelation of a providential, chance encounter. Both characters "work," although within the flexible limits of an accommodating profession, without steady pressure. The same goes for the diverse members of the "great showbiz family." In turn busy or "at liberty," basically masters of their own time, but dependent upon the whims of supply and demand, they belong to a profession that more often than not is an alibi decked out as a vocation. In any case, it is facile. One notch lower down we find the malefactors, the crooks whose business is irregular in both senses of the word. Fleecing people requires, if nothing else, a certain dose of imagination and sangfroid. In no way must we confuse this sort of livelihood with prostitution. Fellini's sentimental or cynical whores possess through everything a certain professional integrity. The client gets his money's worth. The bottom floor in this edifice is occupied by those whose nonworking state is pure, unsullied by any labor. The obdurate *vitelloni*, the millionaire loafers or penniless good-for-nothings watch life pass by, cozily settled down in their own little corner of nothingness.

It has been claimed, and I might add, rather thoughtlessly, that Fellini views this little world with the slightly suspect complacency of the dilettante who enjoys esthetic or other curiosities. True enough, one finds few office workers, laborers, or retired citizens among his favorite characters. But what does this mean? Simply that Fellini himself has known such people only from afar. The rather disordered plan of his own existence, his own encounters, and also—and this is certain—his avowed liking for the strange and out-of-the-way have naturally led him to focus on certain subjects and certain characters. The saintly folk, who, in the name of morality and religion as well, reproach Fellini for his "perverse" tastes ought first to reread certain passages of the Gospel (the would-be thief, the whore who was almost stoned to death), and secondly to realize that dereliction and delinquency are not privileges reserved only for the working classes. To concern oneself with the social problems of an era is useful, high-minded, and honorable, but to take interest in asocial beings is no less praiseworthy, especially when this interest takes the form of a respectful examination in which lucidity and benevolence weigh equally.

In effect, Fellini never becomes a prosecutor who condemns his characters, not even the meanest of the lot, nor does he ever serve as the devoted lawyer who gives them his unconditional support. He is more like a witness for the defense who perhaps (and I do mean *perhaps*) disapproves of the act, and yet at the same time feels an attachment for those beings who commit the act. It is an ambiguous and rather uncomfortable position, one that shocks the filmgoer who likes things to be clear-cut.

In the original conception of these characters we again find the same pendulum movement (attraction/repulsion, closeness/distance, light/darkness) that defines Fellini's artistic nature. Certainly, a continually broken line is not an easy road to follow. To appreciate the underlying coherence of his work, it is necessary to go beyond the pseudoscientific, often oversimplified, notions of individual or social psychology and morality. In their very contradictions, Fellini's characters give proof of their great ontological mystery (and who cares if an ignorant fellow like myself uses such big words).

The first mystery—that subterranean kinship that binds a character in one film to his homologue, his fellow, in a later film—arises from the same kind of creative obsession that has gripped the greatest novelists. In each successive film, Fellini paints the swarming picture of a human comedy in which the episodes intermingle and go on indefinitely. The men or the women who cross the filmmaker's line of vision are arrested, one after the other, in close-up or from the distance. It is as if they were endowed with independent existence and kept reappearing under different names in the mythological world of their creator.

In *I vitelloni,* Moraldo, weary of following paths that he knows will lead him nowhere, abandons the circle of loafers who lulled away the dreams of his dissatisfied youth. What happens to him after the film ends? Perhaps he becomes the morose journalist in *The Marriage Bureau.* Or perhaps the columnist in *La dolce vita,* a man visited by that vague remorse entertained—for form's sake—by the weak, who are defeated by what they like to call circumstances. Perhaps (why not?) he becomes the intellectual imprisoned by his apparently successful career—Steiner in that same *La dolce vita.* Unless, trapped in the more modest meshes of a destiny without style, he grows older bearing the more humble features of Marcello's father, the traveling salesman who prudently joined the ranks.

Masina is dead, long live Masina! At the end of *La strada,* the awkward clown with her big eyes that cry and laugh, disappears as discreetly as one can. Did this strange, scarcely normal child leave any legacy? Most certainly, for here comes the ingenuous Cabiria, devoured by a thirst for life, who offers herself rashly to the lowest bidder, and who listens with the same entrancement to the alluring lies of any charlatan or to the peaceful words of a Franciscan possessed of evangelical grace. To be sure, Cabiria is not crystalline like her original prototype. She is bolder, and marked by the experience of her profession. In the process of transmutation she has undergone physical degradation, but the basic nature of the character has not been perverted or distorted. Behind all the greasepaint there remains the immutable ingenuousness of that Fellini heroine par excellence: Gelsomina.

In the same sense, Zampanò (*La strada*) may be considered the ancestor of Augusto (*Il bidone*), an ancestor who goes back to the caveman, a hybrid whose animal frame barely incorporates that precious spark of humanity by which the human condition recognizes itself. The heaviness of his body, the density of his mind give him the sluggish, aimless, stupid aspect of those beings who have hardly ever been disturbed by the encumbering pinpricks of conscience. Augusto, behind a more presentable exterior, wallows in the same darkness. Like the rough Zampanò, he seems absent, lost, impermeable to the song of the world. In Augusto one sees the possible consequences of a "vitellonism" that has rotted on the vine, possessing no last touch of charm or wit; a sclerotic, desperate waywardness. Desperate? This question will be taken up further on.

In the midst of these worn-out beings, lost in their intellectual, moral, or spiritual emptiness, peers forth another species in Fellini's bestiary—the simple and the mad. They possess grace, insouciance, confidence, and joy. They are messengers of light. Generally a little crazy, they can also be grave and reflective, like the little lamplighter in *I vitelloni*, this peaceful adolescent whose words reverberate like a carefully modulated song. In the very last scene in the film, he walks on a rail, his arms spread out for balance. The same childlike figure exists in *La strada*, in the person of Il Matto (the fool). Il Matto is not only a tightrope walker but also a musician, comedian, and . . . philosopher. He propounds his lessons brutally, farcically, as when he douses and defies Zampanò, or in poetry, when he tells Gelsomina the colorful, subtle fables that she is able to understand.

The death of Il Matto is cruel and sweet, moving and joyous, like a beautiful gag.

Il Matto is a jokester; Picasso, in *Il bidone*, is a swindler. This does not matter, for these comedians are brothers. Picasso knows the value of a smile and of wonderment, the requisite (though not wholly sufficient) qualities one must possess to be the kind of troublemaker who upsets the order of things. This youthful, hilarious crook still has a lot to learn, and we abandon him in full swing, at the exact moment of the film when he takes leave of his accomplices and flies off, God only knows toward what new experience. But Patricia is there to take the baton. She is Augusto's own child: studious, shy, balanced, filled with peace. This lovely schoolchild also belongs to the family of those who stop the merry-go-round of the games. This is even more true of the radiant Suzanna, living incarnation of the three theological virtues. Suzanna, if you recall, is the paralyzed little girl who crosses old Augusto's path. There she is, incredibly alive and gay, savagely optimistic, clear as a diamond, and utterly incapable of concealing the enthusiasm and faith that animate her being. The Absolute, sought more or less lazily by all of Fellini's nocturnal heroes, is effortlessly attained by this peasant child. She is graced both in the secular and sacred sense of the word.

Other meteors graze the heavy surface of reality, and by their presence alone they seem to have power to dispel evil charms: the little nun who takes Gelsomina on a tour of her dilapidated convent; the skipping Franciscan who accosts Cabiria with his clownish appearance,[7] and, yet to come, that other adolescent girl. She is blond and laughing, slender, and completely at ease in her young skin. Suddenly the title of that film in which she appears as guest of honor takes on a meaning entirely devoid of irony—*La dolce vita*, the easy, gentle, sweet life.

Whether serious or irrational, reflective or capricious, all these characters haunt the memory like so many unforgettable apparitions. The list is still incomplete: there is Osvaldo, the sick child in *La strada*; the youthful heroine of *The Marriage Bureau*; and even certain silent figures as, for example, the little baker who contemplates the extravagances of Sylvia and Marcello in *La dolce vita*, as they splash about the Trevi Fountain in the small hours of the morning.

Wise men or fools, clowns or vagrants, heroes or "expedients," brutes or saints, intellectuals or the unlettered, Fellini's characters are destined to chance encounters. For although each follows his own path, all paths intersect, and the weary pilgrim must, by his very nature, listen by choice or by force to the little song of the stranger. Sometimes these encounters are misleading, futile, or left undeveloped. Others are crucial. The most spectacular, and also most famous, forms the dramatic core of *La strada*. It is an encounter with a dual release. It can be simplified to the classic geometric form of the triangle. Both Yves L'her[8] and Geneviève Agel[9] make this point about *La strada*, both expressing themselves with inspired lyricism, and yet without having ever consulted each other. In short, a subtle exchange has taken place. Il Matto, the clear-seeing fool, opens Gelsomina to spiritual awareness. Having assimilated his words, she in turn manages to touch the hitherto inaccessible conscience of Zampanò. Explained in such terms, these special encounters may seem too easy, that is, oversimplified, even silly. But this is in appearance only; the previous pages should restore their subtlety.

Almost every Fellini character both gives and receives, is influenced directly or indirectly by an immediate or delayed form of communication. In *The Marriage Bureau* the moral tranquillity of the journalist is troubled by the disarming confidences of his "victim." Moraldo is penetrated bit by bit by the words of the little railway employee. In *Il bidone*, Augusto experiences a strange uneasiness when he listens to his daughter, and later to the cripple. Marcello is ready to let himself be tamed by Steiner's "wisdom" and by the exuberance of the waitress, Paola. I shall not even mention other encounters not as obviously important, but which mark the personal itineraries of the most insignificant characters. Strange, amusing, joyous, grave, these meetings always engender secret or explicit communications whose consequences cannot at all be foreseen. By some mysterious alchemy, transformations will occur, a mind unfolds, a slumbering conscience is awakened. But take care: none of this is ever automatic or definitive. Fellini carefully avoids the classic hypocrisy of spectacular, irreversible conversions.

The remorse is fragile; the flesh is weak, so weak. Fellini embarks upon exhausting voyages that lead to the lands of disorder and confusion. Whether the trip is eventful, sometimes pleasant, often sinister, and always full of action, its end is like the soft, tentative pause of an organ. In other words, the problems of each personage remain unresolved, and everything is almost ready to start all over again.

Fellini underlines the potential of these encounters because he feels—and makes us feel—the endless depths of anxiety of beings condemned to solitude. His heroes are naturally prone to break their isolation by plunging into the turmoil of collective celebrations: the party, circus, spectacle, orgy, procession, and masquerade form the most elementary, most artificial, but also most tempting remedies against isolation.

Alas, the spell of the fiesta will inevitably disintegrate once the excitement is over. We witness, then, the vertiginous plunges that the next day brings. The laugh grows derisive, and stiffens into a mask. And when the mask is removed the terrifying face of anguish, fear, and bitterness reappears. Again the visage of solitude.

In Fellini's world, dawn signals the moment of truth. . . . The spell is shattered, and a person finds himself once again alone and shivering, abandoned, pathetic, left with neither energy nor illusion. This sudden weight that falls upon the shoulders of the solitary nightwalkers like a cope is still not the final point of his adventure. A new day dawns sadly, but other days will follow, new encounters will arrive. One must continue with the hope of finding, at a bend in the road, the godsend of an eternal smile. Nothing is inexorably negative; everything is marvelously provisional. The most sinister characters, those who create their own nothingness and those who are victims of circumstance, would be insupportable if Fellini did not grant them the benefit of a doubt, and this against all appearances, and counter to the secret wishes of the audience. If Zampanò is vulnerable, then nothing is entirely vain or impossible. Marcello cannot hear the voice of the slender Paola. Is he therefore doomed forever? And what about Oscar? Oscar, the infamous seducer, the perfect traitor, offers in a sudden flash the astonishing sight of a kind of repressed shame. This scene is played to perfection by a François Périer who had not been seen before.

These experts at inertia and emptiness, more pitiful than they are diabolic, are in no way prepared to satisfy Christian morality by turning over a new leaf. But they are pained by a dissatisfied, confused conscience. No, Augusto does not give up his hideous frauds despite the cripple's tears of joy. No, he is not magically overcome by grace. It merely disturbs him, which is far more plausible. Conversely, the marvelous mental, moral, and human balance of Fellini's most affirmative character (I am referring to Steiner) should not have reassured us. He too is alone; he too, uneasy. Things are decidedly not simple.

The end of a film is simply a halt, not a point of final conclusion. The actors take no bows; they continue to live, to doubt, to despair, to hope.

And if poor Guido (*8½*) and poor Juliet (*Juliet of the Spirits*) finally learn to know themselves better and to accept themselves while accepting, for better or worse, the others, they haven't yet come to the end of their road. Eased for the moment, they integrate themselves without further resistance into the community of mortals, aware of their imperfect condition. Resignation? Let us say, rather, wisdom, lucidity, modesty, and sweetness. . . .

NOTES

1. To cite at random: the dunes and the sea at the beginning of *La strada*, again the sea, haunting, before which the *vitelloni* split apart; the eternal shoreline of *8½* and of *Juliet* wherefrom emerge hallucinatory sons of Neptune; the open country in *The Marriage Bureau*; the fields and rugged valleys in *Il bidone*; the wastelands in *The Nights of Cabiria*.
2. *Les Chemins de Fellini*, Éditions du Cerf, Collection "7th Art."
3. This episode was later deleted.
4. Nor must one forget Cabiria's spontaneous flair for mime—for example, when she plays at imitating a tree.
5. *Op. cit.*
6. *Cahiers du Cinéma*, No. 49.
7. This role is played by the clown Polydor, whom we shall meet again in the pathetic scene in *La dolce vita*.
8. *Téléciné*, No. 48.
9. *Op. cit.*

24. Early Fellini: *Variety Lights,*   *Peter Bondanella*
The White Sheik, The Vitelloni

Like most contemporary Italian directors, Federico Fellini began his apprenticeship in the cinema as a part of the complex but little understood phenomenon that film historians label, often quite simplistically, Italian neo-realism. Less well known outside of Italy is the fact that the term refers not only to a number of important early works by such directors as Luchino Visconti, Roberto Rossellini, Vittorio De Sica, and Alberto Lattuada, but also to the early novels of writers such as Elio Vittorini (*In Sicily,* 1941), Cesare Pavese (*The Harvesters,* 1941; *The Moon and the Bonfires,* 1951), Carlo Levi (*Christ Stopped at Eboli,* 1945), and Italo Calvino (*The Path to the Nest of Spiders,* 1947). Thus, the neo-realist cinema was a part of a larger movement in the revitalization of Italian culture after the downfall of the fascist regime.

After a rather inauspicious beginning as a gag writer and assistant to several minor directors, Fellini began a series of associations with various neo-realist directors that eventually led him to co-direct his first film, *Variety Lights,* with Alberto Lattuada. His list of neo-realist credits is impressive and might represent the central achievements of a lesser man's entire career: assistant to Rossellini in *Rome, Open City* (1945); collaboration on the story and screenplay in Rossellini's *Paisan* and co-author of the screenplay for Lattuada's *The Crime of Giovanni Episcopo* (1946); co-author of the screenplay for Lattuada's *Without Pity* (1947); actor and writer in Rossellini's *The Miracle* and assistant to Pietro Germi in *In the Name of the Law* (1948); assistant to Lattuada in *The Mill on the Po* and to Rossellini in *The Flowers of St. Francis* (1949); assistant to Germi in *The Path of Hope* (1950) and to Rossellini in *Europe '51* (1951).

With this background in mind, it is easier to understand why certain French and Italian critics and intellectuals might consider a film like *La Strada* to be a rejection and even a betrayal of what they considered Fellini's heritage, as well as the most promising direction for the development of a truly "critical realism" in the Italian film, a realism with Marxist overtones aimed at a radical critique of existing con-

. . . .

This work is published here for the first time by arrangement with the author.

ditions in Italian society. Fellini did much to establish the legitimacy of a cinema of fantasy and imagination based upon the vision of an *auteur* rather than upon the demands of political doctrines, and the direction his works take after the critical and popular success of *La Strada* is clear and unmistakable.[1] Some twenty years after the polemical debate film historians call the "crisis of neo-realism," it is clear that much of the debate involved political issues rather than dispassionate analyses of films as works of art or a scholarly assessment of whether contending theories of realism or neo-realism actually had any explanatory value in the practical task of film criticism. While left-wing critics attacked what they considered the overtly Christian humanism of Fellini, De Sica, or Rossellini when it seemed to abandon social issues and to revert to what they felt was the bourgeois individualism of prewar Italian culture, the defenders of Fellini and others applauded what they viewed as a necessary and inevitable shift of emphasis from the "realistic" representation of general social problems to a "realistic" but increasingly introspective analysis of the effects such a society had upon the individual living within it.[2]

Interestingly enough, both sides in this debate seemed to agree, in many respects, upon a definition of what constituted neo-realism. Neo-realism was a cinema of "fact" or "reconstituted reportage," in the words of André Bazin, which contained a message of fundamental human solidarity fostered by the anti-fascist resistance.[3] It often involved a rejection of both dramatic and cinematic conventions or traditions, but at the same time it involved idealization or myth. Technically, it was supposed to be characterized by work on location rather than in the studio, the use of nonprofessional actors, and documentary effects. It rejected the montage of an Eisenstein with its ideologically motivated juxtaposition of images and shots and its manipulation of reality for the *mise-en-scène* techniques of a Welles or a Renoir with their penchant for deep-focus photography. Thus, the neo-realist's camera seemed to "respect" the ontological wholeness of the reality being filmed, just as the rhythm of its narrated screen time "respected" the actual duration of time within the story. The most sensitive critic of the period was André Bazin, who sums up the best of this critical thinking with a remark on De Sica's *The Bicycle Thief*, which he defines as one of the "first examples of pure cinema": "No more actors, no more story, no more sets, which is to say that in the perfect aesthetic illusion of reality there is no more cinema."[4]

If many critics ignored Bazin's pointed reference to the *illusion* of reality, and not to reality itself, the best neo-realist directors did not.[5]

Indeed, there are often subtle but unmistakable indications within these films that they should be construed as works of art—illusions of reality—rather than as reflections of any reality outside the camera's eye or the director's fantasy. A few concrete examples from De Sica's works—so central to Bazin's influential theories on neo-realism—will suffice to illustrate the point. No viewer of *The Bicycle Thief* will ever forget the dramatic scene in which Ricci loses his bicycle. Less obvious, but equally important, is the fact that Ricci is busy posting advertisements for a Rita Hayworth film just as the theft occurs. A careful analysis of this sequence uncovers its highly contrived, even choreographed nature that combines various camera positions and angles with tight editing. Even the split-second timing of the traffic lights allows the flow of normal traffic and the scene being filmed to run together as if they were not parts of two different worlds—that of art and of everyday life. Yet, the attentive viewer had already been warned by the director's pointed reference to the film poster that his work is a film, not reality. The mythic structure of the plot, the strange and suggestive music, the crucial role of chance or fortune in the story line—elements ignored by critics who insist upon interpreting the film as merely a depiction of postwar social problems rather than as an exceedingly complex absurdist masterpiece—might have attracted more attention if the critics had followed De Siça's reference to the fact that his filmic "reality" was a product of cinematic illusion. De Sica's rejection of film as documentary is even more marked in *Shoeshine*, in which a documentary film reminiscent of the "Why We Fight" series and ironically titled "News of the Free World" is screened in a prison for juvenile offenders; the screening is then disrupted by a freak accident as the director humorously, but unmistakably, rejects the view that film must necessarily reflect the outside world. Again, De Sica warns his viewer that his intentions are poetic ones and are not limited to a social message. His *Miracle in Milan* actually attacks the very definition of neo-realism canonized in Bazin's essays. Its opening ("Once upon a time . . .") places us squarely in the realm of fable or fairy tale, and the film is akin to the surrealistic works of Chaplin or René Clair (De Sica's favorite director), including special photographic effects, process shots, and a programmatic negation of linear plot, continuous time, and commonsense logic—three elements supposedly typical of neo-realist style or content.

A careful viewing of the major works of other neo-realists will uncover similar self-reflective moments as the director reveals his concern that the viewer distinguish the illusion of reality he produces from reality itself. The controlling fiction of these films is that they are "real," but the directors take great pleasure in emphasizing their films' artistic and anti-mimetic qualities. The recognition by the viewer that the reality experienced on the screen is one produced by cinematic conventions rather than by an ontological experience actually increases the aesthetic pleasure of analyzing the films. An examination of the accepted classics of Italian neo-realism, against which Fellini's works are supposed to react or from which they are presumed to depart radically, is revealing. Through it, we discover that the neo-realist film is not only concerned with the representation of social reality. Furthermore, the interest in fantasy and illusion (as opposed to truth and reality) and the focus upon the individual (as opposed to society), often associated with Fellini's development beyond neo-realism, can also be detected in the very neo-realist films from which his style evolved.[6]

The above discussion is not intended to deny that Fellini's early films—*Variety Lights, The White Sheik,* and *The Vitelloni*—represent a gradual evolution beyond his neo-realist origins. Rather, it is meant to show that critics and film historians have failed to specify exactly how this evolution took place, since they have uncritically accepted an untenable dichotomy between films of reality (neo-realism) and of fantasy (Fellini). The distinction between early films by Fellini and the neo-realists is more a difference of degree than a violent separation. It is not merely a technical change, since Fellini did not depart so drastically from neo-realist techniques or conventions, nor is it primarily a thematic shift, since Fellini continued to share the somewhat vague belief in human solidarity and honesty of neo-realist works and theory. Examine his often cited remark on neo-realism: "Neo-realism is a way of seeing reality without prejudice, without conventions coming between it and myself—facing it without preconceptions, looking at it in an honest way—whatever reality is, not just social reality but all that there is within a man."[7] Compare this to statements by De Sica or Rossellini: "reality transposed into the realm of poetry";[8] "realism is simply the artistic form of truth."[9] All three men attempt to include illusion and reality, artifice and truth, in their definitions of neo-realism, but all three are so hopelessly vague in specifying how this is to be achieved in a concrete cinematic style that any director of whatever school or style could subscribe to their statements.

Fellini's innovations lie, instead, in his conception of character. Recent criticism demonstrates that Fellini shifted the focus of neo-realist works from character as defined primarily by society—characters like Visconti's poor fishermen of *La terra trema,* De Sica's pensioner in

Umberto D., or De Santis's exploited workers in the fields of *Bitter Rice*. Fellini moves from typical figures reflecting the social conditions of a specific historical situation to characters that are atypical and unique and, therefore, more amenable to the personal symbolism and mythology of an *auteur* unrestrained by a political program. Equally important is the fact that his early films begin treating characters philosophically or psychologically, a necessary first step toward his future metacinematic concerns in such films as *8½, A Director's Notebook, The Clowns,* and *Roma,* which examine the nature of the film medium itself.

Fellini's development of a personal interpretation of character parallels and even repeats an operation that his compatriot Luigi Pirandello undertook in his reaction against the conventions of realism in the theater of his day. In each case, a realist conception of character as socially determined was undermined by a fundamental philosophical inquiry into the nature of character itself. Both Pirandello and Fellini move from character as a function of some outside factor to a basically subjective attitude, thus defining it in terms of society's influence—character as "mask"—as well as a reflection of the individual's own subconscious aspirations, ideals, and instincts—character as "face." The title of Pirandello's collected theatrical works, *Naked Masks,* might well serve as a definition of Fellini's early films. In both instances, the thrust of the works is toward an unmasking operation; the masks worn by the characters as they act out their socially defined roles are torn away to reveal something of the intimate personality underneath. In plays such as *The Rules of the Game* (actually better translated as "The Game of the Roles"), *The Pleasure of Honesty,* and *It Is So (If You Think So),* Pirandello moved from the realist focus upon a unified character in conflict with other like individuals to the interplay and clash of mask and face; in addition, Pirandello rejected the idea that character could ever be unified or static or even completely known. Character was flux, an everchanging entity beyond the grasp of human reasoning precisely because its fundamental basis, the face behind the mask, was composed of raw emotions, instincts, and preconscious feelings that could only be expressed outwardly by actions that seemed irrational and incomprehensible without a knowledge of their inner motivations. This fundamental redefinition of the nature of dramatic character was the necessary first step in the intellectual evolution that eventually led Pirandello to question and examine the nature of dramatic art itself in his trilogy of the theater.

Fellini lacks Pirandello's scholarly grounding in European philosophy and literature and probably would have little sympathy for Pirandello's desire to establish his theoretical insights on a programmatic basis; there is no equivalent in Fellini to the theoretical treatise *On Humor* (1909), which preceded Pirandello's dramatic works and contains many of the new ideas on art that would later be developed on the stage. Fellini once declared: "I'm not a man who approves of definitions. Labels belong on luggage as far as I'm concerned; they don't mean anything in art."[10] Fellini's ideas about character in cinema developed largely by trial and error in his early films, although the example of Pirandello may have been suggestive even then, as it certainly was to be in 8½ and *The Clowns*.[11] Although there is no indication that Fellini read *On Humor*, Pirandello's definition of comedy, his view of the difference between the comedian and the humorist, and his concepts of life and form can serve the contemporary viewer of Fellini very well as a guide to his early films.

With *Variety Lights*, Fellini plunges us directly into the world of the variety theater, the world of alluring illusion beneath which co-directors Lattuada and Fellini will uncover a tawdry and mundane reality. The narrative is built upon illusion and its subsequent unmasking in the person of Checco Dalmonte (an insignificant variety show performer with illusions of grandeur), his fiancée, Melina Amour, and Liliana, a stagestruck amateur whose ambition to succeed will cause Checco to betray his fiancée. The plot is circular and static, never revealing any essential change or development in Checco. Besides the now familiar scenes of abandoned *piazze*, which reflect the inauthentic existence, loneliness, and solitude of the characters, as well as the frenzied celebrations by night, which are followed by the inevitable moment of truth at the arrival of dawn, Fellini and Lattuada expand the image of the variety theater as a collection of eccentric individuals into a philosophical abstraction wherein the realms of life and art interpenetrate. Life, too, for the directors can be described as a theater wherein we, as actors, play out our roles.

Nowhere is this concept clearer than in the dramatic confrontation between Checco and Liliana after she has abandoned him for a more promising theatrical producer. Checco waits dejectedly for her return, and when he reminds Liliana of what he has done for her and then tries to assert his rights by claiming she should share his bed for his troubles, she demurely agrees to this proposition without a moment's hesitation. Her acceptance reveals to Checco her essential nature, and for the first time he catches a brief glimpse of her true face beneath the mask of innocence she normally wears. Checco himself, in this mo-

Variety Lights: Checco Dalmonte (Peppino De Filippo) and Liliana (Carla Del Poggio) dancing at a Roman night club. (Museum of Modern Art/Film Stills Archive)

ment of truth, lowers his own social mask; the role he has played until this moment as the worldly actor and man-about-town is set aside and his true identity is revealed to Liliana, who is incapable of appreciating his basic honesty and goodness. He slaps Liliana for agreeing to the very thing he most desires, rejecting her lack of morals and commitment to genuine human feelings. As he leaves her, climbing the stairs toward his hotel, we hear what sounds like applause on the sound track. The poetic necessity of this commentary by the directors is unassailable, even if it would be out of place in any purely representational treatment of the scene. We have, after all, witnessed Checco's finest performance of his career, an act that is both genuine and far removed from the ridiculous roles of the variety theater we have viewed earlier. By setting aside the false mask required of him in his confining social role, Checco has allowed his true personality to guide his behavior in the theater of life for a brief moment, which will not be repeated. The directors applaud him for this and we, as spectators, must agree with their judgment. Suddenly, a tram passes by, and we are now offered the possibility that the applause on the sound track may only be the noise of its passage. However, repeated viewings of this scene fail to pinpoint the exact origin of the applause. Reality and illusion thus blend, as the film reveals its novel conception of character through the dramatic clash between social role (mask) and authentic personality (face).

Moreover, Fellini and Lattuada have gone behind the mask of the theater itself as a social institution in *Variety Lights* and have revealed the underside of this artistic medium just as they have done with the film's characters, underlining the petty jealousies, the irrational reasons for success or failure, the economic motives behind the search for a pure artistic form. In an almost imperceptible manner, by concentrating upon the revelation of the nature of one artistic medium, Fellini has begun his long journey that will eventually lead to the examination of the medium of film art in the later works. And there are hints of these self-reflective masterpieces to come in this work—we are shown the co-director Lattuada as a character who organizes the variety show at the close of the film, and we are given brief glimpses of posters of two earlier films scripted by Fellini, Lattuada's *The Crime of Giovanni Episcopo* and Germi's *In the Name of the Law*.

It would be unfair to Lattuada to bestow all the credit for this film upon Fellini, as critics usually do. Even though they are named as co-directors, a partnership solidified by the fact that their wives play the two female leads, and in spite of the fact that most critics claim to detect the familiar Fellinian universe in the picture, Lattuada was the established neo-realist director with major films to his credit, whereas Fellini was at this time only a beginner. It is, therefore, impossible to attribute the entire conception of the work to Fellini or even to determine which aspects of the work we should attribute to each man. Still, the fact that a film co-directed by a neo-realist like Lattuada could focus so consistently upon the *reality* of illusion rather than the *illusion* of reality should not be overlooked. Seen from this perspective, *Variety Lights* bridges the gap between the end of the neo-realist period and the new cinematic style evolving in Fellini; it is both a coherent first effort by a young director, which embodies an important and innovative idea of character in cinema, and it is also proof of the fact that Italian neo-realists such as Lattuada never embraced the simplistic antithesis of illusion and reality accepted by the critics and scholars. Instead, they conceived these two realms as inseparably linked together in a mutually illuminating manner by the imagination of the director and the aesthetic forms of art.

Whereas *Variety Lights* introduces us to Fellini's new notion of character in film, *The White Sheik* expands and examines it in detail. Once again, Fellini sets his work against the background of the world of art—in this instance, the world of the photo-novel or cartoon-romance, the pictorial equivalent of the pulp magazine or the television soap opera in our own culture.[12] The title is doubly significant, as it evokes the memory of Valentino, the Italian immigrant whose roles in such films as *The Sheik* and *Son of the Sheik* made him an international celebrity. Fellini builds the film around the visit to Rome of a newly wed couple fresh from the provinces. In other works, this situation might have an overtly autobiographical character, as it does in *La Dolce Vita* or *Roma*. In this case, however, the director is more interested in the metaphysical clash of reality and illusion and the resulting tension between mask and face. In fact, Fellini employs the fastidious Ivan Cavalli and his wife Wanda to embody each aspect of this psychological conflict.

Ivan, the typical petit bourgeois husband from the provinces, is trapped within a life of mechanical forms and conventions and is the antithesis of spontaneity and emotion.[13] From the moment they arrive in Rome, he has every minute of their visit planned down to the required stop at the Vatican, the dutiful homage to the monument of the unknown soldier, and even the consummation of their marriage toward evening. Superficial piety and patriotism characterize Ivan's view of life, and these personality traits misled some critics into viewing the film when it was first released as an authentic neo-realist critique of

Italian provincial mores. Wanda embodies a rather naïve attempt to break out of the provincial forms and her conventional marriage into a world of illusion and fantasy, symbolized for her by the white sheik and the *fotoromanzi*, the world of art, and set apart from the real world of her everyday existence. As Wanda steals away from the hotel to visit the editorial office of *Blue Romance*, leaving her bath water running in the process, the film's structure shifts to follow the two characters in parallel action sequences, employing extensive crosscutting between separate stories, and therefore dividing the twin realms of illusion and reality the characters embody in order to comment on them both. As the story line shifts back and forth from Ivan to Wanda, the transitions are most carefully made, the sequences are tightly edited, and the result is a minor masterpiece which belies the impression of carelessness that a first viewing of the film or a reading of the superficial comments of the critics might suggest.

The initial parting of Wanda from Ivan is a typical example of Fellini's attention to detail in this film. As Wanda walks to the editorial office, her path is lined with film posters, all reflecting the illusions that make her character what it is. Moreover, church bells are heard on the sound track as she walks, suggesting the ultimate source of deception and illusion in Fellini's universe. At the editorial office, Wanda declares that illusion is preferable to reality and agrees with Marilena Alba Velardi that "dreams are our true lives."[14] As she leaves the office, she witnesses a strange procession of the characters in the *fotoromanzo*, all dressed in their Arabic costumes, and her fantasy world merges with the real world. In addition, the parade is without any apparent order or structure, reminiscent of figures in a dream. The music on the sound track underlines the point, for it is not a part of the world being filmed but is supplied by the director to support the fantastic nature of the parade.

The transition back to Ivan and the hotel is made by an African priest who discovers the bath water Wanda has left flowing in the tub; this strange individual who speaks an incomprehensible language is the counterpart in Ivan's real world of the falsely made-up Arab with a dark complexion that Wanda takes for a real Bedouin in the office of *Blue Romance*. In contrast to Wanda's mysterious procession with its evocative music, Ivan encounters an entirely different kind of procession as he searches for Wanda, a highly regimented parade of Italian *bersaglieri* (shock troops). The music accompanying this procession is played by the troops themselves, as if to emphasize their location in the world of everyday reality. Fellini then crosscuts to the beach at Fregene,

The White Sheik: Fernando Rivoli, "The White Sheik," (Alberto Sordi) on location for the shooting of the *fotoromanzo* photographs.

where the scenes for the *fotoromanzo* will be shot. Wanda meets her idol, the sheik, and is persuaded by him to dress as a harem girl and to play a role in the next issue of the magazine. Unlike the other actors, however, Wanda accepts the illusion of the *fotoromanzo* as reality and actually lives her part.

As Wanda becomes a part of this world of the imagination, life and art merge in the hilarious sequence during which the stills for the *fotoromanzo* are made. Here, Fellini actually reproduces the process of film montage with still photographs. In so doing, he implicitly rejects the neo-realist approach to editing, Rossellini's in particular, which refuses to "manipulate" reality with dramatic editing. Earlier, Wanda had been asked by Marilena what kind of line might be appropriate for a scene such as the one now being filmed, and she had replied: "Oh . . . I feel so uneasy. . . ." At that time, the line had been described as reflecting "the simplicity of life itself." Now, Wanda repeats this line almost unconsciously while the photographs are being taken, as the realms of art and life merge together on the screen.

At this point, the narrative returns to Ivan who is entertaining his relatives at a restaurant. He too is playing a role, for he must pretend to speak to his lost wife on the telephone in order to convince his relatives that Wanda really exists. But Ivan's role is unwillingly assumed, unlike the role Wanda plays gladly in the *fotoromanzo*, and while Wanda breathes life into her part and causes her reality to merge with the world of illusion, Ivan merely assumes a dead form to protect his social mask. Just as Fellini had made the transition from beach to restaurant by having both groups eat lunch, we now return to Wanda with the transition effected by the restaurant music, which directs our attention back to the ocean ("O sky, o sun, o sea"). Wanda and her sheik leave the seaside and sail out onto the ocean, where she is gullible enough to accept the sheik's fantastic lie about how he has been tricked into marriage by a woman with a magic potion. Just as he tries to force a kiss from her, he loses control of the boom and is struck several times on the head by it. Fellini immediately cuts to the opera house where the frantic applause of the people around Ivan and his relatives conveys the director's judgment of the sheik's accident; furthermore, the opera being performed is *Don Giovanni*, an ironic contrast to the bungling attempts of the white sheik to seduce Wanda.

By this time, both Wanda and Ivan have been frozen in their respective roles—Wanda lives a life based upon empty romantic illusions, which cause her to assume a mask she uses to escape from reality, while Ivan lives a life according to society's demands upon him, which causes him to assume a mask constructed for him by others. Neither of the two is really aware of this comic situation, for neither has a sense of self-consciousness. The director provides the viewers of the film with a privileged position so that we can appreciate the absurdity of their predicament; our sympathies, and those of Fellini, are clearly with Wanda. By this time, each of the characters is considered mad by those around them. When Ivan goes to the police to complain of his wife's disappearance with a white sheik, he is thought to be insane. Returning from the boat to the beach, where his fat, shrewish wife awaits him, the white sheik (now reduced to the lowly status of Fernando Rivoli, a mediocre actor in our view but still the fabulous white sheik for Wanda) calls Wanda crazy when she accuses his wife of forcing him to marry her by means of her magic potion. Returning to Ivan, we see him meet two prostitutes and go off with one of them, thereby breaking his own code of conventional ethics and destroying whatever claim he might have had to respectability. Meanwhile, in contrast to Ivan's truancy, Wanda is returned home by a man whose advances she rejects. Deciding to end her life and bidding good-by to her husband, she exclaims: "Dreams are our true life . . . but sometimes dreams plunge us into a fatal abyss. . . ." Her suicide attempt ends in a comic failure, since the water level of the River Tiber is sufficient only to dampen her spirits. She is immediately rushed to a mental hospital, where Ivan finds her again just a few minutes before they must meet his relatives at St. Peter's Square to visit the Pope and only a short time after Ivan has returned from his tryst with the lady of the night.

The two threads of the narrative, so carefully divided and interrelated throughout the film, have now been rejoined. Now, before the final scene at St. Peter's, Ivan and Wanda are forced to confront each other and their respective illusions in a madhouse. Both have been misguided, for Fellini has demonstrated how a life based upon either social convention or romantic dreams is doomed to disaster. In subsequent films (8½, *Juliet of the Spirits*) Fellini will suggest that only a fusion of masculine and feminine traits can produce a whole personality. Here, however, the protagonists of *The White Sheik*, like Checco of *Variety Lights*, are totally incapable of escaping the roles assigned to them by society or their fantasy life.

Before the entrance to St. Peter's, Ivan decides to live a lie—that he has not soiled the family's honor—while Wanda now transfers her illusions from the *fotoromanzi* to her marriage. In the past, she pursued a more spontaneous life, one directly opposed to her provincial husband's, through a fantasy world created by the romances she read each week. But this reliance upon illusion alone has turned her illusions into dead forms and has destroyed them by bringing them into contact with the world of reality; they are now rendered as meaningless as the empty form of her marriage. Wanda's marriage and her husband represent the encrusted form of convention that has grown over spontaneous life, illusion, and the fantasy world of the imagination. Yet, at the end of the film Wanda tells Ivan just before they enter St. Peter's that *he* is now her white sheik! Her solution is to accept the form of marriage (and the role and mask it entails) as her illusion and, in a sense, to merge the world of illusion and reality. While both Ivan and Wanda vaguely glimpse the true nature of their respective illusions, both ultimately reject an awareness of the truth and take refuge in another illusion. Wanda resolves her search for a dream world by declaring that her reality will suffice; Ivan is now transformed into her new white sheik. Ivan pretends that the honor of the family remains intact, accepts Wanda without confessing his own fall from grace, and thus continues to live out his role of the respectable married man. Now, however, he does so with a guilty conscience. As the couple and their relatives head into the church, their brisk manner of walking recalls the earlier procession of the *bersaglieri*. Here, at the source of the ultimate illusion (or is it the ultimate reality?), a brief shot of a statue of an angel provides an ironic benediction for this final but basically inauthentic reconciliation of illusion and reality. A similar shot prefaced Wanda's ridiculous attempt to commit suicide, and its repetition here is a none too subtle declaration by Fellini that the harmony between Ivan's social pretensions and Wanda's romantic dreams within the form of matrimony as sanctioned by Holy Mother Church will only be temporary. *The White Sheik* is therefore neither a shallow comedy nor a satirical commentary on Italy's provincial life. It is, instead, a serious philosophical statement about the nature of character and the roles we are forced to play as we contend with the conflicting demands of our social forms and the attractions of our personal illusions through the conflict of mask and face.

The Vitelloni represents a further step in the development of Fellini's conception of character and, with it, his interest in the dramatic possibilities of the clash of mask and face.[15] Like *The White Sheik*, *The Vitelloni* was first interpreted as a simple, neo-realist satire of life in the provinces. But unlike Fellini's earlier film, this one was both a critical and commercial success and was the first of his works to achieve foreign distribution, thus helping to establish his international reputation even before the astounding success of *La Strada* in the following year. Like *8½*, *Roma*, and *Amarcord*, *The Vitelloni* draws heavily upon Fellini's childhood memories—or, at least, upon memories invented from a childhood created in his imagination.

Its main characters are five overgrown adolescents—*vitelloni*, in the slang of Rimini, Fellini's birthplace. The most important is Fausto, described by the narrator as the "guide and spiritual leader" of the group; his affair with Sandra Rubini (Moraldo's sister), their subsequent forced marriage, and Fausto's failure at his job selling religious articles receive most of Fellini's attention. Alberto is the most pathetic of the five and is a weak, slightly effeminate individual who lives off his sister Olga's wages, all the while boasting to his friends about how women must be supervised to protect the family's honor. Leopoldo is a would-be poet who wastes his time dreaming of hunting in Africa "like Hemingway," or of the day his pedestrian plays will be performed by the local theatrical company. The most sensitive of the group whose departure from the provincial village finally concludes the film is Moraldo, a figure often linked to Fellini himself and a trace of whom can be seen in

most of the displaced provincials who populate his future works. Riccardo, played by Fellini's own brother Riccardo, is poorly developed
and is simply a very pleasant fellow with a melodious voice.

Whereas the twin protagonists of *The White Sheik* represented each
aspect of the theme of illusion and reality and were closely interrelated
by frequent crosscutting between their respective story lines, Fellini
modifies his narrative structure in *The Vitelloni* in several important
ways. To increase the distance between the characters and himself, he
inserts an omniscient narrator whose voice-overs help to tie the rather
formless plot together and provide a running commentary, as well as
an objective perspective, on the actions. We never know the identity
of this voice—it may represent Fellini himself or it may reflect the views
of a mature Moraldo as he examines his past. This objective element,
from the perspective of which the illusions of the *vitelloni* are judged
and found wanting, is in contrast to a new and more subjective camera
that reflects not the omniscient perspective of the director but the
more limited points of view of his characters.

These technical aspects should not cause us to ignore the fact that
the theme of the film is similar to that of *The White Sheik*; indeed, the
worlds of illusion and reality, and the resulting clash of mask and face,
are here more clearly delineated than ever by this combination of objective narrative voice and subjective camera. More importantly, however, *The Vitelloni* goes beyond the earlier film and provides some
resolution of the dilemma posed but not resolved at the conclusion of
The White Sheik. The plot follows and reveals the different personal
crises of each *vitellone*; first their social roles are outlined, and then
their masks are torn away, forcing them to confront the reality of their
faces and the emptiness of their illusions. Three of the group—Fausto,
Alberto, and Leopoldo—are studied in detail. Riccardo seems to be pur-
posely slighted, as if treating the character played by the director's
brother would have forced Fellini to concentrate on autobiographical
matters. Moraldo, the fifth *vitellone*, observes the crises in the lives of
his three friends and he, alone, reaches a measure of self-awareness sufficient to change the course of his life.

Each of the three is placed in a situation in which the clash of reality and illusion arises naturally from the setting—a beauty pageant, a
carnival ball, a variety theater. Indeed, one of the marks of Fellini's
genius is that the smallest, most mundane particular of everyday life or
milieu can have philosophical import. He has no need to seek out gratuitous philosophical abstractions, for his ideas are intuited by his emotions and embodied in his imagery with ease. We meet Fausto at the

beauty contest that opens the film. As Sandra receives the news that she has been selected "Miss Siren of 1953," Fausto is flirting with another woman. The future course of their marriage is immediately evident. As he had done earlier with the world of theater in *Variety Lights*, Fellini now uncovers the tawdry reality behind the dream world of the beauty pageant: Sandra's fainting spell is a sign to the onlookers that she is pregnant. Here, Fellini shifts from the objective narrative voice to a more subjective perspective as the camera recreates the girl's dizziness and fall as she faints. As a result, we are encouraged to view the sequence from her vantage point, and we must regard her with sympathy and Fausto with disgust. Fausto attempts to escape the burdens of a family and marriage by leaving town. His evasions of responsibility recur throughout the film, for his role as a local Don Juan is incompatible with such adult notions as duty and obligation. Nevertheless, his social mask is progressively destroyed by the director as he is first of all forced to marry Sandra; then, he is fired from his job because of his attentions to his employer's wife, attentions that are predictably rejected; finally, he is abandoned by his wife and child. Reduced to his true identity as a spoiled brat by these failures, Fausto is not the provincial Casanova he pretends to be, and he is finally whipped by his father like the child he still is and will always remain.

Alberto's moment of truth occurs in a similar situation during a masked ball at carnival time, an even more obvious arena than a beauty contest for the interplay of reality and illusion, mask and face, to evolve. Fellini presents a typically frenzied celebration with the inevitable reckoning at the break of dawn. Again, his subjective camera work with its rapid movement through a variety of angles and positions, as well as the suddenly increased tempo and complexity of his editing, give us an insight into Alberto's state of mind. We see him lurching about the ballroom in a drunken stupor, dancing with a huge papier-mâché head or mask and dressed in a female costume that underlines the effeminate qualities that set him apart from his strong and self-reliant sister, Olga. No other image in Fellini's works visualizes so clearly his interest in the clash of mask and face than this surrealistic dance between a man in drag and an empty mask. In his inebriated state, he asks Moraldo the kind of philosophical question he would never understand while sober: "Who are you? You're nobody, nobody!" As he staggers about, and as Fellini's camera takes on his perspective to make us feel almost as dizzy as Alberto, we come to realize that Alberto is really addressing this question to himself and has supplied his own answer. His mask is torn aside and the reality of his miserable life is revealed both to him and to Moraldo. Predictably, the final blow occurs as he returns home at dawn. His sister, upon whom he has depended for so long a time, is leaving town with her married lover. Although he is a somewhat sympathetic figure, Fellini judges Alberto as mercilessly as he condemns Fausto. At the same time, we sense the typical Fellinian sense of complicity with his characters that somewhat softens his harsh assessment of their inevitable failures.

With Leopoldo, the confrontation of reality and illusion occurs once again against the background of the theatrical world, in this case the variety show of an aged homosexual actor named Natali. While Leopoldo believes Natali is interested in his talent and might like to stage one of his wretched plays, the old man is only concerned with seducing the naïve *vitellone*. As Leopoldo accompanies Natali to the seashore, he slowly comes to realize that his literary works are merely the pretext for another and more sinister purpose. Racing away from Natali and the menacing shadows with which Fellini envelops this mysterious figure, Leopoldo returns to his home, his maiden aunts, and his comfortable illusions, sadder but surely no wiser.

Each of the *vitelloni* experiences a crisis as his illusions collide with reality. Each is forced by this shock to cast aside his social mask and to confront his more authentic, but infinitely less appealing face. In all three cases, the truth that emerges from this clash is almost too much for these essentially shallow characters to bear. Their lives move on the surface of reality, and when superficial responses to serious problems are no longer satisfactory, the *vitelloni* lose control and cling to the soothing comfort of their shattered illusions. Moraldo, however, is never forced to undergo the kind of trial the others experience; instead, he is allowed to witness their failures and is permitted to learn from their negative examples. His moment of truth involves a decision to abandon the provinces, and the catalyst for his resolve to do so is his contact with a young boy who works at the train station. He reminds Moraldo of his youth when problems seemed simpler and capable of resolution through facile illusions, but Moraldo realizes that childhood illusions, such as the ones his fellow *vitelloni* never abandon, are unworthy of a mature individual in the adult world. And so, Moraldo sets out, much as Fellini did years earlier. With a brilliant closing shot, Fellini employs a mobile, subjective camera to let us experience Moraldo's emotion as he departs. While the train pulls away from the station toward Rome and Moraldo bids farewell to his young friend, the camera moves through each of the *vitelloni*'s bedrooms, passing over each sleeping *vitelloni* like a nostalgic caress.

Moraldo has put aside childish things and is the first Fellinian character to have experienced a conversion, an epiphany. The nature of this conversion is a philosophical change, a conscious decision to accept the responsibilities of the adult world and to abandon the puerile illusions of the past as the basis for life in the world. It is not, however, a complete rejection of the world of illusion for that of reality, nor is it yet the kind of religious conversion that will mark the lives of Gelsomina, Cabiria, and Augusto in his next three feature films. But it is interesting that the professional actor playing the role of Moraldo—Franco Interlenghi—began his career as the nonprofessional actor in the role of the orphan boy in De Sica's *Shoeshine*. Interlenghi, the actor, has grown up, and the character Moraldo has come of age. Finally, Fellini seems to be telling us that the Italian cinema must do the same. Just as Fellini has retained some of his neo-realist past in *The Vitelloni* (in this case, an actor), so too the Italian cinema must preserve the best of its neo-realist heritage—the honesty, the belief in humanist values, and the sincerity that characterized the masterpieces of neo-realism regardless of their political perspectives or cinematic styles. But it must also, like Moraldo and Fellini, evolve with the passage of time and the exigencies of the medium itself. With *Variety Lights*, *The White Sheik*, and *The Vitelloni*, Fellini absorbed the authentic heritage of neo-realism and its message that the demands of film art are superior and more compelling than the profits of its producers, the intellectual quarrels and often pedantic objections of its critics, and even the mercurial favor of its fickle public. With this legacy of artistic integrity incorporated into his own creative vision, Fellini transcended his neo-realist origins with his new perspective on the nature of film character and the dramatic possibilities of the clash between social roles and authentic feelings, masks and faces. In so doing, he laid the intellectual foundations for the complicated odyssey his career was to take in the future, for all his later works would be shaped, to some degree, by this early interest in the dialectical interplay of illusion and reality.

NOTES

1. For a discussion of the interrelationship of reality and illusion in Fellini after *La Strada*, see the study by Patrizio Rossi and Ben Lawton reprinted in this volume.

2. For a representative sample of opinions on both sides of this debate, see the articles by Aristarco and Bazin, as well as the several early statements

ıade by Fellini concerning his ties to neo-realism, reprinted in this volume. ßazin's essays on neo-realism are for the most part available in English in *What Is Cinema? Part II*, trans. Hugh Gray (Berkeley: University of California Press, 1971). The most comprehensive historical survey of neo-realism in any language is Roy Armes, *Patterns of Realism* (Cranbury, N.J.: A. S. Barnes, 1971); for a critique of Armes' concept of film realism, see the perceptive review by David Bordwell in *Cinéaste*, 5 (1972), 76-78.

4. Bazin, ibid., p. 60.
5. Bazin's theories are discussed at length in J. Dudley Andrew, *The Major Film Theories: An Introduction* (New York: Oxford University Press, 1976); Andrew Tudor, *Theories of Film* (New York: Viking, 1974); and Christopher Williams, "Bazin on Neo-realism," *Screen*, 14 (1973-74), 61-68.
6. This argument will be expanded in a forthcoming study on Italian neo-realism. In the light of recent interest in reassessing the contributions of the movement, two Italian studies are of importance: Pietro Angelini, *Controfellini: il fellinismo tra restaurazione e magia bianca* (Milan: Edizioni Ottaviano, 1974)—a radical Marxist attack on *both* neo-realist films and the early works of Fellini for what Angelini terms their "cult of the subproletarian experience" and their "superficial ecumenical humanism"—and Lino Micciché, ed., *Il neorealismo cinematografico italiano* (Venice: Marsilio Editore, 1975)—an important collection of essays by various hands which calls into question many of the traditionally accepted notions of the movement's origins, characteristics, and lasting achievements.
7. Federico Fellini, *Fellini on Fellini*, trans. Isabel Quigly (London: Eyre Methuen, 1976), p. 152.
8. Vittorio De Sica, *Miracle in Milan* (Baltimore: Penguin, 1969), p. 4.
9. "A Discussion of Neo-Realism: Rossellini Interviewed by Mario Verdone," *Screen*, 14 (1973-74), 70.
10. Suzanne Budgen, *Fellini* (London: British Film Institute, 1966), p. 92.
11. Fellini rarely admits the influence of other writers or directors. Nevertheless, he has stated that "it isn't necessary to read a certain author—say, Joyce—if Joyce has really been important, as he has been, to contemporary culture. Then you come to know Joyce by looking at the layout of a magazine, speaking with people, observing how a girl is dressed." Any crucial thinker, artist, or director is, therefore, "absorbed" into a film director's work through his subconscious awareness of the culture of his times, even if that individual or his works have not been formally encountered on an intellectual level. If Fellini could make this statement about James Joyce, an author little known in Italy until after 1945, it would be impossible to imagine that Luigi Pirandello, Italy's major dramatist and the dominant Italian literary figure of the century, would not have left his mark upon Fellini's work. For the complete text of this interview, see *Federico Fellini's Juliet of the Spirits*, ed. Tullio Kezich (New York: Orion, 1965), pp. 11-65.
12. The *fotoromanzo* derives its name and peculiar character from the fact that the narrative is carried forward by photographs of actual people rather than by cartoons, as in comic strips (*fumetti* in Italian). The *foto-*

romanzo does, however, retain a balloon encircling the character's words, typical of the comic strips.

13. Fellini's association of the mechanical with the comical, ultimately derived from Henri Bergson and Pirandello, is most apparent in his latest film *Casanova*, in which the protagonist's sexual exploits are consistently portrayed as mechanical, are accompanied by the flappings of a mechanical bird, and are finally summarized in a brilliant closing scene where Casanova dreams of his only satisfying sexual encounter (that with a mechanical doll) and performs in his dream a dance with the doll in which he, too, becomes a machine.

14. Federico Fellini, *Early Screenplays*, trans. Judith Green (New York: Orion, 1971), p. 102. Subsequent references to this script will be taken from this edition.

15. For the script of *The Vitelloni*, see Federico Fellini, *Three Screenplays*, trans. Judith Green (New York: Orion, 1970). For a discussion of *The Vitelloni* in connection with *Il Bidone*, *Amarcord*, or Fellini's imagery, see the articles by Aldo Tassone, Geneviève Agel, and Gilbert Salachas reprinted in this volume.

. . . .

25. The Secret Life of Federico Fellini   *Peter Harcourt*

. . . as far as my personal feelings are concerned, the film I'm fondest of is *La Strada*.[1]

. . . I believe in prayers and miracles.[2]

There is a sequence in *La Strada* that is crucial for our understanding of the films of Federico Fellini. It begins with a wedding celebration taking place in the open air. To one side of a long banquet table, really quite unnoticed by the wedding party, Zampanò and Gelsomina are performing one of their tatty numbers, a kind of raggle-taggle conga. Zampanò is seated and is playing the drum, his huge form made awkward by the crumpled position necessary for him to hold the drum between his knees, while Gelsomina is performing her stiff little dance. Bowler hat on her head and clown's make-up on her face, she hops

. . . .

From *Film Quarterly*, Vol. 19, No. 3 (1966), pp. 4-13, 19. © 1966 by The Regents of the University of California. Reprinted by permission of The Regents and Peter Harcourt. An updated version of this article appears as a chapter in Peter Harcourt's *Six European Directors* (Harmondsworth: Penguin Books, 1974).

about in time to the music, thrusting her arms forward on every fourth beat. All about them both is the litter that is always associated with any festivity in Fellini; and although she is ignored by the wedding party, scarcely noticed by the adult world, while Gelsomina dances, a number of children in the background dance in unison with her. They respond in sympathy to what she is doing and imitate her movements. One of the guests offers Gelsomina some wine which, after a hurried sip, she passes on to Zampanò. Then the lady-of-the-house calls them to come and eat, and the sad little performance ends. On her way to the house, however, Gelsomina is led away by the children who have been so attentive to her dancing. There is apparently something that they want her to see.

She is led up a narrow flight of stairs by the side of the house and along a network of corridors where she almost loses her way. At one moment we see a little boy dressed in a black cloak gliding along. We've never seen him before in this film and we'll never see him again; but the magical fascination of his sudden appearance holds us for that moment and gives us the sense of something festive about to take place as well as perhaps of something that we can't quite understand. Who is this boy? What is he doing here? What is going on?

Gelsomina is then led into a large dark room, all the windows shuttered to keep out the sun, at the end of which crouches Osvaldo, a little boy in a big bed. There are two small mobiles suspended above him, little universes that rotate before his eyes. Indeed, his eyes stare out of his misshaped head, for he is apparently some kind of spastic, in the film regarded as a little idiot boy. The children ask Gelsomina to try and make him laugh, but her imitative bird flutterings only strike more terror into the boy's already terrified eyes. Finally, in a moment impossible to describe without limiting its implications, she draws close to him—he staring in confused terror at her, her own eyes opening wide to receive the full impact of this stare. Then abruptly, she and all the children are chased out of the room by a nun.

What is the meaning of this moment in *La Strada?* What is it that she receives from those wild staring eyes? Is it that in this misformed child she recognizes some affinity with her own gentle strangeness? *Un po strana*, as her mother described her at the beginning of the film. Or is it that she senses in this blank unmovable face something beyond the powers of her simple goodness to affect in any way? And is it, then, a feeling of real terror that communicates itself to her, the result of a sudden recognition that at the end of long corridors hidden away in some sunless room there might lurk something terrible, something beyond our understanding, something deeply buried away and kept from conscious sight, but something terrifyingly real nevertheless?[3] In the film, it is a moment of great power as Fellini creates it for us; and like the tatty party and the fleeting appearance of the bright-faced little boy, it is a moment that can remind us of similar moments in other films by Fellini. Yet it is essentially dumb. It defies confident interpretation. Just as the idiot boy's eyes do not fully give up their meaning to the inquisitive Gelsomina, so the scene holds back its full significance from us. It is a moment where something deep and irrational passes between these two people; and if we are temperamentally attuned to Fellini's particular universe sufficiently to receive it, then something equally deep and irrational passes through to us.

But the sequence continues. We cut to the kitchen where Zampanò and the woman are stuffing themselves with food and talking about marriage. She is explaining how her first husband had been as big as he is and that no one subsequently has had any use for his clothes. Gelsomina appears and tries to tell Zampanò about the sick boy she has seen; but she fails to communicate anything to him and is left alone with her meal and with the gradual realization of what is going on as Zampanò and the woman go upstairs together, to see about those clothes.

Then a fade onto a typical Fellini post-festivity scene. The light of day has almost totally disappeared, making the foreground dark while the sky is still luminous beyond. Rags of streamers are hanging down from the house and posts nearby, and a single tree is isolated in mid-frame as one remaining couple carry on dancing to the sound of a lonely accordion player. Suddenly we notice a light-bulb dangling in the upper righthand corner of the frame, appearing comically out of place and apparently without function. But as we draw back a bit, we see that Gelsomina is in fact contemplating this scene from a barn window and the light-bulb begins to make a little more sense.

Zampanò is trying on his new clothes, absurdly self-involved in his new-found pinstriped elegance. Meanwhile, Gelsomina begins to hum her little tune and relates how she had first heard it one day in the rain while standing by an open window. She wonders what it is called and asks Zampanò if he will teach her to play it on the trumpet. But as he continues to ignore her, she gets angry with him and stomps about the barn, finally falling down a hole where she decides to spend the night.

A cock crows as we dissolve into morning. Gelsomina is determined to take her stand. She is going to leave Zampanò and return home, not because she doesn't like the work but because she requires some human recognition. *Io me ne vado*, she keeps screaming to an unresponsive Zampanò and later to the stillness of the morning; but then, after changing back into the togs she wore originally, taking care to return all of Zampanò's property, she sets out on her way, waving in spite of herself at whomever she sees in a field nearby. There is no real sense of where she is going, simply the desire to get away.

After a bit (another dissolve), she sits down by the roadside, apparently in gloom. Then she notices a lady-bug or some such small creature and cannot help but become fascinated by it. She places it on her finger and blows it away. And immediately, without preparation, without a hint of plausibility in any social or psychological terms,[4] a characteristic Fellini miracle occurs. Her sense of wonder is renewed. The impulse to live again surges up inside of her as does her determination to continue her lonely journey in life. A little circus band of three musicians appears in the middle of a field, walking along by the side of the road; and in her turnabout way, she dances after them into town. Once in town she will come across another procession—a religious celebration—and, also in the rain as when she first heard her little tune, she will encounter Il Matto—the Fool—wearing an angel's wings and balancing precariously in the sky. Throughout the rest of the film, we will be aware of a strange affinity between Il Matto and Gelsomina, the stripes on his tights matching the stripes on her jersey as he also shares with her her little tune which he plays on a tiny violin.

> There are more Zampanòs in the world than bicycle thieves, and the story of a man who discovers his neighbour is just as important as the story of a strike.[5]

> I believe that everyone has to find truth by himself. . . . That is . . . the reason why my pictures never end. They never have a simple solution. I think it is immoral (in the true sense of the word) to tell a story that has a conclusion. Because you cut out the audience the moment you present a solution on the screen. Because there are no "solutions" in their lives. I think it is more moral—and more important—to show, let's say, the story of one man. Then every one, with his own sensibility and on the basis of his own inner development, can try to find his own solution.[6]

In essence, the whole of Fellini can be found in this sequence from *La Strada*. His thematic center is here. To begin with, reinforced by the title itself, there is the sense of life as a journey, as a constant tearing away from things known and a plunging into the unfamiliar. Unlike Bergman, however, whose allegoric wanderings are generally from place to place—in *Wild Strawberries*, the journey from Stockholm to

Lund parallelling old Borg's journey along the path of increased self-knowledge—in Fellini, there is seldom any sense of direction or eventual goal. The form of his films tends to be circular, the characters usually ending where they began.

This restlessness of movement can work in different ways. Occasionally, as with the nuns in *La Strada*, there is the feeling that we must give up things dear to us before we get too fond of them; but more frequently there is the feeling that only by moving on, by probing and searching, can we ever come to know the purpose of life. Fellini's fondness for processions is obviously related to this. Indeed, it sometimes seems as if the celebration of movement such as we witness in processions may by itself *provide* the purpose, as if in terrestial terms there may be, in fact, no goal.

Of course, Fellini would reject such intellectual speculations. For Fellini is an intuitive in his response to life, a great muddle-headed irrationalist with very strong feelings and no clear thought. He lives life from the senses, yet his intelligence has informed him that the senses can deceive. Hence, the intellectual indecisions, the apparently inexhaustible interviews with all their self-contradictions. Yet, hence too all the passionate affirmations of his films. It is as if Fellini recognizes that "truth" must lie somewhere, though locked up in subjectivity, but he is unable to seize it with the merely rational surface of his mind. Hence all the turbulence, all the restless energy, the endless travelling along streets and long corridors. Whether it is the Vitelloni wandering about the beach or the town at night or Moraldo setting off at the end on his own for we don't know where; whether it is the peasant families at the end of *Il Bidone* (the little children with ricks on their backs recalling the first shot of Gelsomina) that walk by beyond the reach of the dying Augusto; or whether it is the complete Fellini-Anselmi entourage descending that vast structure at the close of 8½ and dancing round and round the circus ring together in an infinity of perfect movement—whatever the context and whatever the film, this perpetual movement is central to Fellini. And it is also central to his irrational view of life that the movement should be without origin or goal.

But in this sequence from *La Strada*, there are also some examples of the twin experiences that this directionless journey through life must entail—experiences of the freshness and unexpectedness of innocence which are immediately followed by the experience of something dreadful that in a world freed from the devil is now without a name. On the one hand, we have the presence of Gelsomina herself and of the somewhat querulous Il Matto who appears from on high; but more characteristically we have the fleeting image of that little boy in the cloak passing along the corridor that charms us so gratuitously. For it is also a part of Fellini's irrationality that especially childhood innocence should so often play such a formally gratuitous role in his films, that children should simply appear and then disappear—providing us with a momentary pleasure and perhaps renewing our faith in the wonder of life but remaining essentially apart from the troubled business of life in Fellini's adult world. This goes a long way in *La Dolce Vita* towards explaining the floating presence of Paola, the little Umbrian angel, who has so universally been disapproved of as a facile resolution to that troubling, too-long film.[7] Initially, Paola simply passes into a short bridging sequence and passes out again, like the boy in the cloak. We see her setting the table at a seaside restaurant, misunderstanding Marcello's difficulties yet attracted by some quality in him, while deriving simple enjoyment from the loud assertions of "Patricia" playing on the juke-box, a simplicity that is emphasized by the later degradation which we experience towards the end of the film when Nadia strips to the same tune. But Paola has been placed here so that when she appears in the epilogue to the film as a kind of *diva ex machina*, she may suggest a quality in life that has been ignored in the compulsive distractions we have been witnessing. Dramatically in any conventional way, she may leave much to be desired; but she is perfect for suggesting Fellini's sense of youthful trust that, although beautiful, is presented as ineffectual and so exists somewhat apart. And we may remember in *I Vitelloni* Moraldo's child companion of the railways, with whom he discoursed about life and the stars, who is left to return to the hopelessness of the town, balancing precariously along the rails. Or we might remember the children towards the end of *La Strada* who (as if in gentle rehearsal for the end of 8½) are dancing in a ring round a young tree while their mother (we assume) is hanging out her washing and singing Gelsomina's tune. And of course, there are the young people who appear out of the woods at the end of *Le Notti di Cabiria*: "We have lost our way," one of them says as they begin to circle round her while another barks at her in a way that might remind us of the wild compère in the nightclub towards the beginning of the film. In spite of the hopelessness of her present position, the lack of "solution" to any of her problems, she cannot help but return their smiles and their "*Buona sera*." And of course in 8½, when the lights dim and the ring of dancers vanish and even the circus performers disappear from the scene, it is the young Guido Anselmi-cum-young-Federico Fellini who is left alone in the spotlight and who moves with it to the side of the ring, leaving the screen in darkness. Although there's never a solution to any of the problems, there's always the sense of something young and fresh left to carry on.

Yet, if on the one hand there are children, representing the possibility of new forms of life, on the other there is the recurring presence of this dreadful nameless thing, the presence of some form of evil, of some kind of threat.

In all of Fellini's films, there are these disturbing images, moments of disillusion that serve to challenge simple faith. There is the sinister homosexual who so disappoints Leopoldo in *I Vitelloni*, as there had been the more-than-disappointing flesh-and-blood reality of the White Sheik before. But in *I Vitelloni* more powerfully and more like Osvaldo is the woman in the cinema who so easily tempts Fausto and who is again encountered one day on the beach. Within the subterranean depths of Fellini's imagination, she serves as a link between Osvaldo and La Saraghina and simply appears at odd moments as a threat to the flesh. Also in *I Vitelloni* there is the married man in the dark glasses who tempts Olga away. He too is first encountered on the beach; but most ominous of all is the shot of his dark car just before they drive away: it is almost hidden by the early morning shadows in the street while the light glares out above it threateningly, like a scar. And if in *Cabiria* there is of course the deceitful Oscar, more in keeping with the irrationality of these images of threat is the devil-dressed magician who through hypnosis turns innocence towards evil ends.

Excluding for the moment La Saraghina, who is a more complex incarnation of this kind of nameless threat, simultaneously described as "evil" yet *felt* to be beautiful, in *La Dolce Vita* we have a summary of this sort of effect in that strange blob of a fish that pollutes the stretch of beach at the end of the film and forms the imaginative counterpole to the young Paola waving to Marcello across the protective inlet of the sea. It is as if something deep in Fellini recognizes that in childhood and childlike responses to existence, there is beauty and affirmation of a frequently troubling kind, troubling because unconscious of the terrible threats and temptations that can lurk in the unknowable depths of adult life; and in the way that so frequently these polar elements seem more an accompaniment to the main theme than a formally intrinsic part of his films, it is as if at this stage of his development, Fellini cannot consciously work out the exact relationship between these two extremes or even to find a settled place for them within the narrative structure of his films. Constantly he creates situations for which he can find no earthly solution and his characters encounter difficulties be-

La Dolce Vita: Fellini and Marcello Mastroianni examine the monster fish used in the concluding sequence of the film. (Museum of Modern Art/Film Stills Archive)

yond their means to control. So for the end of *La Dolce Vita,* it is as if the gods themselves must be evoked to bring about the closing affirmation. Failing to communicate anything helpful to Marcello, the little Umbrian angel looks straight at the camera, and at us. What do we make of it all? What do we feel about innocence by the end?

> I make movies in the same way that I talk to people—whether it's a friend, a girl, a priest, or anyone: to seek some clarification. That is what neo-realism means to me, in the original, pure sense. A search into oneself, and into others. In any direction, any direction where there is life. All the formal philosophy you could possibly apply to my work is that there is no formal philosophy. . . . A man's film is like a naked man— nothing can be hidden. I must be truthful in my films.[8]

Among many film enthusiasts, especially in Great Britain, Fellini has been undervalued and, I think, misunderstood. Before the appearance of *8½, I Vitelloni* has often been regarded as his most successful film.

And so it is—on the social realist level. Along with *Il Bidone* in its somewhat grimmer way, *I Vitelloni* is the only Fellini film that truly works on the level of social observation. It is balanced in its narrative, minutely observant, beautifully paced, and very funny. Yet from a slightly deeper level, it can also make a more personal appeal. When looked at sympathetically, it is not *essentially* that different from Fellini's other films. Beneath its realist exterior, it too can make its more subliminal appeal.

One of the difficulties that Fellini's films pose for more rational minds—indeed, we could even say, one of the limitations of Fellini's particular kind of cinematic art—is that he has too often been too careless about the surface credibility of his films, confusing and alienating all but the most sympathetic of his viewers as the conventions of his films have seemed so strange. Yet at their best—excluding the colorful excesses of *Boccaccio 70* and *Giulietta degli spiriti*—they are strange only to the expectations of literary narrative and of psychological realism. Fellini's conventions are not at all strange to the language of painting which, beneath the narrative surface of his films, is the language that he most frequently employs.

For there is in all real films—in all films that have the lasting interest that characterizes a work of art—what I find it convenient to call a subliminal level, a level largely of images plus the complex associations of scarcely perceived sounds. Although we are often not really conscious of these vital ingredients, especially on a first viewing, we can nevertheless be immensely moved by their power to affect us. Indeed, it is generally these elements that give a film its atmosphere or mood.

If there are in Fellini certain constantly recurring themes or motifs, there are also certain constantly recurring images and effects that, when responded to, can make an extraordinary impression upon us and which are then cumulative in their power. For these images to be discussed at all, criticism has to lean away from the comfortably confident tone of literary-cum-film analysis and draw upon the tentativeness of art appreciation. For the central fact about art criticism is the elusiveness of the total power of the image when talked about in words and of the apparently greater subjectivity of the way paintings speak to us, moving towards music which is the most subjectively elusive of all. Images and sounds cannot be argued with. They either affect us or they don't. When talking about a painting, there is always so much that we cannot *know*. The discursive element in painting is automatically much less than it can be in literature and the speculative element in interpretation correspondingly that much more. Once again, we might think of that moment between Osvaldo and Gelsomina, the inscrutability of which I've taken some pains to describe; but in Fellini's films, there are images of greater tentativeness than this.

If we look at a painting by Jean Carzou, for example "The Bay of Dreams," there are many things that we might want to say about it, about the gentle flowing lines of the figure in the foreground moving through a variety of shapes and objects in extended perspective to the sharply jagged quality of the mountains in the rear. But one of the most striking formal elements in the picture and part of what is for me the forlornness of its mood is the lateral shadow that cuts across its middle, intensifying its sense of space and further distancing these two contrasting worlds. If we next look at an image from *I Vitelloni*, just after the departure of Moraldo's pregnant sister on her shotgun honeymoon, if we are responding to the impact of the images in the film and not just waiting for the next point of characterization or development of plot to emerge, we might be affected in much the same way. Similarly, if we contemplate the effect of the foreground shadow in Giorgio de Chirico's "The Rose Tower"[9] and remember that the entire proposal scene between Oscar and Cabiria is similarly played in shadow with the landscape and buildings luminous behind, we might feel that by the very light itself, both de Chirico and Fellini, working independently in their quite different ways, have employed these foreground shadows to lend a worried aspect to the scene and yet to suggest that there is something worthwhile in the distance, something worth achieving beyond.

In fact, de Chirico, perhaps because as an Italian he too has been particularly sensitive to Italian space and Italian light, can be used again and again to illuminate by analogy the images in Fellini. Along with images of the sea and of isolated trees,[10] the Italian town square with its fountain in the middle is a recurrent image in Fellini. It is generally seen at night or in the early morning, generally presented as a place of reckoning and is divorced from its more sociable associations of being a place where people meet. In Fellini, the town square is never felt to be the social center of a community. De Chirico too seemed to be sensitive to the empty feeling of such places at unused times of day—indeed, to the very irrelevance of such vast structures to the little intimacies of human life. And so in de Chirico, we find a number of such paintings that depict huge buildings and exaggerated shadows, where the tiny figures serve both to emphasize the hugeness of the structures (as do the miniature trains that we frequently see puffing away on the horizon) and to give a feeling that the little human things don't really belong in such a space. Sometimes this feeling is further emphasized by the presence of some stray object in the foreground, some object made bizarre by being torn from the context of its function—like that light-bulb in *La Strada* or the railway carriage that we see in "Anguish of Departure" in the middle of the square.

So with Fellini, in the much-admired beach sequence in *I Vitelloni*, (admired for its sensitive observation of these five men imprisoned in their own apathy and defeated by the feeling that there is nothing they can do) Fellini emphasizes their own feeling of irrelevance and functionlessness by the many apparently useless structures that we see sticking up out of the sand. Skeletons of summer changing-huts and odd inexplicable bits of wire frequently dominate the scene and create the feeling of something strange with an almost surrealist intensity. Everywhere throughout the film as throughout every Fellini film there is the recurring presence of the bizarre.

In fact, this recognition of the bizarre is at the center of Fellini's world, the physical parallel of his response to the irrational, the source both of his humor and of his sense of dread. For if humor is uppermost in most films by Fellini, beneath the comic observation of the discrepancies of human life there is always this feeling of something beyond our control, something not fully known to our rational selves—like that grotesque fish at the end of *La Dolce Vita* or like Osvaldo in that guarded-over room.

The first image we see in the first film directed by Fellini himself is an image of a structure sticking up out of the sand with a piece of cloth blowing in the wind. In front of this structure with his robes also blowing sits the White Sheik on his horse in all his phony splendor—an opening image of immense absurdity as indeed are so many of the images in this extraordinarily funny film. But it is really in *Cabiria* that this purely visual absurdity acquires its most consistently surrealist force. Constantly surrounding Cabiria's box-like house is a litter of people and objects apparently devoid of function and deprived of any context of psychological plausibility. At one moment as we track along we see a post with a for-sale sign on top and a bicycle leaning against it, a baby in a stroller a little beyond, and a woman squatting in the field further beyond that. At another moment as we see Cabiria stomping back from her unfortunate dunking in the river, wearing her characteristic vertical stripes, we see the bulbous Wanda in the background, beside her some washing, a stray horse, and behind her quite inexplicably a little black creature with an umbrella in the field, and behind all that, above yet another box of a house, there is a kite sailing aimlessly in the sky. But most absurd of all and most characteristically Fellinian is the strangely functionless structure that exists outside Cabiria's house. How did it come to be there and what purpose does it serve? Questions like that can have no answer on any rational plane, but the presence of this structure dominates a number of scenes in the film; and of course it is related both to the beach structures that we've seen more naturalistically in *The White Sheik* and *I Vitelloni* and that structure to end all structures that looms over *8½!* And as in *8½* where throngs of people are always walking up and down this unnecessary construction, so in *Cabiria* little boys are constantly clambering about these poles that exist outside her home. Like the circus itself so important in Fellini, like the apparently gratuitous accomplishments of the clown or aerialist, it is as if this kind of purposeless activity that nevertheless can give pleasure and even a kind of physical meaning to the absurdity of life should exist as an emblem of Fellini's view of the world—movement without direction, life essentially without a goal.

> Visually, I've often made use of the theme of circus life which is a mixture of spectacle, risk, and reality. My characters are often a bit bizarre. I'm always talking to people in the street who seem rather unusual or out of place or who have some physical or mental affliction. Also, there is naturally the theme of beaches that recurs in all my films, but that has been talked about so much that I don't want to go into it! Since all these elements form a part of me, I don't see why I shouldn't introduce them into my films.[11]

So far in this account of Fellini, I have been concerned only with the thematic consistency of his work and with the peculiar force of his imagery. Taken all together, Fellini's films create a world that is uniquely and personally his own. They manage to enact his vision of the universe. But all this, although true, tends to ignore the great differences between Fellini's individual films, differences of surface characteristics but also finally of quality as well. For much as I respond with enormous pleasure to nearly everything that he has produced—even to much of *Giulietta degli spiriti*—I recognize that if Fellini is a man of immense inventiveness, he is also a director of uncertain control over the many elements that his mind, with apparently so little effort, can with such energy invent. Also, if Fellini is a man who has created for us an immensely personal view of life on the screen, I recognize that it is just that—an *immensely personal view of life* which is frequently egotistic, self-indulgent, sentimental, and above all wilfully irrational, courting mystery at every corner and asking from us as much compassion for all these difficulties as he has bestowed upon them himself.[12]

So the critics who have preferred *I Vitelloni* to anything that Fellini has subsequently done—at least until 8½—have probably done so because of all his films, *I Vitelloni* least imprisons us in Fellini's private world. There is in the film such a wealth of surface detail that we can get a good deal from it without being too closely attuned to its more subjective elements. Whereas *La Strada* presents Fellini's private world with a minimum of props.

In *La Strada*, unless we are sensitive to the subliminal level on which the film is really operating and are sympathetic to Fellini's concern through his images to unite Gelsomina with Il Matto and the two of them with the sea while at the same time he is enmeshing Zampanò in his own chains of earth and fire and brute insensitivity, unless we are sensitive to the suggestive power of the imagery, the film will either make very little sense to us or it will seem terribly naive. If by way of "meaning" we carry away from *La Strada* only Il Matto's disquisition on the usefulness of pebbles, then we will come away with what we could rightly call a sentimental experience. But if we have been moved by the little children dancing round that tree and are aware that it is Gelsomina's beloved sea—both her natural home and her constant friend—that is washing up on the beach during that final image where Zampanò lies crushed by a kind of dumb and brutal grief, then the intellectually self-indulgent and sentimental elements will be buoyed up by some sort of aesthetic charge as well, by the sense of some depth of feeling and perception being communicated to us beyond what our merely rational selves can readily receive.

For if it is true that there is nothing in Fellini's films that we can properly call thought, there is nevertheless evidence of an intelligence of a totally different kind. Everywhere in his films there is the presence of a mind that responds to life itself on a subliminal level, that is acutely conscious of the natural metaphors to be found in the trappings of day-to-day life and which struggles to find a structure both flexible and persuasive enough to contain them within his films. Even in a film as distended and episodic as *La Dolce Vita*, there is an intricate interweaving of sounds and images that help to bind together this elongated experience. When the lifeless statue of Christ is being flown to St. Peter's at the opening of the film, only a handful of *ragazzi* follow its shadow through the streets of Rome; while at the injunction of the pneumatic Sylvia to "Follow me everybody," this laughing, living goddess, this beatific creature who is more at home with little kittens than with the temptations of the flesh, gains an active and excited response as people follow her dance about the nightclub floor. I've already mentioned the ironic repetition of the "Patricia" tune which should help to give a slightly more settled place to the presence of Paola—if we're fully attentive to the soundtrack of the film, we should be remembering Paola while we're watching Nadia strip—but also at Steiner's party certain things occur that acquire a formal relevance by the end.

In fact, the portrait of Steiner offers a convenient example of how Fellini's compressed characterization works in this sprawling fresco of his own uneasy mind.[13] As his German name might suggest (and he is played by a French actor!), Steiner is the modern *déraciné* eclectic, a man with only intellectual allegiances. For him, all experience is filtered through the mind. He is a *dilettante*, as he himself says, "too serious to be an amateur and not serious enough to be a professional." He remains outside experience, unattached, and strives to bring to life the order and clarity of a work of art. In his self-created isolation, he draws what sustenance he can from the culture of all nations and epochs. When we first see him, he is carrying a Sanskrit grammar in a modern church and, after a few tentative chords of jazz, we hear him playing a Bach toccata on the organ.

For Steiner, life has meaning only if he can contemplate it as he can a work of art. Even natural sounds, the roar of the wind and the sea, are recorded on tape and listened to like music; and his delight in his daughter is largely the delight he takes in her fondness for words, in her own instinctive gifts as a poet. For Steiner, real life is apparently too much and he tries, through art, to find an escape. Of course, he fails; and through his failure Fellini would seem to be, too schematically, insisting that there can be no path into the future through intellectual activity or through art. Yet, by the end of the film when we're confronted with the final beach scene and by our necessary Paola,[14] we should recognize that those very same sounds of the wind and the sea that Steiner had listened to as music are part of the disturbance that, along with the intrusive inlet of the sea, keeps Paola from communicating with Marcello. They are part of her "natural" protection from his jaded world. And although I shouldn't want to make great claims for the power of such effects to hold together this too insistent film, nevertheless they do reveal the presence of an artistic intelligence of a rare intuitive kind.

> I don't like the idea of "understanding" a film. I don't believe that rational understanding is an essential element in the reception of any work

of art. Either a film has something to say to you or it hasn't. If you are moved by it, you don't need to have it explained to you. If not, no explanation can make you moved by it. That's why I don't think my films are misunderstood when they are accepted for different reasons. Every person has his own fund of experiences and emotions which he brings to bear on every new experience—whether it is to his view of a film or to a love affair; and it is simply the combination of the film with the reality already existing in each person which creates the final impression of unity. As I was saying, this is the way the spectator participates in the process of creation. This diversity of reaction doesn't mean that the objective reality of the film has been misunderstood. Anyway, there is no objective reality in my films, any more than there is in life.[15] . . .

NOTES

1. *Federico Fellini*, by Gilbert Salachas (Éditions Seghers, 1963); p. 103. Translations from the French have been done with the help of Sue Bennett.
2. *Journal d'un Bidoniste*, by Delouche Dominique (bound with *Les Chemins de Fellini*, by Geneviève Agel, Les Éditions du cerf, 1956), p. 129.
3. Geneviève Agel (op. cit.), in the course of an immensely sensitive but predominantly Christian interpretation of Fellini's work, sees Osvaldo as marking one of the four stages in Gelsomina's development. See pp. 5 ff.
4. Although recently Fellini has related how just such a little band did one day improbably appear.
5. *Journal d'un Bidoniste*, p. 129.
6. From an interview with Gideon Bachmann in *Film: Book 1* (ed. Robert Hughes, Grove Press, 1959), p. 101.
7. See for example Eric Rhode in *Sight & Sound*, Winter '60-'61, p. 34.
8. *Film: Book 1*, p. 105.
9. For a better understanding of the painting of de Chirico, I am indebted to Peter Greenaway, painter and film-maker and himself a perceptive student of Fellini.
10. For a more detailed account of Fellini's recurrent imagery, see *Les Chemins de Fellini* (op. cit.) or following that, the excellent chapter on Fellini in John Russell Taylor's *Cinema Eye, Cinema Ear* (Methuen, 1964).
11. From another interview with Gideon Bachmann in *Cinéma 65* (Numéro 99, Sept.-Octobre).
12. Again, see John Russell Taylor's account for the "womb-like" quality of Fellini's affection.
13. This description of Steiner is adapted from an account of *La Dolce Vita* I wrote for the *Twentieth Century*, Jan. 1961, pp. 81 ff.
14. Gilbert Salachas, with nice perception, sees Paola as the guest of honor—"*l'hôtesse d'honneur*"—in *La Dolce Vita*. Op. cit., p. 2.
15. From *Cinéma 65* (op. cit.), p. 85.

. . . .

26. Reality, Fantasy, and Fellini   *Patrizio Rossi and Ben Lawton*

In the two decades following the second world war the importance of Italian cinema has come to be recognized the world over. From the stark realism of *La Battaglia di Algieri*, of *Banditi ad Orgosolo*, to the fantasy worlds of *Blow-up, Giulietta degli Spiriti* and *I Clowns*, it has left a mark on world cinema which every serious director must consider. . . . The apparently irreconcilable opposites, realism and fantasy, did not, however, burst forth simultaneously on the Italian cinematic scene; rather the process was a laborious one, during which the two modes were often, if not permanently, in conflict, and it is only in most recent times that the right to coexistence has been recognized to the genres, singly and in combination. Although no man can be said to be totally responsible for the acceptance of fantasy as a legitimate filmic mode, it was unquestionably Federico Fellini's midwifery which helped it be born of the already established Italian neorealism.

Fellini's earliest battle was directed towards the legitimation of subjective reality in the almost fanatical neorealistic ambiance of post-war Italian cinema, against both critical and financial opinion. He began his career as a scriptwriter in 1943, but it wasn't until 1950 that he had his earliest directorial experience, working alongside Alberto Lattuada on *Luci del Varietà*. The film, an unsentimentalized portrait of vaudeville life, was a critical and financial failure. It was pejoratively compared to "Ridi Pagliaccio" by Angelo Solmi, and Fellini was compelled to return to scriptwriting until 1952 when, working independently, he produced *Lo Sceicco Bianco*. The inchoate elements of the *univers fellinien*, which we have all come to recognize, began to take concrete form in this film which, at the 1952 Venice Festival, was panned by most of the critics, who were unable to understand or accept the director's innovations. Undaunted Fellini went to work on his next film, *I Vitelloni*, which was inspired by the memories of his personal experiences as a student in Rimini. Completed in time for the 1953 Venice Festival, where it was awarded the Silver Lion, it was a critical suc-

. . . .

From *Italian Quarterly*, Vol. 15, Nos. 58-59 (1971), pp. 87-97. Reprinted by permission of *Italian Quarterly*.

cess. The jurors praised the "insights it offered into a previously unexplored milieu of provincial Italy." They felt that in the "excellent portrayal of certain segments of small town society" *I Vitelloni* "achieved
a universal validity by revealing the worst failings of middle class youth
not only in Italy, but in the world at large."[1] These opinions which
emphasized the neorealistic tones of the film were immediately chal-
lenged by the hard-line disciples of that school who perceived that, as
in his preceding works, here too the director had blended objective and
subjective realities. In 1954, however, when *La Strada* was released, it
was met by the almost unanimous condemnation of the Neorealists
who decried the film's international success and accused Fellini of
treachery.

    La Strada was not made merely as a reflex to an environmental situa-
tion in order to eke out a solution for a social difficulty, nor can it be
compared to De Sica's *Ladri di Biciclette* which does not pierce far
enough beneath the surface of the situation it portrays to reveal the
complex subjective, emotional responses deep within its characters.
The Neorealists, although capable of responding to injustice and misfortune in a social context, had not explored the profound consequences
these conditions imposed upon the individual, and it is for this that
Fellini searches. The film's theme is man's anxious attempt to find individual happiness in a world which constantly obstructs and confuses
him in his quest. Fellini confronts the problem by dealing internally
with "atypical" individuals. By drawing on his characters' inner experiences he makes their response to reality highly personal and universally
human at the same time. This unique approach, however, totally inverted the Neorealists' mode of operation and, consequently, aroused
their ire. The neorealist critics' primary objection was directed towards
the director's choice of characters. The one protagonist which Italian
post-war cinema had consistently refused to portray was precisely the
one which Fellini's film brought to the footlights: the tumblers, the
jugglers and the clowns whose very presence acts symbolically to con-
jure up a universe which exists beyond reality. The Neorealists' condemnation of the director was addressed less to his patent mysticism
than to his fusion of neorealistic techniques and poetic statements.
That he should use their methods to convey a symbol-packed story was
to them the most extreme of his crimes against the movement.

    Until the appearance of *La Strada* psychological and aesthetic theo-
reticians had not realized that to initiate a new cinema it was not
enough to introduce hand-picked characters and social environments
into neorealistic film; one needed rather an all-important alteration in

the point of view from which these environments could be seen. The Neorealists felt that *La Strada* was an extremely dangerous threat to Italian cinema. In it they saw the take-over of the world of the "little people," which they had been portraying in such a revolutionary manner, by mystically inspired poetry. As seen by Fellini, this humble world of the common man became the limitless universe of the "poor in spirit," the "wise fool" and the "infantile brute." While the Neorealists felt that this was a dangerous, reactionary turn towards symbolism, the opponents of this school were catalysed by Fellini's innovations. They now had *La Strada* around which they could rally the cinematographic powers not subservient to realism. Fellini became for them the spiritual center of a new movement which they felt would supplant neorealistic cinema with a cinema of pure art.

Fellini did not remain silent in the face of the accusations leveled against him. At first he reacted vigorously to the charges of infidelity by swearing that he was not a subversive, that he had only modified neorealistic principles by taking them in an artistic direction more amenable to his own talents. To understand the full measure of Fellini's resentment in answering his detractors we must remember that the controversy was grounded in political attitudes and inextricably enmeshed with political partisanship. Because of this, critical opinions both for and against neorealism were clearly separated along the issues of the nation's political divisions.

This sensitivity to politics is typical of the Italian literary world as well. In a discussion of the crisis in literary neorealism,[2] the novelist Italo Calvino gives an account of the ways in which various authors attempted to evade the impasse into which the neorealistic novel had run. He explains that he too chose a new direction which was almost totally antithetical to his previous one by drawing inspiration from the *Orlando Furioso*, Ariosto's fantastic epic poem. Calvino is quick to add, however, that he has not abandoned neorealism for a permanent love affair with fantasy, that he still prefers writing novels in the realistic genre. Like Fellini trying to defend his position as a neorealist, Calvino attempts to rationalize his tergiversation by reaffirming his serious moral commitment to his realistic work. He disclaims the validity of his experimentation by relegating it to the status of an inconsequential escapade with fantasy. Fellini, too, had been accused of abandoning his moral commitment to art in favor of making solipsistic films overrun with vague symbolic implications. Indeed, he had great difficulty in facing these charges of "immorality" since he was quite obviously turning away from a cinema tightly controlled by the moralistic theologies of socialism and communism.

When interviewed by Dominique Delouche in 1956,[3] Fellini asserted that, although in principle his films still proceeded as analyses of life's most concrete elements, he was being increasingly drawn towards the illumination of internal, personal reality rather than the external reality of humanity en masse. In the same interview he remarked with irritation: "I have been reprimanded for having presented a couple of exceptional characters, Gelsomina and Zampanò, in *La Strada*; but for me the story of one man who discovers his neighbor is as real and as important as the story of a strike."[4] In 1958, when the echo of *Le Notti di Cabiria* was still lingering in the air and *La Dolce Vita* was already in the process of gestation, Fellini reaffirmed his faith in neorealism, but insisted that the creative film-maker should eventually attempt to transcend the rigid limits imposed by the movement's theoreticians. "I absolutely cannot believe," he said, "in a cinema which constantly returns to dusty, outworn formulae, polishes them up, attempts to pass them off as new and then attempts to justify its actions by claiming that neorealism is exhausted." He insisted that "we cannot ignore neorealism, but we must go beyond it. The neorealistic vision is constructive, deeply human, and concrete."[5]

The following year Fellini's artistic position became even more explicit. At that time he went on to add that although neorealism had been surpassed by new innovations in cinema, it was still of importance for the contemporary film-maker. In response to an interviewer who asked whether it were still possible to speak of a neorealistic trend in Italian cinema, Fellini retorted: "Those who mourn the passing away of neorealism are anti-historical in their attitude, but as a spiritual state of mind neorealism must still be deemed a formative experience of inestimable value."[6]

Two years later in an interview with the English reporter Gideon Bachmann,[7] Fellini once again returned to the subject of neorealism. The director's first films were by this time a thing of the past, *La Dolce Vita* had been completed and *Otto e Mezzo* was already in progress. Many of the political and social problems which had been of great moment to Italian cinema had long been resolved or forgotten, and yet Fellini continued to defend his position as a neorealist. At this time, however, his defense was shorn of the aggressiveness and confidence which characterized his earlier pronouncements. "I was one of the first to write scripts for the neorealistic films," he said in a hesitating, nostalgic tone of voice, "and it seems to me that all my work since then has had a decidedly neorealistic stamp." But he seemed no longer certain of this, and, as if to recognize the voice of the opposition, he added, "even if there are still some people today who do not think so."[8]

Whether Fellini was consciously aware of it or not, *La Dolce Vita* marks the director's total abandonment of the neorealistic principles. Even though the film has been interpreted as a documentary, partially because Fellini did not use atypical characters for its focus as he did with *La Strada*, the social scene which served as his point of departure was insistently depicted in a grotesque, baroque manner. Moreover the "sweet life" of the city's demi-monde is presented in an extremely symbolic manner. In a series of sketches this film portrays a life permeated with a profound sadness and a bitterness which is unalleviated, even momentarily, by an instance of pathos or humor. The expected return to hope, present in all of Fellini's earlier works, is noticeably missing from this film. In his study of Fellini, Leandro Castellani states that the final message of *La Dolce Vita* is the most bitter of Fellini's entire production because in it "the last positive *vitellone*, the one who had succeeded in escaping the emotional prison of his narrow provincial world, Moraldo-Marcello, falls prey to the big city and is spiritually annihilated by it."[9]

Fellini's "grotesquification" (if one may coin a word) and symbolic metamorphosis of reality reached their climax in *La Dolce Vita*. *Otto e Mezzo* and *Giulietta degli Spiriti* simply confirm these achievements. *Otto e Mezzo* is almost entirely composed of flashbacks in which every image is an evocative bit of baroque filigree. The composite image is a mandala of personal symbolism which finally eliminates the last particle of realistic residue from the director's work. *Giulietta degli Spiriti* follows a similar procedure. It detaches itself completely from reality and replaces it with all the grotesque, baroque, and phantasmagoric characteristics which dominate *Otto e Mezzo*. In *Giulietta*, however, the fantastic is emphasized to an extreme degree. The director chose to shoot the film in color to emphasize its dreamlike and often nightmarish quality.

This baroque element of Fellini's art, so obvious in his recent films, was first noticed in his earliest work by the French columnist, Geneviève Agel. In her book, *Les Chemins de Fellini*,[10] she points out those features of the Italian director's work which have an unquestionably baroque twist. By analyzing his films in accordance with the principles formulated by the Spanish scholar, Guido D'Or, in his essay "L'Art Baroque," Miss Agel demonstrates that the characteristic themes of the baroque school—dynamism, depth, and picturesqueness—are all easily traceable in Fellini's work. Miss Agel's individuation of the baroque characteristics in Fellini's earliest films is worthy of comment since it might lead us to believe, erroneously, that the director never participated fully in Italian neorealism. On a conscious level the director was undoubtedly a neorealist, and his work observed the canons of this school as long as he was under the direct supervision of his teacher, Roberto Rossellini. However, as soon as he was alone with his deepest artistic emotions—those baroque tendencies most proper to his sensitivity—he began to develop a highly personalized cinematic art form which strongly resembles the decadent tendencies of the turn-of-the-century art and literature.

Notwithstanding the obvious success of Fellini's works and of those of Michelangelo Antonioni, who likewise abandoned the neorealistic aesthetic to follow a "new art," realistic cinema had not lost its vitality. The classic neorealistic works—*Roma Città Aperta*, *Ladri di Biciclette*, *Umberto D.*—were received with undisputed success during most of the fifties. Moreover, in the early sixties when both Fellini and Antonioni were dominating the screen, realist cinema made a dynamic comeback with such works as De Seta's *Banditi ad Orgosolo* and Gillo Pontecorvo's *La Battaglia di Algieri*. Because of its shocking verisimilitude the latter was prefaced by a disclaimer which warned the public that not one inch of its footage was taken from actual war documentaries. It was with this film that neorealistic cinema once again found itself in the social and historical environment which was capable of giving it nourishment, for *La Battaglia di Algieri* is concerned with a reality comparable to that treated by the earliest realist films: war, and humanity's collective response to it. The experience of mankind at war was the common heritage of World War II and it is this experience which neorealist film-makers had shown themselves capable of reproducing with sublime art.

The experience of Italian cinema, however, does not terminate with the extremely antipodal positions of *Giulietta degli Spiriti* and *La Battaglia di Algieri*, rather it would seem that some of the most recent productions have surpassed the crisis dictated by critical fiat, and have at least attempted to fuse external social realities with personal ones. A case in point might be Fellini's *Satyricon* in which, while witnessing the personal reality of the two youths, we also observe the impact of socio-political upheaval on the most disparate persons, in terms that, notwithstanding the symbolism, are ultimately externally realistic to the utmost. The ultimate debasement of the "typical" man to wealth is seen symbolically, through the eyes of the boys, as anthropofagia, and yet the episode depicts an ill of the consumer society in a manner which the American saying "dog eat dog" expresses equally well, if less forcibly. Fellini would, therefore, seem to be acknowledging the importance and impact of the common tangible experience, while not denying the equally important stimulus present in those experiences which are not relatable on a one-to-one basis.

Fellini, although in large measure responsible for this fusion, has not rested on his laurels. While the greater part of his earlier films dealt with reality, be it external or internal, with *I Clowns* he is confronting the cinema-goer with problems with which the patrons of the theater have been acquainted ever since Pirandello.

I Clowns unites in itself two elements which have been extremely prominent in Fellini's works: the clown and the mask. In this work the director examines forthrightly the character which best symbolizes to him the split between person and personage in a film which portrays Fellini, as Fellini shooting the film of Fellini directing a documentary on the famous clowns of yesteryear. The clowns, in turn, are both themselves in their dotage in the documentary, and the clowns (buffoons) of the film. Fellini, while being the "dottore," is also the "white" clown, that is, the straight man for the most improbable film crew ever assembled. The question at this point becomes not "is the reality internal or external?", but "what is reality?" One can no longer simply sit in a darkened room and accept or reject a temporary reality. Rather we are compelled to question the very nature of the reality on the silver screen, and by extension, in everyday life. With this work Fellini has brought Pirandello's *Six Characters in Search of an Author* to the screen. We see the personages portray themselves, the play within the play—which in this case becomes the film within the film—and, with a touch of *Henry IV*, we are confronted with the King—Fellini—who is a madman-clown and yet may be most totally sane when he is most insane. . . .

NOTES

1. Angelo Solmi, *Storia di Federico Fellini* (Milan: Rizzoli, 1963), p. 138.
2. Italo Calvino, "Major Currents in Italian Fiction Today," *Italian Quarterly,* 4 (1960), 3-15.
3. Geneviève Agel, *Les Chemins de Fellini* (Paris: Éditions du Cerf, 1956), p. 93.
4. Ibid., p. 94.

5. Solmi, p. 19.
6. Tullio Kezich, *La Dolce Vita di Federico Fellini* (Bologna: Cappelli, 1959), p. 30.
7. Solmi, p. 20.
8. Ibid.
9. Leandro Castellani, *Temi e figure del cinema contemporaneo* (Rome: Studium, 1963), p. 63.
10. Agel, pp. 12-17.

. . . .

27. From Romagna to Rome: *Aldo Tassone* The Voyage of a Visionary Chronicler (*Roma* and *Amarcord*)

FELLINI AND THE CRITICS

With each new film of Fellini, certain critics immediately set forth the usual accusations: the use of autobiographical materials, irrationalism, ambiguity, mystification, mannerism, baroque tendencies, and so on. As for the flattering qualifications, they too always remain the same: sorcerer with images, Cagliostro of directing, a medium for directing actors, and so on. It even happens that those who accused *Roma* of being too autobiographical complain that *Amarcord* is not sufficiently so. But when will Fellini decide to do what the critics want? Certain of the more intrepid among them even go so far as to give advice to this author. There are few works like those of Fellini that require the audience to view them with minds free of preconceived critical notions. Precisely for this reason, it is useful to review the most frequent accusations against Fellini's art before examining his last two films. Is it not anachronistic to apply formulas that are twenty years out of date to an author as creative and complex as Fellini?

The accusation of ambiguity no longer has the same immediacy it had during the sixties. In a cinema of ideas what counts, as Rossellini has said, "is not the images but the ideas." And in a cinema of imagery

. . . .

From *La Revue du Cinéma: Image et Son*, No. 290 (1974), pp. 17-38. Reprinted by permission of the publisher. Translated by Julia Conaway Bondanella.

the more or less enigmatic, subconscious meanings remain hidden under the form of the spectacle just as the larger portion of the iceberg remains beneath the water. In a purist cinema of style (that of Bresson) and a cinema of spectacle the richness of life counts more than the purity of language. "I do not like films where nothing happens; I want to include something of everything in mine," the protagonist of 8½ always said. In Fellini's cinema, meaning and image form a particularly indivisible unity. Beyond the level of spectacle, a film by Fellini does not exist: the always allusive meanings are absorbed by the iconography where they dissolve into each other (the "all pervadingness of images," as Pavese would say). "Fellini speaks a language of images," Natalia Ginzburg has written, "and the images must be observed before being understood."

The images always have multiple meanings because they derive, as Jung said about Picasso, from an interior area of the mind located behind the conscience: "The unconscious acts upon the conscious mind from the interior and from the rear. . . . Unlike objective or conscious representation, the procedure and the actions of this interior background are symbolic, that is, they allude in an approximate fashion to a still unknown meaning which seems to dominate and to engulf the author himself." Fellinian ambiguity is not a game. It is the emanation of the mystery of an ambivalent reality. It is complicity with the characters and the will to apprehend all without leaving anything out. Does not reality attract us as much as it repels us? Does it not have a flavor both bitter and sweet like the world of *I Vitelloni* and *Amarcord*, transfigured and described by an artist in whose work poetry always has the upper hand over moral design? The work of art is enigmatic like a text which must be deciphered. "The dream," Freud has written, "intends to say nothing to anyone and, far from being a means of communication, is destined to remain misunderstood." Fellini poses questions without offering solutions, proposes without disposing. Is not the power of suggestion inversely proportionate to clarity, as certain surrealists explain it?

If Fellini's "pendular" adhesion to reality is, then, often taken for a game, the superabundance of his language is sometimes qualified by mystification and a baroque quality. The spectacular aspect of Fellini's cinema, its powerful figurative and visual richness, runs the risk of resembling a sterile quest for effects like those found in the works of certain baroque geniuses who are astounding and too clever. If the baroque is the renunciation of simplicity, the quest for movement without motivation, the effort to create "a falsely dramatic life" as Burckhardt puts it, can one honestly affirm that this is what characterizes Fellini's work? In the frenzy and the variegation, in the visual delirium of Fellini's style, there seems to be no trace of an illusionism that would be in itself alone his own purpose. The magic of Fellini, his taste for spectacle and contrasts, his astounding dynamism rarely bear the mark of effort or predetermination. "It is absolutely necessary to expand and to broaden in order, then, to condense," the director one day confided to me. . . . "Flamboyant collisions of imagery," the parade sequences of the inspired Fellini are not pure exercises of virtuosity and technique as they are for a Ken Russell, in whose work movement and distortion are a veritable mania. To a question I asked him about the present relevance of the baroque, Fellini responded in this fashion: "All that restores authentic emotion to you is of the present. The important thing is not to know if a work has the right to be art nouveau, gothic, baroque or classic; the important thing is to see if the information which it carries to the spectator is vital or not, if it proposes something new or something old."

A certain number of critics vigorously attack Fellini for his autobiographical presumptions. And they miss the Fellini of the sixties who kept one eye wide open on reality, whereas today he seems to fix both eyes like two large beacons on his own subconscious and to fall back nostalgically upon his past. The problem of idealism and the limits of an autobiographical outlook open an unending debate among Fellini's critics, most especially the Italians. To reproach the director for his use of autobiographical materials and label it narcissism is singularly to limit the problem and to reduce a contemplative artist to the role of militant. Aside from the fact that the work of every great artist is necessarily autobiographical, Fellini does not limit himself to telling the story of his life. He does not make vain personal confessions; he writes the history of his time by means of an intermediary. His biography is a filter, a spyglass which he uses the better to capture life as it is. After all, from the moment he speaks to us of life and of death, what difference does it make that the director passes through the catalytic medium of his own experience? What other reality do we know as well as our own?

It is often said that Fellini repeats himself or that he always remakes the same film. In the sixties, the director succeeded in asserting his own style and poetic universe. Subsequently, he won his wager by the unlimited variation of the themes that inspire him. 8½ constitutes the compendium of his art and a sort of exemplary testament delivered to his contemporaries. Afterward, he searched for new modes of expression, but the themes, however, remained the same and the risk of repetition began to make itself felt. After the liberating digression of the exceptional *Toby Dammit*, in which the anxiety became aggravated to the point of despair and the director anticipated many of the themes of his following films, he made his escape into pure dream and myth with *Satyricon*.

Finally, with *The Clowns*, the overture to both *Roma* and *Amarcord*, he returns to his origins. Some critics then asked what Fellini expected from the transformation of his childhood. Pavese has also been reproached for always speaking of his native land. The response of the writer from Turin is valid for the director from Romagna:

> Poetry is repetition, the celebration of a mythical plan. True astonishment comes from recollection, not from novelty. We only admire those landscapes we have already admired previously, and "our" landscapes are limited: it is difficult to add to those which have been revealed to us in infancy when our imaginative structures take form. The most certain and rapid means of being astonished is always to fix one's attention upon the same object. One fine day, we shall have the impression of never having seen it before. The years color the same theme in very different ways. Age is an accumulation of like things which grow ever more rich and profound.

Does Fellini always make the same film? Certainly! But the language of the different chapters of this unique film is incessantly renewed as *Roma* and *Amarcord* prove. "It is precisely because it repeats recurrent motifs that Fellini's fantasy appears unsurpassed," Casiraghi writes very correctly.

ROMA: THE STRATA OF A MYTHICAL METROPOLIS

La Dolce Vita had given us a horizontal panorama of Rome; *Satyricon* had explored her as the classical Rome of myth. With *Roma*, Fellini combs the viscera of the eternal city and her unpredictable underground in eight strata, as the city engineer defined it. *Roma* could be called "The Mysteries of Rome," but not in the sense in which Zavattini understands the term in his film inquiry, which is totally lacking in mystery.[1] Fellini's Rome is everything save a city. "Rome created me insofar as I am an artist, and I—I recreate Rome," the director could say.

And anyone who agrees with Jung that it was Faust who created Goethe and not the reverse could not disagree with Fellini. It is precisely because he speaks of Rome while interposing himself as an intermediary that he ends by saying what every other director ought to take care not to say. *Roma* is a two-headed film. The newly arrived provincial is not satisfied with repeating the two or three things he knows about the city (the family boardinghouse, the music hall, the freeways, the brothels, Trastevere), but he tries to explore the mystery of what he does not know (the subway, the fashion parade, the motorcyclists). In the evocation of this complex relationship between a dreamer and the universe which has most stimulated his artistic imagination, Rome —city as state of mind—presents itself to Fellini under three different aspects: (1) as the incarnation of the eternal feminine; (2) as the personal theater of a director; (3) as a mysterious cemetery abounding in vitality. To review the film briefly in terms of these three aspects (not intended to be restrictive) can be useful in order to perceive the richness of its allusions.

ROME: WOMAN AND SPECTACLE

"The Roman woman has a c . . . as big as that!" joyfully exclaims one of the customers of the Caffè del Commercio in Rimini, adding gesture to word in order to be better understood. It cannot be doubted that Fellini loves to celebrate the opulent forms of the Latin woman. One need only think of the sequence at the prep school in which very fleshy buttocks seen from behind appear among the slides of the monuments of Rome to the hilarious joy of the students and the ashamed despair of the priest! But the portrayal of the Fellinian woman is not limited to a single aspect. She can be the enormous giant (Saraghina) or the "respectable" prostitute with a heart of gold (Susy, Carla); the asexual sister (Gelsomina, Cabiria) or the castrating mother; the abandoned wife and judge (Luisa, Giulietta) or the mythical woman (Silvia, Claudia). In *Roma*, Fellini runs the gamut of his feminine portraits. The monumental mistress of the boardinghouse is an exemplary version of the authoritarian mother, immediately corrected by the Juno-like and maternal proprietor of the restaurant. The she-wolf of the Via Appia is the majestic replica of Saraghina. During the frenetic dance of the damned women in the workingmen's brothel, one immediately notices the maternal smile of an evanescent beauty that seems to distort the love of timid youths and promises a bed never frequented by remorse: it is the sister of the brunette odalisque who, upon stepping out of the glass elevator at the deluxe brothel, plunges the forbidden clientele into a religious silence. In a sequence cut out during the editing, the young provincial even dreamed of marrying this creature, as Guido had dreamed of marrying Claudia in 8½.

In the subway sequence, Fellini even tries to violate this Rome—maternal and good, a corpulent and enigmatic protectress. The voyage of the discovery of phantoms and the dead lends itself, in fact, to a psychoanalytic reading as a sort of attempt to penetrate the fleshy, placental womb of Mother Rome. The director cautiously explores her bosom and her innermost recesses, dripping water and resounding with the rumbling of underground rivers; then he penetrates it as the voracious and phallic countersink bites into the feeble partition that protected the villa with its frescoes. But this ardent attempt to communicate with his own origins and to meet the phantoms from the beyond vanishes in impotence. There is no return to the maternal breast.

Rome, birthplace of the baroque and capital city of spectacle, is the chosen place of Fellini's inspiration. In *The Clowns*, Fellini as a child felt his future vocation as a master of ceremonies born within him while seeing the apparition of a fabulous circus tent surge beneath the window of his bedroom. Later in Rome, while the young Fellini leans out the window of his room, the immense ceiling of a building situated just beneath the boardinghouse slowly divides in two and, as in a mirage, the geometric rows of the seats of a cinema in the open air appear under his eyes. This vision, cut in the French version of the film, seems to be the allegorical anticipation of the call that Rossellini made in 1945 to Fellini, inviting him to collaborate on the scripts of his films. The identification of Rome with the stage of a theater becomes evident at the time of the violent and amusing contact with this worthy successor of the *Ludi Circenses*—the music hall of the forties (the inspiration of the first film of Fellini-Lattuada, *Variety Lights*). For a director who associates spectacle with improvisation, madness, and the macabre nonsense of the circus, the Roman music hall reveals itself as a spectacle of the second order. One cannot very clearly distinguish who are the actors and who are the spectators in this room. By turns, the scene is in the hall and in the hall on the stage! What born actors these Romans are, who oblige the professional actors to leave the stage and who improvise an unexpected but no less picturesque show in a turbulent and boisterous hall.

ROME, CITY OF THE DEAD

Like *Satyricon* and *Toby Dammit*, *Roma* is a nocturnal film, sprinkled with reminders of death. Gone are the luminous nights, the fountains, and the nymphs of *La Dolce Vita*. Roman nights remain, henceforth, without dawns, and the city peopled by ruins and shadows seems an engulfed necropolis. The Tiber, even in a sequence sketch, is described as "a menacing serpent, with no more life than the Dead Sea, which drags an entire fabulous history of candelabra and engulfed statues painfully toward the ocean."

Right in the middle of the variety show, between the jeers of the spectators and the pathetic efforts of the artists to make them laugh, one suddenly hears a cry in the hall: "Help, help, I feel ill." The prostitutes, condemned to perpetual movement and automatic gestures, sometimes voice gloomy complaints: "In fifty years, we'll all be eaten by worms." The faces—of the pope, the saint, the domestics of Domitilla and the prelates—thin and almost cadaver-like, disfigured or emaciated, worn and stiffened, without humanity or vitality, are marked by premonitory signs of an ineluctable and approaching decomposition.

Entire sequences—the freeway, the subway, the motorcyclists—are revealed to be voyages toward nothingness. The peripheral freeway, which girds Rome like a "ring of Saturn" made of fire and mud, leads nowhere. Its convulsive flux, its futile breathlessness become blocked in front of the Colosseum (a variation of the nightmare which marked the opening of 8½). The numerous headlights, distorted by the rain which blurs the windshields, dissolve into nebulous little letters. Prisoners in their automobiles, as if in coffins of glass, their faces reduced to grotesque masks, the passengers become outraged, lose patience or bite their nails. "And what if we cannot move along any further? Suppose we are condemned to remain here forever?": this is the question that the passengers of a phantom Nocturnal Tramway also asked themselves. This sequence, anticipated in the first scenario, has perhaps set the tone for the freeway scene. This metallic and mysterious chariot, shuddering and creaking, was peopled by a crowd of shipwrecked persons asleep with their mouths open as if the trip was the sign of a condemnation, of a spell such as that of the shipwrecked people on the Street of Providence in *The Exterminating Angel* (it would, moreover, be fruitful to study the numerous analogies between Fellini and

Buñuel). Fellini had likewise anticipated filming the crushing of dogs and cats on the highway. The animals that had been hit were to be progressively reduced to mere skins adhering to the asphalt with the successive passing of the automobiles.

The subway sequence seems to be the illustration and the continuation of a dream that Fellini had during the filming of *Satyricon*. He found himself in a subterranean prison. Beyond the wall, situated across from him, he heard noises, and a voice repeated to him: "On the other side there are Romans." The wall, the space that separated him from these unknown people, diminished more and more as the dream came to an end. The subway sequence is an attempt to travel backward in time across the eight strata of the unforeseeable basement of Rome. The subway is like a catacomb that passes through the bowels of the city. Shortly before the countersink fells the last wall, a wall both of time and of the unconscious (the descent into the past is a descent into the cave of occult knowledge), one of the technicians is taken ill. He will soon contemplate his own image, his double—a veiled allusion to a sort of metempsychosis?

Before becoming blurred and migrating elsewhere, the dead depicted in the fresco captivate the stupefied profaners of their tranquillity. The statue of a matron even has her back turned, her eyes riveted to the wall. Who are these dead who are the living in this Roman villa flooded by the water? On contact with the fatal air of the present, the ancient frescoes disintegrate, carried off by the whirlwind of a breeze, which seems to blow from Hades. And like phantasms, the technicians and the crew shoot around the columns in vain and watch, transfixed, the walls henceforth covered over by a uniform and opaque gray. "The prophetic gaze of the adolescent Fellini," as Le Clézio has said, "penetrates through and through the wall of our history of decadence, while illuminating during its passage the whole glacial labyrinth of the galleries of the dead, and menaces our corrupt and perverse society with annihilation, while accelerating the process of disintegration."

The procession of phantoms in *Roma* becomes a spectacular Sabbath when the horde of motorcyclists erupts in the sleeping city. Savages armed with helmets and jackets, these enigmatic visitors (barbarians of a mechanical and brutalizing civilization, angels of the Apocalypse come to announce the end of everything?) angrily surround the monuments. Fellini's eye assails the stones of Rome with ultraviolet light and the ruins with a shock of rumbling and spectral shadows as if he wanted to tear out their inviolable secrets. The silhouettes of the gigantic sons of Zeus on the Quirinal, menacing on the façade of the presidential palace, are blurred. The spectator will long remember the sight of the headlights, which look like meteors all ablaze, crossing the screen like incendiary grenades. It appears that Rome is beginning to burn behind the passing of these black angels and that the scythe (of the first shot of the film) is soon going to reduce the city to a heap of ruins. But the Eternal City does not seem to awaken from its worldly slumber, nor to surrender its secret. There is a famous expressionist painting by the Roman painter Scipione, in which, in a sulfurous atmosphere, the obelisks, the cupola, and the prostitutes go into contortions and convulsions. It is entitled "Roman Slumber" and could well be the design for *Roma*. Though a heap of ruins, the Eternal City does not seem to awaken from her worldly slumber.

Note how all the film's movement, like the route of the tramway, is circular. Think of the half-circles traced by the prostitutes before their clients on the ring of Saturn formed by the freeway or the fashion show on the oval platform or the circle of motorcyclists. The voyage into the bowels of the Eternal City—eternal in the sense that it lives beyond the realm of time, in the deep sleep of death, perhaps awaiting that ultimate end as suggested by the American writer at the end of the film—has no temporal progression. "I want to create a tableau-portrait without precise temporal connotations. Perhaps because I no longer succeed in growing, I no longer succeed in distinguishing past, present and future," Fellini has said in introducing *Amarcord*. The director is seized by the process of decay in everything and by the impossibility of finding peace in the remembrance of things past. His ideal space is the ring of a circus, the labyrinth, the eclipse of a parade whose silhouettes come from no one knows where or cross furtively without leaving any traces of their passing. His time is that of dreams, a mythical, absolute present.

FROM CHRONICLE TO VISION

"The difficulty of art," Pavese has written, "lies in rendering with astonishment the things which we know while treating them in a surprising manner." Fellini renders the surprising aspect of things by emphasizing their characteristic traits, by presenting them under an unusual light and from a disconcerting angle. He makes us discover them as if we were looking at them for the first time with the eyes of infancy.

Although they formed a block of very distinct sequences at the time of 8½, memory and imagination now burst forth from reality, that is, from chronicle, like a natural emanation or a natural extension. Thus, one passes imperceptibly from the record of the real to its fantastic transposition; the documentary becomes in a natural way "fantadocumentary" (document + imagination). The surreal is revealed to us with the same language as the real. In the eyes of the director, they speak the same language. Fellini's manner of storytelling is not so different from that of Buñuel—as one might think at first glance. With a perfectly realistic style, Fellini and Buñuel arrive at the mystery of things from opposite positions; the former, by accentuating the bizarre and searching for the incongruous (the surreal metaphor) which is as if projected upon the real; the latter, on the contrary, by expanding and distorting reality (the actors' make-up, sets, lighting, traveling shots) and by freeing the fabulous aspect that it contains within it. Buñuel, without circumlocutions, makes a cock and an ostrich appear in a room, to the stupefaction of its occupant; Fellini makes a real ocean liner appear, transformed by the lighting and the traveling shot, into a symbol of something else (a surreal metamorphosis). With one eye, Fellini establishes his characteristic reality; with the other, he defines the fourth dimension.

Let us consider the moment in *Roma* when the young Fellini disembarks in the capital. The arrival of a provincial in a railroad station and his admission into a boardinghouse become the magical encounter of an adolescent with an unknown planet. What Peter Gonzales sees in the railroadmen, nuns and priests, *carabinieri* and soldiers, peddlers and hotel lift-attendants in search of clients, pimps, and individuals of every kind, Fellini succeeds in transforming then into unique apparitions by a method specifically his own: first, a series of sinuous traveling shots that interpret the glances of the traveler who is walking on the platform and extract an impression of exploration and discovery; second, the fixity of the expressions, which confers a hieratic appearance upon the two immobile policemen, their eyes staring off into space and at the woman who has trained her eyes in the direction of an invisible traveler; third, a montage that concentrates into the space of two minutes, in an unreal fashion, the presentation of all the kinds of people one might find in an Italian railway station. The result is a series of visions; the chronicle becomes myth. Let us briefly compare this station to the one in *Death in Venice*. The analytical eye of Visconti does not succeed in conferring a fantastic dimension upon the two policemen who are walking amidst the crowd of travelers. Fellini, the visionary that he is, "represents" what he has seen and imagined as if he were in the process of dreaming it. Visconti's station is peopled with extras; that of Fellini is a procession of apparitions.

Furthermore, if one bears in mind the way in which a realist film would have described the arrival at the boardinghouse, what a difference from the evocation Fellini proposes to us, an evocation full of the memory and emotion he experienced when he entered the place for the first time. This is not just any boardinghouse but "that one," the first he knew in his life, inhabited by a humanity as picturesque as it is surprising. Fellini takes us by the hand and leads us into a totally recreated, bizarre world, as the little girl takes the new boarder by the hand and leads him to the attic, far from the world, where a tiny little grandmother, the *nonna piccola*, lives (a reminder of the visit Gelsomina pays to Osvaldo, the little sick boy in *La Strada* who is also closed up in the attic far from the world).

After the savory and popular feast outside, characterized by a joyous realism, where unexpected apparitions are not lacking (among the official musicians, a little old man goes on his way and plays his ballad with a leaf that he makes whistle against his lips), there is the nature-walk in the new town, a veritable piece of magic, all done by traveling shots and lighting effects. The blowtorches of workers, in the midst of repairing the rails of the tramway, shoot out their disquieting flashes of astral light among the sleepwalking mannequins of a fashion boutique and on the quarters of meat hanging in a butcher shop. The hallucinating eye of the solitary stroller discovers the tombs, the gates, the arches of the Via Appia enveloped in mystery. A strange goddess of love appears suddenly among the ruins of the famous road, illuminated just an instant by the headlights of a car. Monumental as the arch of Janus, this she-wolf courtesan "of majestic poses who seems to imitate the proudest monuments" and whose large eyes have the "nocturnal clarity of eternal things" (Baudelaire) could very well be the symbol of the Eternal City (in Italy, moreover, she appeared in a close-up on the poster advertising the film).

The opening of certain sequences, the brothels, for example, is already truly unreal. In the labyrinth of the alleys of old Rome, an entire fantastic universe is concentrated: a man is seated near a car without wheels, an artisan paints a wardrobe with a mirror in the open air, an infant leaps over a metallic bedspring near a fire, a little girl amuses herself all alone inside a rich antique shop while two butchers' assistants, seen in the reflection from the mirror, pass by carrying on their shoulders a row of lambs tinged with blood on a spit. Behind a sheet hung at a window, one perceives the sterile whiteness of a bidet abandoned in a corner of the alley. In this strange climate where time has stopped, three soldiers head for the door of a squalid tenement building. The concierge, a minuscule good-natured woman, shriveled up and shrill, demands the identification papers of the soldiers on leave. The camera crosses to a second door. After a pan of ninety degrees, the eye discovers a long corridor done in white earthenware tile like that in lavatories, narrow like the crates on a freight truck; the clients crane their necks desperately from afar to catch sight of these "artists" whose secret charms the proprietress is praising. The circle of prostitutes then explodes: hysterical or aggressive, ugly or innocent, they wear the monstrous mask of a humanity condemned to live an inhuman existence in this agonizing underworld.

To lead us into hell, Fellini invented nothing extraordinary: he only set up a series of "things seen," gathered together by a metaphysical eye and organized into a voyage toward another reality. The same thing happens with the descent into the subway. The halo of light that searches out the innermost recesses of the gallery, the compact editing, and the linking of the movements transform this documentary passage into an adventure of the human understanding, into a voyage across the "eight levels" of the unconscious in search of one's own identity. Certain apparitions possess an indefinable something of the premonitory and the mysterious. The faceless workers, stiff like statues on their little car, become the Martians of a cosmic expedition. The Mole, the enormous wheel with teeth possessing the phosphorescent eyes of a monster of the depths, becomes the means of exploring the obscure cavern of Hades where we look for the shades of our ancestors. At the moment when the countersink breaks through the wall which envelops the buried city like a sarcophagus—one of the most moving moments in all of Fellini—the spectator clearly understands that it is a question of a dream which concerns him directly. He "sees" the barrier that separates him from his buried ego fall, and in an instant the enigmatic forms of a past which always withdraw further into the subconscious come to light.

A PARADE OF APPARITIONS

Other sequences of *Roma* are a continual parade of apparitions—the freeway and the ecclesiastical presentation. The parade (at the time of *La Strada*, it was the cortege, the procession) seems to be henceforth the preferred form of expression for the director who conceives of each film as a journey into the mystery of time in search of his own identity. A journey into space (the ecclesiastical parade and the subway were journeys in time), the sequence of the freeway departs from the real. But, after the first documentary images, things that are successively less normal begin to march by: a white horse escaped from its cart; a chauffeur who is taking a dog for a ride in a sumptuous car; a man who supports an enormous mirror full of clouds in the trailer of a truck; the somber forms of the cement mixers; the armored cars; ruins eaten by grasses and bushes or gloomily disemboweled; a truck in flames which, in overturning, sprinkles the asphalt with corpses; a cemetery covered with dust in the night. The images become blurred; one only glimpses the halo of the headlights in the rain and, through the windows of the automobiles jammed by the chaotic traffic, the tense, hangdog faces. There is no doubt: we are in one of the circles of hell. When, shortly afterward, the camera films the trees of the Villa Borghese and reveals the razed cupolas of Rome, one has the impression of emerging from the abyss into the Elysian fields.

In the penumbra, the sinister grating of a pulley is heard. As if by enchantment, dusty tableaux arise by themselves on the vertical plane of a wall while a spectral light progressively lights up a surprising portrait gallery containing the gloomy, even menacing faces of old cardinals. Two decrepit servants, candle in hand, go to meet a rubicund cardinal with the face of an old child (a forward traveling shot and a violent light bring the guest of honor in this unusual soiree out of the shadows). Such is the prelude to the ecclesiastical fashion show, the key to the film. Elegant designs for nuns and vestments for sportive priests begin to file by an audience of aristocrats and church dignitaries. One might believe himself to be right in the middle of an operetta, but soon the tone changes and it is the two thousand years of ecclesiastical history that pass before the eyes of the spectators—thurifers, chasubles of all kinds, copes surmounted by windowpanes in an unstable equilibrium. The passage to the imaginary is imperceptible. At that moment, an unexpected guest makes her appearance, the music takes up the apocalyptic motif of *La Dolce Vita*, and the parade is transformed into a *danse macabre*. Like an anxious soul in Purgatory, her visage veiled and corroded by death, a saint glides over the platform through a shower of rose petals. It is the replica of the one who makes the little schoolboy of 8½ flee in horror. Hands clasped on her breast, her head leaning to one side, the saint curtsies, then disappears as if carried away by some secret torment. Is this a silent entreaty for someone to come to

Roma: The ecclesiastical fashion parade. (Museum of Modern Art/Film Stills Archive)

her aid? Is it not also, on Fellini's part, the caricature of the dogma of the resurrection of the flesh?

After a majestic procession of bishops (the camera films them from different angles, calling attention to the mechanical swaying of these automatons wrapped in their costumes), a hearse covered with skeletons posed in menacing positions comes to interrupt the parade once again. The black veils of the hearse glide slowly before the prelates who silently attend the ceremony as if death, touching them, draws them along in her triumphant wake. (It might be noted that Fellini alternated extras and puppets on the tiers on purpose, just as Vigo did in *Zero for Conduct.*)

Preceded by this allegorical *vanitas vanitatum,* the papal apotheosis now bursts forth. The bells ring, the walls of the background are transformed into a gigantic platform, and, triumphant like a sun, Pius XII appears. One cannot detect the slightest sign of humanity or ecstasy on his pallid, statuary face. His doubtful ecclesiastical character is expressed by a kind of gilded fan placed behind his tiaraed head, which produces dazzling illuminations worthy of a show window of Interflora[2] to create a halo of supraterrestrial light around him. The last representative of a triumphant tradition of ecclesiastical power, the Grand Old Man looks into the void, impassive as an idol, in spite of the acclamations of a nostalgic nobility. Fellini examines him several times by repeated traveling shots, from bottom to top, alternating with rapid shots of the faces of the spectators. The director will use the same technique to describe the apparition of the ocean liner *Rex* in *Amarcord*, another symbol of an inaccessible and illusory power. The director closes the papal sequence with a close-up of Pius XII, then extinguishes the lights: the Grand Old Man also belongs to the realm of the dead. "The king dreams he is king and in this delusion, he lives, rules, disposes, governs, and the honors one bestows upon him are written on the wind and reduced by death to dust and ashes. . . . Life is but a dream and dreams are only dreams" (Calderon).

In these different sequences (the arrival in Rome, the brothel, the subway, the ecclesiastical parade), it is not an exaggeration to say that Fellini realizes the dream of every artist, as Pavese explains it: to blend together the richness of our realistic experiences with the profound meanings of symbolism. In *Amarcord*, the apparitions become so intimate a part of the fantastic chronicle that they seem to be natural events—the *Rex* as well as the peacock, the mad motorcyclist as well as the fifty concubines of the emir. The episode that is most abundant in vision—the excursion of the mad uncle, a veritable journey through the magic of nature—has the appearance of a serene picnic.

A-M'ARCORD OR THE PROVINCE, 1930

Three-quarters of Fellini's works could have been entitled *A-m'arcord*, which in the author's mind signifies "do you remember?" or "once upon a time," rather than the too literal and restrictive translation "I remember." Once upon a time, there was a music hall (*Variety Lights*); once upon a time there was a troupe of actors in *fumetti* (*The White Sheik*); once upon a time there were *vitelloni* and *bidonisti*; once upon a time there were a couple of vagabonds (*La Strada*); once upon a time there was a journalist who came from the provinces to Rome (*La Dolce Vita*), etc., etc. Province and city become "a provincial in the city" in all the films of Fellini: that was the title for the ensemble suggested to me by Faiana, Fellini's assistant. In the ideal order, with *Roma, La Dolce Vita,* and 8½, Fellini has written the continuation of *I Vitelloni,* the trilogy of Moraldo in the city.

1) THE THIRD PART OF A TRILOGY

The Clowns, Roma, Amarcord: there is, by all appearances, a profound thematic analogy and an undeniable unity of tone among the three chapters of this trilogy of Fellini's maturity. The chapters burst forth so definitively one from another that it is impossible to consider them separately. From one film to another, the recurring motifs become ever richer in meaning. The initial part of *The Clowns,* a film of total novelty in comparison with the preceding ones, is already situated in the small town of *Amarcord.* It involves anecdotes, little tableaux on the theme "the clowns are among us"; and, in fact, a very comical little nun heads for church, mumbling; Giudizio—the simpleton of the town —recounts and animates with conviction a martial exploit in the middle of the city square; the coachmen at the station squabble like children; and from the windows of the train, children emit incongruous noises in the direction of the stationmaster. These brief and savory glimpses of provincial life, not very well integrated into the rest of the film, were already an indirect anticipation of what was ripening to maturity in the mind of the director. At the beginning of *Roma,* Fellini keenly feels the need of a propitiatory bath in the provincial waters before throwing himself into exploring his secret ties with the city of enigmas (the Cinema Fulgor, the school, the papal benediction, the pharmacist's nymphomanic wife). There, too, the link between these sketches and the meaning of the film is not evident. But Fellini, popular bard and creator of stories, has always enjoyed sprinkling his works with seeds that bloom later on. The sketches the director draws in broad outlines at the beginning of *The Clowns* and *Roma* could be quietly inserted into *Amarcord* and rightfully belong there.

It is not simply that the three films belong to a sort of trilogy or "quest," but also that the same conspiratorial irony, the same melancholy, the same tendency to fantastic expansion of chronicle unite them. Even the title *A-m'arcord* is already suggested in *Roma.* In order to introduce one of the sequences of the film a voice-over says suddenly: "The brothels, do you remember them?" It is as if, while he was occupied in evoking his ties with the circus and Rome, Fellini could not stop his thoughts from surging forward to *Amarcord*, the film that was knocking at the door in search of an author. Certain characters among *The Clowns* reappear identically in *Amarcord*: Giudizio, the simple of spirit who, at the opening of the film, comments upon the dance of the puffballs; the dwarf nun; the successfully drawn figures of the young man and the *vitellone* with the white lock of hair; the fascist officer; and so on. The spirit of *The Clowns* animates the life of *Amarcord*, which abounds in clownish situations. There is, for example, the game of Titta's father, with his bald cranium, topped by a large wart, who pulls furiously at his jaws in the course of a conjugal brawl or bad-temperedly bites his hat before the obstinacy of his brother Teo, while in the foreground a peasant, dumbfounded and dressed like a clown, watches his exasperated gestures and laughs. The presentation of the professors, the fascist parade—with its trial race over the length of the parade route, its slogans interrupted by great fascist salutes—recall from near or far the entrances in the circus. The fascists, in fact, are the white clowns, odious and grotesque.

The theme of fascism appears in the three chapters, enriched each time by new nuances. In *The Clowns*, fascism has the somber visage of an officer who descends from a side car after three symbolic turns around the square, then goes to take his place beside the stationmaster to protect him from the vulgarities of the children. He gazes into the void while smoking a cigarette, his eyes surrounded by the darkest of circles. All the corruption and the threat of the regime is already present in this face. In one sequence of *Roma*, it is the folkloric and spectacular side of the regime that comes to the fore in a comic fashion: the leap across the circles of fire, the parade of very young children against the background of the martial profile of the Duce, his jaws jutting out. In *Amarcord* the two preceding motifs are organized by means of a complex discourse in which irony takes the place of sarcasm. Again one finds the gymnastic exhibition and the face of the Duce, presented frontally this time, his eyes dilated and menacing. Again one finds the parade: after the grotesque apparition of the fascist provincial secretary who appears in a cloud of smoke, the procession heads toward the grandstands at a run. The menace of *The Clowns* has become reality—the firing at the gramophone, the punishment by castor oil. The apparition of the disabled veteran in his little cart in the middle of the procession should also be noted: he is seen in *The Clowns*, in which one glimpses him very quickly from the back along the seashore. During the interrogation of Titta's father, we see again

the brusk movement of the fascist's head when he repeats: "What sad-
dens us is this obstinacy in not wanting to understand that fascism
wants to give them back their dignity."

2) IN THE LAND OF THE VITELLONI

With *Amarcord*, Fellini has given us the first chapter of the story of his
infancy and his generation. Before *I Vitelloni*, there was a kind of
lacuna: the director had to fill the gap sooner or later. Knowing why
he waited twenty years to return to his origins is not really important.
Perhaps it was to gain the necessary perspective. It is more interesting
to know in what spirit Fellini has retraced the route to Romagna, about
which he had long promised himself to make a film that was picaresque,
sanguinary, and adventuresome. During the convalescence after his illness in 1966, he had written a collection of memoirs entitled *My Rimini*, the first draft of his future work. The perspective went no further
than the voyage with Anita, planned at the time of *La Dolce Vita*.
After having exorcised the enigmas of life and death in *Satyricon*, *The
Clowns*, and *Roma*, Fellini was able to return to his infancy with the
wisdom of a second maturity.

Amarcord and *I Vitelloni*, or the thirties and the fifties, are two
frescoes which complete each other. The first is the prehistory of the
second and provides the key to understanding it. The state of mind of
vitellonism is the consequence of being educated by the illusions,
myths, and the immobility of the thirties. These adolescents who dance
in front of the Grand Hotel in the misty autumn become the young
men, now a little older, who participate in the election of Miss Siren in
this same Grand Hotel, dance in the middle of the street when one of
them has returned from his honeymoon, rush into the whirlwind of
the carnival, play soccer in the middle of the night in the deserted
streets, or are disciplined by their angry fathers when they pull their
pranks. On the streets, they again find the brave Giudizio (in *I .Vitel-
loni*, he aides Fausto in transporting the stolen angel from the shop
that sells religious objects, whose shopwindow reappears in *Amarcord*).
At the Cinema Fulgor, Fausto—a twenty-year-old Titta—courts the most
beautiful girl in town. The important seasonal events in *I Vitelloni*,
the "Election of Miss Siren," the arrival of the audience at the music
hall, and the Carnival, are now the Fascist Parade, the Mille Miglia
race, and the passage of the *Rex*.

As one can see, numerous elements in *Amarcord* are recaptured from

I Vitelloni, but they are seen from a different perspective. As Flaiano confirmed to me some months before his death, the subject of *I Vitelloni* was born from the encounter of three friends—Fellini, Flaiano, Pinelli—who were trading stories about their adolescence. Each of the six *vitelloni* who composed the group had his own story, a story halfway between irony and fable. "It was a big joke that I was playing on some friends from Rimini," swears Fellini. In *Amarcord*, the tableau is enlarged: the entire population of Romagna is the protagonist and the author does not limit himself to recounting only the savory adventures but conducts an investigation of familial, social, political, and religious ties and the causes of behavior in this community.

In *Amarcord*, there is a record of failure—the failure of an infancy deformed by the rhetoric of the schools, by fascism and by the religious Manichaeism, closed to all exchange with the outside world, nourished by myths and fears. It is the failure of the one who remembers, for he feels that although this world that was a part of him is irremediably lost, he will never be able to forget it, as the clown, Borio, says referring to the circus. And since it was unique—one has but one childhood—why be surprised that the director's feelings about "these most beautiful years" of disappointment and love are ambiguous? And, moreover, why try to reduce the complex emotions found in each episode to a single one? Fellini feels rage and disappointment as a witness to the comportment of the crowd during the fascist parade and their bovine expectation of the *Rex*; enchantment and tenderness at the arrival of the seasons and in his portrayal of the dreams of the poor in spirit such as Biscein and Teo, the fool; uneasiness in the middle of the fog; and heartrending melancholy on the day of Gradisca's wedding. Yet, his humor bursts forth at the evocation of his experiences at school, at confession, at family meals, during the promenades down the avenues, and with Titta's lovesickness.

3) THREE EXEMPLARY SEQUENCES

We shall analyze here but three exemplary sequences that illustrate the cinematic originality of this work: the *Rex* (the collective myth); the autumn fog (the mystery); and Uncle Teo's country outing (the fabulous evasion). "Where are they going?" asks Giudizio while the whole town heads toward the breaker. The sea seems filled with boats. "Wonderful, Gradisca!"—comments the anglophile proprietor of the cinema when he catches sight of the beautiful woman dressed in an appropriate sailor's uniform. "At what distance will it pass by?" inquires the headmaster, Zeus. "At 4 kilometers," the physics professor responds, "but, thanks to Galileo, at 400 meters." "And how big is it?" "Twice the size of the Grand Hotel plus the arch of Jupiter besides!" one hears among the villagers. It is a scene of general excitement. Nothing ever happens in the provinces, and one always lives in the expectation of something. Little by little, the villagers indulge in confessions. Fellini excels in the art of picking out the random expressions and sentiments of a crowd. Titta's father talks about the origin of the stars. Gradisca admits her disappointments and begins to cry: "Each time, I'm wrong. I would like to have an encounter that would last a whole lifetime." "This girl has a soft heart," the director of the Cinema Fulgor observes ironically. Biscein, the peddler, tells the story of an imaginary adventure with some dolphins. And when the village dozes off completely, the dull noise of a foghorn is heard. A black mountain thicker than the night appears on the horizon and grows ever larger. In the scenario, the villagers had the sensation that the mountain was falling on them like some monstrous apparition. In the production, the gigantic liner glides in front of the boats, decked out with feeble lights like a madonna in a procession.

No longer are we in the disquieting and anxious atmosphere of Herman Melville, but in the fabulous world of Lewis Carroll. This marvelous collective dream ("I don't know if I dreamt it, and then it became real, or if I have seen it in reality, and then it became a dream" says Alice) parades beneath the delighted eyes of the Amarcordians who make it the multifaceted symbol of everything they lack and all that they would like to have. For Gradisca who salutes it with tears in her eyes, it is the symbol of escape to a world of adventure and wealth. For the mayor and the fascist provincial secretary, it is the incarnation of the shining accomplishments of their regime. The *Rex* embodies, in effect, the seductive aspect of power, in contrast to the enormous and terrorizing effigy of the Duce who presided over the parade. Gradisca holds out her arms toward the *Rex* in the same way that she held them out toward the fascist officer during the parade when she cried out, "Let me touch him!" And the blind accordionist, who does not want to be left out, even takes off his glasses in order to see better. For all, it is a magical floating Grand Hotel, the forbidden paradise of all the possible and unimaginable joys. The director explores this papier-mâché monument and records the reactions of the dreamers with the same symphony of traveling shots as he had used for the apparitions of the Duce and the pope of *Roma*. This aquatic comet moves

Amarcord: The passage of the *Rex*, symbol of the fascist regime's power.

away and leaves the Amarcordians in the most total obscurity (the following shot is of the agonizing fog of autumn). The waves formed in the wake of the phantom vessel brusquely draw them from their wonderment. And until the annual automobile race, they are returned to the humdrum of everyday, the "ennui" that "kills," as Marcello's father calls it in *La Dolce Vita.*

The Great Fog, by erasing everything, embodies the void and plunges the grandfather into a solitude that brings him to think of death. "Everything has disappeared! If this is death, it's not very pretty!" the little old man mutters through his teeth, while moving about in the thick cloud which has hidden the house from view and has literally erased the village. For Titta's little brother, the way to school in this opaque universe inhabited by brittle, indistinct noises takes on the aspect of a labyrinth of fear and mystery, which is not without similarity to that of Encolpius—bizarre, fog-shrouded silhouettes parading on either side, mutilated trees reduced to somber forms. A truck passes like a meteor. Suddenly an enormous, enigmatic shadow

bars the way of the little schoolboy who stops short, terrorized like Encolpius before the Minotaur. He feels the mysterious threat of two eyes
upon him, staring at him through the obscurity. But it is only a peaceful buffalo who disappears behind a tree. The clock at the station seems
to be suspended in the void like a metaphysical moon; time has
stopped, immobilized by this phantom universe. On the breaker near
some boats that seem to have come from a Turner painting, there is no
longer anything but a stray dog. In front of the Grand Hotel, closed
from now on and resembling a sleeping dinosaur, the wind piles up the
dead leaves. Titta and his gang explore it in vain through one of the
keyholes and search for traces of a season that has already vanished.
One of them traces the steps of a slow waltz, and in this rhythm each
one improvises some variations while whispering to his imaginary love.
There remains nothing but to accept life as it is and to offer it the
homage of a dance. After having presented the solo of each dancer,
Fellini films them in a long shot as in the finale of *The Clowns* (the
French version unfortunately cut some frames in this section for commercial reasons). Winter follows and the children throw snowballs at
each other in the square, where they are joined by Gradisca, who is
dressed entirely in white. The count's peacock descends on the Renaissance fountain to display his colors like a snow-god, splendid and un-
touchable.[3]

The evocation of the magic of the seasons—one of the novelties of
the film—is of an extraordinary poetic vitality. *Amarcord* could be entitled: "The Seasons of our Illusions." In contrast, the work of Farre-
bique de Rouquier is a precedent that emphasizes the poetic originality
of Fellini's film. Fellini has done for the cinema what Brueghel and
Vivaldi had done for painting and music. It is in part due to these
contemplative digressions on nature that this melancholy film leaves a
spark of vitality in the spectator's soul, a sentiment of joy not felt in
Fellini's films since 8½.

For Teo, a fool "ma non troppo," the countryside represents liberty.
Teo is the prototype of a category of misfits or original characters—
Giudizio, Biscein, the blind accordionist, the lawyers—whose very ab-
normality gives them the freedom experienced by none of the Amarcordians. In this great circus of life, these extraordinary beings have the
task—in Fellini's perspective—of bringing messages from another world,
such as the one brought by the fool of *La Strada* to Gelsomina. They
do what the others no longer know how to do: they smile; they gather
stones in their pockets simply because they are beautiful; they find

enchantment in the spectacle of a wheel, which turns or in the perfection of an egg; they climb trees.

Essentially two things strike one in this sequence, the most original in *Amarcord*: the strong formal suggestion of the images, and the fusion of realism and magic that permits us constantly to understand the episode on two levels, the picaresque and the mythical. The first shot of Uncle Teo behind the bars—a medium shot followed by a slow zoom-out shot—is an intense apparition which gives the right tone to the whole. In the glittering summer light, beside another inmate of the asylum who has a large complacent smile on his absentminded face, Teo, frighteningly thin and dressed in black, has the air of a Don Quixote. The joyous family reunion takes place in an atmosphere of utter delight. A meticulous disposition of the characters—immobile and seen from the back of the open carriage—and the enchantment of the impressionist colors (Miranda holds an umbrella with white and blue polka dots) gives the shot the fixity of a painting. During the trip, Teo gets out of the carriage to relieve himself.

In four shots, Fellini transforms this prosaic incident into a moment of ecstatic identification with nature. Teo's head slowly emerges in the frame of the sky, as if he were looking through a window. In the following shot—a long angle shot seen from behind—the father and son, like two somber statues, stand out in relief against the gold of the wheatfields. The strong summer breeze invades the screen. Our Don Quixote is much too occupied in contemplating nature to think of unbuttoning his fly, and he wets his pants. "The sea over there is a long blue line," he observes in following his train of thought without paying any attention to the comments of the family. Like an imp, the little brother bobs up and down among the blades of ripening wheat. The carriage resumes its quiet passage down the path lined with poplars. The outing is henceforth a voyage into the magical heart of nature. The following images have the flavor of the discoveries of infancy; Titta tries to charm a turkey (in the background, the silhouette of a haystack takes the shape of a strange prehistoric animal). The grandfather tastes a glass of wine with pleasure. Teo is absorbed in contemplating an egg, then a tree. When, drunk with liberty, he disappears in the branches, having become a tree himself, we understand that for no reason in the world would he abandon his position. Teo, like *The Baron in the Trees* of Italo Calvino, feels like and is a God beyond all contingencies and conventions. The only normal beings are the madmen and, happily, there are a few in Amarcord City.

THE OLD AND THE NEW

There are two categories of films in Fellini's works: the great spectacles (*La Dolce Vita, Satyricon*) and the intimate films (*La Strada, I Vitelloni*). *Roma* belongs to the first, *Amarcord* to the second. According to tastes and times, one might prefer one or the other. But that is not the problem: *Roma* and *Amarcord* are two ways of making films. To draw a parallel between the two films permits one better to distinguish their characteristics and to respect their intrinsic nature—the overwhelming vitality of *Roma* and the purified smoothness of *Amarcord*. Among the possible criteria for establishing a comparison, we shall limit ourselves to those of internal coherence and of innovations in the two films with respect to the ensemble of Fellinian filmography.

In *Roma*, Fellini seems to have been deeply preoccupied with the linking of episodes, and the result is not always very felicitous. Certain transitions are only pretexts, such as the introduction of the music hall sequence by means of an operator perched on the arm of the crane that "accidentally" frames the cupola of the little theater of the Barafonda, or the passage from today's hippies to the furtive and forbidden love of yesterday's brothels, as if the voice-over of the commentator would not suffice to present the sequence: "The brothels—do you remember them?" The recourse to a protagonist functioning as a liaison between the different scenes was perfectly justified for the Rome of the thirties, but much less for the Rome of today. What purpose does the presence of Fellini himself behind the camera serve? One has the impression that the director, having become aware of the fragmentary aspect of *Roma*, tried to remedy the problem by inserting an artificial transition between the tableaux of this many-sided work of art, which is annoying precisely because it is not necessary. In *The Phantom of Liberty*, Buñuel juxtaposed sketches without being concerned about establishing a logical tie. Why did Fellini not simply order the sequences in their logical or analogical progression? This question calls forth another. Why did Fellini feel the need to apologize in his film for the limited portrait he intended to draw of the city in the sequence of the Villa Borghese? Was he anticipating the attacks of a certain type of politically committed Italian criticism?

In contrast to the agitated and fragmentary rhythm of *Roma*, the structural homogeneity of *Amarcord* seems most harmonious. The succession of scenes in *Amarcord* has the fluid rhythm of the seasons that punctuate the life of the town. "One has the sensation of seeing nature exist rather than watching a film," Natalia Ginzburg has said. This affirmation applies perfectly to the structure of *Amarcord*. Extras (the lawyer, the distracted motorcyclist), apparitions (the *Rex*, the peacock), dreamlike evocations (the meeting with the prince) are disengaged at the right moment, obeying a musical rhythm. All is natural and necessary in this popular fresco in which no one sequence is more successful than another. For *Roma* one is tempted to think, on the contrary, that certain sequences (the Villa Borghese and Trastevere) could have been cut without damaging the film. The pathetic nostalgia of Conocchia for the Rome of old with its peace and tranquillity, the heckling of Fellini by the students and his response, the charge of the police at Trastevere seem forced and unnecessary. The director has not always avoided inappropriate choices, such as the brief flashback upon the couple awakened from a deep sleep by the vibrations of the "mole." One cannot say that this intrusion of the completely mundane enriches the journey through the Roman catacombs.

In *Amarcord*, on the contrary, the director has edited the film without restraint in creating a spectacle of unusual proportions. And to think that the attempts to dally in this fantastic universe were not lacking! Take, for example, the nights of Gradisca and Biscein at the Grand Hotel. No sooner does the picturesque harem perform a languorous dance, charmed by the magic flute of Biscein, than the director cuts and passes on to something else with indifference. (These few images are enough to make us regret that it was not Fellini who shot *A Thousand and One Nights!*).[4] Of the scenes foreseen in the scenario, only three do not figure in the film. The first—the waterspout—was not shot. The second, of a nondescript realism (the Chinese constrained by Titta's uncle to show his navel in Caffè del Commercio) was expediently eliminated from the montage. The third, of a delicious irony, depicted the fishing out of a ring from a cesspool. The "little countess" of the town had dropped it inadvertently in her chamber pot; the very dignified faces of the little countess and her father observing the work of the laborer from the height of their window was a treat. Inexplicably, Fellini suppressed it in the French version.[5] He would have been better advised to suppress the character of Volpina, the pale and thin replica of La Saraghina, whom he doesn't seem to have felt. Another weakness of the film is the burial of Titta's mother, which the director limits himself to describing in one or two trite images in the manner of Bogdanovich or Rouquier. But the weaknesses in *Amarcord* have the advantage of not spoiling the beauty of the whole.

The novelty of certain sequences of *Roma* has often been mentioned. "Nothing like it has ever been seen in the cinema," Alain Resnais told me, referring to the Freeway. Personally, this sequence forced me to think of *Toby Dammit*, and not only because the musical motif is the same. It seemed to me that the three minutes of the English actor's trip from the airport to the capital foretold the entire sequence in *Roma*, and they were endowed with a remarkable emotional force. The monstrous cement mixers, the disputes among the drivers, the exposition of the lampposts, the traffic jam in front of the Colosseum, the accident in *Toby Dammit* cause the viewer to feel powerfully the uneasiness with which the drugged, intoxicated actor looked at these successive scenes. By comparison, the Freeway sequence seems to be a matter of considerable acrobatic skill in which the ingenuity of the artisan shows through more than the inspiration of the poet, especially because certain images are rather manneristic and forced, like the horse, in the manner of De Chirico, who is trotting among the cars, the armored cars in the style of Bergman, the shrill parade of Neapolitan fans, the prostitutes under their umbrellas, the audacious acrobatic turns of the camera at the top of the "Chapman" (which makes one think of the eye of the dinosaur seen against the background of the vapors arising from an industrial inferno). One observes something similar in the sequence of the motorcyclists who recall the nocturnal journey of Toby aboard his racing car.

Taken as a whole, an apparently "minor" film like *Amarcord* reveals itself to be more moving than certain flashy improvisations in *Roma*. *Roma* stupefies by its excesses, *Amarcord* by its measure. Before works so rich in complementary qualities, one is forced to admire Fellini's ability to be reborn in each film from his own ashes. What is most striking in *Amarcord* is its necessary objective dimension. The narrator who passed for an impenitent Narcissus knew how to select from his memories the only ones endowed with universal significance, which was not the case in *Roma* (see the conclusion of a private order between Fellini and Dolores in the luxurious brothel, and its repetition in the bomb shelter between the same Fellini and the blond German singer). To take up an old dichotomy in the criticism, one could say that the author buried the romantic tendency of such films as *La Strada* on behalf of the purified chronicle of such films as *I Vitelloni*.

In the film that risks being the most autobiographical, Fellini is totally absent as a character. One of the limits of *The Clowns* and *Roma* is the too frequent appearance of the character of Fellini—the little boy of the circus, the young provincial, the investigator of clowns, the director filming himself. In *Amarcord*, Fellini no longer needs to acknowledge himself in a protagonist, neither in Titta nor in any other alter ego such as the six *vitelloni*. The initial appearance of the lawyer is extremely significant in effacing the protagonist and in establishing the tone of affectionate irony behind which Fellini the narrator conceals himself. He appears from afar in the night pushing his bicycle, stops 20 meters from the camera, looks all about himself, then begins in the most natural way to give us a history lesson on the origins of the town. When the camera films him in a medium shot, we find ourselves with one of these learned provincials, both likeable and ingenuous, who knows all the local history but who does not know how to talk about anything else, a provincial of whom people make fun and who laughs at them in turn!

Not resorting to a single protagonist permits Fellini to sketch a gallery of human types who are extraordinarily well characterized and endowed with a powerful vitality: the carefree and romantic Gradisca; the proprietor of the cinema who brings to town all the Gary Cooper films; the authoritarian *pater familias*; the typically Latin mother, affectionate and neurotic; the rubicund and alert grandfather; the impenitent *vitellone* who lives at the expense of others (the fascist uncle of Titta); the authoritarian provincial secretary; the beardless headmaster; the good-natured priest; the likeable braggart Biscein; the ethereal prince; the tobacconist in need of love.

As in a painting in which Brueghel portrays peasant life, each visage in the fresco is captured in its most characteristic expression. Is it accidental or the confirmation of what we said before that Titta, the character who functions more or less as the protagonist, seems to be the most colorless? The result is even more remarkable in that, except for Magali Noël, the group of actors are nonprofessional or come from the music hall and the provincial theaters (especially the Neapolitan and Romagnol theater). An actor, in Fellini's hands, is capable of any kind of metamorphosis. Take the poor devil who goes to sleep under the statue of King Victor Emmanuel: he becomes in turn the emir of *A Thousand and One Nights* on the way to the Grand Hotel and the city streetsweeper on the square in front of the church!

With an unexpected humility (which someone has not missed defining as the nth invention of this mystifier of genius: ingenuity or not, the poetry is nevertheless there), Fellini has burned Fellini as the Amarcordians burned the witch of winter. *Amarcord* no longer seems to be a film of Fellini: Fellinian excesses, obsessions, and phantasms have disappeared. *Amarcord* is pleasing precisely because the director clearly does not want to say "I remember" at all. Before returning to Rimini, he procured a virgin eye in order to retranspose upon the screen what childhood had revealed to him about life without distortions and veils. *Amarcord* is no longer even a film, because it is more than that. It is the Province that lives again before us naturally like a past season of "our" life, our best, our worst years. Is it not curious to state that it is the most personal of the Italian directors who, far from withdrawing into himself, into the "meanderings of his memory," knew how to give to his compatriots the most faithful and compelling portrait of their childhood? After "the circus and I," after "Rome and I," here is quite simply "The Provinces." How can we not agree with Fellini when he says that the only true realist is the visionary?

NOTES

1. Cesare Zavattini's *I misteri di Roma* (1963, *The Mysteries of Rome*), an episodic film more in the tradition of Gualtiero Jacopetti's *Mondo Cane* (1962) than in the neo-realist vein of his earlier *Amore in città* (1953, *Love in the City*).—EDITOR
2. The European counterpart of Florists' Trans-World Delivery ("FTD").—EDITOR
3. The peacock's beauty should not cause the viewer to overlook its sinister symbolic connotations of vanity and, in Italy, of death.—EDITOR
4. This work was actually filmed by Pier Paolo Pasolini in 1973 as the third part of his medieval "trilogy of life," the first two sections being *The Decameron* (1971) and *The Canterbury Tales* (1972).—EDITOR
5. The English version also omits this scene.—EDITOR

28. Spectacle: Magnifying the Personal Vision

Stuart Rosenthal

Fellini: A Director's Notebook ends with a parade of diverse, eccentric people trying to win the director's attention and, hopefully, a part in his next film. Members of the crowd compete for his time by playing the accordion, asking absurd questions, reading from foreign language newspapers, distributing photographs, flexing muscles and hustling artware. These people's appearances match the outrageousness of their tactics. In body type they range from wiry to ultra-muscular to enormously obese, and from child-sized to gigantic. Their faces, expressions, dress and mannerisms are varied, unusual and striking. Although, outwardly, Fellini has greeted his visitors with an air of boredom and annoyance, he admits that he has a deep affection for them. "I am very fond of all these characters who are always chasing after me," he confides to the audience. "They are all a little mad, I know that. They say they need me, but in truth I need them more. Their human qualities are rich, comic, and sometimes very moving."

This manic display is shot from Fellini's point of view as though the lens were his eye. (Once we even see his hands and forearms closing a folder as though he had momentarily glanced down to co-ordinate the movement.) The episode could be described as a "circus," a "fresco," a "sideshow" or even as "a series of vaudeville acts." These analogies give us a key with which to approach the use and place of spectacle in Fellini's films. The scene is typical of Fellini's vision of life and of the human world around him. His final comments on the crowd of prospective movie stars establish a compatibility between his humanistic attitudes and the gaudy exhibitions that run through his work. His words sum up the attraction he feels for the motley crowd of people that move endlessly through his films. From the most peripheral bit player to the central character, Fellini is consistent in his belief that every human life is valuable and interesting.

Clearly, Fellini cannot delve into the life of every extra who passes before his lens. On the other hand, if he were to ignore the minor

· · · · · · · · ·

From *The Cinema of Federico Fellini* by Stuart Rosenthal (New York: A. S. Barnes & Company, 1976), pp. 67-71, 73-75, 77-79, 88-93. Reprinted by permission of A. S. Barnes & Company, Inc.

289

roles in his movies or slide his extras around the set like so many bodies needed to fill a given amount of space, he would be untrue to his respect for the importance of the individual. We know that Cabiria's hopes are riding on her expectation of a miracle at the tabernacle, but the ritual is surely of equal significance to the other pilgrims. Though our attention is focused upon Cabiria, other members of the procession have features that are distinctive enough to enable us to pick them out from shot to shot. We might settle upon the masculine looking old woman with the scarf wrapped around her head—who is often glimpsed behind Cabiria—and wonder what need has brought her to the shrine. Because we can single out specific people in the procession, we realise that the human current which sweeps Cabiria along is composed of individuals, each feeling the intensity of the moment in his own way. When it is understood that the ritual will cruelly wreck the aspirations of a multitude of real people—rather than just disappoint a nebulous, impersonal mass—the true horror of the activity at the shrine becomes apparent. If Fellini had simply called for a hundred men and women of ordinary appearance to take part in the sequence, we would be less likely to realise that the supplicants outside Cabiria's party also have a commitment to the event. Our recognition of the spiritual devastation inflicted upon each member of the procession galvanises the experience for us.

Fellini uses physical features not to stereotype the members of his supporting cast, but to make them distinctly different from each other. In doing so, he preserves the integrity of the individual and reasserts his own wonder at the diversity of human form and temperament. He has a gift for finding people whose faces and bodies seem to reflect a recognisable personality. In this respect his experience as a caricaturist has served him well. By supplementing the natural endowments of his players with carefully chosen clothes, gestures and posturings, Fellini can convey, almost instantly, a complex impression of a character who is in view only momentarily. In *I clowns*, during the child's approach to the circus, the camera tracks past a woman dispensing tickets from a wagon window. She is dark-haired, round-faced and earthy. Her general appearance and the little bit of spaghetti that she is pushing into the corner of her mouth make her register on our memories and even give us an idea of what it would be like to stand near her. The few feet of film in which she appears make an enormous contribution toward establishing a kind of sweaty, human flavour around the manifestations of the big top.

Fellini effectively applies this method to important supporting characters as well as to the constituents of crowd scenes. *I vitelloni* never explicitly explains Leopoldo's horrified reaction to Natali—nor does Fellini give Natali the limp-wristed movements that traditionally identify homosexuals in movies. Rather, by controlling lighting, dress, and the facial expression of the actor playing Natali, the director is able to arouse our suspicions about the "great artist," but reserve the definitive revelation until the last moment. On stage Natali looks like any other ham actor. He does not seem out of the ordinary until we see him talking to the boys through the torn curtain of his dressing room. Away from the stage lights his make-up and lip rouge transform him into a peculiar clown with white skin and cavernous eye sockets. This shot is the first intimation that something is amiss. Later, a single, short shot clarifies everything. Natali, in close up, cocks his head to one side, raises his eyebrows and, in dulcet tones, asks Leopoldo, "Are you afraid of me?" At that moment the odd smile that we saw in the dressing room appears again. It is fuller than before and the space where Natali is missing two upper teeth (we could not see this space earlier) makes the grin demonic. At the same time, we are impressed by how aged the actor is. In less than ten seconds Fellini has told us much about the man while generating the shock that the sequence requires.

Sometimes Fellini will obtain a specific effect by bringing together many people who share a desired quality. Even then he refuses to amalgamate his subjects into a crowd that presents a single, summated face. The spa in *8½* is such an instance. The common denominator there is old age, a prospect which Fellini has always treated with both dread and sympathy. The dread is evident in the very infirmity of those who are taking the cure: the man who needs the support of two attendants to get to his chair, the trembling hand of another visitor as he limps along on his cane, the lady with the stringy hair and flat features who has fallen asleep under the hot sun, the toothless gentleman who shields his head with a newspaper. Not all of the faces are desperate, though. There is the *blasé* lady with the cigarette and oversized sunglasses. We also find several women with parasols, looking like friendly grandmothers. One of them even throws a kiss toward the camera. Like the chubby, giggling nun who chortles as she quaffs her mineral water, these women are pleasant, but irritating because they seem out of touch with the world around them—another symptom of aging. The goal of this pageant, in the context of *8½*, is not to comment upon old age but to evoke Guido's impression of a loss of personal prowess by placing him among the old and sick. In doing so, the sequence displays the ravages of senility. At the same time, however, it generates a great deal of compassion for the sufferers—compassion that goes beyond a conditioned response to a pathetic sight. It is the character that Fellini finds in their faces that makes us react to them as something more than living props.

Spectacle gives Fellini a way to magnify the emotion and significance of a life or an event. This effect helps explain the predominance of spectacle in films that are, at heart, intimate portraits of two or three central personalities. His desire to uphold the worthiness of the story's most peripheral figures justifies the extreme individualisation of the many extras Fellini employs. But why, in the first place, must he mount the private lives of Guido, Gelsomina, Cabiria and the others on such a massive stage? Is it really necessary, we might ask, to bring together a hundred extras just to establish Guido's feeling of dessication?

It is important to remember that the films are built around their protagonists. Guido is fully preoccupied with his inability to move ahead on his film and to put his personal relationships in order. This pressing concern pervades every aspect of his life and he finds reminders of his paralysis wherever he turns. The gathering of old, exhausted people at the springs externalises Guido's depression on a grand scale. The spectacle heightens our sensitivity to his feelings, while the enormity of his vision of everything around him enlarges him for us. This does not mean that we are more easily moved by Guido's problems just because they are presented on an oversized canvas. (As we will see shortly, the effect may be exactly the opposite.) But because his life evinces itself in such imposing patterns, we more readily accept Guido and his difficulties as being worth our attention.

In the same vein, we might dismiss Gelsomina, Fausto, Picasso or Cabiria as small, ordinary, unimportant people who hardly merit our concern or consideration. Yet, our view of them is inseparably tied to high-powered parties and festivities, exotic homes and villas, frightening religious processions and strange night-clubs and entertainments. These individuals are literally enveloped in excitement. Involvement in such gigantic, emotionally supercharged events adds conceptual mass to the characters. The intensity of a spectacular episode clings to the character, strengthening his presence without distracting from the spectacle itself.

If the impressiveness of this sort of sequence is to accrue to a character, however, the sequence must maintain a close relationship to him. A protagonist will reap little benefit, in the way of increased viewer regard, from spectacle that proceeds without referring back to him. Fellini's emphasis upon the subjective pays off handsomely when it comes to tying his characters to various sensational events. Examples from three films nicely illustrate how Fellini uses subjectivity to convert visual exhilaration into significant insight or regard for a character. The sequence at the spa in *8½* transmits Guido's point of view with full force, giving the viewer an idea of Guido's problem as he perceives it. The raucous wedding party in *La strada*, followed by the mystic confrontation with Oswaldo, is a haunting demonstration of Gelsomina's isolation. And the uproar created by the storm at the "Miss Siren" contest in *I vitelloni* leaves us with a sense of the panic and disorder that have just entered the lives of Fausto and Sandra. Each of these examples is an extravagantly mounted set piece which, though stimulating in its own right, adds immeasurably to our familiarity with a character.

All of the cases cited above use a small amount of subjective camerawork to create the primary link between the character and the spectacle. This short footage is enough to diffuse the character's presence throughout the segment. After making provision for this bridge, Fellini develops the spectacle in whatever manner he considers most advantageous. The frankly subjective camera set-ups serve the same end as the shots from behind Fellini's desk in *Fellini: A Director's Notebook*: they establish the correlation between the character and the exhibition on the screen and they remind us of the personal origins of what we are seeing. In *La strada*, the camera sometimes walks in Gelsomina's place as the children lead her to Oswaldo's room. Once they arrive, it tracks in on Oswaldo in his bed. Shortly thereafter, there is a stationary shot from a position near Oswaldo in which Gelsomina approaches him. These shots fully convey the affinity between Gelsomina and the lonely retard. The loneliness embodied in the sequence becomes an important point of reference as we follow Gelsomina's further travels. The intimacy of the Oswaldo episode also sharpens the effect of the preceding wedding feast. There a long, rapid tracking shot reveals the celebrants fighting, eating, throwing food and *confetti*, and chasing each other. The track, so much colder and more impersonal than the near-magical visit to Oswaldo, effectively excludes Gelsomina from the gaiety and camaraderie. Thus a tiny piece of subjective camerawork—as Gelsomina runs after the children—personalises in retrospect what would otherwise seem only a vulgar, but funny spectacle. A more direct effect occurs when Sandra is being congratulated for winning the "Miss Siren" title. The only explicitly subjective work in this sequence occurs as the faces of her admirers are thrust suffocatingly close to the lens. Then the camera suddenly tilts upwards, mimicking Sandra's abrupt fall. Even if one does not immediately guess that her unexpected nausea is a symptom of pregnancy, it is clear that something is terribly wrong. The graphically rendered fainting spell picks up the confusion of the party and the panic created by the ominous storm and focuses them upon Sandra. The wild party then becomes expressive of a huge, personal crisis.

Fellini's emphasis on the personal and subjective aspects of his spectacles endows them with great vitality. It is a remarkable feat, in the first place, to devise something so huge and so out of the ordinary that a person confronted with it will be at a loss as to how to respond. In the cinema, Fellini and Busby Berkeley are the most notable among the few who have had unlimited success with this method. Both of these film-makers have imaginations that operate far beyond the confines of routine human experience. Both know how to open up their gargantuan constructions gradually, in a way that will milk the maximum effect from them. (Berkeley uses what he calls a "disclosure shot" while Fellini continually adds new elements to his "production numbers.") But, Berkeley's camera positions are dictated by the geometry of the musical routines. Neither his facial close-ups nor kaleidoscopic views correspond to anything vaguely in the "first person." In fact, he reinforces the non-involvement by opening and closing stage curtains on his acts. Fellini's spectacles, in contrast, most often start and/or end with the character concerned. The first shot at the springs in 8½ begins with a short pan from two women walking in the distance to another pair of women, back to back, in medium close-up. The shot continues, following a lady in the background until it comes across an elderly man whom it discovers in the foreground. Somewhere during this manoeuvre the pan turns into a track and proceeds without interruption to a seat where an old gentleman hands a glass of water to a lady friend. Immediately, the camera picks up a priest who emerges in the distance behind the chair, and tracks him until he disappears behind a group of white-hatted grandmother types, one of whom throws a kiss toward us. Then, without pausing, the camera moves to take in the nearby orchestra conductor. We can easily make a case for this travelling shot as a subjective rendering of what Guido sees while he walks toward the women dispensing water. In any case, the definitive subjective moment occurs at the end of the segment when Guido fantasies Claudia at the water dispersal counter. This flight of imagination indicates that Guido is the instigator of the spectacle we have just seen.

Unlike Berkeley, Fellini reveals his spectacles in a way that imitates our natural attentive processes, concentrating, if only briefly, upon one element at a time. We tend to notice moving things more readily than stationary ones, so that if something moves across the camera's field of view—the priest in the spa sequence, for example—Fellini will zero in on it. If someone pops into the frame from up close, Fellini almost reflexively shifts the centre of interest to him in the same way that our eyes adapt and readjust when we realign our gaze. So the camera behaves as if it were our own organ of vision under our own control. In the sequence at the spa, it is not until we have had a chance to wander about in this manner, picking up details for ourselves, that Fellini puts everything together with a long, high crane shot. Since we have seen the spa (or Guido's vision of it) as we would if we had been there ourselves, the experience is more immediate than if it were offered as a passively-viewed, Berkeleyesque phantasmagoria.

The camera style in the spa sequence filters the experience through a kind of funnel of subjectivity. At the widest end of the cone are the panoramic vistas like the crane shot and the shots where people walk toward a fixed camera. These give us a broad idea of the arrangement of the space and action. The effect of these views is modified by the feeling of having discovered much of the area ourselves—a "viewer subjectivity" resulting from camera movements which simulate our own system of gathering information. At the neck of the funnel are the shots which are subjective from Guido's point of view, and which relate the total spectacle to him. So Fellini immerses us, at first hand, in the staggering spectacle and then leads us to transfer the impact of the experience to our feelings for his main character.

Fellini has a basic procedure for simulating viewer involvement in the disclosure of a spectacle. He reveals one detail after another, taking care to provide a medium of continuity between the details. The continuity may come from camera movement, a strong sense of place and time, or various rhythmic qualities—both internal (especially cutting tempo) and external (music, for instance). When we survey a complex space or event we can concentrate on only one thing at a time. If we are startled by something in our peripheral visual field while concentrating on something else, we can turn our attention to the new stimulus. But we cannot, simultaneously, continue to view the first item. When several activities are shown in depth in a single frame, the spectator may choose both the order in which he scrutinizes the components and the amount of time he devotes to each. While this generates a useful ambiguity, it removes the man in the theatre seat from the action by a degree. His position is relatively objective and he must act upon the shot—that is, break it down—before he can begin to assimilate it. By providing a governed flow of material, Fellini can guide the viewer's attention, controlling what is seen and the weight given each element. The perception process is included in the film, and like everything else that is projected on the screen, it is magnified, strengthening the viewer's sense of participation.

Most often, the camera movement that supplies continuity between various elements of Fellini's spectacle is the pan. The pan is a natural, quasi-anatomical movement that is the equivalent of a person turning his head. It places the viewer in the centre of everything and can even be used for character subjectivity. When a character's identification with spectacle is unusually strong—as in *8½* and *Juliet of the Spirits* where spectacle is a manifestation of the interior state of the protagonists—the pan is the dominant camera movement. The harem fantasy of *8½*, with its many players and unceasing movement, is handled mostly with pans and variations of pans. Sometimes the camera placement coincides with Guido's position, as during the argument over Jacqueline in which, from a low angle, Fellini pans back and forth among the hostile females. At other times, the effect of head turning is retained although Guido is obviously not the originator of the movement. One such instance is the combination of pan and tilt employed as the women parade their master around the room on a sheet. The camera is actually tracking back in front of the procession. At first it is trained upon Saraghina, who talks about the straightness of Guido's legs; then it pans to the right and tilts downward to look at Guido who is riding close to the ground. Finally, reversing the tilt and panning even farther to the right, it settles on the French actress as she accuses the master of the harem of being a hypocrite. These manoeuvres are natural and help to keep the sequence in the present tense for the spectator. Shortly thereafter, when rebellion breaks out, there are a number of blindingly fast pans in rapid succession. Our eyes would normally conduct themselves this way in a room where a great many things are happening at once. The more studied shots scattered throughout the daydream—the girl with the star shaped hat in silhouette with Guido and his whip visible over her shoulder, or the woman who enters the frame from in front of the camera—do not interfere with the effect of the pans. In fact, they introduce visual excitement of their own, which is swept into the momentum generated by the pans. Many of the other spectacles in *8½* and *Juliet of the Spirits*, including the farmhouse memory and the visits to Susy's and Bhishma's, rely upon panning to put the viewer in the middle of everything.

Long tracking shots are also used, at times, to develop viewer involvement. They are most effective in achieving this goal when the character concerned is walking and the shot gives the perspective of a moving observer (the spa sequence of 8½ might serve as an illustration). But when the character is not moving, the outcome of a track during a set-piece is altogether different. The idea, as with the pans, is that the viewer's relationship to the action should correspond to that of the main character. When the character is not in motion, tracks seem much colder and more clinical. Thus they are ideal for situations where the character is on the outside of the spectacle. In most of Fellini's films the bond between character and spectacle is so substantial that pans predominate. But in two films, *La dolce vita* and *Satyricon*, the characters are estranged from the world around them. The hysteria caused by the "miracle children" in *La dolce vita* is captured in a series of long tracking shots which move at a steady velocity. During the mayhem, Marcello is perched atop a high scaffolding. As he looks on unemotionally his alienation increases; the frenzy of the faithful is certainly not the answer or meaning that he has been seeking. The tracks more than adequately cover the event and convey the horror and madness that permeate it. But the mechanical execution of the shots prevents the impact of their content from affecting our view of the dissatisfied gossip journalists. In *La dolce vita*, tracking shots are used to enforce a psychological distance between Marcello and the spectacle he witnesses. But the "orgy" sequence after Marcello has finally given himself to the debauchery about him is loaded with pans which put both Marcello and us in the centre of the party. The technique makes us aware of Marcello's full immersion in this loose society. . . .

In Fellini's films the relationship between character and spectacle is a reciprocal one. The character benefits because the spectacle "cracks open" his world for the viewer, making it—and the character with it—seem bigger, more important. The extravagant exhibitions fascinate the spectator and engage his attention and interest for the character. In return, the character vitalises the spectacles. His position with respect to these events gives them a personal flavour which increases the audience's emotional stake in them. The measure of a spectacle's success, after all, is the extent to which it produces emotional excitement in those who witness it.

Ultimately, our reaction to one of Fellini's protagonists depends upon our reaction to the spectacle of his life. If we are not thoroughly captivated by what we see, it is not likely that we will care much about him. To guarantee this enthrallment, Fellini relies upon traditional, tried-and-proven forms of spectacle: the music-hall and the circus-carnival. As long as the director can create a state of wonderment in the viewer and then transfer the feeling to the character, a strong audience response is assured.

Straightforward reproductions of circus and music-hall entertainment often provide enjoyable interludes in a Fellini movie. For its first ten minutes or so, *Variety Lights* concentrates upon an actual performance of the troupe and the reaction of their audience. The good naturedness of this sequence starts the film off in an altogether charming manner. An atmosphere of fun is immediately established; its aura will stay with us even during Checco's periods of despondency. The light, rousing character of the film is maintained by this segment and others like it (including the beginning of the party at Renzo's which Fellini handles with a jaunty touch matching that used to show the artistes on stage). Because of the light tone, we are never too dismayed by Checco's set-backs. This film's opening is an example of spectacle which, while pleasurable in its own right, has important ramifications for the picture as a whole. The same is true of several of the cabaret scenes (a close cousin to music-hall) in *La dolce vita*: the clown with the balloons would be moving in any case, but his appearance at the "Kit Kat Club" while Marcello's father is straining to have a good time adds a wistful note which instils the episode with just the sense of loss it requires.

The show at the Teatrino della Barafonda in *Roma* would be amusing even without the heckling audience. Although the content of the acts may, today, be appreciated only by Italians—and then only for nostalgic reasons—Fellini has polished other aspects of the programme so that it has appeal for a modern, international audience. The lighting, *décor*, costumes, and personalities have been made especially attractive and interesting, adding much to the rich, overall texture of *Roma*.

Both the *Roma* and *Variety Lights* music-hall scenes reconfirm the desirability of building spectacle around characters. The numbers at the Teatrino della Barafonda and in the different provincial halls in *Variety Lights* are effective because they project the personalities of the performers. In both films, the crowds respond primarily to the performer—not to the act—as is apparent from the personal nature of the heckling in *Roma* and from the ticket-buyers' lecherous admiration of Liliana as she dances in the *Variety Lights* chorus. The importance of personality is unmistakable if one compares Liliana's *début* in Parmasani's company with the routines she used on the road. Despite its hugeness and the number of dancers involved, the Parmasani act is dull and impersonal; it lacks the vulgar robustness of the performances by Checco's group. The elaborate scenery and mechanical devices are of little interest without a strong personality to animate them. Parmasani's

Roma: The procession of the prostitutes in the Roman brothel. (Museum of Modern Art/Film Stills Archive)

show is Busby Berkeley spectacle, not Fellini spectacle. It is diverting for us only because we know Liliana and appreciate her attempts to up-stage the star.

The circus routines of the different principals in *La strada* are par-ticularly suited to each of them as individuals. Gelsomina is a clown who, though intellectually stunted, has enormous appeal. Zampanò's act is a boasting, brutish exhibition of pure muscle which has meaning within the allegorical framework of the film: he is a strong man trying to break, with a breath of air, the chains that confine him. Il Matto, in his angel outfit, balances precariously on a tightrope while executing audacious stunts. A single miscalculation in his wild movements—or even a strong gust of wind—might cause him to plunge to his death. In our introduction to the madman, Fellini gives us a taste of the risk that is part of Il Matto's life by making it appear, for a moment, that he will fall from the wire.

From his own experiences with the circus, the popular cinema, the music-hall and the night-club/cabaret, Fellini recognises that people put themselves into an emotionally susceptible state when they enter a hall or arena to be entertained. This condition increases Fellini's effectiveness in raising his characters' stock with the audience during moments of spectacle. When the ticket buyer is absorbed and enraptured by the spectacle before him—as in the scenes at the movies in *Roma* and *Fellini: A Director's Notebook*—he will be even more receptive than usual to Fellini's revelations of character. We can observe this heightened vulnerability during moments of relaxation in some of the characters in Fellini's films: Augusto is identified and denounced while taking his daughter to the movies. Cabiria meets Oscar as a result of her adventure in the variety hall. Giulietta's image of her father—an important factor in the psychoanalytic rationale of *Juliet of the Spirits*— is formed mostly from her memories of him at the circus.

The traditional spectacles have also influenced the structure of Fellini's films. Variety shows consist of many acts, one on the heels of the next. The circus not only presents its attractions in rapid fire order, but frequently has several in progress simultaneously. The result is a dense, variegated. programme that moves rapidly through a number of different moods and is constantly stimulating. This last line could serve equally well as a description of any of Fellini's films.

The key to the breathtaking pace of Fellini's work is its density—the packing of a wealth of detail and event into the shortest reasonable time span. The films themselves are episodic—the episode being the structural equivalent of a music-hall act. Each episode is internally cohesive, almost a short, self-contained movie. With respect to the narrative, the episodes often have only casual interconnections. They come together in a given film because they have a direct bearing upon the characters. Through these multiple vignettes, we can observe the characters from many different view points, in a variety of humours, and circumstances. So in recalling *La strada*, we think first of Gelsomina, Zampanò and Il Matto, then of specific segments of the film— the religious procession, the theft from the convent, the wedding celebration, etc. The end product is a tightly packed collection of many different experiences. Because so many incidents are followed to completion, the film seems more concentrated than if it had a solitary plot which was developed in a dramatically linear fashion. In *8½*, *La dolce vita* and *Juliet of the Spirits* the concentration effect increases the complexity of the lead character.

Fellini's insistence upon spectacular density is carried through from the practice of building a movie from discreet episodes, down to the level of the individual shot, or part of a shot. If our attention lags—if a shot or sequence is held longer than the time that we need to get everything out of it—we become restless. Such a breakdown in the steady flow of stimulation will kill a spectacle instantly. On the other hand, it would be senseless to overload the film with detail that will be missed because there is not enough time available to take in all of it. The trick—and Fellini has mastered it—is to tailor the length of time that a shot or point of interest is on screen to the time the viewer needs to assimilate it. Fellini's style of moving from detail to detail (discussed earlier) is an ideal way to ration time to each element of a sequence. When Fellini uses a series of relatively static shots, his editing is generally tight, piling the shots on top of each other and giving the viewer a minimally adequate opportunity to react to each of them. When the thunderstorm disrupts the "Miss Siren" festivities in *I vitelloni*, there is a fast montage of different corners of the dance area. It is as though we have glanced quickly in various directions—pausing at each position just long enough to get an idea of what is happening there. The technique is used in 8½ just before Maya's entrance. There we jump from table to table—from Pace and his starlet to Mezzabotta to Daumier and the American writer to Guido to Carla to the French actress and her agent. The combinations of characters involved in conversations are continually shifting and we frequently hear a discussion at one table while the camera views a different table. Each shot is strikingly composed, especially in terms of lighting, so there is a fresh burst of interest on the part of the spectator after each cut. This brief sequence is as dense and entertaining as any passage of its length could conceivably be.

A moving camera gives Fellini even greater control over the steady parade of visions that constitute a sequence. There are two possible ways to do this with camera movement. The first is to shift camera positions, thereby creating a new composition that alters the viewer's perception of the shot. This technique is employed during the carrying of the child Guido to his bed after the bath in 8½. Initially, the lens tracks the woman who carries the boy to the stairs. As she ascends the steps, the camera dollies through an arc of about 90° and cranes slightly so that it looks up the staircase at the woman and her charge, now visible in silhouette. Abruptly, another woman drying another child pops into the foreground at the foot of the stairs. In a few seconds we have had to adjust to three distinct framings, each of which has a somewhat different effect.

The second way of regulating the flow of attractions with a mobile camera is to let the camera, in a track or pan, reveal one detail after another. When Toby Dammit walks through the Fiumicino airport the camera catches, in quick succession, people with masked features in the waiting area, a covey of nuns in the gate area, Moslems prostrating themselves in a departure lounge, a black girl at the fountain who steps back in horror before the advancing camera, a weird-looking man in a wheelchair and other striking faces. The experience—partially a distortion due to Dammit's less than lucid state, but not altogether removed from the feeling one gets in the Da Vinci air terminal—is like a trip through a sideshow. The visitor is given just enough of a look at each freak to tease his imagination. Then he is hustled on to the next booth before he has a chance to reflect upon the monstrosity and, perhaps, discover its artificiality.

To keep his spectacles rolling like a good circus or sideshow, Fellini allots each element just enough screen time to entice us, but never enough for us to study it. The time necessary is relative, of course, and expands or contracts according to the complexity of the item on display, how badly the audience wants to see it and how clearly it can be seen. The frescoes in the Metro excavation in *Roma* pique our interest enough to make us want a long, close look at them. While Fellini grants them substantial exposure, he is always tracking in and out on them. The movement prevents our eyes from settling upon the frescoes, so we are never afforded the definitive view we would like. In one sense, Fellini does this to save himself because the studio-designed wall paintings, when subjected to close inspection, lack the appearance of authenticity. But it is more important that Fellini commonly uses such camera movement to throw our perceptive faculties off balance. (As examples, consider the gathering of the apparitions and other visions from *Juliet of the Spirits*, Via Albalonga after hours in *Roma*, and almost everything in *Toby Dammit*.) The business of shortening the time interval assigned to each detail is notably absent from *Satyricon*. There Fellini is determined not only to expose his grotesque creations, but to devour them as well. The long periods he spends examining the whores, slaves and other specimens of ancient life result in the slower, more deliberate pace of *Satyricon*, as compared to other Fellini spectacles.

. . . .

*Fellini
Bibliography
and Filmography*

Selected Bibliography on Fellini

I. SCRIPTS AND SCREEN PLAYS

Amarcord. Milan: Rizzoli, 1973 (with Tonino Guerra).
Amarcord: Portrait of a Town. New York: Berkley Windhover, 1975 (with Tonino Guerra).
Boccaccio '70 di De Sica, Fellini, Monicelli, Visconti. Ed. Carlo di Carlo. Bologna: Cappelli, 1962.
Casanova. Eds. Federico Fellini and Bernardino Zapponi. Turin: Einaudi, 1977.
I clowns. Ed. Renzo Renzi. Bologna: Cappelli, 1970.
La dolce vita. New York: Ballantine, 1961.
Early Screenplays. New York: Grossman, 1971.
8½ di Federico Fellini. Ed. Camilla Cederna. Bologna: Cappelli, 1965.
Fellini Satyricon. Ed. Dario Zanelli. Bologna: Cappelli, 1969.
Fellini's Casanova. Ed. Bernardino Zapponi. New York: Dell, 1977.
Fellini's Satyricon. Ed. Dario Zanelli. New York: Ballantine, 1970.
Fellini TV: Blocknotes di un regista / I Clowns. Ed. Renzo Renzi. Bologna: Cappelli, 1972.
Il film "Amarcord." Eds. Gianfranco Angelucci and Liliana Betti. Bologna: Cappelli, 1974.
Giulietta degli spiriti. Ed. Tullio Kezich. Bologna: Cappelli, 1965.
Juliet of the Spirits. Ed. Tullio Kezich. New York: Grossman, 1965.
Le notti di Cabiria di Federico Fellini. Ed. Lino del Fra. Bologna: Cappelli, 1965.
Il primo Fellini: Lo sceicco bianco. I vitelloni, La strada, Il bidone. Ed. Renzo Renzi. Bologna: Cappelli, 1969.
Quattro film. Introduction by Italo Calvino. Turin: Einaudi, 1974.
Roma di Federico Fellini. Ed. Bernardino Zapponi. Bologna: Cappelli, 1972.
Tre passi nel delirio di Federico Fellini, Louis Malle, Roger Vadim. Eds. Liliana Betti, Ornella Volta, and Bernardino Zapponi. Bologna: Cappelli, 1968.
Three Screenplays. New York: Grossman, 1970.

II. CRITICISM AND INTERVIEWS WITH FELLINI

(Studies reprinted in this book have been excluded from the bibliography.)

Angelini, Pietro. *Controfellini: il fellinismo tra restaurazione e magia bianca*. Milan: Edizioni Ottaviano, 1974.
Baldelli, Pio. *Cinema dell'ambiguità: Rossellini, De Sica/Zavattini, Fellini*. Rome: Edizioni Samona e Savelli, 1971 (2nd ed.).
Bazin, André. *Qu'est-ce que le cinéma?* Vol. 4. Paris: Éditions du Cerf, 1962.

Benderson, Albert F. *Critical Approaches to Federico Fellini's* "8½". New York: Arno, 1974.
Betti, Liliana and Gianfranco Angelucci, eds. *Casanova rendez-vous con Federico Fellini.* Milan: Bompiani, 1975.
Boyer, Deena. *The Two Hundred Days of 8½.* New York: Macmillan, 1964. Reprint. New York: Garland, 1977.
Budgen, Suzanne. *Fellini.* London: British Film Institute, 1966.
Chemasi, Antonio. "Fellini's *Casanova:* The Final Nights." *American Film,* 1, No. 10 (1976), 8-16.
Durgnat, Raymond. *Sexual Alienation in the Cinema.* London: Studio Vista, 1972.
Escobar, Roberto. "*Amarcord.*" *Cineforum,* 14 (1974), 269-82.
Études Cinématographiques, special issue "Federico Fellini 8½." Nos. 28-29 (1963).
Fellini, Federico. *Fellini on Fellini.* Eds. Anna Keel and Christian Strich. New York: Dell, 1976.
Harcourt, Peter. *Six European Directors: Essays on the Meaning of Film Style.* Baltimore: Penguin, 1974.
Herman, David. "Federico Fellini." *American Imago,* 26 (1969), 251-68.
Holland, Norman N. "Fellini's '8½', Holland's '11'." *Hudson Review,* 16 (1963), 429-36.
———. "The Follies Fellini." *Hudson Review,* 14 (1961), 425-31.
Hovald, Patrice G. *Le Néo-réalisme italien et ses créateurs.* Paris: Éditions du Cerf, 1959.
Hughes, Eileen Lanouette. *On the Set of Fellini Satyricon: A Behind-the-Scenes Diary.* New York: William Morrow, 1971.
Keyser, Lester J. "Three Faces of Evil: Fascism in Recent Movies." *Journal of Popular Film,* 4 (1975), 21-31.
Kovács, Steven. "Fellini's *Toby Dammit:* A Study of Characteristic Themes and Techniques." *Journal of Aesthetics and Art Criticism,* 31 (1972), 255-61.
Leprohon, Pierre. *The Italian Cinema.* London: Secker and Warburg, 1972.
Pecori, Franco. *Fellini.* Florence: La Nuova Italia, 1974.
Perry, Ted. *Filmguide to 8½.* Bloomington: Indiana University Press, 1975.
———. "Signifiers in Fellini's 8½." *Forum Italicum,* 6 (1972), 79-86.
Pierre, Sylvie. "L'homme aux clowns." *Cahiers du cinéma,* 229 (1971), 48-51.
Quargnolo, Mario. *Dove va il cinema italiano?* Milan: Pan editrice, 1972.
Renzi, Renzo. *Federico Fellini.* Parma: Guanda, 1956.
Richardson, Robert D. "Fellini's *Satyricon.*" *Denver Quarterly,* 6 (1971), 59-71.
Rondi, Brunello. *Cinema e realtà.* Rome: Edizioni Cinque Lune, 1957.
———. *Il cinema di Fellini.* Rome: Edizioni di Bianco e Nero, 1965.
Salachas, Gilbert. *Federico Fellini.* 3rd ed. rev. Paris: Éditions Seghers, 1970.
Samuels, Charles Thomas. *Encountering Directors.* New York: Putnam's, 1972.
Segal, Erich. "Arbitrary *Satyricon:* Petronius and Fellini." *Diacritics,* 1 (1971), 54-57.
Solmi, Angelo. *Fellini.* London: Merlin Press, 1967.
———. *Storia di Federico Fellini.* Milan: Rizzoli, 1962.

Spinazzola, Vittorio. *Cinema e pubblico: lo spettacolo filmico in Italia 1945-1965*. Milan: Bompiani, 1974.

Strich, Christian. *Fellini's Films*. New York: Putnam's, 1977.

Tassone, Aldo. "*Amarcord.*" *La Revue du Cinéma: Image et Son*, 284 (1974), 90-93.

——. "Entretien avec Federico Fellini." *Positif*, 181 (1976), 4-12, and 182 (1976), 34-42.

——. "Entretien avec Federico Fellini." *La Revue du Cinéma: Image et Son*, 284 (1974), 59-67.

Taylor, John Russell. *Cinema Eye Cinema Ear: Some Key Film-Makers of the Sixties*. New York: Hill and Wang, 1964.

Torri, Bruno. *Cinema italiano: dalla realtà alle metafore*. Palermo: Palumbo, 1973.

Wall, James M., ed. *Three European Directors*. Grand Rapids: Eerdmans, 1973.

Williams, Forrest. "Fellini's Voices." *Film Quarterly*, 21 (1968), 21-25.

. . . .

Selected Fellini Filmography
(*Principal Credits*)

1950: VARIETY LIGHTS (*Luci del varietà*)

DIR: Federico Fellini and Alberto Lattuada
SCR: Federico Fellini, Alberto Lattuada, Tullio Pinelli, and Ennio Flaiano
D/P: Otello Martelli
MUS: Felice Lattuada
SET: Aldo Buzzi
EDR: Mario Bonotti
PRO: Capitolium Film
CAST: Peppino De Filippo (Checco Dalmonte), Carla Del Poggio (Liliana), Giulietta Masina (Melina), Johnny Kitzmiller (Johnny), Giulio Cali (Edison Will), Carlo Romano (Renzo the lawyer), Folco Lulli (Conti)

1952: THE WHITE SHEIK (*Lo sceicco bianco*)

DIR: Federico Fellini
SCR: Federico Fellini, Tullio Pinelli, and Ennio Flaiano
D/P: Arturo Gallea
MUS: Nino Rota

SET: Federico Fellini
EDR: Rolando Benedetti
PRO: Luigi Rovere
CAST: Brunella Bovo (Wanda Cavalli), Leopoldo Trieste (Ivan Cavalli), Alberto Sordi (Fernando Rivoli, the "white sheik"), Giulietta Masina (Cabiria), Fanny Marchiò (Marilena Velardi), Ernesto Almirante (*fotoromanzo* director), Ettore Margadonna (Ivan's uncle)

1953: I VITELLONI

DIR: Federico Fellini
SCR: Federico Fellini, Ennio Flaiano, and Tullio Pinelli
D/P: Otello Martelli
MUS: Nino Rota
SET: Mario Chiari
EDR: Rolando Benedetti
PRO: Peg Films—Cité Films
CAST: Franco Interlenghi (Moraldo), Franco Fabrizi (Fausto), Alberto Sordi (Alberto), Leopoldo Trieste (Leopoldo), Riccardo Fellini (Riccardo), Eleonora Ruffo (Sandra), Jean Brochard (Fausto's father), Claude Farell (Alberto's sister), Carlo Romano (Signor Michele), Enrico Viarisio (Sandra's father), Lida Baarova (Signor Michele's wife Giulia), Arlette Sauvage (woman in the cinema)

1953: A MATRIMONIAL AGENCY (*Un'agenzia matrimoniale*)—one episode of LOVE IN THE CITY (*Amore in città*) which includes other segments by Dino Risi, Michelangelo Antonioni, Alberto Lattuada, Carlo Lizzani, Cesare Zavattini, and Francesco Maselli

DIR: Federico Fellini
SCR: Federico Fellini and Tullio Pinelli
D/P: Gianni di Venanzo
MUS: Mario Nascimbene
SET: Gianni Polidori
EDR: Eraldo da Roma
PRO: Faro Films
CAST: Nonprofessionals, including some students from the Centro Sperimentale di Cinematografia in Rome

1954: LA STRADA

DIR: Federico Fellini
SCR: Federico Fellini, Ennio Flaiano, and Tullio Pinelli
D/P: Otello Martelli
MUS: Nino Rota

SET: Mario Ravasco
EDR: Leo Catozzo
PRO: Carlo Ponti and Dino De Laurentiis
CAST: Giulietta Masina (Gelsomina), Anthony Quinn (Zampanò), Richard Basehart (Il Matto, "The Fool"), Aldo Silvani (circus owner), Marcella Rovere (the widow), Livia Venturini (the nun)

1955: IL BIDONE

DIR: Federico Fellini
SCR: Federico Fellini, Ennio Flaiano, and Tullio Pinelli
D/P: Otello Martelli
MUS: Nino Rota
SET: Dario Cecchi
EDR: Mario Serandrei and Giuseppe Vari
PRO: Titanus
CAST: Broderick Crawford (Augusto), Richard Basehart (Picasso), Franco Fabrizi (Roberto), Giulietta Masina (Iris), Lorella De Luca (Patrizia), Giacomo Gabrielli (Vargas), Sue Ellen Blake (Anna), Alberto De Amicis (Goffredo), Irene Cefaro (Marisa)

1956: THE NIGHTS OF CABIRIA (*Le notti di Cabiria*)

DIR: Federico Fellini
SCR: Federico Fellini, Ennio Flaiano, and Tullio Pinelli (with Pier Paolo Pasolini's adaptation of dialect into dialogue)
D/P: Aldo Tonti and Otello Martelli
MUS: Nino Rota
SET: Piero Gherardi
EDR: Leo Catozzo
PRO: Dino De Laurentiis
CAST: Giulietta Masina (Cabiria), Amedeo Nazzari (the actor), François Périer (Oscar D'Onofrio), Aldo Silvani (the hypnotist), Franca Marzi (Wanda), Dorian Gray (Jessy), Franco Fabrizi (Giorgio), Mario Passante (the cripple), Pina Gualandri (Matilda)

1959: LA DOLCE VITA

DIR: Federico Fellini
SCR: Federico Fellini, Ennio Flaiano, Tullio Pinelli, and Brunello Rondi
D/P: Otello Martelli
MUS: Nino Rota
SET: Piero Gherardi
EDR: Leo Catozzo

PRO: Riama Film—Pathé Consortium Cinéma
CAST: Marcello Mastroianni (Marcello Rubini), Anouk Aimée (Maddalena), Anita Ekberg (Sylvia), Walter Santesso (Paparazzo), Lex Barker (Robert), Yvonne Fourneaux (Emma), Alain Cuny (Steiner), Annibale Ninchi (Marcello's father), Polidor (Clown), Nadia Gray (Nadia), Valeria Ciangottini (Paola), Magali Noël (Fanny), Renée Longarini (Signora Steiner), Alan Dijon (Frankie Stout), Giulio Questi (Don Giulio), and numerous minor characters

1961: THE TEMPTATIONS OF DOCTOR ANTONIO (*Le tentazioni del dottor Antonio*)— one episode of *BOCCACCIO '70* which includes other segments by Vittorio De Sica, Luchino Visconti, and Mario Monicelli

DIR: Federico Fellini
SCR: Federico Fellini, Tullio Pinelli, and Ennio Flaiano
D/P: Otello Martelli
MUS: Nino Rota
SET: Piero Zuffi
EDR: Leo Catozzo
PRO: Carlo Ponti and Antonio Cervi
CAST: Peppino De Filippo (Dottor Antonio Mazzuolo), Anita Ekberg (Anita), Donatella Della Nora (Mazzuolo's sister), Antonio Acqua (Commendatore La Pappa), Eleanora Maggi (Cupid)

1962: 8½ (*Otto e mezzo*)

DIR: Federico Fellini
SCR: Federico Fellini, Ennio Flaiano, Tullio Pinelli, and Brunello Rondi
D/P: Gianni di Venanzo
MUS: Nino Rota
SET: Piero Gherardi
EDR: Leo Catozzo
PRO: Angelo Rizzoli
CAST: Marcello Mastroianni (Guido Anselmi), Anouk Aimée (Luisa Anselmi), Sandra Milo (Carla), Claudia Cardinale (Claudia), Rossella Falk (Rossella), Edra Gale (La Saraghina), Caterina Boratto (the beautiful but unidentified woman), Barbara Steele (Gloria Morin), Mario Pisu (Mario Mezzabotta), Jean Rougeul (Daumier, the critic), Tito Masini (the cardinal), Marco Gemini (Guido as a child), Madeleine Lebeau (the French actress), Ian Dallas (Maurice, the magician), Mario Conocchia (Conocchia), Guido Alberti (Pace, the producer), Annibale Ninchi (Guido's father), Giuditta Rissone (Guido's mother), Yvonne Casadei (Jacqueline Bonbon), and numerous minor characters

1965: JULIET OF THE SPIRITS (*Giulietta degli spiriti*)

DIR: Federico Fellini
SCR: Federico Fellini, Tullio Pinelli, Ennio Flaiano, and Brunello Rondi
D/P: Gianni di Venanzo
MUS: Nino Rota
SET: Piero Gherardi
EDR: Ruggero Mastroianni
PRO: Angelo Rizzoli
CAST: Giulietta Masina (Giulietta), Mario Pisu (Giorgio, Giulietta's husband), Sandra Milo (Susy/Iris), Lou Gilbert (Grandfather), Caterina Boratto (Giulietta's mother), Luisa Della Noce (Adele, Giulietta's sister), José de Villalonga (José), Alba Cancellieri (Giulietta as a child), Valeska Gert (Bhishma), Alberto Plebani (Lynx-Eyes), Sylva Koscina (Sylva, Giulietta's sister), Valentina Cortese (Val), Silvana Jachino (Dolores), Elena Fondra (Elena), and numerous minor characters

1968: TOBY DAMMIT—one episode from TALES OF MYSTERY (*Histoires Extraordinaires*) which includes segments by Louis Malle and Roger Vadim

DIR: Federico Fellini
SCR: Federico Fellini and Bernardino Zapponi from "Never Bet the Devil Your Head" by Edgar Allan Poe
D/P: Giuseppe Rotunno
MUS: Nino Rota
SET: Piero Tosi
EDR: Ruggero Mastroianni
PRO: Les Films Marceau/Cocinor—P.E.A. Cinematografica
CAST: Terence Stamp (Toby), Salvo Randone (priest), Antonia Pietrosi (actress), Polidor (old actor)

1968: FELLINI: A DIRECTOR'S NOTEBOOK (*Block-notes di un registra*)

DIR: Federico Fellini
SCR: Federico Fellini
D/P: Pasquale De Santis
MUS: Nino Rota
SET: Federico Fellini
EDR: Ruggero Mastroianni
PRO: NBC-TV and Peter Goldfarb
CAST: Federico Fellini, Giulietta Masina, Marcello Mastroianni, Marina Boratto, Caterina Boratto, Pasquale De Santis, Genius the Medium, and numerous nonprofessional actors

1969: FELLINI SATYRICON

DIR: Federico Fellini
SCR: Federico Fellini and Bernardino Zapponi from *Satyricon* by Petronius
D/P: Giuseppe Rotunno
MUS: Nino Rota
SET: Danilo Donati
EDR: Ruggero Mastroianni
PRO: Alberto Grimaldi
CAST: Martin Potter (Encolpius), Hiram Keller (Ascyltus), Max Born (Giton), Mario Romagnoli (Trimalchio), Fanfulla (Vernacchio), Gordon Mitchell (robber), Alain Cuny (Lichas), Joseph Wheeler (suicide husband), Donyale Luna (Oenothea), Salvo Randone (Eumolpus), Lucia Bosè (suicide wife), Capucine (Tryphaena), Magali Noël (Fortunata), Hylette Adolphe (slave girl), Pasquale Baldassare (hermaphrodite), Luigi Montefiori (Minotaur), Gennaro Sabatino (ferryman), Marcello di Falco (Proconsul), Tanya Lopert (Emperor), and numerous minor characters

1970: THE CLOWNS (*I clowns*)

DIR: Federico Fellini
SCR: Federico Fellini and Bernardino Zapponi
D/P: Dario di Palma
MUS: Nino Rota
SET: Danilo Donati
EDR: Ruggero Mastroianni
PRO: Federico Fellini, Ugo Guerra, and Elio Scardamaglia
CAST: *Film Crew*—Maya Morin, Lina Alberti, Gasperino, Alvaro Vitali; *French clowns*—Alex, Bario, Père Loriot, Ludo, Nino, Charlie Rivel; *Italian clowns*—Riccardo Billi, Fanfulla, Tino Scotti, Carlo Rizzo, Freddo Pistoni, the Colombaioni, Merli, Maggio, Valdemaro Bevilacqua, Janigro, Terzo, Vingelli, Fumagalli; *others as themselves*—Liana Orfei, Tristan Rémy, Anita Ekberg, Victoria Chaplin, Franco Migliorini, Baptiste, Pierre Etaix, and Federico Fellini

1971: ROMA

DIR: Federico Fellini
SCR: Federico Fellini and Bernardino Zapponi
D/P: Giuseppe Rotunno
MUS: Nino Rota
SET: Danilo Donati
EDR: Ruggero Mastroianni
PRO: Turi Vasile

CAST: Peter Gonzales (young Fellini), Fiona Florence (beautiful prostitute), Pia De Doses (aristocratic princess), Alvaro Vitali (tap dancer in music hall), Libero Frissi, Mario Del Vago, Galliano Sbarra, Alfredo Adami (performers in music hall), Gore Vidal, Anna Magnani, Federico Fellini, Alberto Sordi, and Marcello Mastroianni as themselves (Sordi and Mastroianni were cut from the version distributed outside Italy), and numerous minor characters

1974: AMARCORD

DIR: Federico Fellini
SCR: Federico Fellini and Tonino Guerra
D/P: Giuseppe Rotunno
MUS: Nino Rota
SET: Danilo Donati
EDR: Ruggero Mastroianni
PRO: Franco Cristaldi
CAST: Bruno Zanin (Titta), Pupella Maggio (Titta's mother), Armando Brancia (Aurelio, Titta's father), Nando Orfei (Pataca), Peppino Ianigro (grandfather), Ciccio Ingrassia (the mad uncle), Magali Noël (Gradisca), Josiane Tanzilli (Volpina), Maria Antonietta Beluzzi (tobacconist), Luigi Rossi (lawyer), Marcello di Falco (the prince), Gennaro Ombra (Biscein the liar), Aristide Caporale (Giudizio), Alvaro Vitali (Naso), Bruno Scagnetti (Ovo), Bruno Lenzi (Gigliozzi), Fernando de Felice (Ciccio), Francesca Vona (Candela), Donatella Gambini (Aldina), Franco Magno (Zeus, the headmaster), Mauro Misul (philosophy teacher), Dina Adorni (math teacher), Francesco Maselli (physics teacher), Mario Silvestri (Italian teacher), Fides Stagni (art history teacher), Mario Liberati ("Ronald Coleman," the owner of the Fulgor Cinema), Domenico Pertica (blindman), and numerous minor characters

1976: CASANOVA

DIR: Federico Fellini
SCR: Federico Fellini and Bernardino Zapponi
D/P: Giuseppe Rotunno
MUS: Nino Rota
SET: Danilo Donati (based upon suggestions by Federico Fellini)
EDR: Ruggero Mastroianni
PRO: Alberto Grimaldi for Universal-Fox-Gaumont-Titanus
CAST: Donald Sutherland (Casanova), Cecile Brown (Madame d'Urfé), Tina Aumont (Henriette), Margaret Clementi (M. M.), Olimpia Carlisi (Isabella), Daniel Emilfork (Dubois), Sandy Allen (the giantess), Claretta Algrandi (Marcolina), Chesty

Morgan (Barberina), Daniela Gatti (Giselda d'Altemburger),
Clarissa Roll (Annamaria), Marika Rivera (Astrodi), Marie
Marquet (Casanova's mother), Dudley Sutton (the Duke of
Württemberg), Adele Angela Lojodice (the mechanical bal-
lerina)

5-79

JE5 '79